BORN TO BE HURT

BORN
TO BE *Hurt*

THE UNTOLD STORY OF *IMITATION OF LIFE*

SAM STAGGS

ST. MARTIN'S PRESS

NEW YORK

www.stmartins.com

Design by Fritz Metsch

Library of Congress Cataloging-in-Publication Data

Staggs, Sam.
    Born to be hurt : the untold story of Imitation of Life / Sam Staggs. — 1st ed.
       p. cm.
    Includes bibliographical references and index.
    ISBN-13: 978-0-312-37336-8
    ISBN-10: 0-312-37336-8
    1. Imitation of Life (Motion picture : 1959)   I. Title.
    PN1997.I455S73 2009
    791.43'72—dc22   2008029885

First Edition: February 2009

10 9 8 7 6 5 4 3 2 1

To Juanita Moore and Susan Kohner,
with love and admiration

CONTENTS

. . . how to prepare the child for the day when the child would be despised and how to *create* in the child—by what means?—a stronger antidote to this poison than one had found for oneself.

—JAMES BALDWIN
Notes of a Native Son

INTRODUCTION
RECAPTURING THE PAST

APRIL 7, 2004

*F*or a long time, down the years, I've thought about *Imitation of Life*. Tonight, crossing the courtyard to the lobby of the Egyptian Theatre in Hollywood for the forty-fifth anniversary screening, I wonder how future thoughts will evolve. This event promises to be a summing up of the film's emotional grip on me, on all of us here. Moreover, this screening is a late vindication of my own fervor, which has never lessened since the day I saw Douglas Sirk's *Imitation of Life* at a young age, sat through it three times, and finally left the movie house in that small Southern town dimly aware that an indelible lifeline had been crossed.

Tonight is a climax because, unlike those countless other times I've watched *Imitation of Life,* two surviving stars will appear, Juanita Moore and Susan Kohner. Together again—how has time dealt with them? Lana Turner, gone for a decade but strangely extant even before the picture starts, towers as a great unseen entity. That's one of the elusive promises made by movies: Great stars never die.

Crowds have gathered. Fans from Los Angeles and around the country line up outside, stream into the theatre for a facsimile of those glamorous premieres of the old days. But there's a big, big difference. The stars who once made Hollywood so addictive have joined Lana. Tonight, no one alights from long limousines out front, nor do flashbulbs pop. (How could they? Everything is digital.) Rumors circulate that Juanita

Moore arrived quietly half an hour ago, and a sharp-eyed fan saw Susan Kohner slip into the theatre through a side door.

". . . and in their dressing rooms already," someone grouses. "Whatever happened to the star entrance?"

Another chimes in, "It's a black hole in space."

I wish I could pause tonight amidst this Hollywood razzle-dazzle to examine how this picture helped transpose my life to a different key, but here's Ann Robinson and I want to ask her a question.

"Oh, honey, you know what? I don't recall a thing about Douglas Sirk," she replies with a laugh. "I was only on the set for a couple of days, and I can't remember that he directed me at all." Robinson played Susan Kohner's hard-faced, redheaded showgirl roommate in the motel scene near the end of the picture, when the ailing black woman pays a final visit to her light-skinned daughter, who has shunned her and who now passes for white.

Ann's husband snaps a picture of us. As our eyes readjust, fans thrust photos and note cards for her signature, and so our conversation must wait. "My number is 213-250 . . ." she says, and I scribble it down. "Call me anytime, dear."

I know, all too well, that another survivor, Sandra Dee, won't show up. She is desperately ill, with less than a year to live. Nor John Gavin, who left Hollywood to act as Ronald Reagan's questionable ambassador to Mexico. Cheryl Crane, Lana's daughter, is eagerly awaited by some in the throng. "Don't hold your breath," I overhear as I pass through the lobby. "This movie is the worst thing that ever happened to her. Make that the second worst."

Snatches of fan gossip, garish lights on Hollywood Boulevard, the cooling desert at sunset, the faded glory of this very locale, but most of all the picture that's soon to start—all come together to magnetize me with a hybrid emotion. What to call it? More than pleasure, it balloons to edgy euphoria, though it's also flecked with dolor. Movies do that to us. If we take them seriously, or too seriously, after a time they may conjure up all our former selves, those beings who, young and credulous, genuflected to screen romance, to images retouched, to those stupendous divinities on Mount Hollywood before the gods turned into bores.

What if we never watched a movie again after a first passionate exposure? Would *Imitation of Life* hold sway over me if I recalled only its first-day impact? Who would I be, I wonder, if I couldn't recite passages from memory, close my eyes and see the picture unspool as on an old-style projector? Sometimes I feel that I belong to it, which is surely one of those false, proprietary consolations movies give.

These profundities evaporate as an old friend accosts me in the lobby. He has flown in from Ohio, and I half expect to see him with a trunk full of costly *Imitation of Life* memorabilia to spread out for Susan and Juanita like treasures for a caliph. "Look at this half sheet from Larry Edmunds," he pants. "But stills—forget it." Anyone here tonight would know the lingo without translation, but the uninitiated might not guess that a half sheet is a large movie poster, that Larry Edmunds is a famous movie memorabilia shop just down the street, and that, indeed, on the day of the screening, collectors had emptied the store of every still photo from *Imitation of Life*.

As I finally proceed down the aisle and take a seat in this place that's more Egyptianish than Egyptian, I recall the vast ocean of movies I've crossed since I first plunged into *Imitation of Life*. Now the anniversary, and a book to write. How will I tell the story of this key picture, which, more than most, refracts the colors of a lifetime to form a rainbow of emotions? Although I belong to the vast Sirk freemasonry, I must nevertheless stand outside the sect to observe. Will *Imitation of Life*—after the nonstop talk, the adulation and the argument, grave tomes devoted to it by lofty scholars, and tears shed throughout the world—stand up for me at the end, or dissolve like the remnant of some phantom dream? Can it survive adult and contemporary scrutiny, or will it ultimately look small, like this imitation theatre in its faux Egyptianness, a travesty of vanished temples by the Nile?

Now I'm seated in row two, and before the lights go down I try to explain to myself how this picture affected that boy I was, why it still rules my emotional tides at every viewing. Most obvious: the matter of race. Not long after seeing *Imitation of Life,* with its Eastman Color tableaux depicting the ravages of discrimination, I wrote an English class term paper, its topic: "prejudice." This being an unwelcome subject in the South during the civil rights struggle, my teacher responded, "It's not prejudice at all! That's what *they* call it—outside agitators. It's because they don't understand the Southern way of life." Foolish and self-serving though her words were that day, a few years later she told me she believed the changes had been for the better. We stayed in touch for the rest of her life, and I'm convinced she cast off her former bias.

More subtle than race, however, is the message that *Imitation of Life* telegraphed to my subconscious about revolt. About the psychic price that rebels pay, about parental suffocation, and about society's repressions. What I learned that day, though the lesson took years to comprehend, was this: Beware of conditional parental love. Even as it nurtures, so can it wreck our lives. This innocent destruction endures beyond the grave—for Sarah Jane Johnson up there on the screen, and for the rest of us, as well. Mothers especially, whose love can imprison their young like figures in a vitrine, brand the child who escapes their magic vault. That brand is a searing *G,* for Guilt. Like Sarah Jane, we should all "Question Authority"—a bumper sticker from the sixties that has now disappeared, though it belongs on every car in America.

What I couldn't have articulated at my early viewings of *Imitation of Life*: It's a very well-made film, owing to the director, the cameraman, the art director, and a host of Hollywood craftsmen whose artistry I was to comprehend as I progressed beyond a mere fan in the dark. (I hope I'll always retain a fan's enthusiasm. Look what happens to those who don't: Their writings convince you that movies are punishment.)

I glance behind me. Who's that in row eight? She looks different now, I think. Then I realize, so do we all. For it is Lupita Tovar, once a top movie star in Mexico who abandoned her career to marry Paul Kohner, the Hollywood agent. Their daughter, Susan, riveting in *Imitation of Life*, will soon appear once more on screen, tonight, and then in person to loud acclaim.

I recall pictures of Lupita Tovar from 1959, the year of *Imitation of Life,* accompanying Susan Kohner on publicity junkets. The two of them crossing the tarmac in London; mother and daughter emerging from a long Cadillac in Chicago; the Kohners at home in Bel Air. ("I had a strict Catholic upbringing," Susan told me. "My mother chaperoned me and she also spent a lot of time on the set.") Mrs. Kohner, who was forty-nine years old in 1959, was a stylish, lovely woman who still retained her movie-star sheen, though her glamour lacked any hint of Tinseltown gaudiness. Her fine features and upright comportment made her resemble a Mexican Irene Dunne. In fan-magazine photos of the time, Lupita Tovar, still screen-worthy, seemed to stand at the edge of the picture so that all light fell across the remarkable face of her daughter.

In April 2004, Mrs. Paul Kohner, a widow, is ninety-three. Here she is with her son, Pancho, on one side and Susan's sons, Paul and Chris Weitz, on the other. These grandchildren, born after Susan left Hollywood over forty years ago to marry the fashion designer John Weitz, are famous for the *American Pie* movies and other films.

That boy—me, though I must squint to recognize him down the long, gray corridor of time—would have been agog if some fortune-teller had unveiled the future that afternoon as he left the State Theatre in that small town in South Carolina, after seeing *Imitation of Life* for the first three times: ". . . and when you write a book about it, you'll visit Susan Kohner, you'll talk to her on the phone, and Juanita Moore, in her eighties by then, will be a real live wire when you meet her, and that elegant woman you glimpsed at the edge of the photo in last month's *Silver Screen* will talk to you for hours about her daughter's career and her own, and about Old Hollywood in all its goneness."

The house fills up. You can almost discern the clustered emotions around each person here, like auras. Even the few who have never seen the movie suspect they're in for something big. Parsing these emotions would be difficult, however, since *Imitation of Life* galvanizes in all sorts of ways. Worship it, loathe it, laugh, weep—you're bound to react. There is no "whatever."

Perhaps it is this overload of in-house emotion that makes me crane my neck toward the balcony of the Egyptian Theatre, as if searching, most incongruously, for Mahalia Jackson. As though, through special effects, she might rise up to sing "Trouble of the World" tonight as she did at Annie Johnson's funeral in *Imitation of Life*! Was that the most prodigious funeral Hollywood ever filmed?

Then I think, AIDS has robbed tonight's audience of so many. Why have gays always revered *Imitation of Life*? For one thing, there's a message of gay liberation encoded in the script, ten years before Stonewall. When eight-year-old Sarah Jane first denies her black mother in the schoolroom scene, Annie, brokenhearted, declares, "It's a sin to be ashamed of what you are. . . . The Lord must have had his reasons for making some of us white and some of us black."

Being different—is it easier now?

Another minority that reveres this picture: African-American women, several generations of them, who for a rare moment back then recognized themselves on movie screens. Perhaps as the mother, in some cases as the daughter, but always as targets of discrimination. Hollywood pictures of the time abstained from recognition of black people's burdens. The occasional film that took up their oppression typically dealt with happy-ending prejudice, or the ordeals of African-American men, such as racism in the workforce or the military. Black women remained invisible except as maids, jazz singers, or femmes fatales like Lena Horne and Dorothy Dandridge.

What did African-American women find in *Imitation of Life* to claim as their own? To be sure, it offers scant hope. Those postfuneral smiles beamed by Lana Turner and John Gavin won't help Sarah Jane. A misfit among blacks, and disillusioned with the artificial paradise of white America, she has no world of her own.

Perhaps those black women recognized the matriarchal pulse of this mother-daughter relationship, troubled though it is, as their own primal heartbeat. (And, of course, men and women of all races felt a similar arrhythmia. By emphasizing the response of black women, I don't mean to imply that black men respond less emotionally to *Imitation of Life*. I've seen quarterbacks choke up as they watch that funeral.)

Other connections with African Americans in the audience: religious faith as one's greatest comfort, almost compensating for low wages and lower status; colorism, defined as the stratification and prejudicial treatment of individuals in the same racial group based on skin tone, with those who "look white" elevated to higher standing; the traditional African-American respect due one's elders, along with the consequences of violating it.

Today's black woman may state it more directly. Not long ago I was at dinner in a restaurant with Juanita Moore and her godson, the actor and writer Ken Sagoes, when a young African-American woman recognized her and came over to our table. Thrilled to see her idol, the young woman, in her enthusiasm, blurted out, "You should have whipped that girl's butt for talking to you like that!"

It's easier now not to be ashamed of what you are. But in those audiences of 1959, I wonder how many words like "gay" or "Jewish," "Asian," "Hispanic," "poor" or "disabled" could have substituted for "white" and "black"? It's clear today that the picture speaks to a global audience that's boundlessly diverse. In India, I'm told, urban sophisticates weep for *Imitation of Life* as they might not for a Bollywood epic.

Even in distant 1959, however, the arrow hit a subliminal mark, for *Imitation of Life,* we now realize, was a Hollywood milestone. Many who saw it at the time, especially the young, perceived its submerged iconoclasm. Like Marlon Brando's *The Wild One,* although less directly, it helped destabilize 1950s mythology, whose icons enshrined white, middle-class, heterosexual, monogamous, family-valued, church-going, work-ethic America as the bland ideal, with few alternatives on offer.

Many then, and others down the years, took the hint: It's okay to be tragic—but suffer for who you are, not for who you aren't. In that, Sarah Jane functioned as a stern cautionary tale. Spilling her heart's blood for the white race, all she got back was abuse. This subversive idea wasn't written about at the time because no one quite dared. Audiences then saw Sarah Jane as wayward and unfortunate, but directed their sympathy to her mother.

Today, that sympathy strikes a few as misdirected. Some viewers blame the mother for seeking to shackle her daughter's life. A friend shocked me recently with this broadside: "This woman, Annie, deserves what she gets! Because she persecutes the girl—follows her, interferes, smothers her, and won't turn loose. And the daughter so clearly wants to escape." To him, whatever universal appeal *Imitation of Life* may possess comes from the parent-child dynamic: children desperate to flee their family circumstances versus parents who resist that separation. Annie Johnson, however, is scarcely the Hollywood stereotype of an

asphyxiating mother. That would be Shelley Winters, or a tiresome ter-
magant in the world of Woody Allen.

Another example of director Douglas Sirk's subversion: The topic of
interracial romance was taboo in 1959 (*Island in the Sun* had been
banned throughout the South two years earlier), but Sirk included just
such a subplot. Oddly, only one reviewer in the South commented. One
reason for the silence is because the "romance" is filmed as a violent, expressionistic vignette—shocking, in no way romantic.

Troy Donahue, having discovered that Susan Kohner's mother is
black, beats Kohner savagely and leaves her slumped in the gutter. As
the scene starts, slow underscore jazz plays on the sound track. The first
time he hits her, this jazz jumps to a wild bongo beat as if to spur him on
like a fighting cock. The music, the garish colors, the violence, and the
clip-clip editing pack this four-minute sequence so full that virtually no
one noticed the obvious: interracial dating gone sour.

Racist audiences presumably read the sequence as a critique of miscegenation, like the lone Southern reviewer who wrote, in the New Orleans *Times-Picayune,* "This picture is a very strong argument to the
effect that the mixing of the races brings nothing but tragedy over and
over." Others took it, correctly, as a damning indictment of racism. Going deeper, one might decipher the beating scene as metaphoric scorn
for Hollywood's practice of casting nonblacks in black roles (one of the
picture's many "imitations"). Typical of Sirk's prestidigitation and his
subversive irony, these fleeting moments are so jam-packed that it's easy
to miss his primary point, for this brief scene pivots the plot in Sarah
Jane's favor, at least for a time. It justifies her desire to pass. Otherwise,
such suffering is to be her fate.

Filming the scene, Troy Donahue hit Susan Kohner so hard that he
sent her into hysterics. Her face, covered with abrasions, required medical attention, and she missed work for a couple of days. Sirk sent flowers,
with a card inscribed, "Some yellow roses for the blue bruises." Susan still
has that card pasted in a scrapbook.

Tonight, in long retrospect, I'm glad my own miseries and joys have
played out in a gay context, for I have witnessed the grievous results of
closety denial. A paraphrase, half-camp and half-political, of Annie

Johnson's line zips through my head: The Lord must have had his reasons for making some of us gay and some of us straight. Updating the thought, I might rather say that owing in part to such movies as *Imitation of Life* and *Now, Voyager,* we learned to reinvent ourselves—or, in current lingo, rebrand. Put another way, certain movies suggested how to scrape off the false image that biased parties—parents, school, religion, government, and, yes, we ourselves—had painted over our real selves, and to reveal the true design underneath.

This country's tropes of democracy and equality, faulty and failed as they are, perhaps facilitate that kind of identity makeover. But the hidden costs of redefinition may sometimes prove exorbitant. Again, look at Sarah Jane.

Right now, standing in front of the screen at the Egyptian Theatre, tonight's host, film historian Foster Hirsch, opens the program. He says, "Conservatively speaking, you are about to see the greatest film ever made." The audience seems nonplussed. Is he putting them on? I've known Foster for years, and I've heard this before, though I've never decided to what extent his quicksilver statement is tongue-in-cheek. Actually, I want him to mean it literally. Such statements measure one's passion, and his clocks in at fever-pitch. The greatest film . . . ?

Could I say the same—and almost mean it? Whether *Imitation of Life* is greater in anyone's estimation than *Intolerance, Citizen Kane, The Godfather,* or whatever candidate—the answer lies beyond words. Maybe Wittgenstein was right: "What really matters is what we can only be silent about." I do think *Imitation of Life* hits you harder, if you have the right temperament. I do. So does Foster Hirsch, and so do countless others. Perhaps one measure of "soul" is one's response to this film. (I can't picture a hardened Republican like Condoleezza Rice with a tear in her eye.)

The lights dim and the movie starts. Earl Grant sings that haunting, gaudy song:

> *What is love without the giving?*
> *Without love you're only living*
> *An imitation, an imitation of life . . .*

The credits unroll as jewels drop—false diamonds, glass beads cheaply produced—from some imaginary sky and collect in a ravishing pile at the bottom of the frame. Oh yes, I know, some call it vulgar. Let them! I happen to love this Woolworth chichi that Tiffany's doesn't sell. I exult in the florid sentiment, relishing the offense it causes prigs and aesthetes. Something I learned recently about the film's producer: "The Ross Hunter touch was apparent even in the title credits. They were displayed against a background of square, round, and emerald-cut diamonds drifting in slow motion down the screen against a black-velvet backdrop. It was his own design, and he had discovered it at home, using for his experiments a slide projector and a crushed Pepsi-Cola bottle."

Tonight's print of *Imitation of Life,* said to be the only one Universal owns, is slightly worn. For that reason I have the eerie sense of watching a fifties movie in the fifties, one that has been playing for months and now shows the wear.

I recall a conversation with Pauline Kael in 1983. Her book *5001 Nights at the Movies* had just come out, and I asked why she didn't include *Imitation of Life.* "Oh sweetie, I almost choked on the lump in my throat when Susan Kohner showed up for her black mother's funeral," she said, "and at the same time I was laughing. I don't know how I overlooked that one." Kael, who liked to think of herself as a "tough broad," wasn't one to admit shedding tears. So if the picture got to *her,* it must pack more than standard sentimental wallop.

Unlike Kael, I'm not laughing as Susan Kohner breaks through a police line and flings herself sobbing on her mother's coffin. "Mama! Do you hear me? I'm sorry! I'm sorry! Mama! Mama, I did love you." No one laughs tonight. Pauline, of course, wasn't belittling the girl's heartbreak. She was deriding what she considered Hollywood manipulation, the kind that demands a lump in your throat. But *Imitation of Life* is different. Unlike *The Color Purple, Terms of Endearment,* and so many other movies that do indeed extort tears, this one sanctions the release of tears already there. It's a great movie not because it makes you weep, but because the film itself is a threnody for hopeless humanity. The tears also fall inward, on the heart.

Susan Kohner made brilliant acting choices throughout the film, none more so than in this scene. When I asked her about it, she explained her commonsense method: "I pretended it was my own mother in the casket."

Much has been written about Douglas Sirk's irony here and elsewhere in his films. Was it his intention, I wonder, to make audiences flock to see *Imitation of Life* for Lana Turner—the jewels, the gowns, the romance, the scandal—but come out jolted by the performances of Susan Kohner and Juanita Moore?

The film has ended and Foster Hirsch is concluding his introduction of tonight's guests: "And now, the stars of the picture!" The audience starts to applaud. Some of us turn and look around. Applause grows louder.

Enter Susan Kohner and Juanita Moore.

Juanita, holding a cane in her right hand, moves slowly, and Susan takes her left arm to guide her. Annie Johnson's feebleness late in the film echoes down the years in Juanita Moore's geriatric gait. "I'm just tired," Annie said. "Awfully tired." But Juanita herself is feisty, determined to outdo the pitfalls of age.

Applause redoubles, and everyone stands. This entrance suggests the movie's funeral procession in reverse: that operatic cavalcade of mourners, brass band, and horse-drawn hearse moved left across the screen. Now Susan and Juanita, having defied time, move to the right and down the aisle. Reaching the front, they seat themselves in spacious chairs, where both seem rather baffled by the emotional tidal wave. The audience pours out love, gratitude, respect. Also curiosity, for these two women have been out of the spotlight for years. (Juanita says pointblank, "Everybody thinks I'm dead.") But tonight, hundreds have come here to honor this enigmatic pair.

Seeing Juanita and Susan, their characters tragically at odds in the film, together now as friends—in a new century—seems to bestow a benediction on us all. The power of certain films is so great that they overrule our rational mind to create a subtext of absolution. In other words, it's as though Annie Johnson has been resurrected in a place where she is esteemed and adored, and where at last she finds peace with her daughter, Sarah Jane. Their reunion seems to transcend time.

And so, for many of us here in Hollywood tonight, the used-up years have shed all melancholy meaning. We, too, have transcended time and tinsel. Together, we seem to lay hold of something bigger than the sum of this movie's parts. As though celebrating a secular Easter, we behold Annie Johnson's tomb opened and she stands before us in the grand and durable reality of Juanita Moore.

And what of Sarah Jane? Susan Kohner, in real life, has nothing in common with that bad girl, the undutiful daughter. Raised as a proper lady, Susan possesses such old-fashioned qualities as kindness, modesty, and understatement, which seem to be vanishing from our world like the ice caps. Wise, controlled, and considerate, and woven from strong fibers, she might have grown up in a Jane Austen novel if she hadn't lived in Hollywood.

Nor should anyone mistake Juanita Moore for the saint she played on screen, humble and self-effacing, who seldom raised her voice. In the days leading up to this event, those who crossed her learned that Juanita can bite. "At my age I can say anything I damn well please," she proclaimed. (I smile, recalling the time Juanita said something ribald and proper Susan admonished her, sotto voce, "Don't say that, Juanita.")

Becoming better acquainted with Juanita Moore, I've seen her eyes flash with anger as she recalled racist hurts. I've heard her say words that would make God-fearing Annie Johnson scowl in disapproval. On occasion, Juanita and I have laughed so hard that I've shed a different kind of tear. (At first I called her "Miss Moore." Then she said, "Please call me Juanita. Otherwise, you're gonna make me feel too damn old.")

Yes, she's high-spirited and volatile, but also very loving. Once she trusts you, Juanita Moore is your friend for life. At the end of every visit or phone call, she tells me, "God bless you, baby."

In instances of true acting talent, the stronger an actor's performance, the wider the gulf between the person and the part she plays. And no actor wants to be confused with her role. Still, it's ironic and a little disconcerting to see Susan—petite, shy, speaking in soft tones—overshadowed by Juanita, who rocks the joint. Juanita Moore is a large, handsome woman who in her later years might have played Bessie Smith or Ma Rainey. Though soft-spoken in *Imitation of Life,* tonight you hear the boom in her rich, burnished voice. Her eyes speak almost as loudly, for in them you glimpse, by turns, like figures in an allegory, Hurt, Bitterness, Resignation, and Triumph.

In spite of the wrongs done to her, she won. She did so by refusing to let anyone steal her soul. Juanita found the humanity in her life, as she found it in her screen roles. Her anger is not destructive but cleansing. And in her you'll find no trace of the sanctimonious self-righteousness of Ethel Waters in those Billy Graham crusades, nor is she self-absorbed like many in show business. More than any Hollywood actor I've known, Juanita sees herself clearly—meaning that she views the rest of us clearly, too.

As a kid I imagined stars watching their own pictures often and obsessively, like fans. Tonight the remnant of that kid is surprised to hear Juanita Moore answer Foster Hirsch's question, "I haven't seen the whole film in years." Susan's response—"I usually skip the first forty minutes"—draws a laugh.

That day long ago, at my first exposure, I felt used up, as though I had attended an entire, draining afternoon of church funerals in a row. All across the theatre, weeping drowned the script. To be sure, such mourning brings with it luxury, even a peculiar joy. It starts with sad arousal, builds to an ecstasy of sobs, and climaxes in a flood, to be followed by peace and rest. Perhaps grief evolved from the same unlikely part of the brain as erotic pleasure, like birds from reptiles.

And perhaps that's one reason why *Imitation of Life* is such an emotional turn-on: the gorgeous foreplay of a Ross Hunter production, with Lana Turner's splendors and miseries, and the fantastic urgings of showbiz, all mixed up with forbidden impulses and a bitter critique of bourgeois America's cherished icons and mythology, followed by a lavish production number—in church!—that suggests D. W. Griffith crossed with Wagner, as Mahalia Jackson sings the funeral dirge like a diva at the Met. Or Valhalla.

That grand-opera funeral is so thrillingly produced that you almost smell the cloying gladioli, the treacly gardenias. Teeming with its own

Da Vinci code of meanings and interpretations, *Imitation of Life* is passionate, cynical, and laced with irony, a florid valentine with a death's head where Cupid ought to be. As such, it is Douglas Sirk's great final outburst, his bitter farewell to Hollywood—and the America of quiet desperation.

1 | A SMALL GIANT

O n July 19, 1956, just over two years before Sirk's cast assembled at Universal to begin filming, an item appeared in *The Hollywood Reporter*: "Ross Hunter Gets *Imitation of Life* for Musical Film." The piece stated, "Following lengthy negotiations with novelist Fannie Hurst, U-I producer Ross Hunter has tied up the rights for a musical version of the author's highly successful book, *Imitation of Life,* which was filmed by Universal back in 1934. Shirley Booth will play the role originated by Claudette Colbert, while Ethel Waters is set for the Louise Beavers role. Rehearsals are slated for early 1958."

Shirley Booth, unlike Ethel Waters, seems a bizarre casting choice until you fill in the blanks. Although Ross Hunter preferred glamorous actresses with box-office pull for his films, he often used the other kind—aging ladies, some recently redundant in Hollywood, whom he could hire on the cheap. Hunter was known for making inexpensive pictures look costly, and one ingredient in his formula was big names from the day before yesterday. He had recently used Jane Wyman twice, in *Magnificent Obsession* (1954) and *All That Heaven Allows* (1955). He had also employed Ann Sheridan and Joan Bennett, neither of whom was besieged by other offers at the time.

Universal had found its perfect producer in Ross Hunter. By tradition a cut-rate studio, its star roster often shone with hand-me-down actors from MGM, Paramount, and the other majors. Yet Universal wished to sparkle in spite of its financial rolling blackouts, and Hunter could power a hundred-watt bulb from a firefly's back end.

Shirley Booth, who won an Oscar in 1952 for *Come Back, Little Sheba,* seems a bad fit for *Imitation of Life* if you think of her playing the glittery Lana Turner role. But that isn't what Ross Hunter had in mind. In 1956, he seems to have wanted an earthy heroine to contrast with Claudette Colbert's slick unreality in the original film from 1934.

There is some confusion as to whether he intended the property for Broadway or the screen. Oddly, in a letter to Hurst dated August 3, 1956, a couple of weeks after the *Hollywood Reporter* item, Hunter referred to an announcement of the "musical stage version," which he claimed "came as a complete surprise to me—naturally I would love to do it—and I have discussed the project with Shirley Booth . . . I have such good ideas for a stage version—but must wait for the right time." Although scant documentation remains to trace the evolution of Hunter's plan, it's likely that he intended to retain the plot and characters of Fannie Hurst's soggy 1933 novel in his musical version of it.

In the same letter, he refers to a recent luncheon with Hurst in New York, at which they presumably discussed a musical version of her novel and perhaps a subsequent film remake. He ends the letter by telling her, "I hope that we will—some day—be able to do a stage version of your wonderful book—in fact, I've already discussed its possibilities in the not too distant future with my agents, the William Morris Agency."

In Fannie Hurst's novel, the two main female characters are Bea Pullman, a widowed housewife who eventually makes a fortune through her nationwide chain of waffle restaurants, and Delilah, the black woman who supplies the secret recipe. Each woman has a daughter, and both girls bring their mothers grief. The white girl falls in love with her mother's lover, while the black girl denies her race by passing for white. John M. Stahl's 1934 film version adhered to the novel, which explains why his picture moves with a limp.

In due course, we will revisit Fannie Hurst, John M. Stahl, Claudette Colbert, Louise Beavers, and other parties of the first part. Meanwhile, however, let's assume that Ross Hunter realized the necessity of making significant changes in the remake of a picture over two decades old. His first impulse was to make it sing.

Extrapolating from two graceless musicals that Hunter later produced, *Thoroughly Modern Millie* (1967) and *Lost Horizon* (1973), one can imagine his original concept for the *Imitation of Life* remake: Let 'em warble about waffle batter and the loneliness of successful women without men. Throw in a new spiritual about Negroes, white folks, and a non-denominational God for Ethel Waters, give Shirley Booth a wistful ballad and later a knee-slapping "We're-Rolling-in-Dough-and-I-Don't-Mean-Waffles" number, bring back Ethel for some torchy jazz, and hand over the package to a journeyman director.

Georgia Avenue

By the time Fannie Hurst's novel was finally turned into a musical, Ross Hunter had retired. It's unlikely that he saw the show, for it ran only a few weeks at the Norma Terris Theatre in Connecticut, in the summer of 1985. Nor was it recorded. Recently, I visited the composer, Howard Marren, in New York. At my urging, he sat down at the piano and played and sang half-a-dozen songs from the show. When I told him of Ross Hunter's original plans, he said, "In our version, Shirley Booth would have been a good choice."

Joe Masteroff, best known as writer of the book for Kander and Ebb's *Cabaret,* wrote book and lyrics for *Georgia Avenue.* (The title refers to Bea Pullman's address in Atlantic City before she becomes the waffle queen.) Masteroff said, "I thought it was a beautiful name for a musical." Having seen the 1934 film, he always preferred it to Sirk's remake. Although rights to the material were obtained from the estate of Fannie Hurst and not from Universal, *Georgia Avenue* is considerably simplified, like the original movie.

Marren's other musicals include *Portrait of Jennie* and *Paramour,* based on Anouilh's play *The Waltz of the Toreadors.* He describes *Georgia Avenue* as "though composed and largely sung through, more in the lyric theatre vein than a Tin Pan Alley show."

Based on my slight acquaintance with the show—Howard Marren

(continued)

at the piano, and the tape I made of his impromptu samples—I would place it musically somewhere between early Sondheim and the *verismo* of Jason Robert Brown's *Parade,* which ran on Broadway in 1998–99. "There are no take-home tunes," noted *Variety*'s theatre critic. Other reviewers mentioned members of the audience in tears at the show's funeral finale, "Take Her, Lord."

Was Sirk a contender from the start? Possibly, since he and Ross Hunter had already made half-a-dozen pictures together. Then, too, Sirk was not unfamiliar with musicals, having directed Hunter's small production of *Take Me to Town* in 1953 and, before that, several musical romances in Germany in the 1930s. Hunter no doubt sensed that Sirk would both lighten such material and also give it heft and balance. In line with the story, Shirley Booth, a Hollywood plain Jane, looks the part of a hausfrau who stumbles on a million-dollar recipe. Though not a great singer, she could carry a tune. Indeed, she had done so in several Broadway musicals, including *A Tree Grows in Brooklyn* in 1951 and *By the Beautiful Sea* in 1954.

By 1956, when *The Hollywood Reporter* announced a set-to-music *Imitation of Life,* Ross Hunter had so many films in production or on the boards that he lacked time enough to think them all through. In January and February of 1955, he and Sirk had made *All That Heaven Allows,* a hit when released later that year. Immediately following that, the two filmed *There's Always Tomorrow* with Barbara Stanwyck, Fred MacMurray, and Joan Bennett. Sirk then directed *Written on the Wind* with Al Zugsmith rather than Ross Hunter as producer, though Hunter and Sirk reunited for *Battle Hymn* (filmed March to May of 1956, released March of 1957) with Rock Hudson and Martha Hyer. Ross next produced *Tammy and the Bachelor* (1957), starring Debbie Reynolds and directed by Joseph Pevney. Then Hunter, Sirk, June Allyson, Rossano Brazzi, Jane Wyatt, and the rest of the cast and crew flew to Europe to film *Interlude* in Germany and Austria.

By this point, the careers of Hunter and Sirk resemble a square dance, as Ross sashays right to produce *My Man Godfrey* (1957) with David Niven and June Allyson, directed by Henry Koster, while Sirk promenades left with *The Tarnished Angels* (1957) and his erstwhile producer Al Zugsmith. Do-si-do, and Ross changes partners twice for his next three movies: Blake Edwards directs *This Happy Feeling* (1958), Helmut Käutner *The Restless Years* (1958) and *A Stranger in My Arms* (1959).

Circle again, allemande right, and Sirk directs his penultimate Hollywood film, *A Time to Love and a Time to Die* (1958), produced by Robert Arthur and starring John Gavin, who will work once more with Sirk, and with Hunter again and again. Then, in a great and spectacular finale that ends their dance, Ross Hunter produces, and Sirk directs, *Imitation of Life*.

Ross Hunter left behind no archive. After his death, in 1996, and the death of his partner, Jacque [sic] Mapes, in 2002, their personal and professional papers and other possessions were scattered. This loss reverberates throughout film history of the last sixty years, for Hunter worked with half of Hollywood. He was a small giant. (I intend that term as a compliment, contrasting him with so many presumed giants who turn out, in reality, to stand knee-high to a pygmy.)

Because the record is so sketchy, it's impossible to ascertain the complete genesis of *Imitation of Life,* including how long and how seriously Hunter considered yoking Shirley Booth and Ethel Waters. Nor is it easy to establish a chronology, although it seems that after Hunter acquired rights to the novel in 1956, he laid the project aside until spring of 1958, when Lana Turner materialized for the lead. By that time, also, he had the new script in hand, which transformed Hurst's waffle queen, Bea Pullman, into Broadway star Lora Meredith. (In the 1934 film, Bea's famous waffles were flattened into pancakes.)

On paper, at least, Ethel Waters makes sense as the black woman. A few years earlier, in *Pinky* (1949), she played humble and pious Aunt Dicey. It's unclear why Waters was replaced. Hunter's next candidate, however, would have attacked the part with a brassy clang. In an oral history recorded in 1984, Hunter said, "We wanted Pearl Bailey for the role, but Pearl was going to do *Porgy and Bess* for Sam Goldwyn. He would not let her go."

Then Hunter had two new ideas, each one a bit odd. After pondering Marian Anderson for the role of Annie Johnson, he picked Mahalia Jackson, who commanded the devotion of millions for her gospel singing. (He also thought fleetingly of Anderson as the soloist in the funeral sequence.) Mahalia had never acted, nor did she have any interest in taking it up. Ross Hunter persuaded her at least to listen to his pitch, and she auditioned for the role. We don't know how that audition came off, but according to Juanita Moore, a friend of Mahalia's, it was the singer herself who declined. "Child," she said to Ross Hunter, shaking her great head, "I'm a singer, not an actress. But let me tell you somebody who is. Honey, I want you to go call her up right now. My friend Juanita Moore."

The process may or may not have played out so directly. According to a studio press release in 1958, "After interviewing several hundred aspirants, producer Hunter and director Sirk settled on Juanita Moore." Were there really hundreds of suitable African-American actresses in Hollywood at that time? I recently put the question to actor Robert Hooks, who arrived in town from the New York stage not long after. He said, "For that particular role, Juanita Moore's role in *Imitation of Life,* I doubt it. But there were a lot of African-American actors in Hollywood, most of them out of work. So I could understand that for certain roles there might be a call for a hundred fifty to two hundred actors."

Whether or not that many actually read for the part, the studio's statement suggests unease about the role and about the picture. A "safe" actress was essential, someone palatable to the conservative—and, yes, racist—American public. Such corporate nervousness was not misplaced in 1958. Here was a picture trying to "pass" as a Lana Turner vehicle, replete with fashions and jewels and shiny interior decor, but which, in reality, addressed one of that era's hot-button topics: race. No one at Universal failed to grasp the implications of a story about discrimination, passing, and that oblique glance at interracial love, however camouflaged.

In the oral history cited above, Ross Hunter recalls how he met Juanita Moore. "I found Juanita sitting on a bench, and I went up to her and said, 'Are you an actress?' And she said, 'Well, I am an actress, but you know there are not that many parts for black people.' And I said, 'Well, I'm Ross Hunter.' And she said, 'Oh, sure you are.' She didn't believe me. I said, 'Would you come to my office tomorrow at eleven to test for a movie? There's something about your face that was like a magnet. I've been watching you sitting here waiting for the bus.'"

What a pretty story! Why, it almost resembles a meet-cute scene from a Ross Hunter picture. And not at all true, according to Juanita Moore. "No!" she chortled. "I wasn't waiting for a bus. After Mahalia turned down the part, Joel Fluellen took me to see Ross Hunter." Fluellen, who plays Annie Johnson's minister near the end of *Imitation of Life,* was a close friend of Juanita's and a veteran in the struggle for nonsterotypical African-American visibility in films. "Joel prepared me for my audition and my screen test. He made me up, fixed my hair, he did everything for me," she declared. (More on Joel Fluellen later. For now, however, the focus is Juanita Moore, who, along with Susan Kohner, turned *Imitation of Life* into a masterpiece.)

If Hunter had indeed spotted Juanita waiting for a bus, surely Universal's publicity department would have pumped up the story for a press release. How nicely it would have rhymed with Lana Turner's "discovery" at Schwab's. But they didn't. It is true, however, that once Hunter spoke with Juanita Moore, he would consider no one else to play Annie Johnson. According to Juanita, when she tested for the role, she lacked the necessary Southern accent and mannerisms that the studio bosses wanted and that Mahalia Jackson had (Juanita was born in Mississippi but moved with her family to Los Angeles soon after). Mahalia also had name recognition, especially among black audiences. So did Pearl Bailey. Juanita didn't, but Ross Hunter stuck by her until he overcame studio misgivings. He also put her in the hot seat. "Juanita," he said, "I'm going to stick my neck out for you. If you're no good, I'm finished at Universal."

2 | THE GOOD AND FAITHFUL SERVANT

*T*he studio lavished more on Lana Turner's wardrobe ($23,645) than it paid Juanita Moore in salary ($5,550) for *Imitation of Life*. After all, Juanita was playing the role that blacks had always been hired for in Hollywood pictures. If someone had asked her at the time how she felt about the stereotypical part, she might well have echoed Hattie McDaniel's practical comment on her career: "I'd rather play a maid than be one."

But fortune sometimes boomerangs in the picture business, and Juanita Moore won an Oscar nomination for the role of Annie Johnson, that good and faithful servant.* Her luck didn't hold, however, and so for the next forty years she played again and again the same role she had played from the start: This great actress was cast as the maid.

Ultimately, though, she claimed a huge surplus victory, for today, among legions who have watched *Imitation of Life* and wept, Juanita Moore ranks as a celluloid saint. And a martyr of sorts, not only because of Hollywood's long neglect and humiliation, but more strikingly because,

---

*Juanita Moore was the third African American nominated in the Supporting Actress Category, following winner Hattie McDaniel for *Gone With the Wind* in 1939 and nominee Ethel Waters for *Pinky* in 1949. Dorothy Dandridge was the first African American nominated as Best Actress, for *Carmen Jones* in 1954. James Baskette was given a special Oscar in 1947 for his role as Uncle Remus in *Song of the South*.

in the film, her daughter commits an unpardonable sin: She renounces and reviles her mother. Desperate to pass for white, the daughter voices her mother's death sentence: "If, by accident, we should ever pass on the street, please don't recognize me." *Imitation of Life* made Juanita Moore a star, although a funny kind of star after all. A half century later, everyone remembers the tears they shed for her as she suffered and died. Yet many recall no more than that, making her a household emotion, though not a household name.

A terrible racist stereotype, common at the time *Imitation of Life* was filmed, depicted black maids as pilferers from their employers. The irony here is both devastating and hilarious: This time, the maid stole the picture. And how could she not, since Douglas Sirk made a career of turning out some of the most subtly ironic films ever shot in Hollywood. Of his irony-laced movies, *Imitation of Life* is the most heavily saturated, like a beautiful sugary cake that, underneath the icing, smacks of bitter herbs.

Juanita Moore's accomplice was a white actress passing for black in the film, Susan Kohner. Under Sirk's unwavering direction, their anguished characters outdo the film itself. At the time, their visionary performances haunted the nation, like a latter-day *Uncle Tom's Cabin*.

And the picture was perfectly timed.

"How do you explain to your child, she was born to be hurt?" This line from *Imitation of Life* evokes the United States in its last desperate years of institutionalized racism. It seems more than coincidence that Douglas Sirk filmed his masterpiece in late summer of 1958, less than three years after Rosa Parks sat down in that bus in Montgomery and the Rev. Martin Luther King Jr. led the boycott. Only a few years earlier, neither Hollywood nor the American public would have accepted this picture. (Even the 1934 *Imitation of Life,* conservative, safe, and devoid of subtext, encountered roadblocks, as we will see.) In the spirit of those times, what might Juanita Moore's line to Lana Turner—"How do you explain to your child, she was born to be hurt?"—have meant to audiences north and south when the film opened in 1959? What does it mean today? And how might we, in the "progressive" twenty-first century, explain to those audiences at the tail end of a similar era, that so much has changed, and so little?

Imitation of Life is unlike any other picture that Sirk directed or that Hunter produced. It's really two pictures conjoined as celluloid Siamese twins, albeit fraternal, not identical ones. And inseparable, though the favored one got all the milk, while the other languished, etiolated, and became a laughingstock. This bifocal vision was clear from the start, though the passing years have thrown it into more dramatic relief. First, there's what I'll call "the white movie," starring two blondes, Lana Turner and Sandra Dee, as mother and daughter, with Lana playing glamour-puss actress Lora Meredith. Eventually she and her daughter fall for the same man. This side of the picture labors under every false emotion concocted for screenland drama. As such, it delights and depresses, like *Beyond the Forest* or *Valley of the Dolls*. Laughter permitted.

Who could keep a straight face under Lana's barrage of camp lines, and her high-flown delivery of them: (to John Gavin): "You're so—so good for what ails me."; (blithely, to dying Juanita Moore): "It never occurred to me that you had many friends." And her stiff audition sequence for the playwright David Edwards's latest Feydeauesque farce, where she mimes opening and closing doors to discover trysting roués in closets: "Why, Mr. Overmeyer! Why aren't you in Duluth? Oh, Herbert! You, too?" This is the most gaga audition ever filmed, a ludicrous scene on a bare stage that resembles a Beckett landscape, and yet the very silliness of those lines hoists it to some cockamamie pseudo-grandeur. Lora, the neophyte, is already as grande as Vera Charles.

Sorrow and camp: you could annotate *Imitation of Life* with that phrase. They overlap but faintly. The film's second personality might be called "the dark side." Dark in every sense, it echoes one of Lora Meredith's starring vehicles: *No More Laughter*. Juanita Moore's character, Annie Johnson, raises her daughter, Sarah Jane, the "right" way: to be proud of who she is but to bury her pride. In other words, to stay in her place as a Negro. Even as a child, however, Sarah Jane resents living in back rooms and entering through servants' doors. As a light-skinned young woman, she can pass for white and does so. To wear this white mask safely, however, she must renounce her mother and that "dangerous" black skin. "I'm white, white, WHITE," Sarah Jane wails in anguish at their final meeting. But her mother knows, and so do we: Sarah Jane is fooling no one but herself.

About an hour into the film, you realize that a great wind has swept away the floral scent of the first part of the movie. The key has changed, and that backstage opera buffa has modulated into an opera seria that resembles a work by Verdi or Puccini, with similar outsize emotions and stylized taboos. Devoid of identifiable camp, the *Imitation of Life* owned by Juanita Moore and Susan Kohner reaches a prodigious climax with the mother's ornate funeral, thrillingly produced, which pulls out as many emotional stops as E. Power Biggs at the Radio City organ. From there, looking back, you realize that the earthbound, blond side of the picture served as the booster rocket to shoot the black side to transcendence.

In the film, Juanita Moore based her characterization of Annie Johnson on a family member. Here, in her own words, the source of that unforgettable performance: "I had a sister who really was like that character, and I patterned my role after her. She had been to college, but she did the work of Annie Johnson. She was very religious, loved everybody, she was patient and good. My sister was the opposite of me! She saw *Imitation of Life* many times and thought I did it well."

Juanita's parents, Harrison and Ella Moore, made the long train journey from Greenwood, Mississippi, to Southern California toward the end of World War One. For them, as for others in the Great Migration, the trip must have been both wearying and exhilarating, for they had eight children to keep up with, seven girls and one boy. Juanita, the youngest, was a toddler. One thing was certain, however: No matter how arduous their travels, the Moores' departure from Mississippi meant improvement.

California, although far from paradise, lacked the enduring slave-state mentality of the Deep South. Indeed, one might consider California in the early decades of the twentieth century to have been among the least oppressive parts of the country. And Los Angeles, random and full of energy, had suddenly become a company town as the picture industry morphed from infancy to adolescent sprawl.

Like most African Americans of the time, the Moores settled in South Central L.A. Donald Bogle, in his book *Bright Boulevards, Bold*

Dreams: The Story of Black Hollywood, evokes the energetic young city that Juanita Moore's family arrived in: "Los Angeles itself seemed to be changing daily as more and more colored Americans came west. L.A. could still boast of decent race relations. The new black immigrants were able to live wherever they wanted without great restrictions—*at first.* Yet there were areas where black Angelenos knew they were not welcome. From 1910 into the teens, black residents occupied an area in south central Los Angeles known as the Furlong Tract. The main thoroughfare was Central Avenue, which ran north to south and which became black L.A.'s most famous street."

The family prospered, and in a few years Mrs. Moore and one of her older daughters opened a laundry near Twenty-seventh Street and Griffith Avenue. Juanita worked there, and also in her aunt's ice cream parlor. Recalling her after-school job of scooping up ice cream to make cones and sundaes, Juanita jokes, "On my days behind the counter there was very little net profit."

As a musically inclined young child, Juanita sang and danced. She already had her dream. Little girls from respectable families, however, didn't go traipsing around telling folks they were headed for a career in show business. Mr. and Mrs. Moore, after all, were upstanding Baptists. They didn't condone the wild goings-on of Hollywood, nor were they at ease with the slam-bang entertainments closer to home. Central Avenue, the glittering epicenter of black Angeleno joie de vivre, blazed with such rollicking establishments as the Clark Hotel, the Lyons Hotel, the Louisiana Cafe, and clubs like the Alhambra. On weekends, one might almost have mistaken certain raucous parts of Central Avenue for Bourbon Street.

This including the Dunbar Hotel, "home to the black elite," which fascinated Juanita Moore, now in her early teens. She said she used to sneak down there. And what did she do? "I just looked!" No wonder she was dazzled, since "a gallery of famous entertainers might be spotted sitting in its lounge: Bill 'Bojangles' Robinson. Duke Ellington. Louis Armstrong. Langston Hughes. Count Basie." She recalls gazing at Jack Johnson, the heavyweight boxing champion, as he drove down Central Avenue one day "in a Phaeton with a white woman beside him."

Juanita's parents, sensing the rebel in their youngest, encouraged her to become a teacher. Or a nurse. Anything but an entertainer, which, she says with a great laugh, "was almost as bad as a whore." While attending Jefferson High School, Juanita had a teacher named Miss Thompson who heard her sing in the Glee Club. One day the teacher summoned her and said, "Juanita, I want you to sing for me."

Miss Thompson suggested the possibility of a career on the stage. Or in the movies. "During that time," Juanita said many years later, "we didn't have too many choices." Idealistic Miss Thompson, however, repeated those high-minded words (now a part of vanished Americana) that schoolteachers once spoke routinely: "Juanita, you can become whatever you want to be." Young persons, their illusions intact, often believed those slogans. Suddenly, the world looked wider and more inviting to that young girl, Juanita Moore. (Marcus Garvey, the early civil rights crusader, said it, too, addressing all black people: "Up, you mighty race! You can accomplish what you will.")

One day Juanita felt unwell. The illness worsened, she developed fever, a severe headache came on, her neck and back grew rigid, and then came the failure of her legs. At age fifteen, she was stricken with infantile paralysis, a form of polio. "Doctors didn't care anything about blacks in those days," she declared some seventy-five years later, suggesting that she recovered in spite of their ministrations. Her mother and older sisters cared for her. Juanita recalls her mother rubbing her legs with olive oil while reassuring her, "You're going to walk, Juanita. You will walk!" Four months later, she walked again.

While still in high school, Juanita attended a performance of the Lafayette Players, a black theatre company that originated in Harlem in 1915 and remained there until 1928, when a number of the players emigrated to the Lincoln Theatre in Los Angeles. Located at Twenty-third and Central, this showplace was described by *The California Eagle,* the city's leading African-American newspaper, as "the finest and most beautiful theatre in the country built exclusively for race patronage."

"I scrambled up enough money to go and see a play," Juanita recalled long after. "Maybe fifty or seventy-five cents. I was enthralled! I had never seen black actors before." The troupe's first Los Angeles engagement lasted a couple of months, with a different production every two weeks of a recent Broadway play or revival. Juanita remembers seeing

Madame X and *Dr. Jekyll and Mr. Hyde,* among others. "And that," she says, "was one of my inspirations that told me I wanted to be an actress."

In spite of afternoons spent eating up her aunt's ice cream profits, Juanita kept her figure. (She kept it so well, in fact, that years later, for *Imitation of Life,* she had to gain weight to make Annie Johnson look matronly—and to avoid competition with Lana Turner's own svelte shape.)

After graduation from Jefferson High School, Juanita attended Los Angeles City College "just long enough to take a deep breath." Feeling family restraints in Los Angeles, however, she headed for New York and arrived in time for the closing years of the Harlem Renaissance. Perhaps Nina Simone's song, "To Be Young, Gifted, and Black" (from a poem by Langston Hughes) best describes Juanita Moore in the middle-to-late thirties. And beautiful. These attributes, and others, helped land her first New York job: she joined the chorus line at Small's Paradise, on 135th Street and Seventh Avenue in Harlem.

If Juanita Moore had walked out the front door of Small's Paradise and headed in any direction, in ten minutes or so she could have entered any one of an array of similar establishments: the Yeah Man, the Hot-Cha Bar and Grill (where "Nothing Happens Before 2 a.m."), Radium Club, Connie's Inn, Cotton Club, Savoy Ballroom, or the Log Cabin. Not to mention such restaurant hangouts as the Theatrical Grill, Gladys' Clam House, and Tillie's.

Small's Paradise chose well, and so did Juanita. This was one of the Big Three so-called white-oriented clubs, meaning that black entertainers performed for a predominantly white clientele. (The others were the Cotton Club and Connie's Inn.) This spot being black-owned, however, it did not bar people of color, as certain other clubs did. The reason few local African Americans patronized Small's had to do with its steep prices. Thus, Small's Paradise qualified as a "black-and-tan" club, meaning that black people and white people intermingled, sat together, and danced together in spite of prevailing taboos.

Patrons at Small's Paradise, which flourished from the twenties into the forties, paid top prices to hear jazz and watch elaborate floor shows featuring beautiful young women like Juanita Moore. Between shows, sprightly singing waiters negotiated their way among close-packed tables, stopping to spin their trays and dance the Charleston for goggle-eyed ladies and gents who had trekked uptown for precisely such exotica. Adding to the forbidden allure, at one time an all-gay black male chorus line performed as the Internationalists.

Around this time, Juanita appeared in a show at the Apollo Theatre, where Ethel Waters, superstar, commanded the stage. One day, at rehearsal, Miss Waters—highly aware of her status—walked onstage, paused, scanned the showgirls with eyes of disdain, then slowly pronounced the name of the show's head musician. She repeated the man's name. After a long, theatrical pause, she came to the point like a cobra slinging venom: "He's my man, and all you black bitches keep your fucking hands off of him!" Juanita vows that not one of the chorus girls had made a play for Miss Waters's stud. Although the young Juanita Moore didn't headline at the Apollo, she is the star of this anecdote, for her punchline is the same every time I coax the story out of her: "Oh my, Ethel Waters—she was the bitch of all time." (Once, at a dinner attended by a distinguished minister and a retinue of church people, Waters's name came up. Juanita delivered her punchline impeccably and, not missing a beat, bowed in the minister's direction, drawled, "Excuse me, Reverend," and proceeded as though by memorized script. The preacher couldn't stop giggling.)

Eventually, in the early forties, Juanita moved downtown to the Cafe Zanzibar, located atop the Winter Garden Theatre on Broadway between Fiftieth and Fifty-first streets. A bit later, Ella Fitzgerald arrived as the Zanzibar's headliner, and she and Juanita became friends. Reminiscing, Juanita says that "Ella was so shy, and I was very aggressive, so maybe she liked me because I brought her out, made her feel less timid."

Martha Coolidge, in the early sequences of her 1999 HBO film *Introducing Dorothy Dandridge,* recaptures the world of black nightclubs where Juanita Moore, Dandridge, and so many other entertainers made a start. Juanita's years as a chorus girl extended from the mid-thirties into the forties. Along the way, she married Nyas Berry (ca. 1912–1951), one of the famous Berry Brothers, a team of specialty acrobatic dancers who appeared in vaudeville, nightclubs, and in several Hollywood musicals including *Lady Be Good* (1941) with Eleanor Powell, Ann Sothern, and Robert Young. Nyas (short for the biblical "Ananias") Berry and Juanita Moore were married in a Broadway theatre, she says, but she cannot recall which one.

Although overshadowed by the more famous Nicholas Brothers, the Berrys still have a following. (At the outset there were two dancing brothers; later a third joined the act.) A Google search turned up admiring references to their "tap dance, spins, cane work, handsprings, and splits" and also to their "breathtaking, amazingly choreographed and executed dance sequences at the end of *Lady Be Good*." In 1938, at the Cotton Club in New York, the Berry Brothers competed with the Nicholas Brothers in a famous confrontation, a sort of dance-fight for supremacy where the champions used tap shoes instead of boxing gloves. During her marriage to Nyas Berry, Juanita herself was called "Berry" by friends and colleagues. He died of cancer in 1951.

A searing example of the racism encountered in those days, even by elite African Americans: After the Cotton Club moved from Harlem to West Forty-eighth Street in 1936, a stringent new policy was enforced. Uptown, it had been a "black-and-tan" club; in "white" midtown, blacks performed for a segregated audience. Juanita Moore recalls a time when the Berry Brothers were performing, but she was barred from the show. Finally, she received a special—and humiliating—dispensation: The owners permitted her inside the club, provided she would sit alone at an obscure table far to one side. (In *Imitation of Life,* Annie Johnson endures the same insulting treatment in basement dive and highfalutin nightclub alike, when she enters in pursuit of her estranged daughter. Juanita's convincingness in these scenes needed no research: she had lived them.)

After New York, Juanita danced her way into the London Palladium and the Moulin Rouge in Paris. At the start of World War Two, she left Europe and returned home to California. There she found work at the Cotton Club in Culver City. (By this time the racist Cotton Club of midtown Manhattan was defunct.)

No one filmed Juanita Moore's performance in the chorus during those early days of her career. Hollywood, however, did so belatedly in *The Girl Can't Help It* (1956). In this mammary Frank Tashlin picture,

Juanita once again plays the maid—this time Jayne Mansfield's. In a sequence where Juanita, Tom Ewell, and Mansfield watch an Elvis-like rock 'n' roll singer on TV, Juanita starts to move and groove with the beat. Though she dances less than a minute, she comes across as a born dancer—in contrast to trained ones such as Ginger Rogers and Cyd Charisse. In other words, Juanita's dancing is jazzy and less stylized. This brief scene shows a terrific sample of her expertise. At the time, Juanita was close to forty, with the figure of a twenty-five-year-old and a natural yet sophisticated dancing technique that tips you off: This "maid" has more talent than anyone else in the picture.

*J*uanita Moore made her film debut in 1943, although not as a dancer, singer, or member of the chorus. Rather, she sat on a man's lap, and while it may have been fun, the assignment qualifies, technically, as acting. To call this a film debut, however, is misleading, for the vehicle was a "soundie," it lasted less than five minutes, and it wasn't shown in any theatre. It played only on a Panoram, an obsolete apparatus that most of us have never seen or even heard of.

According to the website www.1940.co.uk, "Soundies were a brand new form of entertainment conceived in early 1940, born in January 1941, and then suffered a lingering demise mid-way through 1947. They were three-minute, black-and-white films with an optical soundtrack designed to be shown on self-contained, coin-operated 16mm rear projection machines situated in bars, diners, night clubs, roadhouses, and other public places throughout the United States and Canada. The most widely distributed of these projectors was the Panoram, a complicated device using a system of mirrors and with a screen mounted on top of a stylish cabinet. The range of soundies catered for all tastes and included swing, big bands, jazz, blues, country and western, hillbilly, gospel, Latin American, Hawaiian, dance, musical comedy, vaudeville, and even swimmers, ice-skaters, knife-throwers, and gymnasts! One reel of eight soundies was released each week, with more hitting the Panorams at holidays and other peak periods."

In photographs, the Panoram resembles a jukebox crossed with an early console television set. Like a jukebox, it has a slot to insert coins, and like primitive TV, a rectangular viewing screen roughly the size of the screen on a laptop computer. Thus, forty years before MTV, soundies foretold music videos.

The soundie in question was *Paper Doll,* and it served as visual accompaniment to the Mills Brothers' hit song of the same name. On the screen, the singers are surrounded by beautiful young women, several of whom—Juanita Moore, Avanelle Harris, and Lucy Battle—sit on their laps. Everyone is smiling, except for one wistful Mills brother, who gazes at a photograph of a pretty girl. As they sing, "I'm gonna buy a paper doll that I can call my own," the girl in the phototograph materializes into a life-size cutout doll, who then comes vibrantly alive and starts to sing and dance. The "doll" is twenty-year-old Dorothy Dandridge.

Around this time, Juanita and two friends, Lucy Battle and Myrtle Fortune, formed their own act, the Mossetti Dancers. (Juanita can't recall how they came up with the name.) A high-stepping trio with years of experience in top-notch clubs, they were nevertheless approaching the end of chorus-girl youth. Soon they would all turn thirty. They enlisted Nick Castle Sr., the Hollywood choreographer who had recently staged Duke Ellington's musical revue *Jump for Joy* at the Mayan Theatre in Los Angeles, to work with them on the act. Castle's high-profile professionalism gave the Mossetti Dancers added cachet that led to high-end bookings in nightclubs around Los Angeles and up the West Coast to Seattle.

In the postwar years, however, nightclubs began a long, slow decline as the mood of the country changed. Cocooners creating a baby boom found television the ideal replacement for going out. For Juanita Moore, as for many other nonheadliners, club engagements dwindled.

She took a waitress job at a chicken restaurant on Jefferson Boulevard in Los Angeles. The spot was popular with young actors owing to its reasonable prices and late hours. There she met Joel Fluellen, an actor on the scene in Hollywood since 1937. They would remain best friends until his death, and he would exert great influence on her acting career. Fluellen's first advice was straightforward: learning that she had been enamored of the stage since childhood, he said, "If you want to act, you have to study hard." He took her to the Actors Laboratory Theatre in Hollywood and helped her gain admission as a student. Tuition was twenty-two dollars a week, a steep price at a time when the normal tip for a waitress was a dime or a quarter.

The Lab, as it was informally called, had been founded a few years earlier by former members of the disbanded Group Theatre in New York. Their main reason for establishing the Lab was to provide meaningful work for stage actors who found Hollywood films artistically unrewarding. Among those affiliated with the Lab were Anthony Quinn, Vincent Price, Hume Cronyn, Jessica Tandy, and director Jules Dassin. Several early plays by Tennessee Williams were staged there, as well as contemporary and classic works. A notable student at the Lab was Norma Jean Baker who, as Marilyn Monroe, would later congratulate her old classmate, Juanita Moore, on being nominated for Best Supporting Actress in *Imitation of Life*.

Marlon Brando liked chicken, and he liked it even better served by Juanita. They became good friends. When Brando took her to the set of *A Streetcar Named Desire* to appear in a crowd scene, Juanita was exhausted from waiting tables all night. He led her to an isolated cranny on the set and told her to nap until her scene was called. Recalling her great fatigue, Juanita says, "I curled up in some corner to sleep. Then I started to snore, and it must have grown pretty loud. Kazan, usually so soft spoken, roared, 'What the hell is that?' Marlon woke me up. He told me, 'Juanita, I said sleep, I didn't say snore.'"

Juanita knew Elia Kazan already, for the year before her *Streetcar* snooze he had cast her in *Pinky*, filmed in the spring of 1949 and released later that year.

Pinky

Ten years before *Imitation of Life*, Kazan made *Pinky* minus any trace of irony. Did anyone, then or now, believe that Jeanne Crain's eponymous character had a drop of African blood? Even the dialect in this film rings false: pseudo-Ebonics dreamed up by white screenwriters. For example, Aunt Dicey, played by Ethel Waters: "Oh shame,

(continued)

shame be on you, Pinky. Denyin' yourself like Peter denied the good Lord Jesus."

Aunt Dicey, like some female Uncle Tom, is so humble, pious, and good that even rednecks in her Alabama backwater respect her. Surely it's as wrong to stereotype blacks that way as to make them pimps and hos. Either way, they're robbed of flesh-and-blood humanity.

In the story, Pinky leaves the South for Chicago, where she attends nursing school and passes for white. But this toothless movie makes it all too easy. For starters, Jeanne Crain couldn't pass for anything but white. Nor does her character suffer real conflict over her divided self. Those who forecast a happy future for Sarah Jane in *Imitation of Life* seem to confuse her with upbeat, go-get-'em Pinky, who, although as light as alabaster, eventually claims her "colored" heritage.

Pinky belies Kazan's deserved reputation as an actor's director. Darryl F. Zanuck called him in to replace John Ford, whose quarrels with Ethel Waters threatened to close down production. Kazan considered the script uninteresting, and, by his own admission, "I didn't know how to make a film . . . I was still a stage director." In his eight-hundred-page autobiography, he devotes a mere couple of pages to *Pinky*. Commenting on Jeanne Crain's shortcomings, Kazan does not name her. Instead, he tactfully calls her "my leading lady."

Juanita Moore, cast as a nurse in the clinic that Pinky runs, appears in one scene at the end of the picture. Already she had a professional grasp of film acting and a rapport with the camera. Given a larger role, she might have jump-started this phlegmatic film.

In her scene, Juanita complains to Jeanne Crain about Ethel Waters's character: "Miss Pinky, you'll have to do something about Aunt Dicey. She's been at that new sterilizer again. Every time I start sterilizing sheets, she puts them back. Says they ain't white enough." Juanita speaks these lines as she and Crain descend a staircase. When they reach the bottom, Ethel Waters glares at Juanita, who shakes her pert, pretty head in a gesture of contempt and then flounces back upstairs. On screen and off, these two were antagonists, and it shows.

Juanita worked as a dress extra in several pictures. In others she had walk-ons and the occasional line of dialogue. Among her early films are *No Questions Asked* (1951), *Skirts Ahoy!* (1952), and *Lydia Bailey* (1952). On stage in Los Angeles, however, she had better luck, thanks to Nick Stewart and the Ebony Showcase Theatre. Juanita had met Stewart and his wife, Edna, in New York in 1940 when Nick was appearing in the Irving Berlin musical *Louisiana Purchase*. After the play closed in 1941, the Stewarts returned to Los Angeles when Nick was cast as Lightnin' in the *Amos 'n Andy* radio show.

Although reluctant at first to play a role that many considered an offensive stereotype, Stewart took the part for one reason. His salary— along with earnings from a number of film roles and the voice of Br'er Bear in Disney's *Song of the South* in 1946—would enable him to fulfill a lifelong dream of building a theatre to showcase the talents of African-American actors in roles other than maids, butlers, and train porters. By 1950 he had saved enough money to open the Ebony Showcase Theatre, a converted garage at Washington and Jefferson boulevards. In this small house with one hundred seats, Stewart staged Philip Yordan's *Anna Lucasta* as his first production. The best-known cast member was James Edwards, a tall, handsome, virile black actor who might have had a leading-man career comparable to Denzel Washington's had he arrived in Hollywood a few decades later.

In subsequent seasons at the Ebony Showcase, Stewart staged such Broadway hits as *Three Men on a Horse* and *A Streetcar Named Desire,* with James Edwards as Stanley Kowalski. In 1953, Stewart presented Sartre's *No Exit* starring Edwards, Juanita Moore, and Madie Norman. A reviewer for the *Hollywood Citizen-News* found the play "staged with impressive, incisive skill . . . proof positive that intelligence, artistry, and integrity are emphatically not solely a matter of pigmentation." In the play, Juanita had the role of Inès, the lesbian. But, as she said years later, "I was a man's woman, and I felt unsure how to prepare for that part."

Meanwhile, Juanita had met and married her second husband, Charles Burris, a bus driver in Los Angeles. On his bus route was a lesbian bar, and also a hospital, meaning that Carolyn, head nurse at the hospital, also rode his bus to the bar. Burris, outgoing and friendly with his regular passengers, arranged for Juanita and Carolyn to meet.

Juanita, however, found Carolyn somewhat demure. Feeling that she needed a more forceful prototype for Inès, Juanita went to the bar to search out a more raucous lesbian than Carolyn, then combined the traits of the two in her performance.

Juanita's first meeting with Charles Burris sounds like the opening scene of a movie romance. Crossing Western Avenue, near Adams, she either stepped in front of his bus, or he thought she did. Or did fate intervene? "This bus driver pulled up right at me," she recalled in her late eighties, "and he put on those brakes, very loud. He said, 'You better watch your step, young lady!' I said, 'You crazy-ass bus driver, what are you trying to do, kill me?'"

After hearing that exchange, I wanted to know whether he also asked Juanita for a date. "Not that night," she said with a laugh. "But I think we were supposed to be together. About a week later, we met again. We were married for fifty years." (Mr. Burris died in 2001.)

Juanita continued her association with the Ebony Showcase for decades, appearing in such plays as *Take a Giant Step, Purlie Victorious,* and *Norman, Is That You?*

Considering the limitations placed on her by Hollywood's stereotypical casting, Juanita gave memorable performances in several pictures. Her largest screen role prior to *Imitation of Life* (and one of the largest of her film career) came in *Affair in Trinidad* (1952), starring Rita Hayworth and Glenn Ford and directed by Vincent Sherman. (In his autobiography, *Studio Affairs: My Life as a Film Director,* Sherman misnamed Juanita Moore as Juanita Hall, confusing her with the light-skinned black actress who often played Asians and Pacific Islanders.)

Juanita, normally full of compliments for her directors and costars, wavers when Vincent Sherman's name comes up. "No, he wasn't helpful. . . . He was nice. He would direct and not direct me. I was lucky to have Glenn and Joel" (her friend Joel Fluellen, in a bit part as a fisherman, speaks one word in the film).

"You must put Glenn Ford in the book because he was so helpful," Juanita said not long ago. "He reassured me. This was my first real endeavor on the screen, you know." In this tropical film noir, Juanita plays Rita Hayworth's maid, Dominique. In a white apron worn over a long, full skirt, and a large turban on her head, she's a Caribbean knockout. In the role, she's both a feisty presence and one to be reckoned with. Her attempts to rule over sultry employer Rita Hayworth, an expat American nightclub performer, almost succeed. Juanita's best line in the film: "It is the prerogative of a good and loyal servant to be impertinent."

Juanita speaks affectionately of Hayworth, recalling her as "very sweet, but at that time she was having problems." (One problem being Vincent Sherman, who was her lover while shooting *Affair in Trinidad*.) "I remember so well when I first met her," Juanita continues. "I was scared to death. But when they introduced me to her, she put her arms around me. She said, 'We're going to have a good time.' I had done a few things in movies. She was the only one that allowed me to get close to her."

It's true that Juanita had done "a few things in movies," but much depended on this role. Lacking strong directorial support, she was engulfed by fear and insecurity. It showed on the set. Glenn Ford, she says, "would hold my hand and rub my elbow and say, 'Relax, Juanita, just relax. I'm here.'" He often volunteered to rehearse with her before a take. "I was the underdog," says Juanita, "but so was Glenn, in a way. Everybody knew it was Rita's picture. So he ranked second, you might say."

Following *Affair in Trinidad,* Juanita appeared in a dozen pictures, often uncredited and more often the maid. In 1957, she evaded such typecasting twice. In *Something of Value* she played a Kikuyu woman of Kenya with a shaved head who is beaten until she names the man who initiated her into the anticolonialist Mau Mau.

In the ludicrous Civil War melodrama *Band of Angels,* directed by Raoul Walsh, Juanita plays a slave floozy. As such, she gives the only sexy performance in this oddly sterile picture. Dressed in an orange turban, Gypsy earrings, a scoop-neck peasant blouse, and a gaily patterned skirt, she's the apple of ole Massa's eye.

Speaking in a shrill voice several notches higher than her own, hot-mama Juanita taunts dim Yvonne De Carlo about the carnal pleasures awaiting her as a newly arrived mulatto in New Orleans. (De Carlo, heiress to a plantation, has just been snatched from it upon discovery that her mother was black.) Juanita whispers dirty things in De Carlo's ear, then throws back her head and cackles like a big-time sinner. This is Juanita's best comic acting on screen; what a shame no one realized she's a brilliant comedienne. The director, she says, told her to ad-lib ribald stories for the chaste ear of De Carlo's character.

Two years before *Imitation of Life, Band of Angels* dealt with race and miscegenation in terms of master and slave. But the racial issues in this misguided potboiler are so stylized and stereotypical that anyone could watch the picture and make no connection with civil rights or anything more current than General Beauregard's cotillion. The movie misses even as a campfest. The closest it comes is when hysterical neophyte slave Yvonne De Carlo screams at an assailant, "I'm white! Get out of this room!"

I'm white! White! WHITE! . . . Please, Mama, will you go?"
Thus Susan Kohner, two years later, to Juanita Moore. Their performances didn't finish off the antebellum bodice ripper, of which *Band of
Angels* is one example, nor other genres that stereotyped African Americans. But *Imitation of Life*—and the zeitgeist—did raise the bar, making racial gaminess, and the trivialization of blacks, more suspect, and
less profitable, for Hollywood. Then, too, after Susan Kohner, what studio would dare cast such lightweights as Yvonne De Carlo and Jeanne
Crain as black, or even biracial, women? (A few years later, owing to the
civil rights movement and more leverage by blacks, not even Susan
Kohner would have been so cast.)

In view of her background, Susan might well have been overlooked
altogether. In early 1958, before filming began, she must have seemed an
inauspicious choice: a nice girl on screen and off, straightlaced, lacking
the combustion to play Sarah Jane. (A person affiliated with Universal at
the time told me, on condition of anonymity, that Douglas Sirk didn't
want her for the role but was overruled by Ross Hunter and front office
brass. Susan herself says, "I was not some people's first choice at the
studio.") A year later, however, other serious contenders who tested for
the role of Sarah Jane Johnson—Natalie Wood, Margaret O'Brien—
seemed laughable longshots.

Earlier I said that if Susan Kohner hadn't been a child of Hollywood she might have originated in a Jane Austen novel. When I visited her mother recently at the family home in Bel Air, I thought first of someplace like Pemberley or Mansfield Park. Soon, however, I realized that the Kohner household more closely resembles the lived-in, understated home of the Bennets in *Pride and Prejudice*. Everything at the Kohners' seems connected to the family's past and present. The tone of the place, tasteful but not showy, belies any hint of the nouveau. The money, no doubt, was new at one time, but the one who made it—Paul Kohner, the gentleman alpha agent—lacked arriviste impulses. Grace and manners, discipline and self-control, happy times in the context of ordered lives— these impressions predominate.

Dracula's Unlikely Victim

Lupita Tovar, chaperoned by her grandmother but frightened nonetheless, arrived in Hollywood as a teenager in the late twenties. Having won a talent contest in Mexico, she was summoned by Fox, where she appeared in small parts in several silent pictures. In 1930, Paul Kohner, on the rise at Universal, cast her as Eva in the Spanish-language version of *Dracula* (1931), which he coproduced (he and the actress married in 1932). Many horror connoisseurs consider this version superior to the one in English. Although the same sets at Universal were used for both, each one had a different producer, director, cinematographer, and, of course, a different cast. Even certain characters were renamed; Tovar's Eva, for instance, is called Mina in the English-language version.

Readers who want the full story will find it in David J. Skal's *Hollywood Gothic: The Tangled Web of Dracula from Novel to Stage to Screen*. Meanwhile, I wish to point out that Lupita Tovar in *Dracula* bears a striking resemblance to her daughter in *Imitation of Life*. They were roughly the same age when they made their respective

(continued)

pictures. Susan Kohner has her mother's eyes and facial shape. They sound alike, also—on screen but not off. Both have that unusual mix of throaty resonance, almost an echo.

The first shot of Lupita Tovar in *Dracula* is in Dr. Seward's opera box, where she looks like the prototype of Susan in the box at the theatre, with Juanita Moore and Sandra Dee, at one of Lana's Broadway plays. The similar setup may be intentional on the part of Douglas Sirk.

Mrs. Kohner recalled the rigors of filming *Dracula* in Spanish. "We worked all night. The English cast left, we came in at six o'clock for makeup, and at seven I was on the set. We worked until seven the next morning, with a dinner break around midnight. The director, George Melford, did not speak Spanish. Nor did the assistant director or the cameraman. [An interpreter bridged the language gaps.] Around three o'clock in the morning, I would be so tired. I'd sit while they changed the lights or a camera setup, and then something would drop from the rafters. An electrician up there would send me a Hershey bar; he was a Mexican!"

Mrs. Kohner still gets fan mail for *Dracula*. The day I visited, she showed me her latest stack: letters from Indonesia, Scotland, and one from Kentucky, which she read: "Dear Lupita, I am one of your biggest fans, I have been watching your work since *Dracula*. It would mean the world to me if you would send me a personalized autograph. To make this exchange more equal, I have enclosed an autographed photo of myself, for you." In spite of eye problems in recent years, she answers every letter as though replying to a friend.

When I drove in, I noticed, parked under the porte cochere, an aging blue Cadillac with a license plate from the eighties: "LUPITA K." Later I learned from Susan that the car had belonged to her father. Paul Kohner, by all accounts, wouldn't dream of a self-trumpeting vanity plate, but a wink at his wife via the California highway department shows a sly and winsome side of the man.

After ten minutes with Lupita Tovar Kohner, a fanciful scenario popped into my mind: I imagined her, in earlier years, motoring gaily around town in her husband's Caddy, honking at friends, pulling in at the Dairy Queen, not exactly fixing her own flats but knocking on mansion doors to have someone phone Paul at the office. At ninety-eight, Mrs. Kohner is one of Hollywood's great offscreen ladies, lively, strong-minded, a bit madcap. I say offscreen because she didn't pursue her own career—her last film appearance took place circa 1945—and yet calling on her is like visiting Greer Garson, or Mrs. Miniver, for "Lupita K." is lovely, poised, intelligent, witty, and extremely kind. I feel sure that a beggar knocking at her door would be welcomed and fed and helped.

Time was when the moviegoing public could recite Susan Kohner's life story as they quote Julia Roberts's or Cate Blanchett's today. They knew from reading magazines—*Life, Look, TV Guide, Photoplay,* and other fan publications—that she was born November 11, 1936, in Los Angeles, that her parents' famous friends included John Huston, Charles Boyer, Marlene Dietrich, Mr. and Mrs. Edward G. Robinson, Loretta Young, and other big names in Hollywood, that her godmother was Dolores del Rio, and that despite her wealth and privilege she lacked pretensions, hated snobbery.

The reading public consumed such tidbits as this, reported in *Motion Picture* in September 1959: "She wasn't exactly a million dollar baby, but she did collect $1,000 just by being born. Her dad's best buddy, director William Wyler, and his wife at the time, Margaret Sullavan, made a newlywed bet with the Kohners on who'd produce the first baby. They paid off right after Susie arrived at the Cedars of Lebanon Hospital in Hollywood."

Christened Guadalupe Susanna Kohner, she grew up in the Spanish-style house in Bel Air where her mother still lives. In this sequestered setting, her German governess kept her "scrubbed, primped, and so antiseptic that she never even caught measles until she entered college." Susan, surely, was born to be loved.

Later, when Susan's career made her sought after by reporters, her early years were described as "an idyllic childhood straight out of a storybook. She had her own pink bedroom, bath, and dressing room in a rambling house where huge sycamores edged a mountain stream. On the hill behind it, Susie had her own playhouse and could splash in a pool chipped out of solid rock. When Susie gave birthday parties her playmates were the well-brushed children of her parents' glamorous friends." Her early years in long shot.

Another writer, interviewing Susan after her nomination for *Imitation of Life,* tracked in for a close-up of the young actress: "Susan Kohner leaned back against the pink and grey pillows of the window seat in her beautiful French Provincial bedroom and propped her favorite stuffed panda up on her knees. She gazed absently through the open windows to the gardens below. Out there, her family's 40' by 20' swimming pool lay sparkling in the afternoon sun; out there, her own powder-blue Mercury convertible waited in the driveway; out there, the flowers that grew around the little brook were full blooming and sweet smelling; out there, the air was soft and warm."

Susan and her younger brother, Pancho, attended the Brentwood Town and Country School. Then, at grade six, Susan transferred to the Westlake School for Girls. Among her classmates there were Sharon Disney, Ava Astaire, and Maria Cooper, Gary Cooper's daughter. While at Westlake, when she was fifteen, she began her acting career. Hearing of an upcoming production of *The Girl on the Via Flaminia* at the Circle Theatre in Hollywood, Susan showed up to audition for the part of the young maid. She got the role, but faced the more difficult task of convincing her parents to let her take it. The producer, a family friend, cajoled until he won over Mamá, who declared protectively, "I'll come to the theatre with her every night."

Even with such foolproof chaperonage, however, Papa held out. "You know that education is more important than anything else," he argued. But the man who could best every mogul in town soon faced domestic defeat. "When she finishes school, then she can act in plays," he protested in vain. Lupita and Susan glanced at each other. A deal was struck: Susan would not miss any time from the Westlake School, and her grades must not decline during the two-month run of the play. She kept her end of the bargain—straight A's as always—and soon other plays followed, including a little-theatre production of *The Rose Tattoo* in which she costarred with Jody McCrea, the son of Joel McCrea and Frances Dee.

After graduation from the Westlake School as valedictorian in 1954, Susan spent a summer in Europe. Back in Los Angeles that September, she enrolled at UCLA with a major in theatre arts. Just before midterms in her sophomore year, Tyrone Power, a family friend, came to dinner at the Kohners'. The visit was both social and professional, since Power had business to discuss with his agent. While talking about a new play back east called *A Quiet Place* that he would soon star in, Power kept returning to the ingenue role, so far uncast. Late that evening, as he started to leave, Tyrone Power looked at Susan as he had not before. She had turned into a woman, and a striking one at that.

A few days later, Delbert Mann, director of the play, phoned Paul Kohner from New York. Susan guessed who had instigated the call. Mann wanted her to drop everything, fly to New York, and audition for *A Quiet Place*. Although she was studying for exams, she did indeed drop everything. So ended her academic career, as her acting career entered an important new phase.

The play opened in New Haven, moved to Boston and on to Washington, D.C., where it closed on New Year's Eve, 1955. But Susan was noticed. Elliot Norton of *The Boston Globe,* an influential critic, wrote that "it was obvious here that Susan Kohner had a great deal of unusual talent. At eighteen, very few untrained girls can convey deep romantic feeling. Susan acted with an almost fierce intensity."

Disappointed that the play didn't reach Broadway, she returned to Los Angeles. As it turned out, even a flop with Tyrone Power made her sought after. It helped, also, that she was no stranger in town. Not that her parents pushed her in front of the cameras. On the contrary, they had viewed the picture business from all angles. They knew the pitfalls awaiting even the toughest, the most ambitious. They wondered what might befall their sheltered fledgling.

Although Susan had no real dramatic training, offers came in. She hired an agent: Paul Kohner. In 1955, she made her first film, *To Hell and Back,* based on Audie Murphy's autobiography and starring Murphy as himself. In the picture, Susan plays Maria, a Neapolitan girl that Murphy meets at the end of World War Two. Although girlishly pretty in the role, she is not quite the beauty she would later become. Her Italian accent isn't especially convincing, and the movie is a dud. But how could it not be, with depressive, putty-faced Audie Murphy carrying the picture? (Still, it made a ton of money for Universal.)

From *To Hell and Back* until *Imitation of Life*, the impression Susan made on screen and in her television appearances owed more to her photogenic appeal and her quiet, half-brooding and half-wistful presence than to verifiable acting. One reason she seemed wobbly in those early days can be blamed on lackluster, undemanding parts. Another is that no one had yet polished her natural talent.

Her next picture was *The Last Wagon* (1956), starring Richard Widmark. In it, Susan's character is half-white, half-Navajo. This film, like *Imitation of Life,* deals with racial prejudice—whites against Indians. Unlike many westerns of the time, however, this one is pro-Indian. The Anglos in the wagon train—many of whom could be described as members of the 1870s religious right—are portrayed as villains. Throughout the picture, Susan wears an elaborate red dress that makes her the visual star, if not the actual one.

Meanwhile, she appeared in several TV dramas such as *Four Star Playhouse, Cavalcade of America,* and *Climax!* Her third film, *Trooper Hook* (1957), looks cheap, one of those B-minus westerns thrown together in less time than a *Wagon Train* episode. In it, Susan is Consuelo, the mantilla'd granddaughter of Señora Sandoval, played by irrepressible Celia Lovsky of the unwavering Eastern European accent (never mind that they're on a stagecoach in Indian country; Celia seems headed for Bratislava). The big-name cast in this low-budget venture includes Joel McCrea and Barbara Stanwyck.

A friend of Susan's once told her, "If you're Jewish, you can play anything." She's half (on her father's side), and the adage surely applies: Italian in *To Hell and Back,* a Native American in *The Last Wagon,* a Mexican girl in *Trooper Hook,* and in *Dino,* her fourth film, an Italian American. In subsequent films and on TV, she would play an African American, ancient Hebrew, French (in an episode of *Alfred Hitchcock Presents*), an Irish American, WASP, a Polish Jew in the Warsaw ghetto, and the Austrian wife of Sigmund Freud.

———

I come to praise Susan Kohner, and the few negative remarks made above will not, I believe, draw rebuttal from her. After the *Dino* shoot in 1956, she seems to have inventoried her talent, her training, and her prospects. The latter two slid to the debit side. Was it her destiny to remain "promising" forever?

To an interviewer after her success in *Imitation of Life,* she recalled her earlier decision to break out of the family circles—the Kohner circle, and the less certain one of Hollywood—and to learn the things a great actress must know. To borrow from Thoreau, who went to Walden Pond because he wished "to live *deliberately,*" Susan, too, might have echoed his wish "to front only the essential facts of life . . . to see what it had to teach." In her case, at age twenty, acting and life coincided. Learning one, she would learn the other, and New York struck her as the place to explore life. Her teacher, Sanford Meisner, would guide her to techniques for scraping off the superfluous. He aimed, always, for truth.

Susan Kohner left Los Angeles in January 1957 to enrol in Sanford Meisner's professional class at the Neighborhood Playhouse. Here my earlier Jane Austen metaphor shifts to that of bildungsroman, for no longer did the narrative of her life encompass home, parents, lovely things, young romance, and semisatisfying work. Now the story centered her in every scene, as life unfolded from her point of view, and a young person developed from postadolescence to maturity.

Several years later, Susan spoke at length to a reporter about her time in New York. Since this in-depth interview is one of the longest that Susan ever gave, I quote from it at length in the next chapter to clarify her pivot from neophyte to accomplished actress.

Sanford Meisner

On the wall of Meisner's office hung this framed quotation from Goethe: "I wish the stage were as narrow as the wire of a tightrope dancer, so that no incompetent would dare step onto it." Meisner,

(continued)

like his contemporaries at the Group Theatre Lee Strasberg, Stella Adler, and Harold Clurman, was first exposed to the ideas of Konstantin Stanislavsky in the thirties. In later years, each one of these teachers developed his and her own Method. Meisner's "method" is perhaps the cleanest, the least ego-entwined.

As head of the acting department at the Neighborhood Playhouse in New York for forty years, Meisner (1905–1997) taught thousands of actors, including James Caan, Joanne Woodward, Maureen Stapleton, and Robert Duvall. Among his precepts are these:

- "Living truthfully under imaginary circumstances is my definition of good acting."
- "You cannot escape the impact of emotion, whether it's in a big theatre or a tiny one. If you have it, it infects you *and* the audience. If you don't have it—like Helen Hayes—don't bother; just say the lines as truthfully as you are capable of doing. You can't fake emotion. It immediately exposes the fact that you ain't got it."
- "My approach is a hell of a lot healthier than Strasberg's. I think he takes an introverted person and introverts him further. It's like wearing three overcoats. I'm always trying to encourage truthful behavior related to the situation. All of the training up to the point where it has to do with the creation of a character has to do with my basic premise: what you do doesn't depend on you—it depends on what the other fellow does."

I found it very difficult. Somehow—without my telling them myself, and certainly I never bragged—[my classmates at the Neighborhood Playhouse] had heard that my father was a 'big shot' in Hollywood; that I was rich. Two other strikes against me: I was shy and scared and they mistook my petrified air to be that of aloofness. Also, I didn't dress like them. I wore high heels, stockings, a smartly tailored suit. The other girls wore long black sox, loafers, the most casual, loosest of sweaters and skirts. Most of these kids were barely scraping by to pay for their courses. I didn't have to work. With my background of wealth, my expensive clothes, it was as though I'd come from a different planet. They resented me, made snide remarks.

"I wasn't happy in the home I lived in. [She was staying with family friends.] The people were wonderful, but I had no privacy. They had two younger children who were constantly barging into my room while I tried to work out a scene.

"I moved to the Barbizon Hotel. It was a women's hotel, so I felt I was safe there (and so did my parents). Since I was determined to live on my own money (the earnings from *Dino*), it meant a great deal to me to live in a fairly inexpensive place. My room was about as big as a mailbox and I shared a bathroom with another girl, but I felt wonderful because I was paying my own way. I was on my own.

Dino

Susan's life thus far has been so wholesome that one craves a spot of delinquency. She herself can't supply it, not, at least, until her bad-girl antics in *Imitation of Life,* but Sal Mineo, her costar in *Dino,* had the knack for sexing up small-time hooliganism. Released in 1957, this low-rent Allied Artists picture packs a raw punch.

Mineo plays Dino, a lost, angry juvenile delinquent just out of reform school after three and a half years. His tense, wound-up-tight performance prefigures those of Robert De Niro and Sean Penn. Mineo, smaller than these two, is a pint-size volcano ready to shoot. This movie makes it clear why he became a fifties teen idol: his face and body give off adolescent sex. And anguish. Better than weepy James Dean, Mineo (in my view, at least) met that enormous need of the era's teenagers to see their screen alter egos as lonely, misunderstood, neglected, and frustrated by the system. Here, as in no other role, Mineo resembles Cagney grafted onto a bantam Brando.

His career should have been bigger. Hollywood, however, didn't know what to do with him. One reason may have been that the studios didn't want another homosexual to worry about; keeping Rock Hudson and Tab Hunter in the closet was trouble enough. Like Susan Kohner, but for very different reasons, Sal Mineo missed out on the big-star destiny that seemed assured. In *Dino,* he gave the kind of bravura performance that Susan gave two years later in *Imitation of Life.*

Bold for the time, the movie has several homosexual allusions. To a psychiatrist, Dino snarls: "Did you ever sleep forty guys to a room? What goes on in there—everything you can think of." Later he reports that he was "ganged." He wiggles his butt and undrapes his torso like a Colt model. He's mean: "I'd like to go back there and cut their guts out." And hard as the slum pavement he comes home to: "Cry? You think I'm gonna cry? What arm do you take it in?"

In the film, Susan plays Shirley, a bespectacled secretary in a

(continued)

settlement house in an unnamed place that resembles the tougher purlieus of Brooklyn. Her voice, here as in *Imitation of Life,* seems to come from outside herself, and also from some deep well inside. It's unique. In visual terms, you could liken it to shellac on a bruise. Apparently, it's her acquired acting voice, used increasingly as her career progressed but absent when she speaks offscreen. The sound that comes from her mouth in those early roles, a reedy contralto reverberation, sounds plaintive and poignant, an aborted wail.

Susan Kohner's Shirley is a wallflower until Dino arrives at the settlement house and she asks him to dance. Petite, thin, and demure, Shirley has invisible strength beneath the reserve. (Now, fifty years later, Susan resembles this girl more than she resembles Sarah Jane.) Dancing awkwardly together, Shirley and Dino recall the touching, unpretty realism of Betsy Blair and Ernest Borgnine in *Marty.* The magnificent anomaly of Susan's career remains her unlikely transformation into voluptuous Sarah Jane of the full bosom, swinging hips, fire-flashing eyes, and legs that go all the way to the floor.

Shirley says: "Dino, I'd like to kiss you." And—big news at the time—Susan gives Sal Mineo his first screen kiss. Then his second. And the third is long and tender; with the fourth, he is redeemed from delinquency and crime, and though it's hokey now it must have offered bright hope to many a lonely teen in the grisaille of those Eisenhower years. The fifth kiss means they'll live happily forever, as in a doo-wop song from that era.

In May 1957, the teen magazine *Dig* carried this cover line: "Sal Mineo's First Movie Love Scene." The article inside, titled "Big Smooch," carried three pages of pictures to illustrate this "momentous occasion," the teen heartthrob equivalent of "Garbo Talks."

"After I moved in I realized I had a problem living there. At the Playhouse, each girl was paired off with a boy as a dramatic partner, and each of us would work with him at night, after regular classes were over. But I couldn't have my partner come to my room because boys couldn't go past the lobby of the Barbizon. So I had to go to his apartment.

"The first time I went, I thought I'd die. It was against my upbringing to go to any boy's apartment alone, even though it was for purely professional reasons. I was shaking in my shoes when I rang the bell of his flat. He lived in an old smelly tenement, with lots of people yelling and running around in the streets. The whole thing was very frightening. Even the subway ride scared me; I'd never ridden in a subway before. All those strange people, the tight, crammed-in feeling underground—it gave me a dreadful attack of claustrophobia.

"The fact that I found my partner physically revolting didn't make it any easier for me. He was short and fat, wore thick glasses, looked as though he needed a bath and had a constant sneering expression. His flat was awful; one room with a makeshift stove; his clothes and underwear all over the place. Evidently the place didn't have closets. He was eating eggs when I came and he scarcely looked up to speak to me. I thought he was rude, crude, horribly unfriendly, and I was scared to death of him. It was months later—after I'd come to understand some of the people who'd been brought up in a world so different from mine—that I learned he was very earnest and frightened himself of a world that had always been hostile to him.

"He looked at me in my fine clothes; I looked at his angry, sullen face, his unkempt hair and hands—and we hated each other. He was so radically different from anyone I'd ever known in all my sheltered life. I'd met young actors in Hollywood—even struggling ones—and they were all handsome, charming. When I was face-to-face with this boy, I just wanted to run and run. But I didn't. I remained, and we worked on an emotional, dramatic scene. I was frozen. It was a dreadful evening.

"But I knew I had to go back and work with him a few nights later. I forced myself to return, and somehow, I found the situation a little more bearable. I still found him repulsive, I still quaked when I got out of the subway and found myself in the middle of a noisy, dirty neighborhood, but I knew I had to do it if I was going to last in the class.

"I couldn't take that 'left out' feeling much longer. I decided to dress like the other girls, and tried to act more like them. I bought long black sox and loafers and dressed in shirts and sweaters and skirts—which I didn't bother to press. I wasn't so conspicuous in class anymore, and my whole personality began to change. I felt freer, more casual. I still had no close friends in class, but as soon as I dressed differently and felt more like them, there was a response. By being simple and natural, I began to convince the others at school that I wasn't a snob, and that I wasn't leaning on my father's money or influence. In fact, I went out of my way to cover up any sign of affluence or importance that came my way.

"Once Sal Mineo called me and asked me to go with him to a premiere. But I never told the kids in class that I'd worked with Sal in Hollywood. They'd have thought I was putting on the dog. I went to the premiere, and begged the photographer not to shoot me in the picture with Sal.

"My father used to send me delicacies from a Beverly Hills gourmet shop—wonderful tins of caviar, smoked snails, imported jams. The first time he did I invited other girls from the Barbizon in to share with me. They looked at the expensive little tins and one girl said, rather bitterly, 'I could eat for a week on what that one can of caviar costs.' I never opened up any more of those imported cans again.

"One night, one of the girls was in my room when the phone rang. She picked up and said, 'It's a man who says he's Tyrone Power.' I was so embarrassed, with the other girl around, that I cut the conversation short. 'Was that really Tyrone Power?' asked the girl. I thought, They'll label me Miss Rich-Snob all over again if I tell the truth, so I laughed and said, 'Oh, no, just a friend trying to tease me.'

"Charles Boyer, who was as close to me as my uncle, called and invited me to the Pavillon, one of the most elegant restaurants in New York, and the theatre. He'd promised my father he would take me out, and he is one of our oldest and dearest friends. I didn't dare tell anyone in class. Going to the Pavillon and the theatre with Mr. Charles Boyer required that I dress up in my most beautiful gown. I didn't want any of the other girls to see me. I slipped down the back stairway.

"It was a funny masquerade. And with it all, I was still shy and lonely. I didn't know any young men in New York. I tried to be like the others in the Playhouse, and I was becoming better liked, but they still had their reservations about me. In the Barbizon, most of the girls, who were models, had loads of boyfriends and were always going out on dates. I spent many nights zipping girls into their evening dresses. Then I'd stay in alone. I was too shy to go to the hotel coffee shop at night because that would advertise the fact that I had no date. So I'd often sit in my room munching on a box of crackers. And crying.

"I stayed at the Neighborhood Playhouse for five months. I learned a great deal about acting there, and about people. I also learned a great deal about myself. Having to live with a new group of young people was just as vital to my acting development as were the acting techniques I learned at the Playhouse. I would have been a shallow actress, always, if I hadn't broken the bonds and gotten out of my shell. Lived like other people. Suffered some, cried a lot.

"That period in New York on my own did a lot for me as a person. I became a little more bohemian with the friends I made in New York. One boy came by on a motorcycle, and invited me for a ride. I'd never done a thing like that. I got on the back, and we whizzed in and out of heavy New York traffic. I felt so exhilarated. I learned how to do things on impulse, another thing I'd never done in the careful, rarefied atmosphere of Bel Air."

The foregoing article, excerpted from *Modern Screen* (August 1959), made Susan squirm when I showed it to her. "Mostly hogwash," she said. Claiming that most of it was fabricated by a writer for the magazine, she failed to find in it the charming nostalgic flummery it conjured up for me. If it's mostly dreamed up, at least the writer had imaginative flair: those tins of caviar and jam, the Cinderella-in-reverse of Susan's stealthy glide down the back staircase to meet Charles Boyer, that slovenly boy's plate of eggs. Would any fanzine create such winsome whimsy today? Imagine *Vanity Fair* or *People* actually building a story around an actor's quest to improve her craft.

So there it is, a "confession" that Susan didn't really confess. It belongs to that marvelous parallel world that once drew us out of our own—that great whopper we believed in called Hollywood.

*S*usan Kohner's name, when she returned to Hollywood, was permanently linked with acting, in contrast with many starlets and contract players of her day—e.g., Jill St. John, Tuesday Weld—who were more often linked with dates, and whose exploits ensured splashier coverage. No scandal ever stained the Kohners, least of all Susan. Anyone picking "the Girl Most Likely to Abandon Hollywood and Enter a Convent" might have chosen her, rather than Dolores Hart, as a future Reverend Mother.

During the second half of 1957, following her return from New York, Susan appeared on television in *Wagon Train* and on *The Schlitz Playhouse of Stars*. Late that year she heard from the Broadway star Alfred Drake, who was preparing to direct a play in New York. Scheduled to open in spring at the Helen Hayes Theatre, it was called *Love Me Little*. In this comedy of adolescence, Susan played Emily Whittaker, an upper-crust ingenue blossoming into womanhood. Elliot Norton, writing in *The Boston Globe*, called Susan's role "the showiest part" in the play. It was also the biggest, but Joan Bennett and Donald Cook, playing her parents, received star billing because they outranked the newcomer.

In the play, Emily functions as both narrator and actress. According to Elliot Norton, "She opens various scenes by introducing one phase or another in the life of a lovesick girl; then she steps into action and plays out the role." *Variety*, reviewing the play during its unpolished New Haven start-up, had few compliments. That critic's assessment: "Susan Kohner plays the teenage heroine unevenly, sometimes engagingly, and at other times monotonously. Her most serious fault is vocal, a clanging tone and a tendency to shout." (That "clanging tone" is one of the vocal qualities that served her so well on film.)

Susan recalls, "After New Haven we moved to Boston, then Philadelphia and Washington, D.C. The production used a complicated turntable to transfer scenery from one scene to another. We had endless trouble out of town, because the turntable often got stuck. Actually, *Love Me Little* was loved very little indeed by the critics." The play opened on Broadway April 15, 1958, and closed April 19, after a total of eight performances.

In the Middle of the Night

In the small hours of the morning of April 5, 1958, Lupita Tovar Kohner was awakened by the ringing phone in her bedroom in a hotel suite in Manhattan. Her husband was calling from California, where it was not yet midnight. The reason for his call stunned his wife. It also shocked Susan when her mother awakened her.

Mrs. Kohner had traveled east with Susan for the pre-Broadway tryouts of *Love Me Little*. Paul Kohner's dead-of-night bulletin from Los Angeles was this: "A horrible thing happened tonight at Lana's," followed by details. Lana Turner's daughter had stabbed Johnny Stompanato to death in her mother's bedroom, believing that he was about to harm Lana.

"I knew Lana from way back," Mrs. Kohner told me recently. "She had been my husband's client for a long time. And Lana was a family friend. She came to dinner at our home, she came to tea. I had nothing but respect for her. That night, after the tragedy, Lana called my husband immediately. She was hysterical. He got there right away, because it's a ten-minute drive from our house. He said to me

(continued)

on the phone, 'I need your understanding for Lana.' Susan and I sent her a telegram with our support and prayers."

Susan spoke less generously of Lana's star demands. "My father went through a lot with Lana because of her personal problems," she said. "I believe he became more involved than he wanted to, since she viewed him as someone she could talk to and confide in."

Ross Hunter, a close friend of Joan Bennett's, happened to see *Love Me Little* during its brief Broadway run. A month or so later, when he began casting *Imitation of Life,* he remembered Susan's performance on stage. He phoned Paul Kohner's office, only to learn that the Kohners were all at the Cannes Film Festival, which Paul Kohner always attended, often accompanied by his family. From Cannes, he branched out to meet with his European clients. Ross Hunter finally caught up with the Kohners in Rome, via cable. Learning of the producer's interest, Susan flew back to Hollywood alone. Early in June, she reported to Universal to film the screen test that would stamp her—at least in Ross Hunter's eyes—as the only viable candidate for the role.

Meanwhile, Susan was committed to a summer stock tour of New England in *He Who Gets Slapped.* Immediately after her screen test, she flew east. The play opened in Falmouth, Massachusetts, then moved on to Matunuck, Rhode Island. While there, Susan got word from Hollywood that she had the role. The play finished its run in Westport, Connecticut, in mid-July, and Susan returned to Los Angeles for such preliminaries as wardrobe fittings, makeup tests, and publicity sessions. Her first day before the cameras at Universal was set for August 22.

Although no one at Universal guessed how totally Juanita Moore and Susan Kohner would come to possess the picture, Ross Hunter's instincts told him these two were the right ones for his picture. Still, he had to sell both actresses to the studio. The most efficient way to swing the deal was to put them in a screen test together.

A person who asked not to be named owns what is perhaps the only surviving copy of that test. Viewing it now reminds me of a museum exhibition where preliminary crayon sketches and oil studies are displayed as lead-ins to a great painting. In the screen test, Susan and Juanita, like figures in such drawings, lack the fullness of characterization we know from Sirk's finished film. Wearing little makeup, dressed in their own clothes or at best studio outfits hastily assembled, and not yet at home in their roles, they commend themselves nevertheless to the script, to the camera, and to us.

Sirk was on hand to direct. Susan recalls that he did so with his usual meticulousness. Despite his lingering reservations about Susan, he was, after all, her father's client, so he wanted her to come off well. Cinematographer Russell Metty, who would later shoot the picture, filmed the screen test. All worked long hours. Paul Kohner's assistant, Irene Heyman, sent him a telegram in Rome: "Susan tested exhaustively all day."

If it's possible to enact the film's wrenching motel scene—that final farewell on this side of the grave—in pastel hues, that's how Susan and Juanita do it in the test. Only later, steeped in the turbulent colors of *Imitation of Life*, do they saturate the sequence. Even so, the latent power of their confrontation is evident from the moment of Juanita's entrance in the test.

When she walks into the motel room she finds Susan, wearing a yellow sweater and black shorts, pulling on her shoes. Juanita, costumed here more or less as she will be in the finished picture, has on a black pillbox hat, a long black coat, and earrings. Owing to very little makeup, both women look younger, and lighter-skinned, than they do in the film.

With a few exceptions, their dialogue is the same as in the movie. Susan's line readings are less emotionally inflected than they would later become, Juanita's not markedly different from the film. Here, minus the layers of makeup that make her so haggard, Juanita looks her own age—fortyish—or even younger.

Juanita's line in the film: "If you're ever in trouble—if you ever need anything at all—if you ever want to come home, and you shouldn't be able to . . . get in touch with me . . . will you let Miss Lora know?" has one variant in the screen test. The last sentence is, "Will you let *Miss Bea* know?" That's because Lana Turner's character, at this point, was still "Bea Pullman" in the script, as in Fannie Hurst's novel. (In another draft of the script, she was briefly called "Helen," and Sandra Dee's character "Maggie.")

Missing from Susan's lips in the test is one word that she later ad-libbed, and which remained in the film to great and haunting effect. When Juanita speaks her final line—"Good-bye, honey. You take good care of yourself."—Susan responds, "Good-bye." But in the film, she mouths the word "Mama," like a great silent star who makes a scene immortal with two poignant, soundless syllables.

*J*ohnny Stompanato, the handsome hoodlum stabbed to death in Lana Turner's bedroom on the night of April 4, 1958, kept a little black book that was actually made of tan leather, with a silver lock. In it, Stompanato had written the private phone numbers of scores of well-known people in Hollywood, most of them women. But he also serviced men, especially if they seemed prospects for blackmail. Some of the listings in his book were shopping cart numbers—that is, he intended to dial them, but had not yet done so. Whether Anita Ekberg, June Allyson, and Zsa Zsa Gabor counted him as a close friend remains unclear. Stompanato, like a gigolo counterpart to Ross Hunter, specialized in actresses who, in the late-fifties climate of studio collapse, faced obsolescence. The difference, of course, was that Ross Hunter hired *them*; they hired Stompanato.

Always, the Hollywood treadmill was an easy place to tumble from, but now the studios had virtually stopped renewing long-term contracts. The greatest crisis since the introduction of sound gripped Hollywood. Blame it on television; bad management; the Supreme Court decision that forced studios to divest themselves of their profitable theatre chains. Whatever the cause of calamity, few stars had job security. Hardest hit were actresses on the threshhold of forty. On February 8, 1958, Lana Turner had turned a dangerous thirty-seven.

She had also been nominated as Best Actress, for her portrayal of

Constance MacKenzie in *Peyton Place*—a Fox picture, since MGM had let her go the previous year after eighteen years of stardom and a series of recent flops. When Lana's agent, Paul Kohner, phoned her in Acapulco to break the news of her nomination, her joy was fleeting. Johnny Stompanato had come along, against Lana's wishes, and held her virtual prisoner in their luxurious lodgings. During their six-week sojourn, he knocked her around; humiliated her; held a gun to her head when she wouldn't satisfy him sexually.

Anticipating favorable publicity as a result of the nomination, and attractive job offers should she win, Lana returned to Hollywood earlier than planned. Unable to shake Stompanato, she set about finding a new home for herself and Cheryl, unsure how to dispose of the menacing pest he had become. A few years earlier, Lana had sold her fifteen-room mansion in Holmby Hills to help pay delinquent taxes. Since then, she had lived in rental properties and occasionally taken a bungalow at the Bel-Air Hotel. Now, however, she intended to settle down with Cheryl, minus Johnny. Soon after her return from Mexico in March of 1958, Lana rented the house at 730 North Bedford Drive. A large neo-Colonial, it was built, according to legend, by character actress Laura Hope Crews, who played Aunt Pittypat in *Gone With the Wind*. Lana and Cheryl moved in on April 1, three days before the stabbing.

Just before *Peyton Place*, Lana had bounced to Universal-International to film *The Lady Takes a Flyer* with Jeff Chandler. (*Peyton Place*, however, was released first.) Next, she formed her own production company, Lanturn, which coproduced (with a British firm) *Another Time, Another Place*. Shot in London, that picture costarred Sean Connery, Barry Sullivan, and Glynis Johns. It failed critically and commercially, putting Lanturn in the red.

Lana herself, like her company, might soon have to close up shop, and yet she must go on. As sole support of an aging mother and a teenage daughter, and unable to do any other job, Lana Turner floundered. She waited for someone to call her about a picture, but instead, one spring day in 1957, the phone rang with an offer of love.

He wanted to send her flowers. For a time, the man wouldn't sign his real name on the extravagant bouquets. When they were delivered to

Lana, the card bore a bland but vaguely suggestive moniker: John Steele. Mr. Steele had phoned and phoned, but Lana did not take his calls. When her maid, or her secretary, or a friend, picked up the phone and asked the caller's name, Lana shook her head. Though recently divorced from Lex Barker, and without a man at present, she couldn't be had for the price of a local call. Movie stars must always seem busy and out of reach, even when they're at home all day watching TV.

The man's unyielding flattery made Lana curious. With a sigh, she requested Del Armstrong, her longtime makeup man and close friend, to find out what, exactly, the persistent Mr. Steele was up to. Why not? she thought. Sometimes fans seemed like her only real friends.

"All he wants is to send you some flowers," came Armstrong's report. "I told him there wouldn't be anything wrong with that." More and more flowers arrived, as if for a great wedding . . . or a funeral, though such a ghoulish thought didn't occur to Lana. "Look," she exclaimed to Del Armstrong, "yellow roses. My favorite!" But flowers caressed only two of her senses, sight and smell. Her phantom suitor wished to arouse her completely, and so he sent music, her favorites—Sinatra, Tony Martin, big band, dance tunes. Also candy and sweet liqueurs, though Lana barely touched the candy. She thought of her hips.

Finally, she could resist no longer. She picked up the phone and called him. He told her they had a friend in common, Ava Gardner. He and Ava had dated, he said. And was Lana free for dinner? She thanked him, but couldn't accept. Too busy. A few days later, her house full of blossoms and fragrance and romantic songs, she phoned again to thank him and this time, when he pressed her, she invited him to drop by for a drink. Lana found him as polished as old silver—at first. The romance was on, but not until some months later did Lana find out that John Steele's real name was Johnny Stompanato. She was displeased. She felt tricked, but by then she had passed the point of no return. Wild nights in his arms, crazed sexual desire and its blinding fulfillment, which led to greater, madder desire—who cared if his name was John the Ripper?

Or exactly how he earned a living. True, he did run a gift shop in Westwood, or so he said, and Lana insisted on seeing it. She was no fool, unless she chose to be, and like Carmela Soprano she decided to accept the official version of how he made his dough. She wished so much to believe that his shepherdess figurines and map of movie star homes tea towels really brought in income that she gave the matter no further thought. By the time Lana found out what a dangerous boyfriend she had, he had ensnared her forever. He said as much. Johnny intended to hold on to this dame. Even if he had to beat her, even if he had to kill her.

Since Lana Turner's debut in 1937, writers have tsk-tsked over her hormonal exploits, judging her by the crooked norms of puritan morality. I don't agree. I like to think that Lana enjoyed every man who ogled her in those tight white sweaters, every date, every night spent dancing in nightclubs and drinking champagne. I hope all of it thrilled her: the fame, the romances, the seven husbands, every sybaritic dollar spent on clothes, cars, houses. And why not? She said it best herself: "I find men terribly exciting, and any girl who says she doesn't is an anemic old maid, a streetwalker, or a saint."

Lana stayed Lana. When life, and fame, went sour, she might have become a depressed shipwreck like so many Hollywood ladies who don't even lunch. But Lana had tough courage. Friends adored her, and so did her fans, who formed an earlier Turner network. I've met a number of people who knew Lana well. They don't deny her flaws, nor do they dwell on them. What lingers, years after her death, are memories of her warm heart, her sense of fairness, her lack of bias. (After the scandal, when she was excoriated by the self-righteous press, fans deluged her with letters of support.)

Bob Osborne, a friend of Lana's from his early days in Hollywood, said, "Lana was funny, witty, and you didn't have to know her very long to understand how she survived that scandal. Everybody liked her. She was a good egg." Jeanine Basinger, a Turner biographer, wrote that Lana "was always popular with film crews and most coworkers. Her reputation as a reliable professional is solid."

Betty Abbott Griffin, a script supervisor who has worked in Hollywood since 1950, was a huge Lana Turner fan. Accustomed to movie stars every day at work, Betty nevertheless found herself awestruck in 1957 when she worked on *The Lady Takes a Flyer,* her first time on a Turner film. "I came on the set," Griffin recalls, "and Del Armstrong, who always did Lana's makeup, said, 'Don't stare.' I answered, 'I can't help it.' Well, L. T. walked out of her trailer looking absolutely gorgeous, as always. I just stood there, couldn't move. Del said, 'Close your mouth! And come over here, I'm going to introduce you.'

"She was as sweet as could be. She said, 'Hello,' and she hugged me. She said, 'We're going to have fun.' L. T. wasn't just a movie star, she was also a wonderful person." A decade later, Griffin found Lana equally amiable on the set of Madame X.

Lana's daughter, Cheryl Crane, pays her mother an enduring tribute that might make a proud epitaph for anyone: "For all its other problems, my family had never shown any prejudice. I had never heard either of my parents put anyone down because of race, religion, or sexual preference."

Johnny Stompanato, in a yearbook photo from 1943, the year he graduated from military school, has the furtive, menacing good looks of Chris Moltisanti on The Sopranos. Stompanato was the same kind of violent stud. He slapped Lana around, as he had slapped other women. His abuses have been chronicled elsewhere, and so has the end of Johnny. Little need, then, to rehash the rainy night of April 4, 1958—Good Friday—and what took place at 730 North Bedford Drive in Beverly Hills.

After all, only one person still alive—Cheryl Crane—knows exactly what happened. The rest of us know that Johnny Stompanato was stabbed to death in Lana Turner's bedroom, that Lana supposedly begged Beverly Hills police chief Clinton Anderson, a family friend, to let her take the blame, and that Cheryl Crane confessed and was later exonerated at the coroner's inquest. The jury ruled that, acting to protect her mother's life, Cheryl had committed justifiable homicide. It was brought out in testimony that she stabbed him because she heard him threatening Lana. "You'll never get away from me," Stompanato growled. "I'll cut you good, baby. You'll never work again. And don't think I won't also get your mother and your kid."

The death of Johnny Stompanato triggered one of Hollywood's undying mystery-scandals. It belongs in the same pantheon of foul deeds as the Fatty Arbuckle rape trial in 1921, the ambiguous death of Marilyn Monroe in 1962, and the O. J. Simpson case of 1994–95. In spite of court testimony and official rulings, all of these headline grabbers remain to some degree unsolved. They trouble us because so many facets are unexplored, and also because many principals appear to know more than they revealed at the time. Another reason for our unease is the somber mythology that has overgrown each one of these events. In the case of Lana, Cheryl, and Stompanato, the catalog of myths ranges from campy to creepy.

Sydney Guilaroff, the famous MGM hair stylist, claimed in his memoir, *Crowning Glory,* that on the very day of the stabbing he had gone to a drugstore in Beverly Hills and on his way out ran into Lana, who was leaving a nearby establishment. "What are you doing at Pioneer Hardware?" inquired Guilaroff.

"We needed a new kitchen knife," Lana said.

If this sounds like the opening of *Murder, She Wrote,* the following paragraph might serve as a skit for Dame Edna, especially if you add the word "possums" somewhere in the text: "The next morning, I heard the stunning news on the radio: Johnny Stompanato had been stabbed to death on the pink rug in Lana's bedroom. I got into my car and flew to Lana's house. When I arrived, none of her servants was on duty, and Lana herself opened the door. 'Oh Sydney, I'm so glad you came,' she sobbed, falling into my arms. She wept for a long time. After a while she composed herself a little and began talking. 'Did you ever dream that this could have happened?' she sighed. 'And with the very knife that I bought just yesterday.'" (Not that Guilaroff invented their chance encounter; Cheryl Crane confirms that Lana and Stompanato drove around town that Friday afternoon buying kitchen utensils, including knives. Lana, in her own book, put the knife buying a few days earlier, and recalled that Stompanato himself bought the knife that later killed him.)

Lana's dialogue came off as more convincing, and less flighty, at the inquest than in Guilaroff's story. In fact, it fostered the journalistic cliché that Lana gave the greatest performance of her life on the witness stand that day, April 11, 1958. Who can gainsay this cynical consensus? After all, Lana knew little about the world except as it related to her performances. Was that so bad? Consider Georges Braque's dictum, as applicable to Hollywood as to painting: "As one grows older, art and life become one and the same."

As Lana took the stand that day, "a hush fell over the crowd as the famous actress sat down, removed one white glove, and filled her lungs with a deep, steadying intake of air. For the next sixty-two minutes she sat with her impeccable posture, answering questions. Her performance was flawless, expert in its timing and expressiveness. Photographers, desperate for better shots, stood on their seats, on the arms of their seats, and even on window sills. Soon almost everyone in the crowd was standing on the seats. 'In their precarious, picturesque position,' one journalist reported, 'the audience soon grew frozen and hushed and, except for the click and clatter of the desperately laboring photographers, the throaty, halting voice of Lana Turner seemed to be the only living thing in the room.' She made good use of her training, pausing dramatically at key points and struggling to contain her tears. Midway through her description of how the dying Stompanato made 'the most horrible noises in his throat and gasping'— she took a fortifying sip of water. When her ordeal was over, she returned to her seat next to her attorney, Jerry Geisler, and collapsed in tears."

Indeed, a great performance. And yet, how easy for glib raconteurs to seize on it as "proof" that Lana was not a real actress, that she could perform only to save her daughter's neck, and herself from ruin. Even George Cukor, who directed Lana in one picture (*A Life of Her Own*, 1950), performed a parody of Lana in extremis. According to novelist John Rechy, "I saw him once do a brutal imitation of Lana Turner testifying in that very ugly Johnny Stompanato murder case. He 'did' her on the stand, posing and posturing, and denying she'd committed a certain sexual act. It was very, very cruel."

Guilaroff, Cukor, the slavering journalists and rabid paparazzi— these can be scraped away from the myth like barnacles off a ship's bottom. Not so easily dismissed, however, are certain statements made decades later by Lana herself, and by her daughter.

In 1971 Lana met Eric Root, a hairdresser and former dance instructor for Arthur Murray. They soon became close friends, with Root serving as coiffeur, escort, bodyguard, and major domo to the star. In a book titled *The Private Diary of My Life with Lana*, published in 1996, the year after Lana's death, Eric Root recounts Lana's "confession" that she herself killed Johnny Stompanato.

"We were sitting in our suite at the Plaza Hotel," he writes, "watching a television documentary on Hollywood scandals. Actually, we really weren't paying that much attention. Suddenly, images of Lana, Johnny Stompanato, and Cheryl flashed across the screen.

"'Lana, do you want me to shut it off?' I asked.

"'No,' she said. She watched intently until the narrator went on to somebody else's scandal, then clicked the remote. The screen went black.

"She became extremely agitated and angry. Neither of us spoke for what seemed like a long time. Finally she blurted it out. 'I killed the son of a bitch and I'd do it again!'

"'What!' I exclaimed, shocked.

"'Scratch that,' she said, making a waving gesture."

Root adds that in a couple of hours Lana expanded on her prodigious revelation. According to him, she continued, "If I die before my daughter, you should tell the truth so I can rest in peace. Don't let my baby take the rap all her life for my mistake. . . . Now you know. I've spoken to you and said things I've never told anyone else, until tonight. . . . Someday, when I'm gone—tell it all."

Patricia Bosworth, writing a feature on the Stompanato killing for the April 1999 *Vanity Fair,* questioned Cheryl Crane about Eric Root's assertion. Crane's response: "This idea that Root had in his book is so far-fetched. . . . You know, everybody has something they want to sell. I guess it was the only way he could get his book published."

And yet for one fleeting moment Crane herself corroborated her mother's "far-fetched" confession. In her autobiography, *Detour,* published in 1988, Cheryl Crane recounts how, in 1970, at the beginning of her relationship with Joyce LeRoy, known as "Josh," she felt compelled to make up a story. Crane writes, "There was, I decided, no way she could love a person who had killed someone. I would have to tell her that someone else had been holding the knife." Crane's "confession" tumbled out one evening over cocktails.

"'You know,' I began, 'I didn't do it.'

"She didn't react. I would have to try again.

"'I love you so much more than anyone before in my life, Josh, that I don't want you to think I could do a terrible thing like that.'"

After a significant pause: "'Cheryl,' she said simply, 'I think it was a very brave and noble thing to go to your mother's defense.'"

This odd vignette is the most intriguing part of Crane's book. Elsewhere she states that, in the frightening melee taking place in her mother's bedroom between Lana and Johnny, she pounded on the door, which suddenly flew open. Holding a "gleaming butcher knife" that she had picked up in the kitchen, Cheryl saw Stompanato coming at Lana from behind, one arm raised to strike. "I took a step forward and lifted the weapon. He ran on the blade." That piece of choreography recalls the "Cell Block Tango" from *Chicago*: "And then he ran into my knife. He ran into my knife ten times!" Lana, in her own book, described the event differently: "Out of the corner of my eye I saw Cheryl make a sudden movement. Her right arm had shot out and caught John in the stomach. I thought she'd punched him."

In this welter of confessions, denials, half-confessions, and counter-confessions, one thinks of *Murder on the Orient Express,* where *they all did it*—death by committee, and well deserved. Indeed, Stompanato had it coming. To be sure, the stabbing has great dramatic potential, which, presumably, will be fully exploited if a film is ever made that was announced as "in development" some time ago: *Stompanato,* starring Keanu Reeves as Johnny and Catherine Zeta-Jones as Lana.

Whatever occurred that Friday night in 1958, Lana's residual guilt sounds greater than Cheryl's—that is, if we believe Eric Root's account. Ultimately, one woman of the two seems to have posed her own version of Macbeth's question after he stabs Duncan: "Is this a dagger which I see before me, the handle toward my hand?" To Macbeth's rhetorical question, the answer is yes. But in the latter case . . .

As for Stompanato: Kindly omit flowers.

*M*arch 26, 1958, was a gala night in Hollywood, one of those anniversaries where stars and spectacle dwarf the movies they celebrate. Was any show-business citizen of Hollywood absent that night from the Pantages Theatre on Hollywood Boulevard? Certainly not Marge and Gower Champion, who danced the show's opening. Nor Tony Martin, who serenaded Anita Ekberg with "Love Is a Many Splendored Thing," Betty Grable and Harry James, with their "Lullaby of Broadway" duet, Janet Leigh, Shirley MacLaine, and Sheree North, who performed a sprightly trio of "The Atchison, Topeka, and the Santa Fe," then Tony Martin again, this time singing to Zsa Zsa Gabor "The Way You Look Tonight," followed by Mae West and Rock Hudson, having more fun than anyone else with their famous "Baby, It's Cold Outside," and a smooch at the end—a show-stopping number, unfortunately followed by the enduring anticlimax, Bob Hope, who ended the opening medley with "Thanks for the Memory."

Lana Turner presented the first acting award, to Red Buttons for Best Supporting Actor in *Sayonara*. She seemed nervous, although poised through her jitters. And showing her age. Too much sun in Acapulco had dried her skin. Also, the stress of Stompanato's terrorism showed in her face and demeanor. She seemed beleaguered. Of course, Lana was also up for an Oscar that night, but the look in her eyes seemed one of dread, not hope.

Only two others in the Pantages Theatre, Cheryl Crane and Lana's mother, Mildred, were privy to her anxiety. Years later, Cheryl described their ride to the theatre in a limousine: "I had never seen Mother actually tremble before. Staring at her hands made me sort of edgy myself, because the fingers were twitching as though they were troubled by bad dreams." (Five months later, on the set of *Imitation of Life,* the camera caught Lana's shaking hands. When she reads aloud Sarah Jane's letter to Annie—"Mama, if you really want to be kind, really a mother, don't try to find me"—the page trembles in spite of Lana's efforts to steady it.)

For several days prior to the Oscars, and on the night itself as Lana dressed and applied her makeup, Stompanato had wheedled, then menaced. He demanded that her night of glory also be his. Or else. In the end, however, he could not break Lana's steadfast refusal. This night was too big, too important, and she had too much to gain. She had even more to lose. If word spread beyond Hollywood of her involvement with a gangster—the word caught in her throat—she could well imagine what *Confidential* and the other scandal mags would make of it, not to mention the likes of Hedda Hopper.

Hope Lange and Ronald Reagan followed Lana onstage to present the evening's first technical awards. The seamless parade of old stars and new moved into and out of production numbers, while each presenter and the many winners glided on and off with choreographic precision. Cyd Charisse, Kim Novak, Jennifer Jones. Dorothy Malone and Van Johnson opening the envelope for Best Sound Recording. A stage full of singers, a celebrity choir made up of Shirley Jones, Tab Hunter, Ann Blyth, Jimmy Rogers, Tommy Sands, and Anna Maria Alberghetti, who sang "April Love," one of the nominated songs.

Then Zsa Zsa Gabor announced the station break.

The extraordinary evening danced on: David Niven, Natalie Wood and Robert Wagner, June Allyson, Eva Marie Saint, Gregory Peck, Rosalind Russell, Joan Collins, Sophia Loren; Kirk Douglas and Burt Lancaster sang "It's Great Not to Be Nominated"; Cary Grant read the nominees for Best Actor (Marlon Brando, *Sayonara*; Anthony Franciosa, *A Hatful of Rain*; Charles Laughton, *Witness for the Prosecution*; Anthony Quinn, *Wild Is the Wind*; and the winner was Alec Guinness for

Bridge on the River Kwai); Brando was seen in the audience; Debbie Reynolds sang "Tammy," a nominated song; and John Wayne announced the Best Actress award to Joanne Woodward for *The Three Faces of Eve* (after which she exclaimed, "I've been dreaming of this since I was nine years old!"). The losers were Lana, Deborah Kerr for *Heaven Knows, Mr. Allison*, Anna Magnani for *Wild Is the Wind,* and Elizabeth Taylor for *Raintree County*.

Ending the evening, Gary Cooper presented the Oscar for Best Picture, *The Bridge on the River Kwai,* which beat *Peyton Place, Sayonara, Twelve Angry Men,* and *Witness for the Prosecution*.

Oscar night flew by like a magic carpet, with Lana riding shotgun, and when the ride ended she felt enormous relief that she had not only survived this appearance on live TV—fifty million viewers!—but had come off well.

In front of the small black-and-white TV at his apartment on Wilshire Boulevard, Johnny Stompanato was seething. That bitch kept him away! He could have seen all three of them, Anita Ekberg, June Allyson, Zsa Zsa Gabor, and a dozen others besides, even added some new contacts. He made a decision. He removed a letter from the pack that he had carefully saved, and read, "I miss you and need you so. Dearest love, what ever will I do over here without you? Beloved, I do love you terribly. I'm your woman and I need you, MY MAN, to love and be loved by you—don't ever, ever doubt or forget that." Signed, "Lanita." Leaving his room, he walked to his white Thunderbird convertible, drove to the Bel-Air Hotel, and let himself into Lana's expensive bungalow.

Meanwhile, very late, Lana and Cheryl dropped off Mildred, and then the limousine took them to the Bel-Air Hotel. Following the awards ceremony, they had attended the ball at the Beverly Hilton, where, as Lana later recalled, "The ballroom sparkled with color and life, and there were all those important people paying me compliments and condolences. That night all my tensions just seemed to float away on the waves of sound."

Cheryl, home from boarding school, spent the night with Lana. Their rented bungalow was spacious, with two bedrooms and a living room. In Lana's bedroom, they relived the evening. Cheryl felt extremely grown-up, and she and her mom were getting along well, for a change. After an hour or so of girl talk, Lana reminded Cheryl to scrub all the makeup off her face before retiring. Makeup was something new for Cheryl, permitted tonight by special dispensation.

In her room, her head on a great generous pillow, Cheryl drifted . . . Cary Grant, Tab Hunter, the winner is . . . off to sleep.

"You no-good bitch!" a man shrieked from Lana's bedroom. "How *dare* you tell me to leave! You think you're such a big *star!*" The quarrel grew worse. Johnny made threats—"Don't even touch that goddamn phone"—and hit Lana hard. He slapped her again and again, until she feared he would kill her as he had so often threatened.

Wide awake, frightened but unsure what to do, Cheryl saw the ashy remains of their fabulous night, hers and Lana's, incinerated by Johnny. And yet no one in the bungalow in those violent hours between midnight and dawn could have guessed that in nine days, the problem of Johnny Stompanato would be permanently solved.

9 | "TAKE AWAY THE SWEATER AND WHAT HAVE YOU GOT?"

. . . asked Sam Goldwyn after Lana's brief appearance in his 1938 production, *The Adventures of Marco Polo*. Twenty years later, with Lana's career a heap of smoking wreckage, Ross Hunter produced one answer, at least, by casting Lana as Lora Meredith in *Imitation of Life*.

Another response to Goldwyn might be, "Give her back the sweater"—meaning, bring back the late-thirties and the forties Lana, the sexy, high-spirited Lana often cast in light-comedy parts or in dramatic roles she could handle. As opposed to the fifties Lana Turner, who grew more dauntingly virtuous—and embalmed—in every picture—a shellacked, frigid, self-righteous Lana who always seemed about to order everyone to take a cold shower.

Beginning in 1952, with *The Bad and the Beautiful*, Lana stiffened. In that picture, and in every subsequent role, she seemed perversely intent on proving to herself and to the audience that she wasn't getting any older, and that she was an upright, quasi-virginal, all-American lady uncomfortably miscast as a matron or a slut. Lana, in real life, surely believed only part of it. Onscreen, however, she mistook herself for "Lana Turner."

In *The Bad and the Beautiful*, Lana plays movie star Georgia Lorrison. Her performance in the first part of the film, as a boozy, Diana Barrymoresque bit player, belongs to her limber forties style—competent, enjoyable, believable within the context of studio acting, especially

MGM's. The first hint of Lana's betrayal—i.e., the lofty rigor mortis that so marked her fifties persona—appears in a couple of clips from films-within-the-film, where she's intended to be a bad actress, and she certainly is. Hilariously bad. But this comic brush with badness rubbed off, and stuck. When Georgia Lorrison becomes a star, she turns into the sort of actress Lana herself will become in subsequent roles. This half of *The Bad and the Beautiful* highlights her phony side, the side of Lana Turner that doesn't act, but pretends to act. (In her comedies, she had a knowing twinkle in her eye as she incorporated comic timing as an acting technique. She moved like the good dancer she was. No one made fun of Lana in the forties; she was no more risible than Gene Tierney or Rita Hayworth.) Ingrid Bergman said in 1972, "Lana Turner can act. She's survived a lot of bad movies, but she still goes on, and that is talent."

Perhaps it's unfair to blame Lana for *The Bad and the Beautiful,* which is director Vincente Minnelli's wet dream about Hollywood. Did Minnelli ruin Lana? Her later counterfeit performances led to critical mockery and unkind laughter. Once she acquired that lacquered overlay, it stayed—like Elizabeth Taylor's permanent Dixie accent post–*Raintree County.*

"Something to Offer Films"

Actors view the performances of their colleagues from radically different angles than we do—that is, we the audience, and the critics. Two of Lana's fellow actors from the studio era assessed her abilities with no trace of condescension. In the seventies, Bette Davis placed Lana squarely in an acting tradition different from her own, but equally valid. "When sound came to the movies," Bette said, "and they brought many of us from New York, from the theatre, that created two groups of actors out here. The ones who really made this town were the so-called glamour personalities. Gary Cooper. Joan Crawford. Clark Gable. Lana Turner. Errol Flynn. They had no theatrical

(continued)

background, none of them. What they *did* have was something to offer films, something that was sensational, personality-wise. That overcame everything else. In fact, I think Lana ended up turning into a very good actress. *The Bad and the Beautiful* was a damn good film, and she's never been better—except maybe in *The Postman Always Rings Twice*. And she was very good with Spence [Tracy] in *Cass Timberlane,* which was a fine picture. But what they had, the thing which made this town, was more than the rest of us had who went in solely for acting. My basic interest was the performance, not the offscreen image. Lana was different. She consciously perpetuated the glamour thing. But that was a large, large, large part of the industry back then."

Loretta Young, interviewed by John Kobal in 1971, said, "I think Lana learned to act." Kobal interjected, "In *Madame X,*" to which Loretta replied, "Well, I've seen her do some pretty good jobs before that. I've seen her do a picture which was almost a straight lead with Clark Gable. She played a nurse and he played a doctor during the war [*Homecoming,* 1948] and you couldn't have asked for a better performance. For what it was."

Here's Lana in *The Prodigal* (1955), playing Samarra, the high priestess (i.e., temple prostitute—"I belong to all men," she proclaims) as if it were a role for Helen Hayes, when of course it's closer to *Queen of Outer Space*. What Lana lacked in the fifties was a sense of camp, even a sense of humor. But it's hard for an actress to laugh when, in the eyes of Hollywood, she's gone tomorrow, and barely here today.

Lana's glossy, artificial scenes with Richard Burton in *The Rains of Ranchipur,* also 1955, are as high-flown as a Lora Meredith kite. The performance matches her character's name: Edwina Esketh. (Here and elsewhere Lana played many memorable scenes in cars. At the end of this picture, when she and Michael Rennie drive away, she assumes that noble mask of theatrical suffering—her "troubled" look. It's the look that prompts Sandra Dee, in *Imitation of Life,* to cry out, "Oh, Mama, stop acting!" Other memorable Lana Turner car scenes: her great screaming hissy fit in *The Bad and the Beautiful*; and in 1960, *Portrait in Black*, where Anthony Quinn makes her drive a car when she's never driven before and doesn't know her brake from a hole in the ground; or 1945's *Keep Your Powder Dry*, with petite Lana handling a big army Jeep.)

Ross Hunter's answer to that Goldwynism cannot be neatly summed up. That's because his implied response to "Take away the sweater and what have you got?" amounts to a polychrome collage of Lana Turner's life and career. Thanks to Hunter, in *Imitation of Life* she got her one chance to play an intentionally bad Lana Turner role—and invest it with some sort of crazy greatness.

To Hollywood, Lana *was* her tight sweater. To Ross Hunter, a closeted gay man unaroused by female flesh, Lana without the sweater meant the opportunity to dress her up in two dozen stunning outfits, like a live Barbie doll. Even that famous sweater, in its day, had symbolized a certain kind of heterosexual camp, redolent of locker rooms and burlesque. Hunter, hugely abetted by Douglas Sirk, created an entirely new goddess, a Lana Turner who, like Myra Breckinridge, embodies both heterosexual and homosexual camp while remaining oddly sexless.

Lana as Lora Meredith plays herself, more or less; that is, she plays the Lana Turner she had become by 1959, a star whose professional menopause had arrived. Her self-referential tour de force in *Imitation of Life* recalls Gloria Swanson consigning a chunk of herself to Norma Desmond, or Marlon Brando's autobiographical monologues in *Last Tango in Paris*. If you're familiar with Lana's life and career, you're assembling a mental jigsaw as you watch her play Lora: Lana on the stairs here alludes to Lana on the stairs in *Ziegfeld Girl*; the title of a Lora Meredith play, *Sweet Surrender,* was the name of a perfume in *Somewhere I'll Find You* (1942), Lana's second film with Clark Gable; Sandra Dee, as Lora's petulant daughter, Susie, might almost have been named "Cheryl."

In *Imitation of Life,* Sirk used Lana's limitations to construct a sort of time-lapse collage of the star herself. Call it "Lora Meredith Descending a Staircase." From one angle, there's the biographical Lana Turner. Another dimension exploits Lana's shortcomings that lead into camp, then a shift in perspective shows her cinematic strengths, as evidenced in her forties films recirculated by Sirk to show Lana's poise and timing throughout the picture. Physically, she always hits her mark. You may laugh at Lana sometimes in *Imitation*—I do—but with due respect, recalling that much of the mirth comes from the script. After all, who but a real actress could play a star who thinks herself a real actress, and isn't, but convinces the theatrical establishment that she is, while signaling us that it's smoke and Sirk mirrors? Lana as Lora as Lana is Turner's truest performance, owing to its very falsity. I doubt that even one of the great film actresses, such as Barbara Stanwyck or Bette Davis, could have played the role with such refulgent double-dealing. That's because Stanwyck and Davis were too self-aware for such self-mockery.

Throughout the film, you're viewing Lana/Lora through 3-D lenses. One focuses Lana, the other Lora, and the two women merge somewhere in the middle distance. Before any of that could take place, however, Ross Hunter had to convince Lana to take the part.

A few weeks after the stabbing, Lana moved again. Her mother had located a small house for her at 515 North Roxbury Drive, and there she sought peace from the nightmare that had taken over her life (that house has since been replaced). Realizing that she could rely on neither escape nor denial, Lana eyeballed the calamity at close range.

"I was determined to read every single word that had been printed," she said later. "So I gathered up all the newspapers and locked myself in the bedroom. I read everything, then reread it, attempting to analyze the whole awful happening. And after that I felt totally drained. The press had done their worst, and I'd have to survive it."

By May of 1958, screenwriters Allan Scott and Eleanore Griffin had delivered to Ross Hunter their first draft of the updated, and highly glamorized, *Imitation of Life* script. After reading it, Hunter began serious discussions with Universal. "When they asked who my lead would be," he recalled later, "I said there was only one person, one star for the role—Lana Turner. They thought I was nuts." Lana's name made studio executives break out in hives.

According to Ross Hunter, "Katharine Hepburn wanted it. Crawford wanted it. Bette Davis wanted it. But I held out for Lana. I knew she was going through her darkest period. But, to be perfectly honest, I also wanted her because of the publicity surrounding her private life." (That Hepburn–Crawford–Davis zinger, uttered three decades after the fact, sounds like jiggery-pokery—until you recall the late-fifties films those ladies made, and the ones they didn't.)

About six weeks after the night of April 4, Paul Kohner phoned Lana with news. Ross Hunter wanted a meeting with her. "See him, Lana," her agent urged. "This is just what you need to come back. It's a proven story." Lana, however, shared the studio's fear that no one would come to see her in a picture. "If the movie bombed," she said, "I knew what could happen—I probably would never work again."

But Paul Kohner persisted. "Ross has a great track record," he said. "And listen—it's only you they want. Ed Muhl [head of production at Universal] insists on it. Otherwise, he won't give the go-ahead."

It's unclear whether Ed Muhl had been Lana's champion from the start, or whether Ross Hunter's wiles had won him over. Certainly Hunter's record of box office hits shot on small budgets made his pitches worth listening to. Muhl favored him over other producers because he could get so much on the screen for a dollar. Then, too, Muhl—now forgotten, though a mogul in his day—belonged to that nucleus of improbable Hollywood patrons who knew how *not* to derail potential good pictures, even when not actively nurturing them. Where did self-taught men like these learn to love story, craft, and visual beauty? Their legacy redoubles with each shapeless, tech-weary, megamillion picture foisted on us by today's "educated" Hollywood.

One Sunday afternoon, Lana's maid opened the door to pleasant Ross Hunter, who carried a leather briefcase with two scripts in it. He was about Lana's age, late-thirtyish. Lana said later that "his rosy-cheeked face and his winning smile could have sold me on anything." Ross made Lana laugh, for the first time in many weeks, by dramatizing the parts as he read the script to her. Although Lana on screen gradually lost her sense of humor, in person she was always fun.

In the final scenes, however, laughter changed to tears. The script's naked emotions lacerated Lana's unhealed wounds, reminding her too much of recent days. Her tears overflowed as Hunter read Annie and Sarah Jane's last encounter; Lora at the deathbed; Sarah Jane's outburst as she throws herself on her mother's coffin. The sun had set when Ross laid down the script, put a handkerchief to his own eyes.

And got down to business. He argued that the role offered Lana an "acting challenge." He dwelled on the glamour—after all, this updated script transformed Claudette Colbert's pancake queen from 1934 into Lora Meredith, queen of Broadway, as big in New York as Lana herself used to be at MGM. He reminded Lana that Hollywood, and the world, loves movies with actresses playing actresses. Perhaps he suggested that she might receive another Oscar nomination.

Then, in a coda, he declaimed that Lana had never reached her fullest capability as an actress because she had been a commercial commodity at MGM. Ross told her that in *Imitation of Life,* for the first time, he would combine the two, the actress and the image.

"It was just the kind of offer I wanted," Lana recalled years later. What she said at the end of Ross Hunter's speech, however, was: "No, I can't do it. I'm frightened." Beset by shame and anxiety, she found the vexed mother-daughter relationship especially painful. And Ross understood. Nevertheless, when he left Lana that Sunday evening, he took along only one copy of the script. He begged Lana to read the other one, and to think of herself as Lora Meredith. "Then he and Paul ganged up on me," Lana said, "insisting that the role was the perfect way to show people I could rise above the tragedy."

10 | A PORTRAIT OF THE ARTIST AS HERO AND BULLY

*S*ome movie sets crackle with tension—star feuds, yelling, throwing things, outrageous demands, all perhaps impelled by a temperamental or perfectionist director and goaded by front-office fury at budget overruns. Others resemble a house party, with actors and crew members talking about the weather, golf scores, problems with their kids. Or perhaps some are playing poker while others read mysteries or go over their lines. It is noticed, on occasion, that two cast members have repaired to a dressing room where they will consummate a scene of passion begun in front of the camera.

Since movies are rarely shot in chronological order, one seldom has a sense of forward movement on a set. At times the atmosphere suggests entropy, at other times inertia. Dozens, hundreds of people buzz at their work, but what end? Or else a few perform tasks at a tropical pace while all other activity stops. Actors repeat the same lines in take after take until the director is satisfied with their readings. Then the camera angle is changed, which usually takes some time. Director huddles with producer, then with the script supervisor or sometimes the editor. The cinematographer and the lighting crew, the sound technicians, makeup and wardrobe people, and a myriad others go about their esoteric crafts.

A visitor to the set of *Imitation of Life* might, at first, have imagined herself inside the headquarters of an important, though somewhat uneventful, nonprofit corporation—the Royal Asiatic Society, say, or the

National Film Board of Canada. That atmosphere—smooth, efficient, somewhat abstract—was fostered by Douglas Sirk, as de facto CEO. One reason our visitor might have found the *Imitation of Life* set un-lively is because the cast members seldom met up offcamera. They came on for their takes, then departed. Not one viewed his or her col-leagues as buddies. Although everyone got along, and all were polite, bonhomie was absent. That's how Sirk wanted it, at least for Juanita Moore and Susan Kohner. In fact, these two became friends only later.

"We got along," says Juanita, "but not that well. We didn't know any-thing about each other." Susan adds, "We kept our distance because of our characters. That made it easier to do our work." Both point out that Sirk warned them against friendship, fearing that chumminess would lessen the dramatic impact of their scenes together.

A Universal press release on October 23, 1958, bore this heading: "Garbo's 'I Want to Be Alone' Attitude Puts Actress Juanita Moore in Proper Mood for Demanding Role in *Imitation of Life*." Juanita herself confirms the veracity of the press release, which reads in part, "Miss Moore invariably remained in her dressing room behind closed doors . . . and was seen by the *Imitation of Life* company only when she was called before the camera for her scenes in the film version of the great Fannie Hurst novel . . . 'I was not being unsociable,' she hastened to explain. 'It was just my way of sustaining whatever mood I need for my scenes. I think my part in *Imitation of Life* is the greatest dramatic role ever given to an actress of my race, and I was determined to do it complete justice. My dressing room is my study hall, and for me there is no recess.'"

As for Susan, whose chronic shyness was exacerbated by uncertainty about her demanding role, she went home to Bel Air immediately after work and didn't come near the set on days she wasn't called. One reason for her flight was Sirk himself. "I felt that Sirk bullied me," she says. "He bullied the emotions out of me." The young, sensitive, sheltered girl she was at the time resented his tactics; her feelings were hurt. Susan seems only recently to have realized why he treated her less well than anyone else in the picture: "His bullying helped my characterization because Sarah Jane was a loner in the film. And I was a loner on the set."

I asked Susan for an example of Sirk's bullying. Did he yell, did he threaten like that intimidating legend, Otto Preminger? "Oh, no," she said. "He was very quiet. He would say, 'More, more.'"

That didn't sound so terrible to me, so I pressed her to find out what he wanted more of.

"Well," she laughed, "more emotion. 'Go deeper,' he said. And all I can say is, he was right."

The more she talks now about Sirk, the more grateful she sounds. "I can't look back and say he was wrong, because I had to plumb depths that maybe I hadn't plumbed before. I think he knew how far he could go. He was good at digging out what he knew I had inside."

Susan Kohner is one of the few in Hollywood who felt uncomfortable with Sirk. But don't we all have someone like that stored in our memory—a teacher, an employer, perhaps a parent or older relative who seemed overbearing to us as youngsters, but who, should we encounter them now, might seem smaller, even friendly and wise?

"If this was an ulterior motive on Sirk's part," Susan continues, "to make me angry, to give me a chip on the shoulder, then it worked. It's not that he showed favoritism. But his personality—I found him very dour and Prussian." Although Sirk was Paul Kohner's client, he obviously did what he deemed necessary to get a performance, even if that meant hectoring his agent's daughter.

If Susan sounds like a Sirk survivor, Juanita Moore is a Sirk acolyte. "I loved the ground Douglas walked on!" she says. "He would say to me in his soft voice, when I had doubts about my ability to play the part, 'Now, Juanita, you can do it.'" She says he was unfailingly kind.

In response to Juanita, Susan chimes in: "He scared the daylights out of me!"

My thought is: He had to do it to turn her into Sarah Jane. She's nothing like the character. Susan concedes, however, that while she perceived Sirk as something of a bully, she also saw his nicer side, adding that he congratulated her after the filming.

(An extra feature on the DVD of Sirk's *All That Heaven Allows* contains excerpts from an interview with the director, broadcast on BBC2 in 1979, eight years before his death. Watching this interview, it's easy to understand how he might intimidate: those arctic blue eyes; the intense, unwavering regard turned on his questioner; a no-nonsense answer to each question; and none of the drollery you might encounter with a director such as John Huston or William Wyler. All of Sirk's irony must have gone into his films; little is visible here. He seems self-contained and remote, like a professor at the Munich Film School—which he was at the time, having come out of retirement to teach filmmaking.)

Lana Turner, more than anyone else in the cast, was a known quantity. Or so she might have been the year before. Now, however, she received VIP treatment—"Sirk treated her like the star she was," recalls Susan Kohner—but all else remained tentative, unpredictable: her emotional health; her ability to meet strenuous schedules and demanding scenes that might drain or overburden her; and her reputation—meaning, was the studio filming an automatic flop because of outrage over Lana's scandal? No one said it aloud, because they were on Lana's side. But the thought must have danced on the borders of everyone's consciousness.

Lana kept apart, for more reasons than one. For her, as for Juanita and Susan, the stakes were high. A bad performance, a bad picture, would bury her. Like Juanita, Lana needed the quiet of a "study hall" to sustain the moods of her scenes. It was imperative that she do this role complete justice. Her survival depended on it, and so did "Lana Turner."

Geography explained the other reason for Lana's remoteness. Her dressing room was not the nearby portable kind occupied by her costars, but rather a forty-two-foot custom-built auto trailer with a mirrored dressing room, electric kitchen, and stereo hi-fi. Parked at some distance from the set, this star cocoon seduced Lana. A press release deemed her trailer "the most luxurious ever accorded a film star at Universal-International. . . . It is fully equipped so that Lana may use it as overnight living quarters if she chooses during filming, and on several planned locations within a fifty-mile radius of Hollywood."

A later press release updated this information: the trailer turned out to be too small. After a few days of production it was hauled away for remodeling, including the addition of a twelve-foot annex. "It was large enough for Lana," explained Ross Hunter, "but too small for her movie wardrobe. We added on a wing to serve as king-sized closet."

During filming, Lana's entourage included her stand-in, Alice May; Del Armstrong, her makeup man; hairdresser Patricia Westmore; wardrobe mistress Martha Bunch; and two Pinkerton detectives guarding the million-dollar jewelry that Lana wears in the film. (They were there not only to guard the rocks, but also Lana from vengeful gangsters. She had received a number of death threats.)

Years later, Sandra Dee recalled her initial qualms about working with Lana. "At first," she said, "we didn't know whether we were walking on eggshells around her, but she was wonderful. She helped me, she taught me more than any director. I'll never forget one day on the set, I was sweating under the lights, and I wanted the makeup man located to touch up my face. But the director was ready to call 'action.' He said, 'No, it's okay, leave it alone.' Lana looked at me and said, 'You know, Sandra, on the screen nobody is going to add a little line on the bottom that says, "We didn't have time to powder."'"

Sandra, in turn, gave Lana some pointers. According to a studio press release, "Sandra Dee will serve as technical advisor to Lana Turner when Lana does scenes in which she appears as a photographer's model. Lana has never worked as a professional model. Sandra, on the other hand, was New York's number one teenage model for several years." Lana had played a top model, however, in *A Life of Her Own* (1950), a picture that emphasized high drama over high fashion.

Sirk had little warmth in his heart for American teenagers. They're often villainous in his pictures (e.g., *All That Heaven Allows*, *There's Always Tomorrow*). Even when they're not selfish and manipulative, Sirk sees them as nuisances in an adult landscape. Enter Sandra Dee, as Susie.

Sirk must have found her annoying portrayal perfect. If he wanted a little talking doll that wouldn't shut up, that's what he got. (Sandra Dee herself bore scant resemblance to her character. Guileless, withdrawn, misused all her life, a hard worker, she earned the respect and affection of colleagues. Susan remembers "Sandy" as "a very sweet girl." Sandra's obituary in the *Los Angeles Times* in 2005 included this statement from a family friend: "She didn't have a bad bone in her body. When she was a big star in pictures and a top five at the box office, she treated the grip the exact same way she treated the head of the studio.")

Sandra Dee, like the others, spent little offtime on the set, because she had to attend school on the Universal lot. Sandra called it "the loneliest classroom in the world," since she was its only pupil. School started when she arrived, and let out when she finished. From one film to the next, Sandra's schedule had to include three hours per day of instruction through grade twelve, as stipulated by California law. Her teachers were required to take attendance. "There she sat in class, surrounded by twenty-nine empty chairs. Sometimes she had a teacher who would let her smoke a cigarettte. Other times, the teacher was a strict disciplinarian who would shut down the shooting of a scene moments away from completion in order to get her young charge into the classroom the moment the second hand ruled the time had come."

"I call it 'Imitation of High School,'" Sandra told a reporter. Crew members dubbed it Sandra Dee High. They teased her for being at the top of her class, and also at the bottom. Her favorite schooldays, she said, were those when Sirk needed her before the camera. After a take, she retired to her dressing room to do homework. In addition to strict school-attendance laws, state regulations mandated that juvenile actors could not work on a sound stage after four o'clock in the afternoon, nor could they work more than eight hours per day. When Sandra turned eighteen a few years later, Ross Hunter rejoiced, perhaps even more than Sandra herself.

Among so many isolated actors playing major roles in *Imitation of Life,* straight arrow John Gavin went home every night to his new wife, Cecily. They lived in a one-bedroom apartment in Beverly Hills, and were expecting their first child in the spring of 1959. He considered the persona bestowed on him by the press accurate, and desirable: "Non-Neurotic Newcomer," as *Look* characterized him shortly before he began work on *Imitation of Life.* He didn't care that a synonym for non-neurotic is "square."

In order to evoke Douglas Sirk the director more completely, I'm going to leave the set and talk with several crew members and actors who worked on other Sirk pictures. That's because *Imitation of Life* is atypical—a different kind of cast, which led to an unusual atmosphere on the studio set—and also because surviving cast members, having made a single Sirk film, have less to report than those who worked with him again and again.

Betty Abbott Griffin probably knew "Mr. Sirk," as she called him, better than anyone else in Hollywood except Hilde Sirk, his wife. Born in Rochester and raised in New York City, Betty (the niece of comedian Bud Abbott) came to Hollywood as a young woman and apprenticed as a script supervisor at Universal. She later worked on thirteen Sirk pictures, beginning with *Thunder on the Hill* in 1951. (N.B.: If you look her up on IMDb.com, you'll find only a partial list of her many credits. As I write this, only one Sirk film appears in her entry—a glaring goof for that useful website. Her place of birth, and the date, are also incorrect.)

During the first of many conversations, in Hollywood and by phone, I asked Betty to tell me the things a script supervisor does, and this is what she said. "A script supervisor follows the continuity of everything on the set. She, or he, is responsible for things that have to look like they should look, and match from take to take and day to day. 'Continuity' is really the better word. You work between the director and the editor, and you compile a script for the editor as you shoot it, so that he knows what the director wants to see on the screen and how he wants to see it edited."

I asked whether her work includes props and the like.

"Yes," she said, "props, clothing, makeup, hair. Dialogue, of course. Also doors, windows, pictures, whatever."

My next question was, Are you on the set all the time? Betty answered, "Every moment of shooting. I'm between the director and the camera at all times."

Sirk's meticulousness, and Betty's, helped cement their friendship on the set and off. *Thunder on the Hill,* which starred Claudette Colbert and Ann Blyth, was one of the first films she worked on following her apprenticeship. "Mr. Sirk was wonderful to me," Betty said. "He took me under his wing."

She stayed there. During the fifties, Betty also worked as script supervisor on these Sirk films: *The Lady Pays Off* (1951), starring Linda Darnell; *Weekend with Father* (1951), Van Heflin and Patricia Neal; *Has Anybody Seen My Gal?* (1952), Piper Laurie and Rock Hudson; *No Room for the Groom* (1952), Tony Curtis and Piper Laurie; *Meet Me at the Fair* (1953), Dan Dailey and Diana Lynn; *Take Me to Town* (1953), Ann Sheridan and Sterling Hayden; *Magnificent Obsession* (1954), Rock Hudson and Jane Wyman; *Captain Lightfoot* (1955), Rock Hudson and Barbara Rush; *All That Heaven Allows* (1955), Rock Hudson and Jane Wyman; *Written on the Wind* (1956), Rock Hudson, Lauren Bacall, Dorothy Malone, Robert Stack; *Interlude* (1957), June Allyson and Rossano Brazzi; and *The Tarnished Angels* (1958), Rock Hudson, Dorothy Malone, Robert Stack.

Betty often visited the Sirks at home in Van Nuys. "The house looked rather European," she remembers, "a charming place. There were fireplaces in three of the rooms, including a brick fireplace in the kitchen. Mrs. Sirk was a wonderful cook. A lot of floral prints on the walls, and a lot of flowers in vases. They grew them in their garden. He was a tremendous reader, who kept his many books on bookshelves in various rooms. The house always seemed warm and welcoming. You felt at home, and at ease, the moment you entered. They were warm people."

Recalling Hilde Sirk (née Jary), Betty called her "a dear, sweet lady. In Germany, years earlier, she had been a sort of comic Shirley Temple. Before the war, she was well known and loved as a comedienne. Mostly on stage, I believe. A tiny woman, and Mr. Sirk was tall, at least six feet, I'd say, and blond. When we filmed *Interlude* in Austria and Germany, Hilde Sirk insisted on going into East Germany to take money to her sister. By God, she went and Mr. Sirk would pace the floor at night waiting for her return. She wore several layers of clothing, with money hidden between layers. A feisty lady."

I asked Betty what made Douglas Sirk such a fine director to work with. "His whole attitude toward what we were doing and toward people," she replied. "He would point out many things he considered important on a set that wouldn't matter to other directors. He had everything in his eye. And his attitude toward actors—kind, gentle, but firm. He knew what he wanted, he knew where he was going with it, and that was that. He knew how to make actors feel good, feel important. If necessary, he would tease them into doing wonderful things."

Barbara Rush, whose first important film role was in Sirk's *The First Legion* in 1951 and who later appeared in the director's *Magnificent Obsession, Taza, Son of Cochise* (both 1954), and *Captain Lightfoot* (1955), describes Sirk as "a Viking, very tall, with curly blond hair combed straight back from his forehead, and no part. He had a large face, a big head, and blazing blue eyes." She loved working on his pictures. "A sweet man, very fatherly," she adds. Rush has only praise for Sirk the man, as well as for Sirk the director. When she felt insecure, or concerned about the quality of her performance, he would reassure her: "No, no, it's very good."

In three of the four pictures she made for Sirk, Barbara Rush costarred with Rock Hudson, who constantly initiated madcap antics on the set. "He was hysterical," she recalls, laughing at the memory. "Rock was a great one to laugh when things went wrong or one of us said the wrong line. He would roar, and so would I. We broke up all the time. We fell on the floor—everything had to stop for us! And I know Rock did the same with Doris Day and others." I asked her whether Douglas Sirk joined in the merriment. "Well," she replied, "in a way, yes, but remember, he was a rather serious man. Even so, he had a twinkle in his eye watching us kids. I can't remember him laughing out loud, but that's because his director's mind was constantly on the next take, the next scene." Ross Hunter, on the other hand, would laugh at Rock Hudson laughing, according to Rush.

Hudson himself recalled Sirk as "just plain delicious! I'm proud to say that he took me under his wing. Yeah, he was like ol' dad to me. And I was like a son to him, I think. He liked me and I liked him."

Asked whether Sirk microdirected, Barbara Rush said, "Not at all. He wasn't a Method director who would take you off to a corner and try to make you think about what you were doing from another direction." (Sirk considered himself an "actor's director," although he apparently never huddled with actors as Elia Kazan, for example, so famously did. Every actor I spoke with from a Sirk film agreed that after giving his instructions, he left the rest up to them. If he was satisfied, the take was printed. If not, they shot it again, although with little further guidance from the director. Nor did Sirk devote undue time to scene rehearsals. Rita Gam, who costarred with Jeff Chandler and Jack Palance in Sirk's *Sign of the Pagan* in 1954, said, "Not a lot of rehearsing at all. I mean, there it was: we went on the set and rehearsed a couple of times, and then we shot the scene.")

In 1950, while filming *The First Legion,* Barbara Rush was twenty-three years old, a neophyte in a cast of heavyweights: Charles Boyer, William Demarest, Leo G. Carroll, Walter Hampden, H. B. Warner, and others. When I asked what Sirk told her about how to play the part, she laughed and said, "Not a damn thing! He really wasn't that kind of actor's director, at least not with me. I think Charles Boyer told me more than he did. Sirk only told me: 'We're going to do this' or 'Here's what we're doing next.' "

In the film, Barbara Rush plays a young crippled girl whose Roman Catholic faith "cures" her affliction at the end of the picture, and she walks a few steps—then falls in a heap. Perhaps Sirk's most ambiguous ending, it poses more questions than Sirk, or the film, could ever answer. In spite of this great irony, you can read the final sequence as truly religious, even mystical, because only God knows whether that miracle sticks. And God talks only to God.

Movies of the studio era portrayed the Catholic Church as far nicer than it ever was in reality. The Production Code, and the pious public, wouldn't tolerate the truth—that the church was a monolithic theocracy verging on fascism, ruthlessly dictated by a hypocritical, neurotic, power-mad hierarchy ruled from afar by a principality of Roman despots. Not until Otto Preminger's *The Cardinal* in 1964 did films dare portray the rulers of the Catholic Church as self-serving politicos.

Sirk in 1951 couldn't go far, but he made a film that zigzags from a young priest's crisis of faith, to Catholic Realpolitik, to a phony miracle in which a doctor dupes an elderly priest, ending on a question mark as to whether the girl's "cure" will last, and whether it springs from a supernatural source or from extreme positive thinking. Lyle Bettger, as the free-thinking doctor who tends the priests, says: "Every time a miracle happens, someone gets hurt." Sirk poses the question: Did the earlier phony miracle inspire a real one, or is the "real" miracle merely the naive delusion of a miserable young girl? The picture leaves an astringent aftertaste.

Unfortunately, few saw it then, and few since. (Referring to another one of his films, *A Scandal in Paris,* Sirk stated what applies equally to *The First Legion*: "I adopted a position which brought out the irony, and that doesn't go down well at all with American audiences. They want a cut-and-dried stance, for or against. But the nuances which handle both at the same time and make Europeans smile are completely foreign to Americans.")

Refreshing, even shocking in the era of such twaddle as *Going My Way* and *The Bells of St. Mary's*, *The First Legion* shows two priests who question their vocations and threaten to leave the Jesuit order. Sirk couldn't make the picture he probably wanted to, but he still did the almost unthinkable for that era: refusing to sentimentalize the Catholic Church or those who run it, he represented the lesser clergy as human beings, not as bloodless holy men. Thus, the death of Leo G. Carroll, as Father Rector Paul Duquesne, affects believer and unbeliever alike. It even prefigures the death of Annie Johnson in *Imitation of Life*. Sirk's characters got a magnificent send-off to the hereafter.

Spanking the Actor

Like everyone else, Sirk could be less than noble. Filming *Summer Storm* in 1944, he had shot sixteen unsatisfactory takes of a scene with Linda Darnell when she grew "tired, embarrassed, and was almost in tears. Finally Sirk ordered, 'Everyone take a breather.' Putting his arm around Linda's shoulder, he said, 'Now I want you to relax.' Suddenly, he yanked her across his knee and spanked her hard. 'Now you go out there and do that scene right!' he snapped. The spanking so shocked and infuriated her that she went back on the set and made the scene one of the best in the picture. 'After that, Sirk and I got along better than ever,' she said." Darnell apparently held no grudge. When Sirk requested her for *The Lady Pays Off* in 1951, she was happy to work with him again.

Jimmy Hunt, a child actor in *Weekend with Father* (1951), broke his arm while rehearsing the potato-sack race with Van Heflin. Sirk demanded another run-through, either assuming that the boy exaggerated, or—as Hunt told an interviewer in 2003—he was simply insensitive to the boy's pain.

(continued)

On the set of *All I Desire* in 1953, Sirk lost his temper with Lori Nelson. The young actress ran, crying, to her dressing room and wouldn't come out. The studio phoned her mother, who wasn't home. Then someone thought to call Rock Hudson, whom Nelson looked upon as a surrogate big brother. Though he wasn't working that day, Hudson made a special trip to Universal, explained to Nelson what Sirk wanted and why he had lost patience, and walked her back to the set.

11 | SIRK DU SOLEIL

ouglas Sirk's career falls into five periods: theatre director in Germany, 1920–1937; film director in Germany, 1934–1937, overlapping his theatre work; minor film work elsewhere in Europe and in Hollywood after fleeing Germany in 1937; pre-Universal films in Hollywood, 1942–1950; and his Universal-International years, 1950–1959, for which he is best known. *The First Legion,* produced by Sirk and Rudolph Joseph and released through United Artists, was the last film he directed before moving to Universal, where he remained until he left Hollywood forever in 1959, following *Imitation of Life.*

As my chapter title suggests, he really has become a sort of Sun King to a coterie of auteurists and academics, many of whom write bad-posture English that slumps on the page. Fortunately, Sirk has also been taken up by good writers and also by several cinéastes, among them Todd Haynes, whose *Far from Heaven* (2002) is an all-out homage to *All That Heaven Allows.*

The best sources for Douglas Sirk's life and work are mostly out of print. Without them, however, it's impossible to approach this complex and elusive director. Jon Halliday's *Sirk on Sirk,* first published in 1972, remains the single most important book, but only when paired with the second edition, which came out in 1997 and includes some twenty-five percent more material than the first. Halliday explains, in the introduction, his later inclusion of material that Sirk asked him to omit during Sirk's own lifetime, and the lifetime of several other persons.

Next in importance is Michael Stern's 1979 assessment, *Douglas Sirk*. Like Halliday, he interviewed the director at length, as did James Harvey, who devotes several chapters to Sirk's films in *Movie Love in the Fifties,* published in 2001. Elisabeth Läufer's *Skeptiker des Lichts: Douglas Sirk und seine Filme,* published in Germany in 1987 and as yet untranslated, contains valuable biographical information and career insights. In the brief biography that follows, I draw on the work of these four diligent authors, and on interviews with others who knew Sirk in Hollywood, and later, in Europe.

Although 1900 is usually given as the year of Sirk's birth, Jon Halliday discovered that the date on his passport was 1897. Another frequent inaccuracy has Sirk born in Denmark. He told Halliday that he was born in Hamburg, but spent several years of his childhood in Denmark. Indeed, his father was Danish, his mother German. Their son's original name: Detlef Sierck.

After attending the universities of Munich, Jena, and Hamburg, Sirk married Lydia Brinken, an actress, and in 1925 their son, Claus Detlef Sierck, was born. Taking time off from university studies, Sirk worked for a time as a newspaperman at the same paper as his father, a wellknown journalist of the time. During the 1920–21 theatre season, Sirk took the job of assistant *Dramaturg* (i.e., play reader and adapter) at the Deutsches Schauspielhaus in Hamburg. From that lowly position he gradually worked his way up to director, translator, and playwright at theatres in various German cities.

Even before Hitler came to power in 1933, Lydia Brinken had joined the Nazi party. Meanwhile, she and Sirk divorced, and he remarried. His second wife, Hilde Jary, was Jewish. For that reason alone, Sirk's ex-wife was able to obtain a court order preventing Sirk from seeing their son. She enrolled the boy in the Hitler Jugend, a Nazi paramilitary organization for young people. Owing to her own connections, both thespian and political, Brinken was able to propel the boy into an acting career. He subsequently became the leading child star of Nazi cinema. According to Halliday, "Sirk was never able to meet or talk to his son again. The only way he could see him was by going to watch him in the movies, where his son sometimes played a young Nazi." Sirk's poignant estrangement from his child perhaps prefigures Annie Johnson's wrenching separation from Sarah Jane in *Imitation of Life*. Since Sirk often reshaped scripts before and during filming, his own parental pain may well be embodied in dialogue, as well as in certain scenes, camera angles, and directorial touches.

It would later be learned that Claus Detlef Sierck, age nineteen, died in action on the Russian front in the spring of 1944. Lydia Brinken died the following year.

In 1936, Hilde Jary Sirk left Germany under unusual circumstances. Nazi officials issued her a passport—and confiscated her Protestant husband's. They thought, apparently, that by forcing Sirk to remain in Germany he might continue making films. After all, several of his pictures at UFA had done very well, both artistically and financially. Could he be cajoled—or compelled—to make films showing the Third Reich in a flattering light? Nazi officials hoped, also, to coerce Sirk into divorcing his Jewish wife. Thus unencumbered, his Aryan looks would offer an attractive fringe benefit to the propaganda campaigns of the master race. Although certainly aware of his left-wing politics and his distaste for totalitarianism, the Nazi overlords seem not only naive but also uncharacteristically forgiving toward Sirk. Others of his persuasion were arrested early on. So eager was the Nazi leadership to benefit from Sirk's talents that, after his departure, Goebbels wrote to him in Paris, predicting a glorious career in Germany, and stating that even the Führer wished him to return. Should he come home to Germany, Goebbels promised, he would be allowed to send money to his wife. Sirk said he flushed the letter down a lavatory.

During this dangerous period, Sirk benefited from several right-wing, although non-Nazi, patrons. His luck held until finally, after a series of nervy adventures worthy of a Weimar James Bond, Sirk escaped in 1937. After sojourns in Switzerland, France, and Holland, he and his wife, now reunited, arrived in the United States in 1939. They headed for California, where Sirk puttered at unrewarding tasks for several studios.

Unable to find steady film or theatre employment, he decided to leave show business. Later he said, "With my last one thousand dollars

I bought a small chicken farm in the San Fernando Valley. I spent a year or more on this farm and in some ways, although I was completely broke, it was maybe my happiest time in America." Later the Sirks sold the chicken farm and invested in a second place, where they grew alfalfa and avocados and raised cows. "I thought my American movie career was probably over," he recalled, "and eventually the Hitler business would be finished and I could go back to pictures in Germany."

After Pearl Harbor, and conscription, Sirk was forced to sell his second farm because, as he later explained, "I couldn't hire any labor to harvest the alfalfa." Again, however, good luck of a sort followed bad. He said, "About this time the movie industry decided to hire all the emigrants. Paul Kohner, my agent, persuaded me to sign a contract with Columbia—this must have been about mid-1942. I was hired as a writer, not a director. I got about 150 dollars a week, which was nothing in Hollywood." (Except for a brief hiatus, Paul Kohner remained his agent until Sirk left picture making after *Imitation of Life*.)

Sirk repeatedly asked Harry Cohn, the churlish head of Columbia, to let him direct, but Cohn refused. "Between Mr. Hitler and Harry Cohn, I lost more than ten years of my life," Sirk said.

Later that year, Sirk's old friend from Germany, Rudolph Joseph, approached him to ask whether he would direct a quickie anti-Nazi film, envisioned as a propaganda vehicle and, in Sirk's words, "not even a B-feature, but a C or D feature." Thus, Sirk's first Hollywood film, *Hitler's Madman,* was shot in one week in 1942 as an independent production, bought by MGM, and partially reshot by Sirk before release. Virtually unknown even by cognoscenti and votaries in the cult of Sirk, *Hitler's Madman* is such an unusual film that I have devoted the following chapter to it.

By the time Sirk began his Hollywood career, the great adventures of his life were past. He and Hilde lived quietly in Van Nuys, apart from Hollywood's premieres, night life, and headlines. Once, at a party given by producer Al Zugsmith in his lavish Los Angeles home, Sirk was shocked to see "naked women frolicking in the pool." After that, the Sirks preferred to stay home and read, grow roses in their garden, and savor the hearty Old World dishes that came from Hilde's kitchen.

After *Hitler's Madman,* Sirk directed one picture a year throughout the forties, all on small budgets with name stars, each one well-crafted and with enough of that ineffable touch of early Sirk to set it apart from the output of studio assembly lines. I often think of Sirk's forties work as resembling the paintings of a lesser-known Impressionist such as Caillebotte or Sisley. Like those artists, whose work eventually received wide appreciation, so Sirk's lapidary early films may eventually be esteemed by a wider audience. They include *Summer Storm* (1944), starring George Sanders and Linda Darnell; *A Scandal in Paris* (1945), George Sanders, Signe Hasso, Carol Landis; *Lured* (1946), Lucille Ball, George Sanders, Boris Karloff, Cedric Hardwicke; *Sleep, My Love* (1947), Claudette Colbert, Robert Cummings, Don Ameche; *Slightly French* (1948), Dorothy Lamour, Don Ameche; *Shockproof* (1949), Cornel Wilde; and *The First Legion.* (Connoisseurs of movie camp lines will appreciate this one from *Shockproof,* spoken by Cornel Wilde to Patricia Knight: "You've got to change your brand of men.")

Sirk's first picture at Universal, *Mystery Submarine* (1950), anchored him at the studio, and there he remained for the rest of his directing career. After a half-dozen more pictures, he teamed up with Ross Hunter, setting in motion the greatest professional events of both careers.

By the time Sirk arrived in Hollywood, his big adventures were behind him, except for an especially harrowing one. In 1949, Sirk decided to return to Germany for a year. There he planned to investigate the possibility of once more making films, even though the Americans had dismantled UFA and, in effect, destroyed German cinema for decades to come. That destruction, and the postwar situation, soon convinced him that a return would cause greater frustration than would staying in Hollywood.

While in Germany, Sirk spent time searching for his lost son. "I went to Berlin and looked at the notice boards," he said, "trying to get some news of him, but I never found anything." (In *A Time to Love and a Time to Die,* John Gavin searches among such notices in the vain hope of locating his parents. Watching that scene today, one recalls New York in the shellshocked weeks after September 11.)

Taking off from New York en route to Germany, "a smaller plane crashed through the roof of the plane he was in and ended up inside the passenger area of the larger plane. Sirk suffered head and neck injuries. The company offered the passengers a choice of a rest in New York, or immediate transportation. Sirk was the only person who opted to take the next plane to Europe, a decision he said he made because he was so desperate (and to which his wife attributed his [subsequent] backaches and headaches)." This initially untreated trauma may also have contributed to Sirk's eventual blindness in old age.

Douglas Sirk died, in Switzerland, in 1987. His wife, who suffered from Alzheimer's disease, lived on for several years, and eventually died in Israel, where she had been cared for by family members.

*S*irk's first Hollywood picture, *Hitler's Madman,* starred John Carradine as Reinhard Heydrich, the so-called Reichsprotektor of Bohemia and Moravia, who was ambushed and shot by Czech freedom fighters on May 27, 1942, outside Prague. Heydrich died on June 4. Six days later, in reprisal, the Nazis destroyed the Czech villages of Lidice and Ležáky after murdering their inhabitants. *Hitler's Madman* was released exactly one year later, on June 10, 1943.

In addition to Carradine, other stars of the film are Patricia Morison, Alan Curtis, and Blanche Yurka (uncredited). The very young Ava Gardner has a bit part as a university student terrorized by the Nazis. Patricia Morison, interviewed in *Scarlet Street* in 2004, added this background on *Hitler's Madman*: "It was financed by German émigrés, particularly a man named Erwin Brettauer, who had financed many German films. Apparently they didn't have enough money to finish it, though, so Metro took it over and completed the film. We'd been working at one of the small independent studios and then MGM took it over. Douglas Sirk was a lovely man and a fine director."

Soon after the holocaust of the Czech villages, Edna St. Vincent Millay wrote a long poem titled "The Murder of Lidice." Like much of her work, it's lofty doggerel, though in this case crudely effective. As Sirk's film opens, a narrator declaims, in voice-over, several lines from the poem, lines about the village's history during six centuries, its peace and prosperity before the Nazi invasion of Czechoslovakia. In a montage at the end of the picture, the ghosts of murdered villagers arise to march across the screen as the flames of Lidice leap behind them. With frightful force, these dead recite Millay's closing lines:

> They entered our country and slaughtered and slew,
> And then, O never forget the day,
> On the tenth of June in '42,
> They murdered the people of Lidice.

I saw *Hitler's Madman* on television when I was eight or nine and never forgot its impact. Prints of the film being hard to come by, I intended to devote a mere paragraph to it. That original paragraph ended like this: "Insofar as childhood memory can be trusted, I believe the picture ranks higher than Sirk's assigned grade of C or D." (He dismissed it as "not even a B-feature.")

Then, just before publication, I obtained an unofficial copy of *Hitler's Madman*. Again, I was shocked. First of all, by the theatrical power of satanic evil as incarnated by Carradine's Heydrich, with his marsupial face, spectral body, and elongated head that seems to caricature the Aryan ideal. Shocked, too, by the roiling pain inflicted on the innocent, which takes place in most films about the Nazis, but which here seems more immediate, as though we were watching it with live actors on a stage. That immediacy is owing to the low-budget rawness of this film, which precludes familiar big-studio suffering. (We actually witness very little. Most is by suggestion, except for a startling scene in which Heydrich shoots dead the Roman Catholic priest of Lidice during a religious procession, an act whose violence most directors would have deemed taboo in those days.) And, finally, I was astounded by Sirk's adroitness in making this picture on the fly, and on a minuscule budget.

Hitler's Madman was not about fine acting, camera work, art direction, editing, or any of the aesthetic rewards we normally associate with Sirk. Planned and executed as a propaganda film, it was shot and assembled in a quasi-documentary style. It's the only Sirk film that might be called "informal," a cinematic feuilleton. As such, its relation to big-budget studio productions is like the work of self-taught, "naive" painters to a Goya exhibit at the Prado. One might even think of it fleetingly as akin to something like *Reefer Madness,* or an Ed Wood concoction minus the craziness, while on a higher plane you detect the influence of Russian silent films: Eisenstein's operatic pageantry (the final moments of *Hitler's Madman* echo *Alexander Nevsky*), and Dovzhenko's veneration of the soil—here, in low-angle shots, wheat brushes the sky like slim cathedral spires. Sirk, in his deft use of available stock footage, shows prewar Czechoslovakia as a lyrical, Jean Renoiresque landscape, and Prague in long shot seems framed by an anonymous master. (A note to collectors of movie *hommages*: In *Imitation of Life,* Sirk's shot of young Susie and Sarah Jane rolling a beach umbrella off an embracing couple alludes to a similar shot in Eisenstein's *October (Ten Days That Shook the World)*; there, a young Bolshevik rolls an umbrella off a bourgeois couple on the banks of the Neva River.)

On a darker level, you sense Sirk's indebtedness to German silents. And to Von Stroheim. In a sequence perhaps inspired by a grim funeral sequence in *Greed,* a villager is taken off by the Nazis one morning for interrogation. At nightfall, his body is brought home in a wooden box. The man's wife collapses, while his little boy, oblivious to sorrow, takes up a loaf of fresh bread and munches like a household pet. In another allusion to *Greed,* the German puppet mayor of Lidice crams food into his mouth as greedily as the vulturine guests at the wedding of Trina and McTeague.

A shot at the beginning of *Hitler's Madman* parodies Riefenstahl, whose camera, in *Triumph of the Will,* practically fondles the Junkers plane bringing Hitler to Nuremberg. Sirk's plane, flying through clouds over Czechoslovakia, transports the partisans who will assassinate Heydrich and organize a wider Czech resistance. Sirk parodies Riefenstahl elsewhere in the film, as well. His stock footage of prewar Prague echoes her sumptuous travelogue through the mellow old city of Nuremberg. Sirk's score incorporates strains from Czech composers, as if to gainsay Riefenstahl's ominous marches. Both filmmakers learned much of their craft from the Russians—the power of rhythmic editing and montage, the aesthetic use of angles, especially low-angle and high-angle shots— an influence dramatically evident in both *Hitler's Madman* and *Triumph of the Will.* Sirk's most brazen and ironic bit of mockery comes at the end, when, in a Brechtian touch, the dead villagers debouch into the frame to exhort the living. These victims are recalled to life, while Riefenstahl's ambiguous soldiers file past her camera like silent ghosts—presumably Wehrmacht, though they might also be read as the "fallen comrades" commemorated in "The Horst Wessel Song" that ends her film. Since nothing in Sirk is accidental, I'm convinced he intended somehow to deconstruct her evil masterpiece. Both endings, however, Sirk's and Riefenstahl's, owe a debt to Eisenstein's *Strike* (1925), where, in the final frame, the face of a fallen Bolshevik reappears, followed by the title: "Remember, Proletarians!"

Lofty and cut-rate—how to explain the hybrid, even schizoid, personality of *Hitler's Madman?* Sirk, of course, was unable to exert full control; others "helped." Perhaps the main reason it alternates from stately to cheesy is because it was shot by two wildly antithetical cinematographers, Jack Greenhalgh and Eugen Schüfftan. Greenhalgh, who's given screen credit, did little of the actual cinematography, according to Sirk. The footage he shot bears the stamp of his B-picture career: over two hundred quickies with titles like *Border Caballero* (1936), *Escort Girl* (1941), and *Robot Monster* (1953), his last.

Schüfftan, on the other hand, who is responsible for the photographic interest of this film, received credit as "technical director." Born in Silesia, which was German at the time and now forms part of Poland, he fled first to France to escape the Nazis, and later, in 1940, to the United States. "I brought him in on the picture," said Sirk, but owing to union rules at the time he wasn't allowed cinematographer's credit. Enter Greenhalgh.

Schüfftan's distinguished career prior to *Hitler's Madman* explains why Sirk used him on this film and on two subsequent ones, *Summer Storm* (1944) and *A Scandal in Paris* (1946). In 1927, Schüfftan worked on special effects for Abel Gance's *Napoléon*. He did trick photography for Fritz Lang's *Siegfried* (1924) and special visual effects for *Metropolis* (1927), shot Robert Siodmak's *Abschied* (1930), G. W. Pabst's *L'Atlantide* (1932), Max Ophüls' *La Tendre ennemie* (1936), Marcel Carné's *Quai des brumes* (1938)—in short, he had worked with some of the best filmmakers in European cinema. Later he shot Franju's *Les Yeux sans visage*

(*Eyes Without a Face*), in 1960, and won an Oscar the following year for Best Black-and-White Cinematography on Robert Rossen's *The Hustler*, starring Paul Newman.

Hitler's Madman has yet another of Sirk's deathbed scenes, this one the malevolent Reinhard Heydrich's, the antithesis of saintly Annie Johnson's. With Himmler at his side, John Carradine's baleful Heydrich, begging for morphine, seems as tormented as Milton's Satan "rolling in the fiery gulf."

Sirk praised the performance. "John Carradine," he said, "*was* Heydrich. Carradine was a stage actor and, more particularly, a Shakespearean stage actor, with a reputation of going overboard. A lot of Nazis behaved like Shakespearean actors." Sirk was exceptionally well qualified to compare actor and real-life prototype, for he had encountered Heydrich in Berlin.

"It must have been at one of the awful parties UFA were always throwing," he recalled. "Anyway, I didn't know who the heck he was, but being a very optical man, I got a good impression of his face, and it was very interesting." Sirk said that both he and Heydrich had attended the German Naval Military Academy at Mürwik, in northern Germany. "Anyone who'd been there was considered a colleague of anyone else who'd been there," he explained. "He must have heard I'd been to Mürwik, and so he came over to me at this party. He was in mufti, but he had the Nazi button and he looked and behaved just like Carradine. He had the same edginess of speech, a certain dry theatricality, which is just what I wanted."

Hitler's Madman, like Orson Welles's *Othello,* reveals every seam. (Welles's film was made piecemeal over a period of years; often he couldn't pay the actors.) In both instances, however, you sense the immediacy, and the precariousness, of filmmaking. The grab-'em-and-shoot circumstances, and each director's choice of monumental subjects, make both pictures exciting because there's no safety net beneath. Sometimes a master filmmaker's rough draft says more than a polished, predictable bestseller.

(Copies of *Hitler's Madman* may be purchased from Eddie Brandt's Saturday Matinee, in North Hollywood; www.ebsmvideo.com.)

The Other Madman

Fritz Lang's *Hangmen Also Die!,* which, like Sirk's film, treats the as-sassination of Heydrich, was released by United Artists in April 1943, two months earlier than *Hitler's Madman*. The timing, and also Lang's reputation, his ample budget, big-ticket production values in-cluding cinematography by James Wong Howe, and a running time of one hundred thirty-four minutes, insured that Sirk's minor vehicle foundered in its wake. (Lang's cast—Brian Donlevy, Walter Brennan, Anna Lee—was scarcely more stellar than Sirk's.)

Lang's picture lacks the desperate moral energy of *Hitler's Mad-man*; it's more mystery than wartime thriller. As such, it recalls early Hitchcock. The rhythm is that of a silent picture: images held several extra beats, a leisurely amble during the first hour as the camera vis-its one Prague household after another to set up the story. Most of all, it lacks the pointedness of *Hitler's Madman*. After a couple of scenes at the beginning, Heydrich (played by Hans Heinrich von Twardowski, who had an uncredited moment in *Hitler's Madman*), is seen no more. His shooting, and subsequent death, take place off camera. The Czech villages are not destroyed. In place of Sirk's tense drama, the plot of *Hangmen Also Die!* resembles a well-made play, with many a tidy coincidence in which half the populace of Prague conspires to outfox the Nazis.

A worthy film, Lang's nevertheless lacks the gut-punch of Sirk's. At times, *Hangmen Also Die!* veers toward trivialization: what those pesky Nazis deserve is a visit from the Czech Miss Marple.

THE SHAKY MEGASTAR AND
THE SEPIA HOLLYWOOD
HOPE

*W*hen Lana Turner walked on that set, every eye turned toward her; you knew that a star was there." That's how Ross Hunter remembered August 5, 1958, the first day of shooting *Imitation of Life*. Lana made her entrance with a brave smile. Head high, shoulders back, the posture of her MGM girlhood, she projected poise and control she didn't feel. In fact, she was terrified. But the press had come today, as well as director, producer, costars, Lana's agent, Paul Kohner, and other well-wishers. They would witness Lana's first battle to take back her career and all that went with it, including her self-respect and well-being. Lana beamed a bright smile, the actress emblem of self-confidence. So far, her performance was working. Feeling tension subside, all those on the set gave Lana a cheering round of applause.

Ross Hunter, and Universal, had made the savvy public relations decision to leave the set open to the press at almost all times. Even though a movie set was usually closed on the first days of shooting so that the company could get to know one another, this one seemed as friendly and welcoming to visitors as Andy Hardy's backyard. "Lana needed all the friends she could get," said a studio PR man.

Dressed for one of the movie's early scenes set in 1947, Lana wore a simple blue-and-white gingham dress. Ross Hunter drew huzzahs from the crowd when he proclaimed, "Lana looks just as good in gingham as she does in mink." Her short hair, lengthened by a platinum fall, gave

her the intended girlish look of young widow Lora Meredith, the impe-
cunious actress and model who has not yet congealed into Lana's latter-
day specialty, star aspic. (According to Universal's production budget for
Imitation of Life, the studio provided Lana with two three-quarter falls,
each one costing $275. This simple gingham dress, plus a duplicate of it,
cost a total of $670. It was the least expensive item in Lana's movie
wardrobe.)

Politely but firmly, Lana informed the gathering of reporters that one
door was shut: "And that is the door on my private life during these very
difficult recent months. I'm sure you understand that I want to speak
only of the future." Then she flashed them the green light with another
smile, and they began, predictably, to quiz her on that future: career,
love, her hopes for coming days.

"Are you nervous?"

"Yes," Lana admitted, "I am. But then I'm always nervous when I
start a new picture." Her eyes darted, her beautifully manicured hands
twitched slightly—the only betrayal of the strain she was under.

Most of the reporters seemed kind and avoided the obvious questions on her recent ordeals. But then one woman asked about the killing
and its aftermath. Lana smiled at her and said, "I don't believe we'll discuss that, thank you." Soon after, the journalist said good-bye and left.
Later Lana confessed that, in a way, she felt grateful for the experience
because it proved she could stand up and handle whatever might come.

Answering another question, Lana said, "Cheryl may come and visit
me on the set." Cheryl, at the time, was living by court order with her
grandmother, Mildred Turner, pending a final custody hearing set for
September. "She always does," Lana added.

Someone asked whether Cheryl might be interested in becoming an
actress.

"Well, I'm not sure," Lana mused, as if her daughter's interests had
never crossed her mind. "Cheryl's artistically inclined. She draws and
sketches, but I don't know about acting."

Just then a huge bouquet of flowers arrived on the set. For Lana,
from Ross Hunter. She thanked him, kissed him on the cheek, and
mentioned to the crowd that in her shiny trailer dressing room were
eight other bouquets from studio officials and friends. (Lana made

arrangements for the flowers to be delivered to a children's hospital in Los Angeles.)

To conclude her official welcome to the set, Lana told colleagues and reporters: "Everyone has been so kind, so considerate." As she spoke, her eyes filled with tears. "It's even a little frightening." Then, in a quicksilver change of mood, she added, with an airy toss of her hair and its extension, "With so much excitement, sometimes I can hardly remember my own name."

Cheryl Crane did visit the set. There she found her mother in full bloom as top star on the lot, courted and coddled by Ross Hunter, who, in Cheryl's brittle estimation, "was famous for the way he massaged the egos of his maturing lady stars . . . Mother seemed to purr with delight over the flowers and favors and gifts, the old MGM perks such as waiting limousine and music in her dressing room with someone hired to play the records."

According to Cheryl, after the Stompanato affair, Lana had begun playing movie star even at home. "Suddenly, Mother would metamorphose into the great star. Her back would straighten, her bottom tighten, and her eyebrows float to a level of mild surprise. I would look on amazed as her voice took on more expression and her hands, which were calm and natural a moment before, assumed a sweeping theatricality."

These same mannerisms, sprinkled through *Imitation of Life,* suggest that Sirk stopped at nothing to get the performance he wanted from Lana. He encouraged her to play Lana Turner playing Lora Meredith as Lana Turner. Remember the famous exchange near the end of the picture when Lana, chin high like a statue of Queen Boudicca, says to Sandra Dee, "If Steve is going to come between us—I'll give him up. I'll never see him again," and Sandra delivers what is surely her best line in this or any other picture, "Oh, Mama! Stop acting!"

Did Lana grasp how totally Sirk had wound her in his coils? In the film, Lana's fifties grandeur and faux sincerity eventually add up, as if by odd algebraic equation, to the portrait of a quasi-honest first lady of the American stage: Lora Meredith, the Toast of Broadway. (By many accounts, those actual first ladies such as Helen Hayes, Lynn Fontanne, and Katharine Cornell acted with high disregard for psychological truth, like Lora in her David Edwards comedies. Truth? That's what closes on Saturday night, while arch great-ladyness keeps lights ablaze along the Great White Way.)

Cheryl concedes that her mother indulged this grande-dame pose "as a defense mechanism, a role she could slip into to keep people back." Whatever Lana's quirks at home, at the studio her movie-star persona paid off. Accessible to the press and endlessly cooperative, she helped *Imitation of Life* garner more in-production publicity than any other film in Hollywood that year.

Lana, in a highly publicized appearance at Town Hall in New York in 1975, was asked about Sirk. "Such a gentle man," she said. "Very quiet, but the wheels were going all the time. When he would give you direction, it was not sitting in a chair saying, 'Hey babe! Do this, and that and the other thing.' Mr. Sirk would ask, 'May I speak with you?' and sit down and say, 'I think this should be done this way. And how do you feel about it? Do you feel it that way?' He didn't yell or throw his weight around. Everyone had the most marvelous respect for him because he was a true craftsman."

Sirk rarely commented on Lana. He did say, however, that "she was very compliant through the whole shooting. She trusted us. And I might add that she wasn't sorry—she was very happy with the picture."

"Douglas Sirk was color blind," said Juanita Moore not long ago, remembering the man who directed her greatest performance. In her recollection, others in the cast and crew were equally so. That was not always the case, however. On other sets, slights sometimes occurred. "They'll call you Juanita even when they don't know you," she said. On a much later film, *Paternity* (1981), she recalled that Burt Reynolds, the star, anticipating such disrespect masquerading as informality, announced to the technicians on the first day of shooting, "This is *Miss* Moore. Miss Juanita Moore." She has never forgotten his gallantry.

Another instance of late-fifties discrimination: the fan magazines. Normally open to newcomers, especially on a notable production like *Imitation of Life*, the leading ones such as *Photoplay, Modern Screen,* and *Motion Picture* would typically feature (if only in a sidebar) an actress of Juanita's importance. In her case, the obvious slant would be that after a decade of bit parts and small roles, at last she had arrived. Yet a search of these magazines at the Academy of Motion Picture Arts and Sciences, and elsewhere, turned up virtually nothing, even after her Oscar nomination. True, Juanita didn't qualify as a starlet, though she certainly possessed style, beauty, and an eventful past. Then, too, her age suggested character-actor status, a category of scant interest to fan magazines. (Harry Belafonte, Dorothy Dandridge, and Sidney Poitier, as "exotic" candidates for stardom, occasionally made those pages.) To these magazines, Juanita was an invisible woman.

Not so in the black press. Such papers as the *Chicago Defender,* the *Pittsburgh Courier,* and the *California Eagle* covered Juanita from casting to premiere, and beyond. "WIFE OF NYAS BERRY GIVEN ROLE IN *IMITATION*"; "JUANITA MOORE GLITTERS IN REVISED VERSION OF PIX *IMITATION OF LIFE*"; "JUANITA MOORE NOMINATED FOR SUPPORTING OSCAR"; "LABEL JUANITA MOORE LATEST 'MISS SEPIA HOLLYWOOD' HOPE."

Although not the nominal star, Juanita's pressures mounted nearly as high as Lana's. Ross Hunter had put it to her at the outset: his stock at Universal would nose-dive if she didn't give a great performance. Sirk also said, "If you're no good, the picture's no good." ("Wasn't that a hell of a burden to lay on me?" she said recently, savoring a fifty-year-old memory.) As that newspaper headline suggested, she bore the hope not only of black actors but also, in a sense, of African Americans generally. In those days, a visible black person soon came to represent his or her race in the eyes of black—and white—America. For Juanita herself, the role of Annie Johnson meant the culmination of years of study, hard work, and the desire to show her full talent. Her big break at last—which might never come again.

As usual, Joel Fluellen coaxed and supported her at the studio and away. "Oh, Joel was my right-hand man," she said. "He believed I had some talent, and whatever success I attained, he was behind it. He did my hair, helped with my makeup. I listened to Joel, didn't go any place without him. He took me over until I met my husband, and then Joel liked both of us."

Off the set, Fluellen served as Juanita's unofficial dialogue coach. "He came from Louisiana," she said, "and he taught me how to talk like a Southerner. I grew up in Los Angeles. I'd go over my lines with him and he would correct little things. He'd say, 'No, no, that's a little too cultured for Annie Johnson.' He schooled me. Then, if I tried to lose the cultured line reading, he'd say, 'Hold on—not too much. I don't want you to sound like a mammy.'" She recalls his coming to the set almost every day, even though his small role as Annie Johnson's minister required only four days before the camera.

In a recent conversation, I mentioned Fluellen's comforting presence as Annie Johnson's minister at the end of the picture. "Joel was always a great comfort to me," Juanita said. "I wore his shoulder out! I'd finish work on *Imitation of Life,* come home sometimes crying, sometimes happy. And sometimes very displeased, but Joel would be right there. He often came home with me from the studio. We lived not far from each other at the time. I lived on Washington and he lived between Venice and Pico."

On unhappy days, Juanita's displeasure was self-directed. Sirk she considered "the kind of director every actor wants." He would lower her emotional temperature by saying, "We have no reason to rush. Let's try it again and see what happens. This time, think about your dog." When a take wasn't perfect, he would guide her to a better one. Sometimes, watching the rushes of a previous day's work, Juanita and Sirk would decide that her facial muscles betrayed the wrong kind of tension. They would discuss how to adjust this as Sirk prepared to reshoot the scene.

Several commentators have wondered whether Sirk, in his love stories, actually believes in love. Indeed, many of those stylized liaisons fall short. His most convincing romantic scene, however, occurs where you least expect it: a quarter hour into *Imitation of Life,* between Lana Turner and Juanita Moore. After watching the scene, you may wonder why Lora Meredith didn't say to Annie Johnson, rather than to Steve, "You're so good for what ails me."

The day after Annie's arrival, she and Lora sit down at the kitchen table to address envelopes, and Lora tells her that she can keep the money from this batch. "It'll pay you for staying today and cooking and . . ." On the sound track, "Lora's Theme" starts up, a vague spin-off from the title song that later underscores Lora's love scenes with Steve Archer.

Annie responds, "Uh-uh. That money goes into our kitty."

Lora (beaming her a look that's both puzzled and pleased): "*Our?* Seems as if you intend staying." Lora, looking down, plays coy, de rigueur for an actress in a scene like this, although not with a fellow actress.

Annie: "Seems like I do, if—if you want it."

Lora (tenderly): "You know I do, but you can see how bad things are."

Annie: "Miss Lora, we just come from a place where—where my color deviled my baby. Now anything that happens here has gotta be better."

As Annie finishes her line, Lora melts into a smile (a warmer, more unguarded smile than she ever gives Steve or David Edwards). She reaches across the table and touches Annie's arm.

Lora: "Oh, Annie!"

Annie is startled for a split second, perhaps embarrassed by Lora's intimacy. Then her face registers delight and incredulity at the prospect of equal partnership in the household. (By the next scene, however, she is once more the unequal servant.)

Few directors would have seen to it, as Sirk did, that each actress received visual parity throughout the sequence. A paradigm goes like this: Both women framed in medium shot as they sit at a table, favoring Annie; reverse shot, favoring Lora; camera tracks in to frame them in medium close-up in a series of alternating reverse-angle shots: Annie, Lora, Annie, Lora, to end of sequence, which ends with both in medium close-up.

This little sequence, as carefully constructed as a sonnet, exemplifies Sirk's subtlety, his sense of cinematic style, his deft touch with actors and camera, his subversive wit, and also his determination not to privilege Lana over Juanita. Although lesbianism is nowhere implied, we see that the two women love each other. And even though it's a parody of movie love scenes—husky voices, subdued lighting by the kitchen sink, a deliquescent vulnerability in both women—it's also genuine: Lora's self-absorption notwithstanding, she really does love Annie. Even more, one might argue, than she loves her daughter. Annie, on the other hand, loves Sarah Jane without limits. And she loves Lora . . . enough. (Structurally and emotionally, this scene parallels the intimate one at Annie's deathbed, when Annie comforts Lora: "No need to cry, honey.")

Scenes like this explain why some of us revere Sirk—and why he unsettles others.

On a number of days, filming took place away from the studio. According to a press release on September 5, 1958—halfway through the shoot—"the number of locations within a fifty-mile radius for a single major production is believed to be a new Hollywood record." Only the Moulin Rouge, a famous nightclub of the time, "played itself" in *Imitation of Life*.

Other locations around Southern California doubled as New York, Connecticut, and the Atlantic Seaboard. Ross Hunter, sounding like a character in *The Last Tycoon*, said, "We have all the 'New York' we need right in our own back yard." Originally, he had planned to fly east and film the picture's opening scenes on Brooklyn's most famous strip of public beach, Coney Island. On second thought, however, Hunter canceled the trip. The reason: crowd control. "It would take the marines who landed on Iwo Jima to manage that mob," he said. "And with Lana Turner on hand, we'd need Carlson's Raiders, as well."

Instead, a portion of the boardwalk at Long Beach stood in for Coney Island's seaside setting during two days of filming. And yet the real Coney Island made it into *Imitation of Life* after all, in a couple of panoramic long shots of the Cyclone roller coaster, the Wonder Wheel, and thousands of summertime New Yorkers on the sand and in the water. Two second-unit men flew to New York, where they were joined by a local hire for the special location photography. The third shot, a seamless match for Coney Island until you pay close attention, is Long Beach, with its own extras and boardwalk. The remaining beach scenes in the final cut were all filmed there, with some thousand extras hired to populate the beach. If you contrast these long-, medium long-, and medium-shot extras in California with the milling throngs in New York, you'll notice that the former seem almost choreographed. They move in casual, uncluttered patterns, all planned and supervised by Sirk and executed by the assistant director.

Lana enters—or rather, her legs enter—the picture from frame right, a low-angle shot. She runs along the boardwalk calling her lost daughter: "Susie! Susie!" A large sign attached to the boardwalk railing announces "The 1947 Coney Island Mardi Gras, Sept. 8th thru 14th," an event held from 1903 to 1954 in late summer, rather than the day before Ash Wednesday, owing to weather. Soon the camera shows us all of Lana's Lora Meredith. This is a mother increasingly desperate to recover her young. She speeds up, runs behind the sign and against foot traffic, those dozens of moving bodies in Dantesque procession on the boardwalk who pay scant attention to this lone figure. She leans over the railing to call out again and again for Susie.

Michael Stern, in his book on Douglas Sirk, points out that many of the director's films "begin with similar shots, showing first the feet then pulling back to reveal the context and the character. It is the perspective from which we see Naomi Murdoch (Barbara Stanwyck) return to town in *All I Desire*. Similar openings take us into *Weekend with Father* and *Lured*. In *Summer Storm,* the first shot following the titles is a close-up of a pair of feet walking hesitantly along a cobblestone street. In each case Sirk shows the movement first, then the goal or purpose or direction." Sirk did it yet again in *Shockproof* (1949), where we first see women's feet and legs moving briskly along Hollywood Boulevard before Patricia Knight is revealed in full shot.

In *Imitation of Life,* Sirk's stylistic device also alludes to Lana's sensational entrance in *The Postman Always Rings Twice*. There, the camera first introduces her feet, then tilts slowly up those shapely legs, stopping at the knees. Cut to John Garfield's startled face, cut back to Lana, in full shot, a white apparition. The camera feasts on her, from white high heels to tight white shorts, bare midriff, white halter top, libidinous face, and white turban over platinum hair. (Pauline Kael once wrote that these dazzling duds seem to conceal the character's "sweaty passions and murderous impulses.")

As for those many other legs on the boardwalk moving in counterpoint to Lana's—men's, women's, some bare below their shorts, others covered by casual slacks, sailor suits, dresses—a casting call went out early on for two hundred pairs. "We are not interested in faces or figures," Sirk said. "Just legs. Dramatic legs, and they must be very talented." All kinds turned up at the studio: from legs à la Betty Grable to those desperate for a makeover. The pairs selected for the sequence presumably met Sirk's tongue-in-cheek criterion: "They must be able to register anger, surprise, coquetry, indecision, decision, and joy—and all without any assistance from the rest of the body."

The Man on the Beach

"I oughta knock your blocks off!" the fat man snarls at the mischievous little girls who have balanced a beer can on his capacious belly while he slept. In real life Billy House (1890–1961) was not at all irascible; a reporter once referred to his "offstage charm." The context of that observation was the reporter's assertion that, despite the actor's claim never to have attended school a day in his life, his affability, and his grammar, belied the supposed lack of education.

Billy House owned a cottage on Cape Cod named Mattapoisett, an Indian word meaning "Place of Rest." There, between assignments on Broadway and in Hollywood, he grew roses. Lest anyone miss their superior quality, he posted a sign over the garden gate that read, "Through These Portals Blossom the Most Beautiful Roses in the World."

Born William Howard Comstock in Minnesota, he lost his father as a child and subsequently took the name of his stepfather. The family

(continued)

moved to Oklahoma, where Billy, in his late teens, joined the Gentry Brothers Dog and Pony Show, a scaled-down circus. Originally hired as property man, he was soon promoted to comic singer. Perched on a horse, and surrounded by "a spangle-clad bevy of circus beauties," he warbled "Meet Me Tonight in Dreamland." (Someone apparently did; obituaries listed a son as his sole survivor.)

After winning a Fat Man Contest at a Texas theatre—he weighed over three hundred pounds—House entered vaudeville and toured throughout the Midwest. In 1924 he finally arrived in New York, and four years later made his Broadway debut in *Luckee Girl,* a musical starring Irene Dunne. Next he appeared in Earl Carroll's *Murder at the Vanities,* during the 1933–34 season, and finally, in 1936–37, as a bathing suit manufacturer from Brooklyn let loose in the Austrian Alps in *White Horse Inn,* a massive quasi-operetta starring Kitty Carlisle.

Meanwhile, House had made his movie debut in Michael Curtiz's *God's Gift to Women,* in 1931. He continued to work regularly in Hollywood for the rest of his life, most notably in Orson Welles's *The Stranger* (1946). There he plays Mr. Potter, a drugstore proprietor and town clerk in the small Connecticut town where Welles, as a Nazi war criminal, hides out. House's character is so obsessed with his ongoing checker games that customers must pour their own coffee, retrieve their own medicines off the shelf, or face Mr. Potter's resentment at being distracted from his checkerboard.

In late August, when the schoolroom scene was filmed—young Sarah Jane, passing for white, runs from the classroom and renounces her dark-skinned mother—the studio searched for forty-five youngsters willing to go back to school several weeks early. Although some children disdained even imaginary lessons on the Universal lot, their ambitious mothers quickly supplied the studio's required head count.

Elsewhere in Southern California, the New Fox Theatre was used for Lora Meredith's audition for playwright David Edwards, and for her subsequent Broadway triumphs, as well. According to a studio press release, this was "a former Hollywood Boulevard legitimate theatre resurrected to play the setting for a Broadway stage hit." Sirk, with his theatre background in Germany, cleverly made the one venue double and redouble as several Broadway houses. Scrutinizing Lora on stage for initial audition and subsequent opening-night curtain calls, I discovered only a couple of telltale similarities: the same red seats in several shots, the same backstage concrete-block walls painted ivory and aquamarine. The actual New Fox Theatre, as it was called in 1958, later became a movie house renamed the Pix. Later still, it received its present-day name: the Henry Fonda Music Box Theatre, at 6126 Hollywood Boulevard. (When I looked in recently, I found it greatly changed, like all else in Hollywood. Only a few touches remain of theatrical glory: old-fashioned plaster rosettes on the ceiling in the lobby, a gleam of stately brass here and there.)

According to a studio press release, "Lana played leading roles in two plays in a single day [at the New Fox]. Her stage performances were for the benefit of two color cameras and a paid audience of extras during a play-within-a-play sequence for *Imitation of Life*." Actually, we see Lana onstage four times: the audition, and then curtain calls for *Stopover, Born to Laugh,* and *No Greater Glory.* Except for that notorious audition, we're deprived of Lora's thespian endowments.

Preparing to film the brief onstage sequences, Lana was quoted as saying, "That will never happen in real life. I grew up in movies and that has been the only medium in which I have acted." Beginning in the seventies, however, Lana did go on the stage. She toured in a regional production of *Forty Carats,* and later starred in dinner theatre productions of such crowd-pleasers as *The Pleasure of His Company* and *Bell, Book, and Candle.*

A house in Mandeville Canyon seemed perfect for Lora Meredith's Connecticut estate, and its exterior was used as such. All interiors of her homes, however—the coldwater flat and the Connecticut house—were built as studio sets. The Reuss Ranch, north of Los Angeles in the foothills of the Santa Susana Mountains, stood in for an idyllic New England picnic spot where Juanita Moore, Sandra Dee, Lana Turner, and John Gavin spend a summer afternoon. A later scene in the movie, with

Sandra Dee and John Gavin riding horseback, was also filmed at the ranch. (Years earlier, a scene or two in *Gone With the Wind* had been shot there.)

The scenes of Susie's high school graduation were filmed at the Town and Country School, which Susan Kohner, and later Cheryl Crane, had attended. In her book, Crane recounts a visit to Lana one day "when they were shooting on location at a boarding school. The scene was the graduation of the Broadway star's daughter. They chose to use my old Town and Country School, and it felt odd to walk around campus, deserted in summer. I sensed I would never be part of any graduation ceremony, mock or real, but there I stood getting my diploma in the person of Sandra Dee. Pert, pretty, and blonde, she looked more like Mother's daughter than I did."

The Ziegfeld Mothers Club

Tucker Fleming, for years a man-about-Hollywood who was a friend of George Cukor, Lana Turner, Ross Hunter, and many other celebrities, told of a party he attended in the sixties. "A fellow I knew gave a *Ziegfeld Girl* party in his little A-frame house in West Hollywood. There were about fifteen guests in all. Naturally, he invited the three glamorous stars of the 1941 picture, and all accepted: Lana, Judy Garland, and Hedy Lamarr. On the night of the party, however, Lana phoned to say she felt rotten and could she send Cheryl in her place.

"So Cheryl arrived with a girlfriend, and both were decked out in leather, which looked rather surprising at the time. I passed by a bedroom right behind Cheryl and her friend. The door was open, and Hedy and Judy were sitting on the bed. I sat down with them to chat, and they were shaking their heads over Cheryl's outfit. Judy said, 'Oh, look at that! You know, Lana's not a very good mother.' I was astounded. Judy Garland and Hedy Lamarr—and it's Lana who isn't a good mother!"

*T*hat first day on the set, Lana not only received flowers; she also sent them. When Terry Burnham, who plays her daughter, Susie, at age six, reported to Universal for her first scenes, she discovered a large bouquet in her dressing room. Attached was a good-luck telegram from Lana that said, "Best wishes to my 'movie daughter.' This is your first film. Welcome to the club."

Although *Imitation of Life* was Terry Burnham's first picture, she already had appeared in several television shows. She made only two other movies, *Key Witness* (1960) and *Boy, Did I Get a Wrong Number* (1966), and a handful of subsequent TV appearances. In *Imitation of Life* she's easier on the nerves than most child performers. A year or so later, in *Key Witness*, Burnham had changed from a cute, feisty little blonde girl to a dark-haired, gangly one who seemed headed for homelessness.

A nagging question: Did Lana, or someone on the picture, also send flowers to young Karin Dicker? Her chiaroscuro portrayal of Sarah Jane, age eight, is one of the best performances in the film, disturbing and full of shadowy nuance. I hope the real Karin wasn't as overlooked offscreen as her character is in the picture, where we wince to see this beguiling little creature wounded by unintentional slights and exclusions.

Karin Dicker was born in 1947, which makes her eleven years old when *Imitation of Life* was filmed. IMDb.com lists only two additional credits for her, a *Lassie* episode in 1959 and *Goodyear Theatre* a year later.

In the early stages of researching this book, I almost interviewed Karin Dicker. Or so I thought. Her adult weirdness proved as unsettling as her Sarah Jane performance, although certainly less pleasing. Here's what happened. In December 2002, when this book was still a distant prospect, a friend of mine, Dwayne Teal, came across the sound track album from *Imitation of Life* offered for sale on eBay. The seller's description began: "I was blessed to play Sarah Jane as a child in this movie, made in 1959. I have already years ago sold other items, including the script."

As a collector of Hollywood memorabilia and a passionate fan of *Imitation of Life,* he immediately e-mailed Karin Dicker with compliments on her performance and also several questions, which she answered. He asked, for example, whether she stayed in touch with Terry Burnham. (She didn't.) He mentioned that some years earlier he had acquired a Spanish lobby card picturing Dicker, Burnham, Lana Turner, and Juanita Moore in the scene where Annie Johnson is telling the girls the Christmas story. Dicker responded, "My favorite scene was the Xmas scene— 'Was Jesus white or black?' I love the way I roll my eyes."

Throughout 2003 and later, Karin Dicker purveyed various memorabilia via eBay: a scrapbook kept by her mother, with candid shots taken at Universal and on location; a souvenir program in Japanese; a congratulatory letter to Karin from Ross Hunter, dated October 28, 1958, in which he tells her he has just seen a rough cut of *Imitation of Life* and "I want you to know that you are simply marvelous in the picture . . . you are a fine young lady with a natural talent"; and various other candid shots and publicity stills.

Meanwhile, Dwayne Teal asked Karin whether he might pass along her e-mail address to me. She replied, "Thanks for asking me first. It is fine." A bit later, I sent an e-mail explaining the general scope of the book and asking whether she and I might speak by phone. A week or so later, having received no answer, I re-sent the e-mail. Again, no response. Fearing that my e-mails had gone astray, I next wrote her a letter and mailed it to the Los Angeles address on the package label of merchandise shipped to Dwayne. She never responded.

My various correspondence was sent in 2003. Then, in the spring of 2004, when a date had been set for the *Imitation of Life* screening at the Egyptian Theatre detailed above, I once more sent Karin Dicker an e-mail informing her of the time and location and assuring her, on behalf of Foster Hirsch, the host, that everyone in attendance would be thrilled to welcome her.

On the night of the screening, Foster introduced notable members of the audience, among them Susan Kohner's mother, her brother, and her sons. Then, having been told that Karin had accepted the invitation and was in the audience, he said, "Let us welcome Karin Dicker, who gave an excellent performance as young Sarah Jane." A great round of anticipatory applause, and then a middle-aged man stood up to announce that Karin Dicker had planned to attend but had fallen ill that day. I believe that everyone who had just watched her on screen was as disappointed as I was.

Later, on "Karin's eBay Homepage," I came across her present-day photograph. She looks exactly the way Karin, grown-up, should look: large, purposeful dark eyes, a stylish coiffure, earrings, and chic black dress. A certain resemblance to Marlo Thomas and a big welcoming smile—for her customers, but not for me. I'm baffled by her quirky elusiveness. Or is it just the behavior of one more Baby Jane Hudson? I'd still like to know: What Ever Happened to Karin Dicker?

16 | "WAS JESUS WHITE OR BLACK?"

*J*always chuckle as the scene starts: "Santa Claus has many names in many different countries. In Holland, he is called Sinter Klaas . . ." It's typical of Sirk to open on that earnest, spinsterish teacher with the unfortunate chin; cut to rapt little Sarah Jane at her seat; and then subvert a happy childhood tableau with Annie Johnson's knock at the schoolroom door. Underlined by the teacher's stricken look when she learns that Sarah Jane is black, tension spikes like blood pressure. Or rather, it rebuilds, for already the shot preceding the classroom scene roils with disturbing Sirkean overtones.

I refer to an exterior shot of the public school that Sarah Jane attends. On the extreme left of the frame, as though to jab us in the eye, sits a dominant red fire hydrant. This looming beacon augers not only danger but unspecified anxiety, as well. Sirk uses the hydrant as a device to beam portents of race and racism, sexuality, and coming conflicts in the Johnson family. Along with broken hopes, for it's the Christmas season, and Christmas means sorrow and discord in a Sirk film.

Red, the Christmas color; a decorated tree in a corner of the classroom, and the teacher lecturing on Santa Claus—cues for heartbreak. When Annie knocks, Sarah Jane slides down in her seat, as if to go, literally, through the floor with embarrassment. Her mother spots her, Sarah Jane slams the book and runs into the blizzard, mortified that her secret is out. In front of the school, in the howling storm (it howls visually and also on the music track), they pause in their desperate chase, which begins now and will end only with death. Annie kneels to tie a scarf around Sarah Jane's head. She says, "What do you want to do, catch pneumonia?" and Sarah Jane spits out a venomous reply: "I hope I do! I hope I die!" Followed by, "Why do you have to be my mother? Why?" There is no peace or good will in the offing, for Sarah Jane's first rejection—her Christmas present to her mother, as it were—takes place before a sign that reads, "Xmas Trees, Special Orders," surrounded by a little forest of evergreens dusted with snow.

This is a key sequence in the picture because, for the first time, Sarah Jane's fate, and Annie's, take unmistakeable shape. The previous sequence foreshadows it, when Annie tells Lora that Sarah Jane cut Susie's wrist to compare their blood because a kid at school claimed that "Negro blood was different." We don't witness that harmless little bloodletting, but it's a potent image nonetheless.

Maida Severn

She was perfect for the role of old-maid schoolteacher (in various movies), airline passenger (in *Airport 1975*), secretary (*Mr. Hobbs Takes a Vacation*), and maid (in *But Not for Me* and a number of television shows). Had she progressed to larger parts, someone surely would have nabbed her for *Arsenic and Old Lace*. Maida Severn (1902–1995) was born in New York and started out as a child actress on Broadway and in summer stock. Later, she studied at the American Academy of Dramatic Arts and at Richard Boleslawski's Theatre Workshop. On radio, she specialized in dialect roles and sang French, German, Italian, and Spanish songs on NBC's *Continental Varieties*.

In 1956 she came to Hollywood, where she appeared frequently on television and in local stage productions (*Waltz of the Toreadors*

(continued)

at the Pasadena Playhouse, *Write Me a Murder* at the Civic Playhouse in Hollywood). In the early seventies, she spent a year and a half on the daytime soap *General Hospital* and worked steadily in commercials, where she sold products as diverse as Mr. Kleen and State Farm Insurance.

Christmas may be Sirk's Rosebud. Whether personal or professional it is not known. If the latter, it might derive from the snow motif in *Citizen Kane*—the deep snow of Kane's Colorado childhood, the sled named Rosebud, which he wields as a weapon against the man who rips him from his mother, and the glass paperweight with a snow scene encased inside that drops from Kane's hand and breaks at his death. Although not specified, Christmas grief seems to hover around Charles Foster Kane. In Sirk, holiday angst is more explicit.

In *All That Heaven Allows,* Jane Wyman's two selfish children, who have pressured her to break up with Rock Hudson, leave her all alone at Christmas. They do, however, send an unwelcome gift: a TV set. The salesman who delivers it assures her that here she will find "drama, comedy, life's parade at your fingertips." In one of Sirk's most famous shots, we see Jane Wyman's disconsolate image reflected on the blank TV screen. Outside, snow falls softly and a group of children pass in the street chirping carols that go unacknowledged by the seemingly dead inhabitants of dead houses. (In his films, Sirk demythologized Christmas to show how suicidally depressing it had become in the hands of American merchants and sentimentalists.)

In his 1952 comedy, *Has Anybody Seen My Gal?,* the Blaisdell family hits rock bottom around Christmas time, a sour pharmacist rushes into the street to berate an organ grinder for making so much noise with "Silent Night," and gruff old Charles Coburn topples a Christmas tree when he pushes another character into it. In *There's Always Tomorrow* (1956), Fred MacMurray functions as a de facto Santa Claus: he's a toy manufacturer in a lonely workshop of cheerless playthings, such as Rex, the battery-powered robot. This Father Christmas is esteemed by his wife and children for the "presents" he provides—the trappings of middle-class comfort—but not as a person with needs and feelings.

Apart from *Citizen Kane*, Sirk might have realized the cinematic possibilities of Yuletide dismay from watching the films of Erich von Stroheim. In *Greed*, ZaSu Pitts's character is murdered on Christmas Eve; in *Walking Down Broadway*, a character standing under a sign wishing "Peace on Earth, Good Will to Men" is fired from her job.

Or maybe Sirk's inspiration was some grotesquerie he saw on television, such as a Bing Crosby Family Christmas Special. Not that Sirk, or anyone, needed a specific trigger to OD on Christmas glut. By the middle of the last century, the holiday had become a juggernaut that annexed all of December. By century's end, it had metastasized to the day after Halloween.

In *Imitation of Life*, Sirk stretches out his Christmas snowstorm through several sequences. Back in the apartment after school, when Lora tries to comfort both Annie and Sarah Jane, Annie ends the sequence with her terrifying question: "How do you explain to your child, she was born to be hurt?"

Following that, Steve Archer arrives. He has come to propose, but in the narrow hallway he and Lora are interrupted in their love scene by a burly man with an armload of Christmas presents who squeezes through. They're interrupted again by a call from Lora's agent, offering her the chance to read for the playwright David Edwards. Cut to Edwards's fancy apartment, with a butler mixing drinks, and through the window we see the storm raging on. When Steve forbids Lora to meet her agent and the playwright, they quarrel and Lora bids him goodbye—"Forever!"

Then another Christmas tableau, with another tree: Lora and Annie, and their daughters, at home on Christmas Eve. Annie tells the girls about the birth of Jesus in Bethlehem, as "secular" Lora passes back and forth, studying the flibbertigibbet scene for her audition. Occasionally she regards herself in the mirror until Sarah Jane interrupts Annie's Nativity story with an odd question: "Was Jesus white or black?"

Lora, always well-intentioned toward both children, answers soothingly: "He's the way you imagine him." Lora's anodyne response is psychologically right. Here, and in other scenes, she functions like an aunt to Sarah Jane: possessing a degree of detachment, aunts can answer questions that stop a mother in her tracks. (Annie surely considers this question impertinent to the point of sacrilege.) Throughout the picture, Lora attempts to defuse racial dynamite. Despite good intentions, however, she's always wide of the mark with Sarah Jane. Thus, it's also psychologically fitting that Sarah Jane answers her own question, since no adult response would satisfy: "He was like me . . . white."

Belying the cozy Christmas in the apartment are Steve's persistent phone calls, which Lora refuses to take. Each time Annie answers, Steve asks: "Has she come in yet?" Annie, who lives her religion, is unwilling to lie. Instead she evades: "I'm sorry," until Steve gives up.

The snow melts, and we don't see it again until Annie's funeral, which takes place in the dead of winter. Always, as those white horses pull the hearse that bears her coffin, I half expect to see a stark Christmas tree in a storefront along the route. But this time Sirk didn't need one. Yet the feeling lingers, that just out of camera range hovers the world's saddest little cedar tree, half-dressed in extinguished lights and faded gewgaws, an existentialist Christmas tree stripped of Christmas. Such irony would be obvious. After all, in Sirk, as in Pinter, what's unsaid often counts for more than what is spoken. And so, unannounced, Sarah Jane finally gets the White Christmas she's always dreamed of.

*S*usan Kohner and Juanita Moore filmed their first scenes together on Friday night, August 22, 1958. These scenes were also Susan's first ones for the picture. Earlier that day, her father had sent her a telegram using the German phrase for "break a leg": "Hals und Beinbruch, Darling. Love, Pop."

Although new to *Imitation of Life,* and unseasoned in the ways of Sirk, Susan, like Juanita, realized the director's intention of making the sequence—Annie and Sarah Jane's confrontation in the street outside Harry's Club—one of the most powerful in the film. And one of the fullest—dramatically, visually, musically. Bringing Susan and Juanita together for the first time in these loaded scenes may well have been a director's trick by Sirk for head-on emotional impact.

In the previous sequence, Annie Johnson has discovered her daughter singing and dancing "in that low-down dive"—and of course, passing for white. It's understood by the management of Harry's Club—and tacitly accepted by 1959 audiences—that when the truth about Sarah Jane's race is revealed, she's fired. The club's host, rudely, to Annie Johnson: "Go on, beat it! She's through, anyway." In the next shot, Sarah Jane emerges onto the street from the service door of Harry's Club—a subtle point, but typical of Sirk's narrative compression and encoded content. She's wearing an olive-drab blouse and tweed skirt. A blue suitcase in each hand, coat draped over right arm, she's fed up with her mother's meddling.

Here the jazzy, dissonant music explodes like a time bomb: bass-note piano played to a bongo beat, ominous and noir. It recalls Henry Mancini's "Peter Gunn Theme" from the hit TV show that first aired in 1958, and no wonder: Frank Skinner, who composed the *Imitation of Life* score, was high in Universal's music department, Mancini a contract composer there. Skinner, a studio veteran, was entitled to use, as needed, and to take credit for, the work of lower-level composers like Mancini, who had been at Universal for only a decade. Although today such unacknowledged contributions resemble plagiarism, in the studio era they were considered bona fide collaboration. According to IMDb.com, Mancini contributed to the *Imitation of Life* score, although his work is uncredited. In his 1989 autobiography, *Did They Mention the Music?*, Mancini himself doesn't mention the picture.

Annie Johnson, in a matching coat and hat of night-sky blue, stands half-hidden in a shadowy alcove clutching her large black purse. Stepping into the street as Sarah Jane stalks past, she grabs her daughter's arms, telling her, "If it ever got back to the teachers' college that you were mixed up in such a place, they'd never let you in." A middle-aged couple, passing on the sidewalk, eyes this intense, troubled pair suspiciously, and hurries off.

Sarah Jane: "I wouldn't be found dead in a colored teachers' college!" Then, outpacing Annie, she steps off the curb. A huge yellow taxi honks, speeds by, barely missing her and her mother, who rushes to keep up. (I consider this near-miss one of Sirk's rare visual clichés. What an overused device in movies—a whizzing car that almost strikes a character in distress. A friend of mine disagrees, pointing out that the yellow taxi chimes with Sarah Jane's "high yellow" status, a term in common use at the time, referring to African Americans with light skin. In earlier scenes, Sarah Jane wore a yellow dress—no coincidence with Sirk, a director whose eye for color and color motifs matches that of a great painter.)

As Sarah Jane disappears down that forlorn street, the music rises from heavy boogie-bass to a shrieking, overwrought, brassy, high-pitched climax accompanied by a keening, gospel-tinged vocalise. (Foster Hirsch has described this sequence as "sorrow set to music—we hear the street wail.")

We've heard that musical disharmony earlier. In the schoolroom scene, when Annie brings red galoshes to Sarah Jane on a snowy day, and Sarah Jane, who has been passing, flees the classroom, that same shrieking vocalise—like a choir of banshees—rises in the air. It matches the severe emotional dischord between daughter and mother. A variation on this musical desperation also occurs in the beating scene. There, however, Sarah Jane's screams of pain and humiliation supply the vocal track.

The later street scene outside Harry's Club, with its deep shadows, saturated colors, darkened shop windows, puny streetlamps, and looming red delivery truck, resembles similar ones in such girl-going-bad German films as *The Joyless Street* (1925) and *Pandora's Box* (1929), both directed by G. W. Pabst and both veering from expressionism toward deep, disturbing realism. Sirk, having come of age in Germany during the tumult of the twenties and the early thirties, knew such works intimately and showed their pessimistic influence throughout his career. Indeed, the silent films of the Weimar era and the later German sound pictures formed his cinematic birthright. Thus, he had every right to use a similar haunted and garish mise-en-scène. Many of Sirk's Hollywood films equate, at least implicitly, the stagnant materialism of American middle-class life in the fifties with the economic desperation and moral poverty of Germany on the eve of Hitler.

Here, on this end-of-the-world nightmare street in *Imitation of Life*, the wet pavement implies that many tears have been shed already, even as Annie Johnson sheds more on the stoop where she has sunk down, suddenly deflated and old. "Ohhh, Sarah Jane," she mourns, as her "baby" vanishes. Like a thief in the night, that grown-up baby has dealt a mortal blow. After this, Annie will rarely rise from her bed. Only once will the two women meet again.

(This remarkable sequence, a semiotic rain forest in its richness, lasts less than two minutes. It was shot on the Warner Bros. lot, a mile or so from Universal, because a fire on Universal's backlot a year earlier had damaged an acre of permanent street-scene sets, including the studio's New York Street. The various theatre marquees that trumpet Lora's Broadway success, and the exterior of young Sarah Jane's grammar school, were also filmed at Warner Bros.)

———

Cut to: Miss Lora's Connecticut estate, a morning pierced by sun. A big, black Cadillac glides up the drive, delivering Lora from a glorious location shoot in Italy. Fellucci wanted her for the part of Rena in *No More Laughter,* and he got her. Sirk the ironist never rests, for that Cadillac foreshadows Annie's funeral cortege, an event that has been speeded up by the harrowing scene just ended.

*R*eferring to the scene inside Harry's Club, when Sarah Jane sings "Empty Arms" and does her flouncy dance, I asked Susan Kohner whether she had done her own singing. She laughed. "No," she said. "I barely did my own dancing!"

The interior scene was shot a couple of weeks after the street scene of the previous chapter, which follows it in the film. The shooting script sets it up like this: "Spotlighted in the center of a small stage, wearing a wisp of a costume, is Sarah Jane. She is singing a risqué ballad, wiggling and gyrating." The continuity and dialogue script expands the "wispy" description: "Sarah Jane is dressed in an abbreviated black, sequined, corset-like costume, with a short, feather-ruffled skirt." She also wears large rhinestone earrings and black fishnet stockings.

They Could Go on Lip-Synching

Jo Ann Greer's voice, though not Jo Ann Greer herself, appeared in a number of famous movies during the fifties. As a "ghost" singer, she supplied the throaty songs that appeared to flow from Rita Hayworth in *Affair in Trinidad* (1952), *Miss Sadie Thompson* (1953),

(continued)

and *Pal Joey* (1957). Greer also worked as vocal stand-in for Gloria Grahame in *Naked Alibi* (1954) and Esther Williams in *Jupiter's Darling* (1955). The last actress she dubbed was Susan Kohner in *Imitation of Life*.

Greer, who began singing with Les Brown and the Band of Renown in 1953 and stayed for the next forty years, left ghost singing in 1959 for a less anonymous career as a visible singer. She also worked with such band leaders as Ray Anthony and Charlie Barnet. In the sixties, Greer married a member of Lawrence Welk's orchestra and made an appearance on Welk's TV show, where she sang "Strangers in the Night"—a racy number for Welk's early-to-bed crowd.

In 1991, Jo Ann Greer and two other "voices" who had sung for the stars—India Adams and Annette Warren—appeared together in a cabaret act at the Hollywood Roosevelt Hotel's Cinegrill. Preceding each one of the singers was a video projection of scenes from films she had dubbed. Then, individually, they re-created one of the film numbers and added a few reminiscences from the set. A reviewer for the *Los Angeles Times* remarked that "the performers—all within sight of sixty from one direction or the other—are still fairly reliable singers." He added that Greer's voice "showed absolutely no signs of wear." Jo Ann Greer died in 2001.

Gary Gabriel, who worked at Universal in the late fifties, delineated the two processes that are often lumped together as "dubbing." He explained that "dubbing was done in films from time to time, but more often it was lip-synching. For example, let's say that Jane Doe was hired as the voice of Ava Gardner. Jane Doe recorded the song, then Ava was photographed pretending to sing it in a scene. That was lip-synching. If Ava sang it herself before the camera, and later Jane Doe's voice was substituted by a sound engineer, that, of course, was dubbing."

Gabriel pointed out also that "in the later years of Hollywood musicals, stars like Judy Garland and Doris Day pre-recorded, for

(continued)

quality, then lip-synched to their own voices." Sometimes, also, a star such as Marilyn Monroe would record her songs (as Monroe did for *Gentlemen Prefer Blondes*), then Jane Doe was brought in to dub—i.e., insert—some of the trills and high notes. Gabriel explained that "it was a dubbing mix because some of Monroe's voice—the low notes—remained on the sound track, enabling Darryl Zanuck to swear at a press conference that the voice on the track was Marilyn Monroe's." Actually, Gabriel added, "the ghost voice and the star worked very closely together so that the singing voice matched the speaking voice as much as possible." Certainly that is true with Jo Ann Greer and Susan Kohner—they sing and act in the same key.

Eight years before Kander and Ebb's *Cabaret* opened on Broadway, Harry's was Douglas Sirk's own Kit Kat Club, a garish chunk of prewar Berlin resurrected on a sound stage in Universal City. No doubt Sirk instructed his art directors and set decorators on the cheesy trappings of the place, for he had seen "Kabarette" all over Germany.

Pink and blue Japanese lanterns dangle incongruously from the ceiling. On the wall behind the stage hang two pairs of bone-white masks, one of Sirk's expressionistic touches. The first pair are masks of comedy and tragedy. As the camera pans left, a second pair grabs the eye, for these are skeletal and sinister. Gray smoke rises into the reddish-purple light. We spot hip-swinging Sarah Jane, who seems to attempt a Rita Hayworth imitation, in long shot, her back to us, as she goes into her song.

Still singing as she shakes her tail feathers, she moves off the stage and circulates, stopping at a table where two men with wasted, lecherous faces leer up at her.

An empty purse can make a good girl bad.
You hear me, dad?

The two men emit crude guffaws as she strokes the face of one of them. On their table is a phallic candle in "Sirk red," that riveting shade that seems to exist nowhere but in the films of Douglas Sirk. These two old men, who rot before our eyes, might have metastasized from a savage drawing by George Grosz, such as "Night Cafe" or "Parasites," both from the desperate years of World War One.

Sarah Jane hops onto a nearby table and tosses her legs in the air. If the censors blanched, they kept quiet about it, but one verse of her song proved too suggestive for enforcers of the Production Code. When the script was submitted for approval, they instructed Universal to delete it. No damage done, however: this is still the most sizzling scene of Susan Kohner's career. Here's that "scorching" lyric that proved too hot for Hollywood:

> Although my equipment is fine
> Hate to complain but will you explain
> Why nobody's using mine?

Imagine Douglas Sirk, who had directed *dames* in musical numbers— Zarah Leander in *La Habañera* (1937), Carol Landis in *A Scandal in Paris* (1946), Dorothy Lamour in *Slightly French* (1949), Ann Sheridan in *Take Me to Town* (1953)—suddenly faced with timorous Susan Kohner. As a nightclub singer—Hollywood's euphemism for a prostitute, or the next thing to it—he expects her to seduce. Instead, she's scared stiff.

"How did you learn to be such a vamp?" I asked.

"What can I say? For a sheltered, private-school girl, that's acting!" What a good answer. But Susan expands her thumbnail response. "We all have several people inside us, and sometimes we're able to bring them out."

My next prompt: "I wonder how much of it you learned from watching Hollywood movies."

"That's possible," she said. "They gave me a recording of that 'Empty Arms' number. I took it home, and that evening, as well as a couple of other times before I had to shoot the scene, I played it outside on the patio. I would go through the number in front of a captive audience: my mother and father, my poor brother, our housekeeper and her husband, even the kids from next door. I don't know whether vamping came naturally to me, but I worked hard at it. I had taken some dance lessons of one kind or another."

Unable to drop the subject, I added: "A friend of mine said that in *Imitation of Life* you have one of the sexiest slinky walks on the screen. Was that stride part of your characterization, with your head tilted slightly down, and those burning, devouring eyes?"

"I'm inclined to think that's how Susan Kohner walked then!" A great laugh followed, and, as an aside: "All these nice things are coming out." Then a surprise revelation: "My mother told me I walked a bit like a duck, with my feet out. I always thought my walk wasn't too great."

"Nothing ducklike about that walk in the movie," I assured her. "Tell your mother."

Yes, Susan's dance in Harry's Club is a bit hokey. She told me that her sons, the filmmakers Chris and Paul Weitz, who like *Imitation of Life,* sometimes make fun of her in this scene. (When I asked Paul Weitz about Harry's Club, he said, "She looks deeply uncomfortable!" He also told me that he and his brother, as adolescents, would show *Imitation of Life* to any new girl they wanted to impress. "I don't know if it made us look at all good," he added, "but they liked my mom.")

Susan's discomfort works, as Sirk surely knew it would. After all, Sarah Jane isn't supposed to be good. She's a rank amateur whose bravado is skin deep. Susan's mother made this point when I spoke with her, adding a few details on Susan's patio rehearsal: "My daughter came home crying. She said, 'I can't do it,' meaning the dance at Harry's Club. So I show her." And Mrs. Kohner stood up and danced a merry jig to illustrate how she coached Susan—more shimmy than nightclub solo, perhaps, but wonderful just the same. (Lupita Tovar Kohner seems to enjoy every moment of life, and I imagine her as something of a Bel Air Auntie Mame during the past seven decades.)

She often accompanied Susan to work, part dueña, part fan, and no doubt reliving her own career. "I sat in the back," she said, meaning she tried to be the opposite of a pushy stage mother. "I would watch, then we had lunch and then we would come back home."

I asked what she remembered about Sirk shooting the Harry's Club number. "The director was rock hard, German and like a sergeant," she replied, echoing Susan's mild distaste for Sirk. "He said, 'Are you ready for the scene?' and when she finished it he got up and came and kissed her on the forehead and said, 'That's what I wanted!' And from then on Susan got, you know, the self-assurance."

"After a day at the studio," I inquired, "did you and Susan come home and discuss her work in *Imitation of Life?*"

"She might ask how I thought she played a scene. I tried to impress on her that Sarah Jane is not yet a professional. I said, 'You are *trying* to be.'"

If Sirk had not been satisfied with Susan's number at Harry's Club, he would have hounded her until she'd gotten it right. But she gave what he wanted in a few takes. Sarah Jane, photographed as leggy and voluptuous—the opposite of slender Susan Kohner—reveals the mantrap trying to break out. We see what Sarah Jane cannot: her showgirl deficiencies foreshadow a downward slide.

Random songs included in a film, such as Sarah Jane's "Empty Arms," are known as source music, to distinguish them from underscore, which is instrumental music (usually without lyrics) played to "underscore" the emotions in a given scene. Source music, then, comes from a source outside the film score itself. In this case, "Empty Arms" was composed by Arnold Hughes (music) and Frederick Herbert (lyrics).

Although Frank Skinner received credit for the *Imitation of Life* score, if you listen to the Dixieland jazz before and after Susan Kohner's "Empty Arms," you realize it's distant from Skinner's style. Jazz wasn't his forte; he specialized in romantic, wistful, highly dramatic scores, some of them even tear-stained. For that reason, I nominate Henry Mancini once more as Skinner's pinch hitter.

In his book *Hollywood Cinema,* film historian Richard Maltby, discussing periods of "time-out" in movies, cites "the suspension of narrative for autonomous spectacle such as musical numbers." To be sure, this downtime obtains that end in most film musicals and in many dramas, although not, typically, in a Douglas Sirk film, and certainly not in Susan Kohner's two musical sequences in *Imitation of Life.* Harry's Club in New York and, later, the Moulin Rouge in Hollywood function rather as tense, and efficient, plot pivots. The former opens the chasm between Sarah Jane and her mother; the latter makes that chasm a grave. Neither slows the action because each lasts only a few moments (the first, two minutes, the second, two and a half) and is fully integrated into the structure of the film.

On September 5, 1958, Universal's shooting call sheet for production number 1884—*Imitation of Life*—specified that Juanita Moore was due at the studio's hairdressing department at 6:15 a.m. and in makeup one hour later. Susan Kohner was to report to makeup at 6:15 and hairdressing at 7:15. Both would leave the studio at 8:15 and arrive a quarter hour later at the Moulin Rouge, on Sunset Boulevard near Vine Street. Some four dozen technicians also traveled in the studio caravan.

The entourage included forty male extras—"well dressed"—and thirty-five women, also dressed up, as members of the audience in the landmark Hollywood nightclub. These were to report directly to the Moulin Rouge, along with five male waiters, one "girl cashier," thirty-three Moulin Rouge showgirls and seven male dancers, and two men in tuxedos, one to play the maître d'. Also, an eleven-piece orchestra, and stand-ins "D. Harris for Miss Moore" and "L. Montgomery for Miss Kohner." And Ann Robinson, her name misspelled on the call sheet as "Robertson," who plays a showgirl on the Moulin Rouge carousel and Sarah Jane's roommate in the following sequence at the motel.

Frank Sennes's Moulin Rouge, to use its official moniker, opened in the early fifties. Sennes, a West Coast showman, took a risk with his swish nightclub, for in postwar America such splashy joints already looked passé. The namesake of the older Moulin Rouge in Paris, this California version patterned its shows after those "ooh-la-la" spectacles that supposedly made visiting Americans so horny. Sennes gave his revues Frenchy titles such as "Voici Paris," "Ça C'est Paris," and "Paris Toujours." He staged recycled Follies Bergère numbers, and Latin ones, as well, along with carnival acts featuring acrobats, aerialists, and a trained elephant. Jimmy Durante, Johnnie Ray, and other headliners appeared regularly.

In 1956, when the Moulin Rouge had seen better days, *Queen for a*

Day pitched camp there for its daily airing on NBC. "A chamber of horrors," one critic once called the show, whose contestants spilled out desperate stories of tragedy, mayhem, and direst need to prove themselves worthy of a day of luxury. One woman wished for tires and gasoline to help transport her newly adopted blind Chinese toddler to San Francisco for medical treatment. Another sought an iron lung for her brother, who had lost his home when a small plane crashed into it. Unctuous host Jack Bailey, who showed signs of heavy drinking, never tired of nostrums and benign wisecracks to "cheer up" suffering, sobbing contestants.

Ross Hunter arranged to film the *Imitation of Life* sequence in the Moulin Rouge, using a production number from Donn Arden's revue, "Pariscope," which was currently packing 'em in (though the Moulin Rouge closed not long after). Hunter said, "It would have been foolish to go to all the trouble of devising a special musical sequence at the studio when Mr. Sennes had exactly what we wanted." Only one change was made: the substitution of Susan Kohner and Ann Robinson for two of the showgirls in Arden's "Rocking Chair Blues" number. Costumes by Madame Berthe, and the setting by Harvey Warren, were also photographed as used in the revue.

So was Donn Arden's staging. When the camera hits in midroutine, you see a meagre line of hoop-skirted, Ziegfeldesque girls who sway like forlorn willows in a squall. A great deal of costumed foot traffic crosses the stage, in no particular order, like a stylized version of crowds at the Gare Saint-Lazare. Showgirls prance around the stage, while featured hoofers kick and twist in the foreground. When you stop blinking from the impact of Madame Berthe's turquoise-and-mustard outfits, you see that the show could have been called "Forty Dancers in Search of a Choreographer." They seem lost. Only the rocking chair girls have a focus: toasts, and humping leg raises. Call it "Toujours Champagne!"

Perhaps I'm too hard on the showgirls and dancers—after all, they *had* been at work all night. Signed en masse by Universal for the *Imitation of Life* scenes, they performed two shows the previous evening, which kept them at the club until 3:00 a.m. Four hours later, they reported back to the Moulin Rouge for filming, which meant that, during a long day, they either worked or waited for camera setups until 6:00 p.m. Then, after a dinner break, they put on costumes again for the club's two regular shows, the first of which began at eight o'clock.

Ross Hunter complimented their stamina and professionalism. "They were wonderful," he said. "They worked very hard without a whimper."

Donn Arden, Father of the Feathers

That's the fond epithet bestowed by one of his former showgirls, Debbie de Coudreaux, on her website of the same name. As choreographer, producer, and director, Arden (1916–1994) created spectacles from New York to Rio, though his most dazzlingly gaudy shows fueled the fleshpots of Las Vegas. He is credited with developing the Vegas showgirl image: a statuesque dancer in sequins, plumes, feathers, and a tall headpiece. When he introduced topless showgirls in 1958, the city's high muck-a-mucks scratched their collective head and wondered why nobody had done it sooner.

Arden started out in Cleveland, where he staged shows for a certain brand of "entrepreneur." "I hate to use the word 'mafia,'" Arden once said, "but they shared my vision of female beauty, and were willing to finance it."

Although Arden's "Pariscope," a piece of which appears in *Imitation of Life,* looks cheesy and dispirited, what Arden unleashed was a high-camp maestro. His girls performed in ultraexpensive settings, massive stage sets with overwhelming special effects that often derived from famous disasters. In "Jubilee," at Bally's, he resank the *Titanic,* with survivors in a lifeboat sailing across the stage to enormous applause. At another casino, a muscleman Sampson reenacted the destruction of a pagan temple as Delilah and her slave girls writhed among collapsed columns, and the audience shivered in biblical glee.

But Arden's gorgeous bad taste didn't stop there. As the "Master of Disaster," he restaged the San Francisco earthquake and other

(continued)

events of human misery. For his "Hello, Hollywood, Hello" revue, he crashed the Hindenburg on stage, with stuntmen falling from the fly-loft in flames. "They expect it of me," he said with a straight face. "It's a contrast to the beauty and the feathers." Arden's two regrets in life were that he wasn't allowed to reburn Atlanta (Margaret Mitchell's estate wouldn't authorize it), nor re-create the parting of the Red Sea. In the latter instance, it was unclear whether Yahweh, or the Egyptian government, held production rights.

Susan Kohner and Juanita Moore speak not a line of dialogue in the Moulin Rouge sequence. Language would be superfluous; they act with their faces, their bodies. ("Good actors are good because of things they tell us without talking," said Sir Cedric Hardwicke.)

Susan, riding that turquoise rocking chair as she pantomimes pouring champagne from bottle to glass, is the focal point, and the climax, of the sequence. Sarah Jane seems stricken with joy. At last, her charade has overtaken reality: white, and a showgirl, aglow with sexual happiness, she winks at two men seated near the stage. One is her date, the other her roommate's. They're picking the girls up at their motel right after the show. Sarah Jane's dark secret lies buried. At last, she possesses herself.

Until a shadow falls. The shadow of her dying mother, soon to be transfigured to a shade. Annie Johnson, in that same matronly, night-sky coat and hat she wore to Harry's Club, or an outfit like it, slinks into the Moulin Rouge like Orpheus into the underworld. Always on the far rim of life, she eyes the club's host, then slips past. Lost, she roams the vast nightclub spaces as though suffering from senile dementia or night blindness. But Annie can't be far past forty, though she looks much older now.

Her religion and her race make this woman a stranger to "sinful" places such as this. To her, it's another "low-down dive," though the clientele seems enraptured. Like Dante in hell, she stands disoriented at the foot of the stage to gaze up at tail-twitching showgirls. Annie Johnson is dwarfed and overpowered by this explosion of grotesque color and lurid flesh, by splendors unknown to her. The maître d' approaches from behind to say (if I read his lips correctly), "Would you mind moving away?" He might be telling her this club is for whites only, except that the camera spots a black woman at a nearby table. (In *Imitation of Life* and other films, Sirk employed many African-American extras. They're visible at Coney Island, in theatre audiences at Lora's plays, and of course, at the funeral.)

At this point, the Moulin Rouge sequence morphs into a muted chase, or, more precisely, a grim parody of one. Sarah Jane, gymnastically up and down on that turquoise chaise that resembles a Lazyboy recliner more than a rocking chair, bobs up and down behind it, throws her fanny out, flings one arm into the air, and . . . Stop!—for a split second. She spots a pursuer. Frowns. Is it . . . ? Sarah Jane suspects it is. Only one person could cause that shiver. She sits in the chair again, kicks her leg high, hoists the champagne glass, and glides offstage with the other showgirls as though descending from a carnival ride.

"What's the matter, honey?" asks Ann Robinson, as the curtain whisks by.

"I don't know," Sarah Jane answers. "Just a funny feeling."

As the girls head to their dressing room, a series of long shots: Annie, peering, searching. Before leaving New York, she told Miss Lora: "I've just got to see my baby once more." That time has come, but the camera observes the mother as a stalker. We see her fading to a ghost.

19 | THE LADY AND THE BULLFIGHTER

*A*nn Robinson, who played Susan Kohner's red-headed pal at the Moulin Rouge, told me recently that when they filmed the scene in the motel room, she had no idea of its significance. "Now I do," she added. "My son kept telling me, 'Don't you realize, Mother, you're in the most powerful and important scene in the movie? That's because you come in and validate everything that Sarah Jane has been saying to her mother.'" That comment says more than a stockpile of critical writing.

In the motel, Sarah Jane has just howled, "I'm white! White! WHITE!" (As she speaks, a dark shadow edges her forehead.) For Sarah Jane, it's a curse to be black in America. To remove the taint, she must flay her mother and herself. This is when tears well up in the audience, for that final encounter jabs a primal nerve.

How typical of Douglas Sirk to interrupt the most intimate, tender, cruel, heartrending scene of the film with this cold-hearted trespasser, who stands in for racist America. A commentator on Sirk's pictures has pointed out similar instances: "Sirk's films are filled with such brief and strange occurrences: the entrance of the masked figure in *The Tarnished Angels*, of the boy on the mechanical horse in *Written on the Wind*, of the Christmas shopper who disrupts the lovers' quarrel in *Imitation of Life*. . . . These intrusions are often terrifying confirmations of hopelessness." Even more blatant is the German tourist couple in *There's Always*

Tomorrow, who violate Fred MacMurray and Barbara Stanwyck's pivotal love scene on the terrace of a Los Angeles hotel to ask whether the Hollywood Bowl is open.

Certainly, the motel scene ends without hope and without release. The obtuse redhead blunders in, looks around, remains oblivious. She condescends to Annie Johnson: "Say, listen, if you're the new maid, I want to report that my shower is full of ants." Grimacing at her racist assumption, we loathe her because she blocks catharsis—Sarah Jane's, and ours. This girl's presence obstructs Sarah Jane's tears.

Nor would Sirk let them flow. He hammered home the sorrowful point: Annie Johnson's departure from the room, bleak and inconsolable, is a memento mori. A Teutonic pessimist, Sirk said, "Everything, even life, is inevitably removed from you. If you try to grasp happiness itself your fingers only meet glass. It's hopeless."

Poor Ann Robinson! I resented her intrusion for years. How dare she say that to Annie Johnson, and then, in a mocking faux-Southern accent, to Sarah Jane: "So, honey chile, you had a mammy!" I'm afraid she's won few friends among the faithful.

But then I met her, and she won me over. She's like a nice L.A. lady you might chat with at the Farmers' Market. Like so many of those, she has a vivid backstory. And her own cult following, as well, for she costarred in the classic sci-fi film *The War of the Worlds* (1953).

The daughter of a banker, Ann Robinson grew up in Los Angeles, in a large, comfortable house in Los Feliz, and graduated from Hollywood High. She broke into movies the hard way—as a stunt girl. One of her first jobs was to climb over a fifteen-foot barbed-wire fence at Tehachapi Prison for Women, in lieu of star June Havoc, for *The Story of Molly X* (1949). On another assignment, she had to jump off a truck going twenty-five miles an hour. She punched it up in a knock-down-drag-out fight with another girl, and was also thrown from a runaway stagecoach. Moving up, she worked, uncredited, as an extra or bit player in close to a dozen early-fifties pictures, including *A Place in the Sun, The Damned Don't Cry, Goodbye, My Fancy,* and *A Life of Her Own* (Ann's first appearance in a Lana Turner film), before her lucky break in *The War of the Worlds*.

During those years, she continued to live with her parents. In a 1952 interview, Ann said: "My life is pretty much the same as any twenty-year-old girl who lives at home. [Born in 1929, she was actually twenty-three at the time.] The boys I date can't afford to go to the high-priced places along the Sunset Strip, so we go to drive-ins, or take drives along the beach." This sounds like virtuous press agentry, but Ann herself confirms her strict upbringing. A couple of years later, when Ann was dating actor Jerry Paris, her mother wouldn't allow the couple to take a weekend excursion unless Jerry's parents chaperoned.

In 1954, Ann played a leading role in Jack Webb's *Dragnet*, the big-screen tie-in to his popular television series. That same year, she appeared as Queen Juliandra in several episodes of *Rocky Jones, Space Ranger* on TV, the beginning of a flourishing career on the smaller screen. Without these television credits—*Cheyenne, Perry Mason, Alfred Hitchcock Presents,* and many others—her résumé might be a quick read, for her film roles after *The War of the Worlds* grew smaller and less frequent.

In the mid-fifties, Ann dated Steve Cochran for a time. One night, director Andrew L. Stone and his wife invited the younger couple to dinner. Afterward, they played charades. "We had so much fun," Ann recalls, "that this lovely man asked me to come in for an interview. He gave me the script of *Julie* [the 1956 picture in which Doris Day, as a flight attendant, must land an airliner whose pilot has been shot] and said, 'There are three parts here. Pick out the one you want.'"

Ann chose the part of Valerie, a flight attendant who appears in the tense climax of the picture. "I suppose I should have chosen the role of Doris Day's roommate," Ann muses. "It had more dialogue. But I wanted to go on location." She reveals that the director had originally planned to shoot the entire film in the air, but owing to Doris Day's fear of flying it was shot on the ground instead, although in the fuselage of a real plane, not a mock-up. "They squeezed the cameras and lights into toilets, cockpit, everywhere they could," Ann explained, adding, "Not many realized what a superb dramatic actress Doris Day was. For the final sequence, we went on location to the Sacramento airport. That day, one plane came in and blew a tire on landing! If only we'd had the cameras going, what terrific footage. As it is, Doris lands the plane a bit too smoothly and professionally."

At the time of Ann's TV appearances on *Cheyenne* in 1955, a Warner Bros. press release detailed her background, then threw in these starlet talking points:

- One of Ann's most alluring physical attractions, outside of her red hair and beautiful, athletic figure, are her long, thick eyelashes. She began brushing them with castor oil and curling them at age twelve, and has continued this care.
- Ann likes to sleep in Chinese mandarin pajamas with the pants legs rolled above her knees.

The author of that press release overlooked two points of interest. One, she was chosen by Willy's of Hollywood, the stocking king, to receive a Golden Calf award for her shapely legs; and two, her main diversion, bullfighting, which was fostered by director Budd Boetticher, a matador manqué. Here, Ann recounts how that interest came about, and what it did to her:

"I always laugh and say that Budd Boetticher brought on the downfall of my career. My very first stunt work took place for him when he was directing *Black Midnight* [1949]. I was hired as stunt rider for Lyn Thomas, who starred in the picture opposite Roddy McDowell. We were on location at Lone Pine, California, and in the evenings, Budd was teaching Roddy the art of bullfighting. I was fascinated, and I watched them intently. They caught me copying all the cape work. Soon I began reading every book I could find on bullfighting. A little later, I went to my first bullfight with Jerry Paris. I fell in love with it!"

Fast-forward to 1957. Busy with her career, Ann took a day off to attend the bullfight in Tijuana. There, on the afternoon of July 7, she met Mexican matador Jaime Bravo. They married that night. "It blew my career right out of the water," she says with minimal regret.

Previously, her husband had been married to actress Francesca de Scaffa, whose nano-career ended when it was revealed she had served as a tipster to *Confidential* magazine. She fled the country in 1957 to avoid a court appearance when the magazine's publisher went on trial.

Ann Robinson and Jaime Bravo remained together for ten years. During that time, they followed the bullfight circuit throughout Mexico and South America. The year after her impetuous marriage, Ann returned to Los Angeles to attend her mother, who had undergone surgery in June of 1958. While there, she was cast in *Imitation of Life*. With so much going on then, she has forgotten who hired her for the role, or why, though Ross Hunter seems her likely benefactor. "I used to run into Ross from time to time," she recalls, "and I couldn't remember how I knew him. But he remembered me quite well. He always came over to say hello." She has no memory of Douglas Sirk, and wasn't aware, until I informed her, that *Imitation of Life* made more money for Universal than any other picture the studio had produced up till then.

Ann Robinson remembers a showgirl from the Moulin Rouge who came to coach her and Susan Kohner a day or two before they filmed their "Rocking Chair Blues" number. "We rehearsed at Universal," she says, "in a dance studio with a huge mirror on one wall. Susan and I copied her, in front of the mirror, in rocking chairs. We had to rock back and forth and hold onto a champagne bottle and an oversized glass, extend one leg up in the air as we rocked back and forth and *undulated*." She laughs as she overpronounces this word. "When I look at that scene now, I think it was pretty suggestive for those days."

I asked whether the actual filming, in those corsetlike costumes, was harder than the rehearsal. "I was a lot stiffer!" she laughed. "It was okay during rehearsal, but when we actually had to shoot the scene—well, I had been using muscles that hadn't been used for a while. Also, I had just had a baby four months prior to that. Fortunately, I was still extremely thin, which was a plus." Ann worked three days on *Imitation of Life*: a day of rehearsal, the day at the nightclub, and the third day, back at Universal, for the motel scene. She earned $250.

Although Ann had no scenes with Lana Turner, she did have, as she slyly puts it, "great comings and going with her—and my husband!" She guffaws, and I detect a savory story. "Tell me more," I deadpan.

"Oh, tell me more, tell me more," she teases. After a theatrical pause, she dangles a tidbit. "You see, Lana just loved bullfighters." If she had demanded payment at this point, I'd have forked over the dough. But Ann was generous. She gave it to me gratis.

"She was in pursuit of my husband. She chased him all over the place."

"What did you think of that?"

"I thought it was amusing. Lana made a picture in Mexico in 1965 called *Love Has Many Faces,* and my husband appeared in it as a bull-fighter. She pursued him while we were in Mexico. I sort of lost track of the story, but Jaime came to Los Angeles for some reason and I stayed in Mexico to do another movie. I finally got back to L.A. and when I answered the phone one day, a woman's voice said, 'I'm calling for Jaime Bravo.'

"So I said, 'May I ask who's calling?' and she said, 'Lana Turner.' Then she added, 'Anita, is that you?'

"I said, 'Yes,' and Lana said, 'What are you doing back in L.A.?'

"I said, 'Why are you calling my husband?'"

And Lana's reply?

"What could she possibly say?"

But, Ann says, holding no apparent grudge, "Lana was an awful lot of fun. Even though she was sneaky. She sneaked around trying to get my husband. And no wonder. Jaime was a very handsome, dashing bull-fighter. All the women loved him."

"Did Lana get him?" I asked.

"I'm sure of it," she said, with a loud burst of laughter. "She and a lot of others. Finally, it got to be too much for me. I decided I'd had it, and we divorced in 1967." In 1987, Ann remarried. Her second husband is Joseph Valdez, a real-estate broker.

Jaime Bravo died in a car accident in 1970, at the age of thirty-eight.

Their two sons are Jaime Bravo Jr., a director with ABC Sports, and Estefan, an entertainer. "My boys love their mother," Ann says. "They're quite loyal." On a recent visit to her elder son, Jaime, and his wife, Ann's daughter-in-law brought out a video copy of *Imitation of Life* for Ann to autograph. "You have to sign this for your grandchildren," she said. On the package, Ann wrote: "I'm in here somewhere."

She signs lots of autographs these days, and has done so since the silver anniversary of *The War of the Worlds* in 1977, when she was rediscovered by aficionados. Since then, she has done speaking engagements, lectured in schools, and appeared on TV and radio shows. In *The War of the Worlds,* Ann plays Sylvia Van Buren, a wholesome fifties girl who "emotes" throughout. (Small wonder that her fans from this earlier film are often astonished at her *Imitation of Life* showgirl, who's been around . . . and around.) Sylvia screams a lot—at spaceships, deadly rays, and danger high and low. But her nerves are always soothed by Gene Barry's strong arms and soft lips.

The real stars of the picture, it turns out, are the special effects, which are better, in my opinion at least, than those later "improvements" by the likes of Steven Spielberg and George Lucas. Spielberg used—or misused—Ann Robinson and Gene Barry in his own 2005 *War of the Worlds.* They make a five-second appearance at the end of his disappointing remake. That hurried quick shot seems more insult than homage to both actors. Why include them at all as mere needles in his noisy, hyperactive haystack?

From 1965, when Ann appeared in an episode of *Gilligan's Island,* to 1988, and her starring role in *Midnight Movie Massacre,* she remained out of touch with show business except for her past triumph in *The War of the Worlds.* Although she lived in Hollywood, she worked only on a few voice-overs and some looping for foreign films (Ann is fluent in Spanish). Her exile was at least partially self-imposed. "Working in films," she told an interviewer, "is just too difficult when you are trying to raise two children by yourself."

20 | NO BEEFCAKE, PLEASE, WE'RE REPUBLICAN

*T*he only time my shirt comes off is when I go swimming with Lana Turner," said John Gavin on the set of *Imitation of Life,* "and even then I put on a robe. As far as I'm concerned, it's time the button-down collar, white shirt, and tie became the uniform of Hollywood's male dramatic personnel. There are no bare-chested, pectoral-showing parts on my film calendar." The reporter who took down Gavin's pronunciamiento added, at the end of that last sentence, "he declared vehemently."

That swimming scene wasn't filmed, so our leading man kept his shirt on after all, at least until Hitchcock made him shed it a couple of years later in *Psycho.* And a year after that, he and Susan Hayward did a swimming scene in *Back Street* that showed off his six-pack abs. The vehemence of Gavin's bare-chest declaration never transferred to his acting, which began and ended as invertebrate, self-righteous, and by rote. You can almost imagine him coached in flimsy dramatics, as in right-wing politics, by his friends Ronald and Nancy Reagan. (Like that pair, he sometimes forgot: the year before *Imitation of Life,* he had appeared shirtless, and in a bathtub, in Sirk's *A Time to Love and a Time to Die.*)

Gavin approached acting as another one of his capitalistic enterprises. In 1958, he insisted that he had never wished to be an actor and that he looked upon his career as "a business opportunity with great growth possibilities." His other business ventures, at the time of *Imitation of Life,* included a financial interest in a Mexican housing project, an egg business in Panama, plantations in South America, and a partnership in Panama-Boston Industries, manufacturers of vegetable oil, soap, and detergent. A month before he began work on *Imitation,* he told an interviewer, "I was thinking about a mining deal in South America before this movie business came up, and I just might try it next."

Gavin made his movie IPO in 1955. Recently released from active duty in the navy, he approached a family friend, film producer Bryan Foy, about a job as technical advisor on a navy film, *Battle Stations,* that Foy was to produce. "Why should I hire a lieutenant when I can get admirals for nothing?" the producer demanded. "Why don't you try acting instead?" Foy took Gavin to Henry Willson, the Hollywood agent best known as a purveyor of male flesh on the hoof, and Willson sold Gavin to Ed Muhl, head of production at Universal-International. (Bryan Foy, known as "Keeper of the B's," produced over two hundred such pictures from 1924 to 1963. Ironically, his final production was the higher-grade *PT 109,* the story of John F. Kennedy's experiences in World War Two. Earlier, Foy had produced such propaganda films as *I Was a Communist for the FBI* (1951) and *Little Tokyo, USA* (1942), a racist anti-Japanese melodrama, as well as such titillating "sociological" pics as *Elysia, Valley of the Nude* (1934) and *Tomorrow's Children* (1934), a controversial story about forced sterilization that was banned in New York for its use of the word "vasectomy.")

According to some sources, Universal intended to groom Gavin as the successor to Rock Hudson, one of its top stars owing partially to his work in Douglas Sirk films. Studios liked having surrogates for their big moneymakers. They could use the newcomer to scare a star into submission, and should mayhem or scandal make the star unbankable, they imagined the replacement as foolproof insurance. (It seldom worked out that way. "New" Marilyn Monroes, for instance, included Sheree North, Jayne Mansfield, and a parade of lesser floats.)

Since Rock Hudson's homosexuality made him a risk for the studio, the advent of a handsome proxy served as insurance in the event of moral turpitude. One reason for Gavin's reluctance to disrobe may have been to distance himself from Hudson. (The two men reportedly got on well together and viewed each other as colleagues, not rivals.) The fact of Henry Willson as his agent made Gavin suspect, and also nervous, since Willson was known as the doting—and sexually demanding—mentor of Hudson, Tab Hunter, Guy Madison, Troy Donohue, and a stable of ornamental studs, most of them rechristened by Willson with the butchest names in the business. (John Gavin's birth name was John Anthony Golenor, and he resented the change. Once, when a studio executive phoned him at home, he answered: "There's no Gavin here, but I can put Mr. Golenor on the phone.") Some of Willson's clients were gay, others bisexual, still others straight. Nevertheless, if Willson was your agent, the heterosexual burden of proof rested on you.

Gavin left Willson's agency after a year. Fifty years later he explained why: "Quite frankly, this may sound prejudiced, but you got a lot of eyebrow-raising if you said Henry Willson represented you."

Gavin, who was born in 1931 (or 1928, according to some sources), grew up in Southern California. His well-to-do father had mining interests in Mexico; his mother was born there, and her family was related to early Spanish settlers in California. Gavin attended St. John's Military Academy in Los Angeles, Beverly Hills High School, and Villanova Preparatory School at Ojai before he entered Stanford University, where he majored in political science and economics.

At Universal, John Gavin made his debut (credited as "John Gilmore") in a small role in *Raw Edge*, a 1956 western starring Rory Calhoun and Yvonne De Carlo. His subsequent pictures as a contract player include *Behind the High Wall* (1956), *Four Girls in Town* (1957), and *Quantez* (1957).

In 1957, Sirk was casting *A Time to Love and a Time to Die*, based on Erich Maria Remarque's antiwar novel. The director wanted Paul Newman for the part of Ernst Gräber, the young German soldier in World War Two who awakens to the horrors and futility of war. Universal, however, pressured Sirk "to build a new star," namely Gavin. Years later Sirk said, "Gavin, naturally, was not nearly the actor Newman was . . . but for this picture I felt, after extensive tests, that he could be just right because of his lack of experience. He was fresh, young, good-looking."

Sirk's ambiguous remarks suggest a weak satisfaction with Gavin's performance. He made no other explicit statement about Gavin, although he did cast him the following year in *Imitation of Life*. The crucial difference was that in *A Time to Love* Gavin had to carry the picture, while in *Imitation of Life* he functioned as Lana's drone. In both films, Gavin is a foreign body: he slows them down like a virus that must run its course.

A Time to Love and a Time to Die, released in 1958, was Gavin's big career opportunity. What he did in this picture, however, he did in all the others—or rather, it's what he didn't do: he didn't act with his face, his eyes, his voice, or his body. He resembles a chiseled monolith, and his facial muscles move as rarely as Nicole Kidman's. That pretty-face performance, tiresome and jejeune, emasculates this poignant story of a German soldier in World War Two. *A Time to Love,* like Edward Dmytryk's *The Young Lions,* released the same year, shows the humane instincts in some conscripts of the Nazi army. In that, these two films differ radically from the usual Hollywood portrayal of German soldiers as generic brutes. To play such a controversial role a dozen years after the end of the war required the talents of a Brando, who played a sympathetic German in *The Young Lions.* Gavin, by contrast, is a vacuum. From the outset, critics have called Gavin "wooden." But that critical cliché tells only half. If heartthrobs like Rock Hudson were dreamboats, then Gavin is a glass-bottom boat—in dry dock. His depthless transparency exposes his shortcomings.

Other factors that made *A Time to Love* such an etiolated film, one of Sirk's most disappointing, include its supporting cast, an international stable of wan talents: Liselotte Pulver, Jock Mahoney, Dorothea Wieck, Keenan Wynn. The anorectic script, adapted by Orin Jannings from Remarque's novel, cannot support the story. Jannings, an unprolific screenwriter, had previously written only three minor films: *Mr. Soft Touch* (1949), *A Force of Arms* (1951), and *She's Back on Broadway* (1953).

In the right hands, this film might have approached the power of *All Quiet on the Western Front* (1930), Lewis Milestone's version of Remarque's other famous war novel. With a strong cast and robust script, Sirk could have made a film statement of moral grandeur about World War Two, and about all war. But bad choices on both sides of the camera turned it into a dispassionate bore.

———

Ross Hunter, Sirk, Universal—everyone knew that *Imitation of Life* must balance on the tightrope of public opinion and audience appeal. Too far to one side and it would plummet into the smoking ruins of Lana Turner. On the other hand, Lana in all her glory must not be overshadowed, not by her female costars and certainly not by the male lead. Casting that part required the diplomatic legerdemain of a mission to Moscow. Rock Hudson, for example, always near the top of box office favorites in those years, looked too big in every way; he would detract from Lana owing to his presence and his personal charm.

And yet the audience of women Ross Hunter hoped to attract with Lana and her fashions and jewels presumably wanted to ogle male eye candy. The solution: John Gavin, low-calorie but filling, and incapable of stealing a scene (although he did study for a time with the actor Jeff Corey, who became a respected teacher of fellow film actors). Testing Gavin and Lana together to see whether he looked old enough to play her lover, the filmmakers might have slapped themselves on the back. Indeed, they had found the perfect dim bulb for their glittery chandelier. Anything he could do, Lana did better. (Those who poke fun at Lana Turner for what they perceive as a vacuous performance often go easy on John Gavin, a subtle reversion to the double standard.)

Off the set, Gavin lived an antiseptic life. Louella Parsons reported that she saw him and his wife on Sundays at the Church of the Good Shepherd in Beverly Hills, a Roman Catholic celebrity parish. Gavin had married Cicely Evans a few days before leaving for Germany to shoot *A Time to Love*.

On location in Germany, Cecily Evans Gavin worked as an extra in her husband's film. In a nonspeaking appearance, she was shown in a bomb shelter during an Allied air raid. Her photogenic qualities in this brief scene persuaded Douglas Sirk, at Gavin's behest, to use her again the following year in *Imitation of Life* as a good luck charm, for the picture was thought to need all the luck it could muster.

There she plays Gavin's girlfriend in a party scene when he reappears in Lana's life after a ten-year hiatus. He introduces her to Lana: "Oh, Lora, I'd like you to know Louise Morton." Cecily Gavin's two lines in the film are, "How do you do, Miss Meredith. I loved your performance."

Lana thanks her grandly, then introduces her old beau to the other guests: "Steve Archer . . . everybody. A very old and dear friend." Then, as an afterthought: "Oh, and uh—Miss Morton."

"Don't get the idea that I want my wife to become an actress," Gavin stated on the set. "One actor to a family is plenty." She agreed. "At first I thought it was a cute idea," she said, "but now in *Imitation of Life* I find myself in a part that runs through three sequences." (She's glimpsed once more in the party sequence, and in the audience at one of Lora's plays.) Cecily Evans Gavin made no further screen appearances after *Imitation of Life,* and she and Gavin divorced some years later.

Hitchcock's wizardry in *Psycho* cannot fully explain how he extracted a near-performance from John Gavin. By all accounts, the director, finding little to admire, used Gavin only because "budget constraints forced Hitchcock to choose him over top contender Stuart Whitman. Gavin could be borrowed from Universal for six weeks at $30,000. 'I guess he'll be all right, Hitchcock shrugged'" after watching Gavin's performance in *Imitation of Life.*

Shooting the hotel room sequence, Hitchcock "grew visibly more riled as take after take failed to thaw Gavin's icy reserve. Finally, the director called 'Cut!' and engaged Janet Leigh in a huddle on the sidelines." Leigh reported that Hitchcock told her, "I think you and John could be more passionate. See what you can do!" She revealed a bit more to Stephen Rebello, author of *Alfred Hitchcock and the Making of Psycho.* According to him, "In discreet but descriptive terms, Hitchcock requested that Leigh take matters in hand, as it were. Leigh blushed, acquiesced, and Hitchcock got a reasonable facsimile of the required response." In other words, Gavin needed a crank and she groped him. Nevertheless, Hitchcock considered Gavin such an unpromising entity that he nicknamed him "the Stiff."

Reviewing Kubrick's *Spartacus* (1960), the *Time* film critic wrote of Gavin, who plays the young Julius Caesar, that he "looks as though he never got to the first conjugation, let alone the Gallic Wars." Kubrick, unaccustomed to being gainsaid by members of his cast, squabbled with Gavin over the exposure of Caesarean flesh. This picture, despite its classy pretentions, amounted to a sword-and-sandal epic, and one appeal of that genre included male skin on parade. Gavin, however, wished to cover up as though the story were set not in pagan Rome but in the papal states. Again, he seemed obsessed with concealing flesh, rather than exposing the truth of the character he portrayed. Kubrick won, however, and Gavin takes it off at the baths.

Although Kubrick directed him well, Gavin's role amounted to a series of walk-ons. Then, too, Kubrick appears more interested in Caesar's foreshadowing presence in Roman politics than in a sketch of him as future ruler. Thus, he employed Gavin as absorber and reflector of the vociferous acting of Charles Laughton and Olivier in his brief scenes with them.

In the sixties, Gavin appeared in several more Ross Hunter productions, including *Midnight Lace* (1960) with Doris Day, *Tammy Tell Me True* (1961) with Sandra Dee, *Back Street* (1961), and *Thoroughly Modern Millie* (1967). In *Back Street*, Gavin gives a déjà vu performance. His character's extramarital affair with doggedly determined Susan Hayward goes on for decades. (Hayward, by this point in her career, was still a firecracker, although a slow burning one.)

Vera Miles, as Gavin's socialite wife, drinks and falls down a lot, but Gavin soldiers on. (Miles later said it was easy to be nasty with him because he was such a poor actor.) *Back Street* is a pastel view of misery smothered in American materialism: money, mansions, big gliding cars, impersonal decor, passions neutered except those, like Miles's alcoholism, that lead to calamity. And love means never having a good time, or even a good night's sleep.

Based on a Fannie Hurst novel, *Back Street* had been filmed twice already, in 1932 with Irene Dunne and John Boles and in 1941 with Charles Boyer and Margaret Sullavan. The Ross Hunter version, made two years after Douglas Sirk quit Hollywood, shows how much Sirk's hegemony restrained Hunter in their long fifties partnership. Lacking the astringency of Sirk's direction, this *Back Street* billows with Ross Hunter's fussy literal-mindedness. Call it *Imitation of Sirk*.

Minus Sirk, however, Hunter's dreams of bourgeois opulence lacked the wormwood that previously gave them dramatic bite. Here, an odorous dream-fluid seeps from set to set, suffusing every bland or over-wrought tableau with unpleasant reflux. The attempt at pathos—Gavin's death scene, and Hayward's chalky face of grief, plus her subsequent embrace of his orphaned children—don't elict tears. You're more apt to reach for the room deodorizer.

Ross Hunter's post-Sirk pictures can maim you. If you were a kid during the years when this sort of perfumed depression played in the movie theatres you went to, a latter-day viewing is about as pleasant as looking through your high school yearbook with your friends cut out and only the creeps remaining.

Throughout the sixties and the seventies, Gavin appeared in low-grade movies and made guest appearances on television in *The Alfred Hitchcock Hour, The Doris Day Show, The Love Boat,* and others. In 1974, he married the actress Constance Towers, a soap-opera regular and some-time musical comedy star who appeared with Yul Brynner in a Broadway revival of *The King and I* in 1977–78.

Since his college days, Gavin had wanted to try diplomacy, and Ronald Reagan's election in 1980 enabled him to enter a field better suited to his talents than acting had been. Or so Gavin believed. When Reagan appointed him ambassador to Mexico early in 1981, however, a howl of jeers and protests went up from the host country. "Diplomatic sadism," one columnist called it. "A mockery," cried another. "If they're going to send us an actor, why not Bo Derek?" chortled a newspaper editor. "Or Wonder Woman?" A government official in Mexico City, upon hearing about the Gavin appointment, remarked sourly, "Perhaps we should name Cantinflas as Ambassador to Washington."

Gavin was widely regarded as a joke. Then, too, he had long been rumored to work for the FBI or the CIA. These rumors, which were never actually proven, he naturally denied, claiming that they arose from his 1961 appointment as special advisor to the secretary general of the Organization of American States and from his various business enterprises in Latin America.

By the end of his first year in Mexico City, Gavin was described by one journalist as playing "a two-sided role in Mexico. He has the reputation for being rude to reporters and bad-tempered with his staff, but he is considered competent and accommodating by diplomatic officials and businessmen." His most egregious clash with the press took place when he pushed a television cameraman into a flowerpot. Gavin claimed he was feeling ill and rushing to the bathroom when the cameraman got in his way.

When Gavin resigned from his post in 1986, after serving for five years, a Latin American specialist of the Council on Foreign Relations reviewed his tenure, calling him "a controversial ambassador because he made no bones about saying what was on his mind. He broke with the old rules, publicly refuting Mexican criticism of the United States on trade and other issues instead of filing diplomatic protests in private."

Despite the controversies surrounding some of his diplomatic exploits, John Gavin has an old-fashioned gentleman's reputation in private life. Sidney Skolsky, writing in 1961 at the height of Gavin's popularity, remarked that the actor was "socially correct at all times." Susan Kohner told me he sent her a condolence letter when her husband died in 2002. Susan's mother speaks warmly of Gavin as a family friend of long standing, though she advised me of the futility of trying to interview him. "He does not want to be reminded that he was an actor," she added. "Isn't that funny? He's a very nice man."

Then Mrs. Kohner told me about a letter he wrote to her while serving as ambassador. "He sent me a Mexican stamp with a question: 'Señora Lupita, this looks like you. Is it you?' Now, my own family [i.e., her siblings in Mexico] had not recognized me on the stamp, but John did. You see, I was the first film star to appear on a Mexican postage stamp." (Issued in 1981, the stamp honors Lupita Tovar and her costar in *Santa*, Mexico's first all-talking picture, on the fiftieth anniversary of the film's release. It bears the legend "Cincuentenario del Cine Sonoro Mexicano.")

Gavin has made no film or television appearances since 1981. He lives in semi-retirement in Los Angeles, and, as Mrs. Kohner pointed out, avoids reminders of his days as an actor.

"A Good Snapshot Stops a Moment from Running Away" (Eudora Welty)

In *Imitation of Life,* John Gavin plays a freelance photographer who first meets Lana Turner at Coney Island when he snaps her picture as she frantically seeks her lost child. In preparation for his role, Gavin took lessons from two celebrity photographers in Hollywood, Bob Willoughby and Zinn Arthur. To practice for his scenes, he shot several rolls of film, using as candid subjects Lana Turner, Sandra Dee, and other cast members. With a do-it-yourself developing kit, he produced the results in the evenings at home.

Originally, Douglas Sirk and Ross Hunter intended to include a sequence showing an exhibition of photographs taken by Gavin's character, Steve Archer. The actual photographs were to be the work of Bob Willoughby. In a recent e-mail, Willoughby told me that the studio filmed that sequence, although it wasn't used in the picture. He continued, "I was heartily disappointed at the time. Most of the images they used were part of an exhibit I had at the Museum in Los Angeles, and the title was 'Through the Looking Glass.' I did augment the ones they selected with some others to fit into the scheme of the film, but that's about all I can remember."

In the script, that deleted sequence follows the Moulin Rouge and the motel scenes. Lora and Steve plan to attend the screening of her Italian film, and she asks Susie to stay home with Annie: "Ever since she came back from Los Angeles she's changed. And Doctor Miller's quite concerned about her condition."

After the screening, Steve and Lora go late at night to the museum where his pictures are on display. Their dialogue goes on for three pages. They discuss her new picture: "All that gushing afterwards," she says. "I thought I'd scream. Everybody telling me how great it was." To which Steve responds: "But it was. I don't think I've ever seen you better."

(continued)

Lora adds that she's fed up with plays and films and has just turned down a good play that her agent, Loomis, sent to her in Europe. Then she asks Steve whether he remembers the scene at the end of her picture when she's dying. "I had a strange experience when I was doing it," she reveals. "Lying there, I kept thinking—if this were real—if I were really dying—what would I have missed? . . . Steve, I'm in love with you." Sirk was smart to cut this sequence, which amounts to lofty throat clearing.

I asked Willoughby whether he took the photos of Lana at Coney Island ("Mother in Distress") and "The Man on the Beach," and he replied that he did not. He added, "John Gavin was a really nice guy, and I spent many hours with him, and his then wife, Cecily. I liked them both."

Willoughby's disappointment at the time is understandable, for he was thirty years old and had worked for the studios since 1954, when Warner Bros. assigned him to photograph Judy Garland on the set of *A Star Is Born*. He started out taking photographs for *Harper's Bazaar* and became one of the first "outside" photographers to work on previously closed studio sets. In 1955, Willoughby's work was included in "The Family of Man," an exceptionally popular exhibit curated by Edward Steichen at the Museum of Modern Art in New York, and subsequently seen by some nine million people in thirty-eight countries. The exhibit was turned into a book by the same name, which sold more than four million copies.

Willoughby took photographs on the sets of 120 films, including *From Here to Eternity, My Fair Lady,* and *The Graduate*. His work has been exhibited in many museums. Since Willoughby didn't take the photos shown in *Imitation of Life,* they were presumably shot by Zinn Arthur, Gavin's other instructor. A Universal press release on July 22, 1958, stated that in addition to instructing John Gavin, "Arthur will shoot layouts on the film version of the Fannie Hurst novel."

(continued)

NO BEEFCAKE, PLEASE, WE'RE REPUBLICAN | 159

Zinn Arthur, who died in 2003 at the age of ninety, was a noted big-band leader before World War Two and toured with Irving Berlin's "This Is the Army" show. As the big-band sound lost popularity in the postwar years, Arthur moved on to a second career as a celebrity photographer, taking pictures of Elizabeth Taylor, Marilyn Monroe, Kim Novak, Burt Lancaster, and scores of others for magazine covers (*Look*, *Life*, *Esquire*) and publicity layouts. He worked as the still photographer on sixty-six films, including *The King and I*, *Cat on a Hot Tin Roof*, and *Picnic*. In his later years, he went on to a third career as a restaurateur with several establishments on Long Island and in south Florida.

The walls of his restaurants were lined with signed pictures he had taken during his years as a celebrity photojournalist, which suggests the possibility that those photographs lining the walls of "Rodney's," where Lana and John Gavin have their first lunch date, and the office walls of Lana's agent are also the work of Zinn Arthur.

*T*he worst fate of all," said Seneca two thousand years ago, "is to be stricken from the roster of the living before you die." Sandra Dee, still young, erased herself from life, retired to her bedroom with a bottle, and seldom emerged, during her last thirty years, except for appearances on a dozen schlocky TV shows.

When Sandra and Lana Turner met on *Imitation of Life,* Lana brought a surprise for her movie daughter: the original sweater that boosted Lana in *They Won't Forget* (1937), and that started the drooling Sweater Girl myth. "Wear it for luck," Lana said. "It's in good condition, and on you it looks even better." (Few would agree with Lana's compliment.) But Sandra's luck ran out early. Lana, who buoyed up across a lifetime of troubled waters, must have been lined with cork. Poor Sandra, like Ophelia, "fell in the weeping brook" and sank to "muddy death." But not for a long time. Sandra endured until 2005, when she was past sixty.

Whose Birthday Is It, Anyway?

Sandra Dee always gave her date of birth as 1942. Her son, Dodd Darin, in his book *Dream Lovers: The Magnificent Shattered Lives of Bobby Darin and Sandra Dee by Their Son,* insists otherwise. He writes: "I'm looking at this [newspaper] article about my mother. It appeared in April of 1957, only days after her birthday, and the photograph is of a girl so young and innocent looking, she could be nine. The caption reads, 'This Is Sandra Dee, Barely Fifteen Years Old.' But she was nowhere near fifteen. The lie her mother told, advancing her age by two years, had been set in concrete. Alexandra Zuck was not born in 1942, as all her biographical notes say. My mom was born in 1944." Sandra's mother added two years to her daughter's age for psychological as well as practical reasons. Manipulating the little girl's age fitted her scheme of ironclad domination, and those two added years also made Sandra a more exploitable commodity on the model market.

Sandra dropped from the womb into the workforce, skipping childhood like a crack in the sidewalk. Around the age of eight, she became a top Conover model who earned seventy thousand dollars a year. Her mother, Mary, a New Jersey Russian, married young, bore Sandra (née Alexandra Zuck) at eighteen, then divorced her alcoholic husband. Like all relentless mothers, Mary considered her bizarreries in the best interest of her child. She remained oblivious to the damaging oddity of feeding Sandra with a spoon until her daughter was six. Had there been a Little Miss Sunshine contest in the forties, Mary would surely have dressed her child as a baby strumpet and set out for the pageant.

Sandra, around eight, and with a mere two years' practice in feeding herself, adored her new stepfather, Eugene Douvan. And he her—too, too much. In his sixties, Douvan was some forty years older than his young bride. Or brides, for he often told Sandra, "I'm not marrying your mother. I'm marrying both of you." Little Sandy took it up, saying, "When *we* married Daddy." Like her mother, Sandra also took his name, which she later shortened to "Dee" at the request of her modeling agency.

Douvan began fondling Sandra even while he and Mary were dating. On their honeymoon (Sandra went, too, of course, since she was cowife), he placed her between him and Mary in the bed, an arrangement that Mary thought darling and that became the norm. Soon his sexual abuse was a commonplace. "I didn't understand what was going on," Sandra said many years later.

One day at breakfast, Sandra's stepfather patted her tummy and said, "Too many pancakes." His remark was a corny joke, but the girl took it literally. She felt as if she had dropped through a hideous trap door. Lifelong horrors often begin in reaction to a careless word or phrase heard in childhood, and his heedless sally that morning, along with the pattern of abuse, triggered Sandra's enduring anorexia. "From that day on," she recalled, "I did everything I could to destroy my body. I ate almost nothing but lettuce one entire year." During another protracted period, she lived on broiled shrimp.

On the set of *Imitation of Life,* no one guessed the real meaning of Sandra's meagre appetite, since everyone in Hollywood was on a diet. When I mentioned Sandra's anorexia to Juanita Moore, she recalled telling Sandra more than once, "Baby, you've got to eat something." And, because everyone looked up to Juanita and came to her for strength, Sandra sometimes obeyed. "I would hug her," Juanita recalled, "and try to treat her like a daughter. She would often sit at my feet, and then I could get her to eat half a sandwich." Bud Westmore, the head makeup artist on *Imitation of Life,* sometimes bribed Sandra. "I'll give you this special new lipstick," he said, "if you'll drink a malted milk." She tried, but couldn't force it down. How Sandra, first as a child, then as a teenage movie star, maintained the earmarks of health—lustrous eyes, sleek hair, pellucid skin—remains a medical mystery.

Carol Lynley, who, like Sandra, was a child model, told me that she knew Sandra from about the age of thirteen. "We were really good buddies," she said, "then I basically never saw her again. I would run into her mother from time to time. Mary meant well, but it's as though they were one person. Like the mirror image of each other. I don't think it was a healthy situation." Sandra herself said, "My mother wanted a cripple.

She wanted to live her life through me, and she wanted to make me a part of her." She referred to her mother as "the best girlfriend in the world. And the worst mother." Indeed, they looked like sisters, Sandra the wholesome child-woman, Mary the slightly older coquette.

In 1956, the stepfather died during heart surgery. A few days later, Sandra's agent phoned. His big news: Ross Hunter had come to town and wanted to meet Miss Dee. Sandra had never heard of him, but, dressed in black, depressed and in mourning, she made her way to Universal's New York office. After a long wait, she finally had her chance to read a few lines of script for the youthful producer. Then she went home with no expectations and little interest. Who was he, anyway?

Hunter was in New York looking for a new young actress to costar with John Saxon in a picture to be called *The Restless Years*. Later he described Sandra's face at their first meeting as "so white it looked like it had been dipped in flour. All except the black circles under her eyes."

A few months later, when Mary and Sandra had all but forgotten about Ross Hunter, he surprised them with a pair of plane tickets to Hollywood, where Sandra made a screen test with John Saxon. The result pleased Hunter so greatly that he arranged, early in 1957, for Sandra and her mother to move to California.

Before Hunter cranked up the star machine for Sandra, he loaned her out to MGM, where she appeared with Paul Newman, Joan Fontaine, Piper Laurie, and Jean Simmons in *Until They Sail*. It's possible that Hunter waited to see how Sandra looked in MGM's picture before risking her in his own. *The Restless Years,* with a storyline that echoed *Peyton Place,* was considered somewhat daring at the time. Sandra plays Melinda Grant, the illegitimate daughter of Teresa Wright. When John Saxon, new to the local high school, falls in love with Sandra, small-town gossip and lies assail the young couple.

Almost fifty years after they made the picture, Saxon recalled certain odd statements from Sandra on the set: "She would say something seemingly out of context that I didn't understand. For example, 'I hated my stepfather so much, I couldn't even go to his funeral.'" Such remarks added up for John Saxon only many years later, after Sandra, in a 1991 *People* magazine revelation, told the story of her long molestation.

Summing up her early career, Sandra said: "My first year and a half in Hollywood, I did three films. Then in 1959 I was in *Gidget, Imitation of Life,* and *A Summer Place.* After that I was a star."

America craved virginity, and Sandra seemed to possess every qualification for its Junior Miss division. She told an interviewer, "I wear pretty clothes, have my hair done well, look clean. Older people see me as the daughter they would like to have—there's no scandal about me." Moviegoers adored Sandra Dee in daylight, but at night their fantasies turned to fast girls like Tuesday Weld and Diane Varsi. Sandra's on-screen innocence mirrored the denial at home, where she and Mary suppressed all memory of what took place during their "marriage" to the same man. On screen, Sandra got away with goodness because—well, she was good. In *A Summer Place,* when she asks Troy Donahue, "Have you been bad, Johnny? Have you been bad with other girls?" it's a question her character sincerely wants answered. The camp rhetoric is an afterthought.

Shortly after Sandra's debut in *The Restless Years,* Louella Parsons summoned her, and Sandra trotted obediently to Louella's lair. The published interview, so innocently lewd that it lies somewhere between Nabokov and John Waters, starts out with a typical wobbly sentence. "Not since the days when Judy Garland and Deanna Durbin were teenagers has there been more excitement over a young girl as [sic] there is over this peach-melba type honey with golden blonde hair and the big brown eyes," Louella swooned. And Sandra swooned back: "You know, Miss Parsons, the most important FIRST of my career is this, being interviewed by you. It means I'm really getting somewhere."

One of Louella's probing questions: "I asked her if she is 'dating' Johnny Saxon off the picture as well as in it." (Imagine Waters filming this scene with Mink Stole as the otiose columnist and Divine as chaste young Sandra.) "Oh, I don't date yet," Sandra replied. "My Daddy is dead, you know. He was such a wonderful man. He encouraged me in all my ambitions, but when I was twelve years old he made me promise I wouldn't date too early. He said, 'Don't have life come at you too quickly. Enjoy being a little girl while you can.'"

———

Sandra Dee's talent was small but genuine. Seldom superfluous on the screen, even in superfluous pictures, she gave her best performances in *The Reluctant Debutante* (1958) and *A Summer Place* (1959). In the former, a zippy comedy directed by Vincente Minnelli, Sandra plays the daughter of Rex Harrison. Stepmother Kay Kendall sets out to present her to London society, which the young girl isn't keen on joining. It's surprising how well Sandra, as a stereotypical ingenue, holds her own with veteran actor Harrison and the brilliant Kendall, a comedienne who makes pratfalls look like *grandes jetées*. Without Minnelli's sure-footed direction, Sandra might have given the kind of predictable performance that seems called for. Instead, she underplays. She even steals, or at least borrows, a few scenes from her elders, including Angela Lansbury. John Saxon again plays Sandra's swarthy lover. (He said, "She had a great knack, a technique of acting. She knew timing. She knew changes. She knew where all the points were.")

On location in Paris for *The Reluctant Debutante,* Sandra started a diary. Years later her son, Dodd Darin, came across it in a box of his mother's papers. Although Sandra began the diary, recording anodyne events and impressions, her mother soon commandeered it. At first, Mary only corrected Sandra's spelling. Soon, however, she began adding entries in Sandra's voice. "By the end of the first week," Darin writes, "all the entries were Mary's—writing as if she were her daughter." This creepy, real-life version of Mother Bates and Norman helps to explain the robe of scars Sandra wore beneath her pretty clothes.

In *A Summer Place,* directed by Delmer Daves, Sandra used intelligent restraint in a role where she could have discharged teen anguish by the gallon. When Constance Ford, as her sex-phobic mother, shakes her violently while Sandra screams in terror, the scene convinces almost too well. It strikes with the same shock power as the beating scene in *Imitation of Life.* (Discussing this scene years later, Sandra said that Ford asked Mary Douvan, Sandra's mother, to leave the set. Then, said Sandra, "She beat me. I saw stars! My mother came back and found her daughter on the floor. But Constance Ford was a wonderful woman. She told my mother, 'I didn't want you to see that but I had to do it that way.'" Half joking—but only half—Sandra said, "She didn't have to do it that hard, to be honest.")

Reunions

During her long decline, Sandra was beset by health problems in addition to alcoholism and anorexia. Although she battled her infirmities, she invariably reverted to drink and semistarvation. For a time in the early 1990s, however, she was on the wagon and able to appear on stage with John Saxon in a production of A. R. Gurney's *Love Letters* in Los Angeles.

In 1997, Sandra (no longer sober) and Troy Donahue attended a New York screening of *A Summer Place* sponsored by American Movie Classics at the start of that network's summer season. In July of the following year, they appeared together once more, this time in San Francisco at the Castro Theatre's "Summer Beach Party." Sandra was fifty-three, Troy sixty-two, and both showed the ravages of alcohol (and in Donahue's case, drug abuse, as well), even though he had been clean since 1982.

In front of the theatre, the two emerged from a late-fifties sedan, signed a few autographs, then made their way inside and onto the stage to be interviwed. Sandra seemed to have trouble walking, and Troy guided her as though she were an elderly lady. (The producer of the show told me, "I never saw anyone so drunk as she was when she got off the plane." But, he added, "She was never unpleasant, and she pulled herself together before going on stage. The audience loved her.")

Sandra comported herself like the pro she was. Yet who can forget the frightened eyes, the air of befuddlement, and her slight discombobulation? Sandra's nervousness took the form of small, talk-show emotions enlarged by theatrical, drag-queen gestures—waving arms, fluttery hands, head thrown back, a parody of something Sandra herself had never been. Although still attractive and well groomed, she might almost have been a death camp survivor: from certain angles, one glimpsed the skeleton beneath her skin.

The audience, of course, was on her side, and so was San Francisco

(continued)

TV and radio personality Jan Wahl, who conducted the onstage interview with tact and affection. Asked by Wahl about her film career,
Sandra said: "I never got a good review. I would read the reviews and
go into hiding and cry."

When, near the end of the interview, Troy talked to Jan Wahl
about his victory over drugs and alcohol, Sandra gazed at him trans-
fixed. What was the emotion that predominated—admiration, or despair that such a victory eluded her? When he finished, she looked at
him, and spoke softly: "Beautifully said," she whispered, and kissed
her old friend and long-ago costar for the last time.

In *Portrait in Black,* where she portrays Lana's stepdaughter, Sandra
plays several scenes like a developing actress. Soon, however, she reverts
to poisonous cuteness. In a café scene with John Saxon (their third film
together), she declaims, with a petulant shake of the head, "If I'd known
we were going to a beatnik joint for coffee and word jazz, I'd have worn
my tights."

In August 1960, Sandra flew to Italy to begin work on *Come September,*
starring Rock Hudson and Gina Lollobrigida. In the film, Bobby Darin,
who had appeared briefly in a few previous pictures, made his real debut. The offscreen plot ended up better than the script, which is a
chastity farce parading as a sex comedy.

Darin's great desire was to star in movies and to marry a movie star.
Already, at twenty-four, he had won four gold records and two Grammys.
He had broken attendance records at famous nightclubs, and fans besieged him. The way he went about winning Sandra Dee recalls the plot
of a vaguely incestuous screwball comedy, for he began by courting her
mother.

The first time Bobby and Sandra met face-to-face he called out, "Will
you marry me?" and she replied, "Not today." So he set to work on Mary
Douvan. Every day he sent her flowers and buttered her up with flattery.
On the set of *Come September,* it was thought that Bobby and Mary were
an item, and why not? Darin was only ten years younger than Sandra's

mother. Mary seems to have known all along that his attentions were directed past her, toward Sandra. Sandra, however, didn't respond.

One day Bobby dropped by to visit Mary, and while there he said nonchalantly to Sandra, "Why don't we go for a carriage ride?" To his surprise, and her own, Sandra responded, "All right." Beginning the next day, Bobby sent flowers to Sandra Dee and not to Mary Douvan. Eighteen yellow roses arrived daily. "He told Mary that Sandra was going to marry someone someday, so she'd better get used to the idea" that her daughter was going to marry him.

Mary wanted Bobby's blood. Saner adults also cautioned Sandra. Rock Hudson, who had become a friend during the shoot, advised her not to marry Darin. When Sandra telephoned Ross Hunter from Rome to tell him she had fallen in love, Hunter demurred. "But, honey, you can't," he said. "You haven't even necked in cars yet."

Bobby Darin finished his work on *Come September* and flew home. Sandra stayed in Rome to complete the picture, and when her plane landed in New York he met her with an engagement ring. They married on December 1, 1960, separated in May 1966, and divorced a year later.

Sandra began drinking during the early years of her marriage. Divorce notwithstanding, she and Bobby remained close, and when he died in 1973 her alcoholism redoubled. After that, the years dragged by like a long, sleepless night. Eventually Sandra no longer bothered to look through the window, for it mattered less and less whether morning had come, or midnight. And yet, by all accounts, including her son's, she was a loving, attentive mother.

During her years of stardom, Sandra played Gidget and Tammy, along with a jumble of other pastel roles. (*Gidget* was based on the novel by Frederick Kohner, Susan's uncle.) Today those Sandra Dee vehicles melt together like a vat of Slurpees, but until the mid-sixties she remained a top box office attraction. Then, suddenly, America's upheaval. Overnight, the kids who had dreamed of being Gidget, or dating her, laughed at anything so square. Sandra herself, like a silent star oblivious to the mutation engendered by sound, expected to continue as Universal's pert young lady, the studio pet.

In December 1965, Bob Thomas, a respected reporter on movies and movie stars, wrote a feature for the Associated Press that began, "Something of a milestone in Hollywood history passed entirely without notice recently. Sandra Dee ended her exclusive contract with Universal." Pointing out the historical significance of the unheralded event, Thomas explained that Sandra was "the last big-name movie star to remain under contract to a major studio."

Thomas wrote that he "detected a trace of bitterness about her departure from the home set." Sandra told him, "I thought they [the bosses at Universal] were my friends. But I found out I was simply a piece of property to them." Although no longer a contract player, Sandra made several other pictures at Universal. Finally, in 1968, following a blowup that began when the studio reneged on a verbal agreement with Sandra that she would not have to appear in a TV movie, she left the studio forever. Her son sums up the result in a sentence: "She shot her career right through the heart." Sandra's last picture for Universal was *Rosie* (1967), with Rosalind Russell and Brian Aherne. Although far from immortal, it boosted Sandra once more into the box office top ten. Divorced from Universal, she didn't work for three years. Her next picture, *The Dunwich Horror*, in 1970, was made by American International, the kind of descent that's nearly always fatal. Sandra Dee was finished.

In a very real sense, she wasn't heard of again until *Grease* (1978), which paid her a number of left-handed compliments. That picture's heedless mockery lingers like cheap perfume. When Sandra died, it proved irresistible to facile eulogists like Daphne Merkin, who ended her piece on Sandra in the *New York Times Magazine* like this: "Look at her, she's Sandra Dee, lousy with debility. Tickets, anyone?" (Gore Vidal had every reason to dub that Sunday supplement "the graveyard of American prose.")

In *Grease*, it's Olivia Newton-John who plays "Sandy," a bland Sandra Dee surrogate and a bad choice for the role. The real Sandra had more presence and personality, even at her most Deeish, than the insipid Newton-John. It's Stockard Channing, however, as Rizzo, the "bad girl," who slaps on a blonde wig and performs the best number in this frantic but etiolated musical:

Look at me, I'm Sandra Dee
Lousy with virginity

(Sandra herself reportedly giggled over *Grease*, but then she was always too nice.)

Throughout the musical, Sandra Dee is the controlling motif. Newton-John starts out as a Sandra clone who, after her "Good-bye, Sandra Dee" finale, is no longer goody-goody but cool, hip, ready to live and have fun. The movie's unintentional cruelty is that Sandra herself didn't have much fun at all. As the lone student in that classroom at Universal, she missed even the paltry good times of high school. And in her early shove into the terrible knowledge of adulthood, she never got a chance to wave good-bye to Sandra Dee.*

---

*In *Beyond the Sea*, Kevin Spacey's 2004 bio pic of Bobby Darin, Kate Bosworth plays Sandra Dee. Bosworth looks like Sandra, moves like her, and uses vocal tones and inflections we know from Sandra Dee movies minus the gushy too-muchness that spoiled many of Dee's performances. Neither Bosworth nor Sandra is well served by the script, whose imagined biographical drama rises only so low:

Bosworth/Sandra: "Bobby, what's gonna happen to me?"

Spacey/Darin: "No matter what happens, baby, you'll always be Sandra Dee."

22 | "IF TROY DONAHUE CAN BE A MOVIE STAR, THEN I CAN BE A MOVIE STAR"

*S*o proclaims Bobby, in *A Chorus Line,* and it's probably true. After all, what did Troy Donahue have that catapulted him to the top of Hollywood's heartthrob roster? He looked uncomfortable on the screen, always seeming to ask himself subliminally, "What am I supposed to do?"—and getting no reply.

He came across better in magazine layouts, where he resembled a Sno-Cone ready for consumption. Donahue's fan base of teenage girls, who wrote him seven thousand letters a week for a few years circa 1959–1963, weren't looking for talent. In him they found a kindred spirit, blandly insouciant, unthreatening, the perfect icon of youth to a huge slice of the American public—with a nasty streak beneath the blond. (Did he pass some weirdly recessive gene to the likes of Chad Michael Murray and Ashley Parker Angel?)

According to the fanciful bio concocted by Universal, by Donahue's irrepressible agent, Henry Willson, and by Donahue himself, Merle Johnson Jr. (his birth name) was the scion of a wealthy General Motors executive and a former stage actress. The family lived in a twenty-seven-room mansion on Long Island, where Merle Jr. assumed the role of protector to his mother and younger sister upon the death of the father in 1950, when the son was fourteen. A few years later, while a journalism student at Columbia University, the future Troy Donahue began appearing

in stock productions, which led him to Hollywood and an almost simultaneous contract at Universal-International.

More reliable sources, however, omit the Ivy League connection. A
writer for *TV Guide* in 1961 stated that after his father's death young
Merle Johnson "began waiting tables for tuition at New York Military
Academy. Then, bitten by the acting bug in school productions, he decided to try Hollywood."

Writing in *McCall's* in 1962, the future novelist Judith Krantz profiled Donahue, who was then at the crest of his stardom: "This is the
story of a twenty-five-year-old youth who shot from obscurity to instant
stardom, a young man no more talented or handsome than many a one
you might find in any college or working in a supermarket. As Merle
Johnson, Junior, he was an undisciplined high-school sophomore who
never did manage to graduate; his best subjects were dating, dancing,
and dressing; his teachers, because of his nice manners, his good vocab-
ulary, and his normal IQ, always hoped he would improve his low
marks."

If Donahue's academic record remains as questionable as George
W. Bush's, there is little ambiguity about his success. Krantz chronicled
the conquests and the possessions of "the most worshiped young male
star in America." Studio insiders, she revealed, called him "the blond cobra of sex." A reporter who knew him well dubbed Donahue "a large
handsome male body surrounded by women." Krantz reported that his
salary was two thousand dollars a week. His public appearances
matched those of Elvis Presley: screaming teenage girls tried to rip the
clothes from his back. Krantz also revealed that Donahue possessed a
Cadillac and three hundred sweaters.

But Judith Krantz's profile of Troy Donahue included more than
clothes and carnality. She quoted a Donahue crony who spoke on condition of anonymity "because he didn't want Troy to take a sock at him."
Troy's home, claimed the source, "was always an open house, and the
worst people in Hollywood and along the Sunset Strip took advantage of
his hospitality. Some of his friends avoided visiting him for fear of a police raid."

That paragraph hints at goings-on not typically brought up in women's
magazines in 1962. Chez Donahue sounds rather Sodom and Gomorrahish,

but savvy readers were supposed to fill in the blanks with something like "opium den." Whatever the implied sexual content of Troy's "hospitality," it would have been mainly hetero, and thus legal—up to a point—under California laws of the time. (He was bi-curious—how could a blond cobra be otherwise?—and, in later years, made no secret of his bisexual encounters.) From the start, drugs and drink took precedence over the craft of acting.

In her article, Krantz draws a neat distinction between the discovery of Troy Donahue, which took place in 1957 when he landed a low-paying contract at Universal, and the invention, a couple of years later, of the male ingenue that Warner Bros. needed for *A Summer Place*. In the beginning, Henry Willson conveyed Donahue to Universal, where Ed Muhl, head of production, trusted the agent's eye for knock-out youth. There, he appeared (often uncredited) in some dozen pictures, including *Man of a Thousand Faces*, Sirk's *The Tarnished Angels, Monster on the Campus*, and *Imitation of Life*, where he was noticed for the first time, but for the wrong reasons: sadistic blond hoodlums who beat women were not in vogue on screen. After a couple of years, he was made redundant.

Warner Bros., meanwhile, having paid a bundle for rights to Sloan Wilson's "sensational" novel *A Summer Place*, wanted someone different from all the actors currently available. Undesirable were sullen rebels, beatniks, ethnic types, and hip-and-pelvis rock 'n' rollers. After testing dozens of actors to star opposite Sandra Dee, Warner Bros. executives cried out "Eureka!"—or the smoke-filled-room equivalent—when they viewed the four-minute screen test that paired all-American Troy with petite, virtuous Sandra in a love scene. Here was a guy, they assured one another, with star quality. He was fresh, clean-cut, soft-spoken—but all man!—romantic, well-bred. He knew from sex, but he looked like a kid who would treat a nice girl nice, open doors ahead of her, get her home on time.

During his two years with Universal, Donahue appeared in a number of TV westerns. Later, at Warner Bros., he seemed a natural for sun-bleached roles in *Hawaiian Eye, Surfside 6*, and the like. Although frequently included with beefcake gods in fan magazine layouts, he looked unacquainted with the gym, and more tofu than beef.

Even after his Warner Bros. makeover, however, Donahue qualified, owing to his role in *Imitation of Life* and to his offscreen punch-ups, as a delinquent, and a *mean* one, not a sensitive, misunderstood boy like James Dean or Sal Mineo. Without the clean-up at Warner, he might have inherited the roles of Elisha Cook Jr.

Sidney Skolsky reported in 1961 that Donahue had "a terrible temper . . . he can be violent, to himself as well as others." A month after Skolsky's column, the starlet Lili Kardell spent two days in Cedars of Lebanon Hospital in Los Angeles as a result of being beaten, she claimed, by Donahue, to whom she had been engaged. Several newspaper accounts contradicted her, reporting that Kardell struck first in a fit of jealous rage when she discovered Donahue talking to another woman on the patio of his pink-and-brown house off the Sunset Strip. Her lawsuit for assault and battery was settled out of court for an undisclosed sum. Earlier, in 1958, Donahue was sentenced to fifteen days in jail owing to a series of five warrants for speeding, a term apparently suspended.

Skolsky, in his column, added that Donahue "is extremely generous and kind." He seems to have possessed a conscience. After the Lili Kardell imbroglio, Donahue professed contrition: "The violence I have been associated with, or accused of, is something I would have avoided and do not like in any way. I am a God-fearing person. I feel that to do wrong and not learn from it is sinful." During the confrontation between Native Americans and the U.S. government at Wounded Knee in 1973, Donahue joined Marlon Brando, Jane Fonda, Carroll O'Connor, and others in chartering a small aircraft to drop food supplies to the tribal occupiers.

In January 1964, Donahue married Suzanne Pleshette. They separated in June, and in September she was awarded a divorce on grounds of extreme cruelty, which, despite the legal terminology, in this case amounted to low-grade churlishness. On one occasion shortly after their marriage, he told her he would be home by midnight but instead stayed out until 5:00 a.m. Returning home, he found the door locked and so climbed in through the bathroom window, loudly accusing her of locking him out. She explained to the judge that she had been afraid to leave the door unlocked while in the house alone. On another occasion, the actress said, when she gave a small dinner party her husband was extremely rude and left the table without eating.

Donahue was later married to actress Valerie Allen for two years; to Vicki Taylor for two years (he arrived at the church on their wedding day in a King Kong outfit, to the surprise and reported delight of bride and guests); and to Alma Sharp, a city administrator, for three years. At the time of his death, in 2001, he was engaged to opera singer Zheng Cao, who had been his companion for many years.

Delmer Daves, who directed Troy Donahue in the four pictures that made him a star—*A Summer Place* (1959), *Parrish* (1961), *Susan Slade* (1961), and *Rome Adventure* (1962)—offered the pithiest explanation for Donahue's succès fou: "He looks like Young America wants to look." Although Daves apparently made his statement without irony, it highlights America's zestless self-image in those years, and its collective ideals. The public craved—or was it force-fed?—bland youth; WASP looks, values, behavior; the provincial "good life" of the middle classes; implied chastity, or at least a carapace guarding and obscuring sexual impulses; mild intelligence, which must never threaten the less well endowed (remember Troy's teachers, who admired his "normal" IQ). Indeed, the national motto might have enjoined, "In Normalcy We Trust." Those stereotypes of Young America saturated the land, beamed across this superpower as relentlessly as Soviet propaganda in the other one.

And especially in movies. Troy Donahue's zenith coincided with the breakdown of studio-ruled Hollywood, a schizy period when moviemakers sought to transgress sexual, political, and cultural statutes while still adhering to public notions of good taste and to the crumbling strictures of the Production Code.

For instance, *Imitation of Life,* which qualifies as both schizoid and revolutionary: surface safety that conceals hidden explosives, and not only because of race. Like other Sirk films, it pictures the dreamy suburban values of American materialism as desirable, even as it undermines the Aryan virtues of Young America. One striking example of the film's counterclockwise optics: Troy Donahue's Frankie, insipidly handsome, and with a wimpy voice, reveals himself as an American Brown Shirt.

Frankie is the film's disturbing white extremist. The other characters on what I call the "blond side" of *Imitation of Life*—good people, all of them, or good enough—live superficially. They imitate. Imitation, to Sirk, is a synonym for normality, a state no artist aspires to. Unlike Annie Johnson and Sarah Jane, the whites do not cross-examine themselves. To Lora Meredith, Susie, Steve Archer, David Edwards, and Allen Loomis, imitating life means conforming. It's hard to condemn them for that; after all, life aches less if you imitate Young America. Indeed, Sarah Jane yearns to do so. Yet because of her race, she cannot. No one lets her forget she was born to be hurt.

Sirk's ubiquitous mirrors hang not only on the walls. Figuratively, he hangs fractured mirrors to face one another and thus create a rotunda of deformity. One such distortion would be to imply, patronizingly, that Annie Johnson and Sarah Jane, in their misery, are somehow more authentic than the white characters. I do believe, however, that their anguished self-interrogation, with its implied indictment of society, bestows on them a degree of truth not available to the others. (They live "life at the bone," to quote Thoreau, who was Sirk's favorite iconoclast.)

A vexed question: Would Sarah Jane and Annie prefer the imitation happiness they see around them to their own pain? Sarah Jane thinks she does. I have no answer. Who but Nietzsche would privilege outright suffering over imitation happiness? On the other hand, isn't a happy life less desirable than one that's lived-in? And since Annie and Sarah Jane are not case histories but made-up characters, we can only judge them aesthetically. From that angle, they perhaps lead more heartfelt lives. But a thin membrane, no more, separates blond existence from black. As Sirk said, "If you try to grasp happiness . . . it's hopeless."

In later years, Troy Donahue told a troubling *Imitation of Life* story that seems oddly congruent with his character in the film. Appearing with Sandra Dee at the Castro Theatre in San Francisco in 1998, he was prompted by Jan Wahl, the onstage inteviewer: "You had to play a really tough role in *Imitation of Life*."

Sandra chimed in, "He was a rat!"

As a lead-in to his story, Troy said, "Ross sent me the script, and I read and read but my character didn't turn up. Finally, I got to the scene and I said, 'I don't want to do this!' This guy does something so terrible, and says something so despicable, that I called Ross and said, 'I can't do this. I'll lose all my fans.' Of course, I didn't *have* any fans yet.

"He said, 'Read it again.' I did, and finally I relented. All actors relent, I guess."

Then came the story: "A few months after the movie was released, I was on a personal appearance tour [for *A Summer Place*] and I went to Birmingham, Alabama. After the screening, there was a whole contingent of black people waiting for me." Here he paused, implying with a smirk that the crowd, angry over his violence to the black girl in *Imitation of Life,* was out to get him. But the punch line took a twist: "To shake my hand for smacking a girl who's passing for white."

He told a slightly different version to Robert Hofler, author of *The Man Who Invented Rock Hudson,* a scurrilous biography of Donahue's agent, Henry Willson. "After that film came out," Donahue claimed, "black people would come up to me and thank me for treating Susan Kohner like that. Twenty years later, the NFL had a lot of black players named Troy."

The point of his story, of course, is that blacks loathe other blacks who pass for white. While pockets of fierce resentment do exist, both versions of that story ring not merely false but preposterous. First of all, African Americans in Birmingham in 1959–60 had more pressing business than congratulating white actors for racist portrayals. In Birmingham, as in much of the South on the eve of the civil rights upheaval, blacks would have watched *Imitation of Life* from the segregated balcony. Second, Southern modesty and politeness would shun unseemly praise for such onscreen thugishness, whether the victim of it was black, white, or passing. Then, too, although Donahue's ego apparently convinced him otherwise, his one scene, although powerful, wasn't the memorable one for black people, or for anyone else. Audiences left the theatre overwhelmed by the performances of his betters: Juanita Moore, Mahalia Jackson, Susan Kohner, and Lana Turner, who made the picture unforgettable.

Finally, Donahue's white delusion that scores of black parents named their newborn boys, the future stars of the NFL, in his honor is ludicrous. That's as absurd as imagining that August Wilson named Troy Maxon, the protagonist of *Fences,* with Donahue in mind. Ironically, of all the Troys in football, the leading one is probably Troy Aikman, former quarterback for the Dallas Cowboys. Born eight years after *Imitation of Life,* he's as white and blond as Troy Donahue.

An audience-reaction story that does ring true is this one, reported by Hilton Als in his 1999 profile of Richard Pryor in *The New Yorker:* "He was stationed in Germany, where he was involved in a racial incident. A young white soldier laughed too hard about the painful black parts in the Douglas Sirk film *Imitation of Life,* and Pryor and a number of other black inductees beat and stabbed him. Pryor went to jail."

Parrish, the first picture in which Donahue received star billing, might have been titled "Nicotine Road" because of its setting: a high-end tobacco farm in Connecticut. To this rural Peyton Place come Claudette Colbert and Donahue, playing mother and son, she to take up residence as ladylike role model to upper-class slut Diane McBain, who soon puts the make on Troy, her chaperone's willowy, blond offspring. Lower-class slut Connie Stevens, who labors in the fields with Madeleine Sherwood and Sylvia Miles (!), lusts mightily for him, too. She rubs a soothing balm on Troy's aching back, gets pregnant by someone else, and Parrish, Troy's character, escapes both girls by joining the navy. Meanwhile, Colbert marries Karl Malden, the rival of her employer, Dean Jagger. The movie is a bizarre mix of class struggle, agribusiness, etiquette, hormonal peasants, and teen angst. Colbert, well-tailored in her screen comeback (and last film), brings a minty whiff of old-style glamour to the picture.

Karl Malden said, "What was fascinating to me about making this film was having the chance to watch two different schools of acting in action. Claudette was the consummate pro. One or two rehearsals and she was ready for a take. What was at the time the younger generation— Troy Donahue, Connie Stevens—had a completely different style. They were often unprepared and relied on blocking time to learn their lines.

They had been thrust into leads too fast. . . . These kids weren't up to the task."

Already, Donahue was addicted to everything. Years later, after becoming sober, he told an interviewer that for twenty years he lived the life of Charles Manson, except for the killing. Homeless, he spent several months in Central Park, with everything he owned stuffed in a backpack. Yet he never went for long without work of some sort. Throughout the sixties and seventies, during his deepest addictions, he turned up at least once or twice a year on TV or in a cheapo movie.

Then, resurrected, he appeared in 1974 in a great film, *The Godfather: Part II*. Donahue and Francis Ford Coppola had known each other in military school as boys, and, as an in-joke, the director named Donahue's character "Merle Johnson." Donahue, as the opportunistic boyfriend of Connie Corleone (Talia Shire), makes a fleeting appearance in three scenes, and speaks two or three lines of dialogue.

He hoped the role might lead to a comeback, but Troy Donahue— the concept, if not the man himself—was out of date, and had been for a long time. Just a year later, the character in *A Chorus Line* cracked that joke, "If Troy Donahue can be a movie star . . ." Even earlier, almost as soon as the last frame of *Rome Adventure* had faded from the screen, Donahue seemed a blur, undifferentiated from so many who had been big in the fifties.

Faye Dunaway, on the threshhold of edgy sixties stardom, had a small part in *Hurry Sundown,* which was filmed in small towns around Baton Rouge, Louisiana, in 1966. One weekend, she, Michael Caine, Jane Fonda, and others in the cast drove into New Orleans, and while sitting in a bar on Bourbon Street they noticed that a small crowd had recognized them as movie stars. "Finally," said Faye, "one of them lurched toward us, stopped at the table, and said, 'Which one of you is Troy Donahue?' Finally we realized he was referring to me."

Faye Dunaway at that time was unknown. Tall and lanky, she probably did resemble Donahue. Besides the blond hair, both had similar puffy eyes, protruding lower lip, and a camera-ready half-smile on the verge of a pout. But a year or so later, not even a tipsy tourist would have confused the two, for Dunaway had the onscreen aggression that Donahue himself, and the studios, suppressed. To attract so many nice girls back then, he had to be denatured.

That silly mistake in New Orleans, however, carries symbolic freight, for a year later, *Bonnie and Clyde* helped redefine Hollywood forever. Its megaton impact blotted out the era when Troy Donahue and Sandra Dee and Ross Hunter could be players. It turned them, and their ilk, into laughingstocks. Those late-Eisenhower, early-Kennedy avatars and purveyors of Young America, so vibrant and loved a short while earlier, had disintegrated like forgotten cans of nitrate stock.

Why Faye Dunaway Wept at Imitation of Life

Each one of us carries a private *Imitation of Life*, which screens simultaneously with Sirk's. If that hidden version causes extreme pain, we shut it up inside, a notorious secret. The submerged *Imitation* is like a microchip embedded in the heart.

Faye Dunaway has a more intimate connection to *Imitation of Life* than just being mistaken for Troy Donahue. In her 1995 memoir, *Looking for Gatsby,* she recounts the picture's impact on her when she saw it in college. In a passage that reveals a vulnerability rarely evident in her performances, Dunaway confesses that conflicts with her own mother made *Imitation of Life* a wrenching experience. Her overwhelming reaction to the picture explains not only her own tears, but the main cause of similar reactions in every audience.

"The character who moved me so on the night I first saw the movie," she writes, "was Sarah Jane, played by Susan Kohner. Our stories were not all that different. As Sarah Jane slips into . . . the white world, she sheds the old, disowns her mother, and leaves behind anything that would connect her to her black ancestry. As I

(continued)

watched the story unfold, I knew in my heart I wasn't that different from Sarah Jane. I was ashamed of my mother and trying desperately to compete in a world of which she had no real understanding."

Watching the movie, Dunaway was engulfed by painful emotions, realizing that her mother "was hopelessly out of place in the polite, educated society that she wanted me to travel in. Because in my heart of hearts I adored my mother. I loved her deeply and I still do. As the lights went up and the theatre emptied out, I sat in the back of the theatre sobbing. In leaving the South, like Sarah Jane, I was also leaving my mother behind."

23 | FURTHER DOWN THE CREDITS

This biography of *Imitation of Life,* like any behind-the-scenes profile, leads inevitably to a deconstruction of the finished film. Not in the recondite sense of the word used by theorists of literature and cinema, but more literally. To dismantle the film, so to speak; to draw back a curtain long closed in an effort to view it as those hundreds of people at Universal-International experienced the construction of it in late summer and early fall of 1958. I want to evoke their everyday work, and their ultimate accomplishments, as they shaped and reshaped the picture, word by word on blank page, plank by nail by paintbrush on the sound stage, from low-end apartment set to grandiose estate in suburban Connecticut, and, in the case of actors, as they transformed themselves into different personae, bringing life and sound to the silent dialogue in a script.

Such deconstruction inevitably reshuffles *Imitation of Life,* allowing us to view it from new angles. For a time, the entire film functions differently, as the order of images disintegrates, loses coherence. Time flows out of sequence as chunks of the movie unspool this way and that. Ultimately, of course, the picture reconstructs itself before our eyes on the screen in all its sound and color. We participate once more in that familiar formal assemblage, except that we now know "secrets" from beyond camera range.

How quotidian, and yet how evocative, to read, on pages 6 and 6A of the studio's production budget, a typed list of some three dozen sets built for the picture, along with the construction cost of each, the number of days it was used, and the cost of striking it. Because the items on that list amount to vertabrae on the backbone of the picture, I reproduce them here, along with a few of their dollar amounts.

*Int. Coldwater Flat—6½ days—$4,500—$350 to strike
*Ext. Door Coldwater Flat
*Int. Rodney's Restaurant
*Int. Loomis Agency Corridor,
   Reception Room, Private Office—2 days—$3,880—$400
*Int. Grammar School
*Int. Theatre Dressing Room #1—½ day—$800—$100
*Int. David Edwards' Apt.—¾ day—$3,300—$425
*Int. Connecticut Home (Lower Floor)—4¾—$16,300—$1,750
*Int. Connecticut Home (Upper Floor)—4½—$5,500—$750
*Ext. Park
*Int. Bocce Restaurant
*Int. Harry's Club
*Int. Motel Room—½ day—$600—$100
*Int. Photographic Exhibit [Deleted from Release Print]
*Int. Theatre Dressing Room #2
*Int. Church Closeups
*Ext. Rear Connecticut Home
*Int. Steve's Office
*Ext. Connecticut Home, incl. Tarped Window [with painted
   landscape]
*Ext. Boardwalk & Beach
*Ext. Harry's, Grammar School, Theatre Marquees
*Ext. Empty Theatre #2 and #4
*Ext. Pinecrest School [i.e., Town and Country School]
*Ext. & Int. Moulin Rouge
*Int. Church
*Ext. Bridle Path and Picnic Grounds

*Int. Shoddy Photo Studio—Process [elevated train seen through
  window]
*Ext. Rodney's Restaurant [not used in film]
*Ext. Theatre Marquee
*Ext. Coldwater Flat

Not included on this list are several off-site locations used in filming. A
few, such as the exterior of Rodney's Restaurant, were edited from the
final print.

Glamour in a cold-water flat demands pluck, and Lora Meredith has it.
Although she's destitute—can't pay the rent nor even the milkman—
her dazzling platinum hair betrays no neglect, nor do her makeup and
manicure. And her well-tailored wardrobe surely didn't come off the
rack at S. Klein. To be sure, she is not your typical denizen of a cold-
water flat. Although the term means literally an apartment lacking hot
water, it is also used more broadly to describe one without modern conveniences. Neither description, however, quite fits Lora's place, which
is equipped with gas range, refrigerator, and hot-water tank. It is sans
washing machine, of course, like many New York apartments then and
now. We know this because Annie handwashes Lora's things on her
first morning there.

It's not surprising that the interior of the so-called cold-water flat
cost more to construct than all but a couple of others, since it comprises
a warren of small rooms: sitting room, kitchen, that "little place off the
kitchen" where Annie and Sarah Jane sleep, linen closet, and Lora's bedroom, which she shares with young Susie. Not to mention the staircase
and hallway outside, which belong to this set.

Dressing the set, and supplying it with props, cost only a few hundred dollars. No doubt the studio owned many of the furnishings already: Lora and Susie's brass bed, lamps and endtables, a long blue sofa,
armchairs, bookcase with books, a kitchen table, and mirrors, the sine
qua non of a Sirk picture.

The ostensible location of the flat is Brooklyn, although Lora's line to
Susie while they're still at Coney Island—"We have to go back to the
city"—suggests Manhattan. (Brooklynites don't travel into Manhattan—

they "go to New York" or "to the city.") Another clue: When Susie tells photographer Steve Archer where to deliver copies of his "fat man on the beach" picture, that address is 450 Prescott Place—a Brooklyn street.

David Tomack

On her deathbed, Annie Johnson recalls the character played by David Tomack, telling Lora, "I want Mr. McKinney to have a nice, clean fifty-dollar bill." Lora has no idea who that is, and so Annie explains that he was "the milkman at the old cold-water flat. He was so nice and understanding about the bill. I always sent him a little something at Christmastime in both our names." A few scenes later, we see Mr. McKinney in the church at Annie's funeral.

A couple of years before *Imitation of Life,* Tomack played Jayne Mansfield's milkman in *The Girl Can't Help It.* As she walks by, her cartoonish breasts preceding her, a bottle of milk he's holding blows its cap and the contents gush out.

David Tomack was born in New York and died in Los Angeles in 1977, at the age of fifty-eight. He appeared in a few movies, usually uncredited, and often on TV in the fifties. Like other nerdy, bespectacled characters of that era, Tomack was used cruelly onscreen. His Reddy Kilowatt face and body nudged audiences: here's a sap you can laugh at. Perhaps Sirk placed him at the funeral to add poignance, and to underscore Annie's loyalty and kindness. *Variety*'s brief obituary for Tomack, which ends like a melancholy haiku, has its own poignance: "Before entering the hospital, he was working as a grip at 20th Century-Fox. Survived by two cousins, a nephew and a niece."

On their first date, Lora Meredith and Steve Archer meet for lunch at Rodney's. She asks to go there, telling him "it's a little place on Forty-fifth and Eighth. Unemployed actors can afford it. Sort of a poor man's '21'." Rodney's is a stand-in for an actual theatre mecca, Jim Downey's, which stood near the same location. Downey's, like this "poor man's '21'," also had photographs of actors on the walls, although not actors who actually ate at Downey's. By the time they were that big, they ate at the real "21".

Rodney's is a long room with round tables and a partition separating the bar from the restaurant. On every space, images of actors—head shots, caricatures, photos of scenes from plays. It is realistically populated with a lunchtime crowd, for the studio hired, in addition to the actors, three waiters, two bartenders, and thirty-six extras. Lora and Steve chat briefly, then another unemployed actress (played by Peg Shirley) calls out, "Lora!" She informs her that "they're beginning to cast a new Tennessee Williams play." Since this is 1947, that play would be *A Streetcar Named Desire*. Lora rushes off to find the agent who presumably can help her land a part, but learns instead that "it's bound to be a blockbuster— but all cast." Jessica Tandy and Kim Hunter got there first.

The art directors on *Imitation of Life* cleverly used the photos and partitions of Rodney's to link that sequence visually and psychologically with the following one, which takes place in the reception room and private office of Allen Loomis, theatrical agent. When Lora Meredith walks in, she finds herself encircled by actors—live ones awaiting their appointments with Loomis, and dozens of show-business photographs on the wall. These gaze down like secular saints. Here, too, a partition separates the outer office from Himself, suggesting a pen to contain those supplicants who have turned out for a cattle call.

On her way to Loomis, Lana Turner is photographed in long shot, walking down a corridor that stretches halfway to the vanishing point. In spite of Lora Meredith's beauty, ambition, and poise, she is dwarfed by her surroundings, and by the daunting quest for an agent. Once among the "cattle," however, Lora breaks out with a stroke of chutzpah, announcing herself as Miss Meredith who has been sent by Robert Hayes of International Pictures. This is one of the more obvious imitations in the story. Although her glamour pose intimidates Loomis's secretary, played by scratchy-voiced Sandra Gould, to us she's no more convincing here than later, when she's imitating a megatalented stage actress. Sirk is having a bit of fun with Lana in his foreign-flavored, good-natured satire on the lure and duplicity of American showbiz.

Sandra Gould

They don't make character actors like Sandra Gould anymore, but they should. She belonged to the Thelma Ritter school of comedy: street-smart New York accent, cynical wisecracks, accentuated dowdiness, and possessing all the qualities of your favorite aunt. It's no surprise that she was born in Brooklyn. The year was 1916, although later she successfully subtracted ten years from that date. Her revisionism skewed chronology. Journalists, for instance, wrote that she made her first Broadway appearance at age nine in *Fly Away Home,* starring Montgomery Clift. But Sandra was nineteen when the play opened in 1935.

She started out in radio, eventually making more than a thousand appearances on popular shows of the thirties and forties hosted by the likes of Jack Benny, Bob Hope, and Red Skelton. In the midforties, she replaced Shirley Booth on the hit broadcast *Duffy's Tavern.*

In the fifties and sixties, Sandra became a familiar face in television comedies and dramas such as *I Love Lucy* and *The Twilight Zone.* Her TV career lasted almost until the day she died, for she appeared on an episode of *Veronica's Closet* in 1999, the year of her death. Her biggest break, however, came in 1966, when she was offered the part of Gladys Kravitz, Samantha's nosy neighbor, on *Bewitched,* replacing Alice Pearce, who had recently died. At first Sandra refused, for she had been a good friend of Pearce and felt that it would be too painful to assume her role. Then, too, Sandra was still mourning her husband, broadcast executive Larry Berns, who had recently died after a long illness. Eventually she did accept the role that made her known to millions of viewers. On several occasions, however, when the director absentmindedly called her "Alice," Sandra burst into tears and ran to her dressing room. (Sandra Gould and Alice Pearce both appeared in the 1964 film, *Dear Heart,* starring Glenn Ford and Geraldine Page. Their one scene together

(continued)

occurs at a national convention of postmasters in New York, when Pearce, wearing a hat that looks like an inverted white cabbage, almost collides with Gould in a hotel lobby.)

Sandra played small roles in some thirty pictures, designed costume jewelry that for a time was sold by Saks and other department stores, and wrote two books: *Always Say Maybe,* a tongue-in-cheek manual on how to catch a man, and *Sexpots and Pans,* an illustrated guide to cooking for forty-seven different kinds of men. As a Sunday painter, she claimed to have sold more than two hundred of her pictures. In addition to her acting career and her avocations, Sandra was a volunteer with several charities, including Meals on Wheels, and Actors and Others for Animals. Her devotion to her first husband during the years of his illness was greatly commended in Hollywood, for he was hospitalized forty-eight times. Her second husband, director Hollingsworth Morse, also predeceased her.

Although remembered for her comedy roles, Gould started out as a dramatic actress and occasionally appeared in little-theatre dramas around Los Angeles. After one such play, Jimmy Durante, with whom she had worked many times, greeted her backstage with these words: "Geeze, kid, I didn't know you had *talent.*"

Robert Alda, playing the sleazy agent Allen Loomis, almost steals the long sequence—seven minutes—from Lana Turner. (It's actually a two-part sequence, the first of which takes place around midday, the second when Lana returns to his office that night.) This may be Alda's best film performance. To be sure, he possessed the qualities to balance, and to counterbalance, Lana, and Sirk exploited Alda's imposing physique and his stage expertise to that purpose.

Since the camera feasts on Lana throughout the sequence, many actors would have succumbed. But Alda had actor's tricks up his sleeve, the first one sartorial. His initial preparation for the role of Allen Loomis was to have his wardrobe made by his own agent's tailor, a stroke of Method realism not governed by the Actors Studio. Although he had appeared in only two plays prior to *Imitation of Life,* Alda had mastered important stage techniques, along with the ability to adapt them to film acting. (For his Broadway debut, he created the role of Sky Masterson in *Guys and Dolls,* and remained with the show throughout much of its run, which lasted from 1950–1953. He won the 1951 Tony Award for Best Actor in a Musical. Alda's other Broadway appearance prior to *Imitation of Life* came in 1956, when he and Linda Darnell costarred in *Harbor Lights,* which closed after two performances.)

Actors with stage training can, in a sense, act circles around those with experience before the camera only. Sometimes that training serves them well, at other times it's a handicap, especially when it leads to showy, self-conscious acting. Many of the best cinema actors honed their skills on Broadway, and built film careers that incorporated their stage background: Barbara Stanwyck, James Cagney, Bette Davis, Spencer Tracy, Marlon Brando. Conversely, it's usually apparent when a top movie star lacks such seasoning: Lana Turner, Marilyn Monroe, Frank Sinatra, Rita Hayworth, William Holden. I don't mean to denigrate these stars, or others, whose screen acting, though of a different species, can bring enormous aesthetic and emotional pleasure, just as stage actors on the screen can stumble on their own technical arabesques; think of the Barrymores, Helen Hayes, Geraldine Page. Actors of this ilk prove that less technique would be more.

Earlier I referred to Robert Alda's tricks, a term not meant pejoratively. They belong to a good actor's arsenal and include gestures, bits of business, and body language that supplement the actor's voice, costumes, and physical presence. When Sandra Gould ushers Lana into his office, Lana sits down in a chair and faces him across the desk. There she remains, a sumptuous statue. Alda, meanwhile, deftly establishes Allen Loomis as a busy and successful theatrical agent, as well as the kind whose cologne is a bit too apparent, and who sucks on breath mints before entering elevators. As soon as Lana sits down, he picks up a cigar from a box, unwraps it without taking his eyes off her as they exchange dialogue, asks, "Do you mind?" then sits, lights his cigar with a heavy silver lighter, and replaces the lighter on his desk. He turns on the oily, faux charm to answer a phone call from "Lillian." Alda uses eyes, eyebrows, face, hands—his whole body—as well as props to show us Loomis. Lana, on the other hand, only *tells* us who Lora Meredith is. She relies on dialogue—plus her looks and her outfits—so that twenty minutes into the picture she's still an acquaintance, not an intimate.

At the end of the sequence, when Lana, outraged because he made a pass, flings the mink coat at him, Alda regards it, baffled. As he caresses the fur, we see him thinking . . . of the next pair of shoulders he'll drape it over. In his subsequent scenes throughout the picture—all of them brief—Alda plays Loomis as weak, overpowered by the supposed talents on whom he makes money: Lora Meredith and other stars of the theatre, and the playwright David Edwards. Alda, with his Mephistophelian looks and weapons-grade portrayal, makes it clear that Loomis is brutal under the cheap charm. For instance, when Lora's audition goes sour, and David Edwards dismisses her, he demurs: "I might as well confess, David. She's not really my client."

Like all good actors, Robert Alda communicates comfort in his environment. In that, the art direction serves him well, for his private office looks expensive, "classy" with just enough flash to impress his dependents. In it we see a wet bar, a green leather sofa—the casting couch—and a mink coat that female clients can check out like books from a library. ("I haven't been seen with a girl without a mink since the heat wave of '39," he informs Lora.) Renoiresque paintings hang on his walls, and an antique poster for "La Vie Boheme." These may well have belonged to Ross Hunter, for he often lent his own art works—covered by studio insurance—to tone up the look of his productions. The walls themselves are painted in hues of lilac and almond, with curtains of a soft golden peach. Surely an ironical view of such places, which more often resemble the Dickensian purlieus of the Marshalsea prison.

Cinematography, especially in the second part of the Loomis sequence, also underlines his character. After her initial lunchtime foray, when Loomis invites her to a party, Lora Meredith presumably takes the subway back to Brooklyn, changes into a slinky black sheath cocktail dress, and reappears at the agent's darkened office in the evening.

When she enters the deserted reception room, we might be watching a German film made at UFA thirty years earlier—or a forties film noir: low angles, shadows, foreboding compositions. This outer office, abuzz with theatre folk during the day, now is deserted and ominous. Lora sashays through the swing door that separates outer office from inner.

Behind her, it flaps back and forth like a gallows. She wheels around as though under attack. And no wonder. Precoital jazz underscore sets the place up not as the scene of a murder, but of Loomis's intended ravishment.

To start with, there was Alfonso Giuseppe Giovanni Roberto D'Abruzzo. With an array of given names to choose from, the young man removed the *o* from Roberto and joined the first two letters of Alfonso to the first two of D'Abruzzo. Hence, Robert Alda. Born in New York in 1914, he studied architecture for two years at New York University. Later, he recalled how he earned money for tuition: "I was paid $24.50 a week to work as a draftsman on plans for what finally became Radio City. Then I entered a singing contest, and won. The prize was $25—fifty cents more than I made in a week. I said, 'This is for me!'"

Alda sang on the radio, in nightclubs, and in various semiprofessional shows, performing in Borscht Belt resorts in the Catskills as a singing straight man in late-thirties burlesque. Elsewhere in burlesque, he appeared with Abbott and Costello and Phil Silvers.

One day in the early forties, a Warner Bros. executive from Hollywood spotted Alda walking down Broadway. Recognizing him from burlesque, the executive stopped Alda to tell him the studio was planning a bio pic about George Gershwin. He could almost guarantee Alda the role if he would go to Hollywood and make a screen test. Alda recalled that "when Perc Westmore, the makeup man, got through with me I *was* Gershwin."

In the film, Alda is upstaged by those Gershwin tunes, but it doesn't matter. This picture required a minimum of acting, since it's more about the talent than the man. Although *Rhapsody in Blue* was filmed in 1943, it was held for release until 1945. Meanwhile, Warner Bros. insisted on keeping Alda hidden away so that he would be a fresh face when the picture finally came out. The actor grew restless. His long period of enforced inactivity soured him on movies, yet in order to meet contract obligations he was forced to make over half-a-dozen pictures before he could escape to the New York stage. These include such run-of-the-mill works as *Cinderella Jones* (1946), *The Man I Love* (1947), and *Homicide* (1949).

Ironically, Alda is probably known to more fans for a schlocky horror movie made during this down period than for any other role: *The Beast with Five Fingers* (1946). It's another one about piano playing, although this time a severed hand tinkles the keys. Peter Lorre, conveying the desperate insect side of his nature that turns him into a sick allegory, probably accounts for the film's cult status. Robert Alda, here as elsewhere, specializes in smooth insincerity. He dusts every sentence with light irony like sugar cookies on a tray, e.g., "This way to the grieving relatives."

The rest of Alda's career, up to his death in 1986, reads like a roadmap of zigzag diversity. In 1950, he made *Tarzan and the Slave Girl,* the following year *Mr. Universe*. On TV he hosted *What's Your Bid?* for several months in 1953 and appeared on countless television shows in later decades, from *The Lucy Show* to *Trapper John, M.D.* In the midfifties, he moved to Italy, where he made a number of films with titles like *Il sepolcro dei re* (released in this country as *Cleopatra's Daughter*). Soon after his arrival in Italy, he met the actress Flora Marino, whom he marrried after an acrimonious divorce from his first wife. (The actor Alan Alda is from the first marriage. Antony Alda, also an actor, is from the second.)

Lee Goodman, as the photographer in what the production budget labels a "Shoddy Photo Studio," is none too nice to poor Lora Meredith. He obviously doesn't know she's going up and up and up. "How could you sneeze?" he chides when she ruins his focus. Then: "You were wonderful, Henry," he pointedly compliments the drooling Saint Bernard, as if to underline that Lora wasn't.

Goodman, at the time, was a seasoned comedian of the Carleton Carpenter–Tommy Tune brand, meaning lanky, with a studied airiness. As a child (né Leonard Goodman, in 1923) in Beechhurst, Queens, he was so hyperkinetic that a physician diagnosed Saint Vitus' dance, a grim medical slipup, apparently, since the same doctor prescribed tap dancing as the cure for the little boy's caffeinated energy.

And it worked, according to Goodman's sister, Effie Grubb, who spoke to me recently about her late brother's career. "He became a fabulous tap dancer!" she exclaimed, so good, in fact, that tap, along with his other showbiz talents, landed him a job on *The Children's Hour*, a New York radio show. Since the passing of time menaced the career of a child performer, "my brother stayed nine years old for five years," laughed Effie. On Broadway, the youngster made his debut in Noël Coward's *Conversation Piece* in 1934, followed a year later by a small role in *Dead End*.

After high school, and three years in the army, Goodman teamed up with the playwright and novelist James Kirkwood Jr. in the late forties to form the comedy team of Kirkwood and Goodman. Performing skits and comic routines similar to the later ones of Rowan and Martin and the Smothers Brothers, the two young men tried out in an amateur contest at the Number One Fifth Avenue Bar, a popular club. They won. The prize was a two-week engagement, which stretched into twenty weeks owing to their popularity. Kirkwood and Goodman later appeared in other New York supper clubs such as Le Ruban Bleu, Cafe Society, and in Hollywood at the Mocambo.

On June 20, 1948, the pair were guests on the very first telecast of *Toast of the Town* (later renamed *The Ed Sullivan Show*), along with Dean Martin and Jerry Lewis, Rodgers and Hammerstein, and other variety acts of the kind much loved by Sullivan. In 1950, they appeared in the Broadway musical revue *Dance Me a Song*, along with Bob Fosse and Wally Cox. Goodman's later Broadway shows include *A Funny Thing Happened on the Way to the Forum, Company,* and *On the Twentieth Century*. He also toured with Chita Rivera in the out-of-town production of *Sweet Charity*. When Goodman died in 1988, Rivera offered his family a room in her newly opened restaurant on Forty-second Street for the memorial service.

Lee Goodman's sister told me that when *Imitation of Life* opened its sell-out run in New York at the Roxy Theatre, his mother and his aunt eagerly queued up to see him in it, both very proud. When the picture ended, however, these ladies, like many others, were still dabbing their eyes when they reached the powder room.

24 | JACK WESTON AND THE CITIZEN'S ARREST IN BEVERLY HILLS

*I*n 1937, at Glenville High School in Cleveland, Ohio, two nice Jewish boys tried out for the lead in the class play. Jack Weinstein got the part; the loser was Martin Fuss.

Twenty-one years later, in Hollywood, pudgy-faced Jack Weston, né Weinstein, is playing the stage manager in a play-within-a-film. The film's producer is glamorous Ross Hunter, né Fuss. This play is *Stopover*, by David Edwards, and it marks the Broadway debut of Lora Meredith, "an actress who heretofore has been hiding her light under a bushel," as stated in the pastiche of a *New York Times* review. (*Stopover* is a Sirk in-joke. It's the title of the novel from which his 1953 film, *All I Desire,* was adapted. Sirk wanted *Stopover* as the film title, but was overruled by Ross Hunter, who preferred the more florid one.)

At the audition, Weston's stage manager isn't very nice to Lora. "Come on, come on!" he snaps. "Let's have your offstage line." When Lora blows the audition, his instincts are vindicated: "Okay, sister, this way out!"

But the playwright reconsiders, Lora lands the part, and on opening night, as the crowd roars its approval long past the final curtain, she borrows a dime from this very stage manager to call her young daughter, Susie. "I'll pay you back," she assures him, but like all of New York, he is now at her feet: "Don't rush. You'll be around a long time," he fawns.

Queen Bess

"This should be a Pulitzer Prize play for David Edwards, for tonight we saw the ranking comedy of the season, marvelously performed by Geraldine Moore and Preston Mitchell." Just one of the raves for *Stopover*, whose leading lady, Geraldine Moore, is played by Bess Flowers, aka "the Queen of the Extras." In real life, Bess was never the lead in anything, yet the number of her screen appearances exceeds that of virtually everyone else in Hollywood. At last count, she had 750 film and TV credits on IMDb.com, with others yet to be discovered. Look for her especially at dressy occasions such as cocktail parties and evenings at the theatre.

After writing about Bess Flowers in a previous book, *All About "All About Eve,"* I received several letters asking more about her. How did she get her start in pictures? Where is she buried? One might say that Bess, who wasn't well known, is well remembered.

At that time I had not read the article that film scholar Anthony Slide wrote in 1984 for *Films in Review*. He points out that "Bess Flowers was noted for the style, quality, and quantity of gowns in her wardrobe, and it was her ability to wear costumes with panache that gained for her the title of 'Hollywood's Best-Dressed Extra.'" Over the years, she purchased many of the elegant outfits she wore onscreen, with the result that studios would often telephone to ask whether she owned a particular kind of gown. If so, they hired her on the spot.

For her *Stopover* curtain call, Bess wears a high-fashion black gown; at the cast party afterward, one that's equally chic, though obscured by a silvery-blue silk or taffeta wrap. Both outfits rival Jean-Louis's creations for Lana, and properly so, since Geraldine Moore, at this point in the story, is David Edwards's big star—but soon to be replaced by Lora Meredith.

Bess was born in Sherman, Texas, in 1898. In her early twenties, she pinched money from her mother's sugar bowl to buy a train ticket to New York and become a Broadway actress. At the station,

(continued)

however, she suddenly decided to try California. Later she said, "I got a job the first day I ever went to an interview." Although she didn't recall the film's title, she told Slide that the studio was Metro, and the year 1922.

The following year, she appeared—uncredited—in Chaplin's *A Woman of Paris*. In it, she plays the statuesque mannequin "who is naked except for a band of cloth wrapped around her body which is slowly unrolled as she stands on a podium." In 1923, Bess married Cullen Tate, one of Cecil B. DeMille's assistant directors. Following Tate's death in 1947, she married an executive at Columbia, William S. Holman.

Before extras had their own union, they often endured demeaning conditions in the workplace. Not Bess. For years, she refused assignments at Universal because of dirty toilets, a situation surely rectified by the time of *Imitation of Life*. At another studio, she was interviewed by a man who made himself a bit too comfortable for her liking. "I walked out," she recalled. "I don't approve of a man meeting a woman with feet up on the desk."

By the time of her sixty-fifth birthday, Bess had reigned long enough. The Queen of the Extras abdicated after *Good Neighbor Sam* in 1964. For a while, she worked as the rental agent for an apartment complex, then retired to a bungalow at the Motion Picture Country Home in Woodland Hills, where she died in 1984. Her remains were scattered in the Rose Garden of Chapel of the Pines Crematory in Los Angeles. Surveying her long and unusual career, Bess Flowers said, "I made a good living. I'm lazy, so I never took anything that was hard. I was always good to Bess."

Anyone looking for a screen example of the schlemiel might name Jack Weston, but that designation would cover only one of his facets. He also played crooks and killers: in *Wait Until Dark,* he and Alan Arkin terrorized the blind Audrey Hepburn until her excruciatingly tardy rescue.

After army service in World War Two, Weston got a job in *South Pacific* on Broadway in 1949. Other theatre work followed until 1958, when

Weston and his first wife, Marjorie Redmond, who were performing in *Bells Are Ringing*, abruptly gave notice to the play and set out for Los Angeles in search of bigger parts and more money. Planning to stay for a few months, they remained for eighteen years. Weston worked steadily in television and in a number of pictures, including *Stage Struck* (1958), *Please Don't Eat the Daisies* (1960), and *A New Leaf* (1971), directed by Elaine May. Years later, he also appeared in her famous turkey, *Ishtar* (1987).

Weston's best comic role was surely that of Gaetano Proclo in *The Ritz*. As a Cleveland garbage collector who takes refuge in a gay bathhouse from his murderous gangster brother-in-law, Weston gave an unforgettable performance on Broadway in 1975–76. Richard Lester's film adaptation of Terrence McNally's farce failed to capture the madcap effervescence of the original, though at least it preserved a likeness of Weston's comic portrayal, as well as those of Rita Moreno, Jerry Stiller, and others from the play.

Jack Weston didn't like living in Los Angeles. But he hadn't liked Cleveland, either, and like all New Yorkers, he complained endlessly about the city. He once declared that he hated every minute of his long sojourn in Southern California except when he was in front of the camera. "Every afternoon at three," he said, "something hits this town. It's called 'flash boredom.' If you're an actor and not working and you don't play tennis or golf, you can go stark raving mad."

Did a sudden attack of flash boredom account for Weston's bizarre dust-up with the police in 1964? Or did he just dislike what Barry Goldwater threatened to do to the country if elected president? Maybe it was just an instance of cross-eyed fate. Too bad someone didn't film the episode as part of a TV series. But *Seinfeld,* the best fit, was not yet a gleam in the eye of ten-year-old Jerry.

Peter Bart, writing in *The New York Times* in March of 1965, mentioned Jack Weston as one of those character actors whose names are generally not well known but whose "faces are vaguely recognizable to every regular moviegoer and TV fan." Bart continued his report by noting that "in recent weeks, oddly enough, Jack Weston's name has been cropping up constantly in trade gossip—but not in an especially flattering light. Indeed, the curious, Kafkaesque saga of Jack Weston shows signs of becoming a minor cause célèbre in show business circles and a major embarrassment for the entertainment industry."

One small incident on October 14, 1964, set in motion a series of increasingly comical—and sinister—events. (Proof that history repeats: One could change the dates and the names and have a CNN story redolent of Bush-era Stalinism.) Scheduled to have lunch with an old friend at a Beverly Hills restaurant, Weston pulled into a parking space, got out, and was sliding a coin into the parking meter when he felt a light pressure against his shoulder, almost as if a large bird had touched down. Turning, he discovered an American flag half enveloping him. Somehow, the flag had become dislodged from the pole where it was mounted.

Weston took the flag in his hands, as anyone might, trying to decide what to do with it. But: the actor had parked his car in front of Goldwater for President headquarters, 9388 Santa Monica Boulevard. Suddenly, he heard a shrill uproar: two shrieking elderly ladies who flew out the front door of Goldwater for President.

Epithets flew—"Pinko," "Commie rat"—along with much invective besides. Soon the peaceful, patriotic sidewalk had become a war zone. But Francis Scott Key, had he happened along that day, would have seen that the flag was still there. And that one of the ladies was trying to make a citizen's arrest of the burly actor.

Weston tried to explain that the flag had toppled on him, not vice versa. He later said, in droll understatement, that his credibility was not especially enhanced in the ladies' eyes by the Lyndon Johnson–Hubert Humphrey stickers plastered on his car.

The melee went on until finally, in exasperation, Weston told his accusers to "Go to hell," and drove away. His adversaries, however, wrote down the license plate number and phoned the cops. The incident was evidently not considered a national emergency, for it took three days for the police to arrest him on a charge of desecrating the American flag, disturbing the peace, and malicious mischief. Weston was booked, fingerprinted, and released on five-hundred-dollars bail.

At first, Weston relished the comic side of the donneybrook. The media had other ideas, however, and next day the headlines carried banners such as "Actor Arrested for Defiling Flag." This was no longer funny. Weston decided to fight the charges in court. In December of 1964, the month after Goldwater's landslide defeat by Johnson, Jack Weston was acquitted of the charge of disrespect to the flag. He was found guilty, however, of the lesser charge of disturbing the peace.

During the eight-hour trial, "the ladies presented their case and contradicted themselves at various points of their testimony. Weston repeated the explanation he had offered the ladies. Municipal Court Judge Jacques Leslie dismissed the charges, noting, 'It is inconceivable to me that Mr. Weston, who fought for this flag as a combat machine gunner through the battle of Cassino, through the near-tragedy of the Anzio beachhead and on through the campaign of the Po Valley, could by any stretch of the imagination . . . treat or allow the flag to be treated in any manner but with the honor to which it is due.' The judge levied a fifty-dollar fine against Weston, however, for telling the two ladies to go to hell—a violation of a Beverly Hills ordinance."

No headlines announced the judge's decision. A small item appeared deep inside the *Los Angeles Times,* headed, somewhat misleadingly, "Actor Found Guilty of Disturbance." Like the *Times,* Hollywood dwelt on the minor guilty verdict rather than the more important acquittal. TV producers were especially reluctant to hire Weston, although he did get a film role in *The Cincinnati Kid* (1965). Meanwhile, hate mail continued to arrive for a long time.

Pauline Kael once wrote, "The movie industry is always frightened, and is always proudest of films that celebrate courage." Indeed, Jack Weston scared the daylights out of Hollywood, which had absolutely nothing to fear. As if to provide a Q.E.D. to Kael's assertion, his first TV assignment after the ludicrous fiasco was in an episode of *Twelve O'Clock High,* the ABC series patterned after the 1949 film. This series chronicled the adventures of the brave men of the 918th Bombardment Group of the U.S. Eighth Air Force, which was stationed in England and flew bombing missions into the German-occupied nations of Europe during World War Two. Weston was vindicated, at last, through fictional bravery.

I have this theory," said playwright Suzan-Lori Parks, "that the soul is like a lizard's tail. If you pull it off, another one will grow back in its place. But repeated abuses will give you a lot of scar tissue."

Joel Fluellen, like many African Americans in Hollywood, must have borne considerable scar tissue, though it's invisible on the screen. For half a century he played roles for which he was overqualified, yet he triumphed as any good actor would wish: He brought something fresh to each characterization, no matter how fleeting. It's a pleasure to watch such an actor, whose every gesture, facial expression, and intonation has a reason, yet his technique is hidden out of sight.

As Annie Johnson's minister in *Imitation of Life,* he consoles the dying woman with the quiet strength of his presence. At the end of her funeral, as the coffin is carried from the church, he recites Psalm CXXI—"I will lift up mine eyes unto the hills, from whence cometh my help"— with resonant authority. Fluellen might have declaimed the psalm, like a Shakespearean exhibition; some actors would not scruple to steal a scene from a corpse. No doubt Joel had the vocal skill to do so. Instead, he reads from the Bible like a well-spoken minister. (In earlier times, clergy, like actors, received vocal training as a professional basic.)

Those who knew Joel Fluellen well recall his loyalty, and his cooking. At his memorial service in 1990, Sidney Poitier drew knowing laughter when he said, "I carry two extra inches on my waist because of that man." (Poitier and Fluellen appeared together in two pictures, *Porgy and Bess* [1959] and *A Raisin in the Sun* [1961].)

Born in Monroe, Louisiana, around 1910, Fluellen moved to Chicago as a young man. There he worked as a milliner and also as a store clerk. An aspiring actor, he met Louise Beavers, one of the stars of the 1934 *Imitation of Life,* who took a motherly interest in the dapper young man. She suggested he come to Hollywood, and in 1936 he did so.

A year later, Fluellen played a bit part in the all-black gangster film *Dark Manhattan.* He appeared, uncredited, in other black-cast films and eventually in mainstream productions such as *The Flame of New Orleans* (1941), starring Marlene Dietrich. Like most African-American actors, he had few choices beyond servant roles, and those usually minus screen credit.

Having gained a toehold in pictures, however, Fluellen succeeded in breaking out of stereotypical roles. In *The Jackie Robinson Story* (1950), he played Robinson's brother, Mack, who had been a silver medalist at the 1936 Olympics in Berlin, but who, even with a college degree, could find work only as a street cleaner. As a florist in *Walk Softly, Stranger* (1950), starring Joseph Cotten, Fluellen edged away, once more, from the roles black actors were expected to play.

In *Seven Angry Men* (1955), which starred Raymond Massey as the abolitionist John Brown, Fluellen played the stationmaster at Harper's Ferry, the site of Brown's electrifying raid in 1859. One can imagine Fluellen being gratified by this role, small though it was, because the picture dealt with events seldom pictured on movie screens. His tenacity seems unwavering, for he worked steadily in films and on television for fifty years. By midcareer, Fluellen was playing roles that any actor might be proud of: the minister in *Imitation of Life,* Bobo in *A Raisin in the Sun* (1961), and Tick in *The Great White Hope* (1970). Bobo is a small role but an important one: he delivers the devastating news to Walter Lee Younger (Sidney Poitier) that the third partner in their scheme has absconded with the family's insurance money, thus plunging the Youngers into a desperate crisis.

In *The Great White Hope,* Fluellen plays the manager of Jack Jefferson (James Earl Jones), a black boxing champion based on Jack Johnson. In one of his biggest screen roles, Fluellen at last can exercise his versatility. When Jefferson's career hits the skids, he and his entourage perform a demeaning, and painfully ironic, stage version of *Uncle Tom's Cabin*. As Topsy, Fluellen uses a Butterfly McQueen accent, then sings a Dixieland jive number. (Had Fluellen lived in later decades, he might have played this kind of bitter satire in films like Spike Lee's *Bamboozled*.)

Near the end of *The Great White Hope*, when Tick brings in the corpse of Jefferson's lover, Eleanor Backman (Jane Alexander), Fluellen keens his line: "She threw herself down the well, busted her neck." Here he echoes a subsidiary character from Shakespeare, whose plays Fluellen might have performed had he belonged to a later generation of actors. After delivering that line, he weeps hysterically, like a lost child, for the Jane Alexander character was Tick's one true friend.

Fluellen's best performance may be in *The Learning Tree* (1969), directed by Gordon Parks. Although allotted no more than five or ten minutes of screen time, he gives the one real performance in this earnest picture by an inexperienced director. As blind Uncle Rob, in blackened glasses, Fluellen swivels his head in odd, arrhythmic beats to show that Uncle Rob's *ears* focus, rather than his eyes. Head bobbing as though attached to springs, Fluellen accomplishes the difficult feat of creating a vivid character without showing us his eyes. In other scenes, guided by his cane, Fluellen takes jerky microsteps with the unnerving precision of a blind man in a D. W. Griffith silent. Every step must have been measured out by Fluellen and not by the director, who was innocent of nuance, and yet not one movement looks calculated.

Watching *The Learning Tree* now, we may flinch if we know what lay ahead for Joel Fluellen. It's poignant, and eerie, to see him portray the blind man with such acumen, for twenty years after, in the late eighties, Fluellen himself went blind from diabetes and glaucoma. Eventually, blindness so depressed him that he committed suicide.

Fluellen's other memorable roles include *Friendly Persuasion* (1956), in which he plays an escaped slave who works as a farmhand in Indiana for the Quaker family headed by Gary Cooper and Dorothy McGuire; *The Autobiography of Miss Jane Pittman* (1974), where he plays Uncle Isom, an older freed slave who cautions his fellow freedmen to remain as workers at the plantation rather than facing the dangers of the unknown

North; and *Man Friday* (1975), a rum update of the Defoe novel told from Friday's point of view.

Only scattered biographical details exist on Joel Fluellen. The fullest account of his life in Hollywood was assembled by Donald Bogle, the author of many valuable books on African Americans in show business. Bogle, however, shows a peevish disdain for Fluellen in two recent books, *Dorothy Dandridge* and *Bright Boulevards, Bold Dreams: The Story of Black Hollywood*. Since Bogle himself did not know the actor, his unflattering characterization of Fluellen comes from informants in the Dandridge circle: Dorothy's sister, Vivian; Geri Branton, Dandridge's closest friend; and Dorothy Nicholas Morrow, Dandridge's sister-in-law. These women, intimately involved in Dandridge's family conflicts and privy to the pressures and frustrations of her career, seem to resent her close friendship with Joel Fluellen. This dynamic is common in a star's entourage, where each member wants exclusive rights to his or her commodity. I consider such testimony on Joel Fluellen's character and his motives suspect, seemingly tinted by obscure jealousies and internecine squabbles. Friends and colleagues like Juanita Moore and Robert Hooks have only positive things to say about Joel. When I asked Juanita, who knew everyone in the Dandridge circle, she confirmed my suspicions of envy and jealousy vis-à-vis Fluellen.

Robert Hooks said, "Joel knew his craft, and he was the kindest and most respectful person that I've ever met. And respectful not just of his colleagues, but of everyone. People loved Joel because he was kind and real. Nothing phony about him. He was a man at peace."

Bogle's references to Fluellen as a "social climber," a "ruthless snob," and a "gossip" notwithstanding, he sketched the actor's career, and his long friendship with Dorothy Dandridge, in more detail than any previous writer had done. In the following paragraphs, therefore, I follow Bogle's account, minus the epithets.

According to him, "When *The Green Pastures* was being filmed [in 1936], Fluellen joined the extras who were picked up by a studio truck to go out to Warner Bros. Finding it hard to adjust to the city, he briefly returned to Chicago, but the lure of the klieg lights soon brought him back to L.A." In addition to working as a studio extra and in bit parts,

Fluellen "also designed hats and catered parties" during his early years in Los Angeles.

Bogle places Fluellen not only in the context of black Hollywood but of gay Hollywood, as well: "At one time he had an affair with a wealthy older white man who kept him dressed in the latest fashion and entertained with giddy nights on the town. At another time, he dallied with one of Hollywood's big athletic stars." Robert Hooks said, "We knew he was gay, but those outside the industry didn't."

Remaining friends with Louise Beavers, Fluellen also befriended Hattie McDaniel and Billie Holiday. Bogle claims that Fluellen made a point of charming Ruby Dandridge, Dorothy's mother, and Ruby's female lover, Ma-Ma, for the sole purpose of snaring Dorothy in his net. But since Fluellen was, in Bogle's own words, "an attractive man—tall, solidly built, brown-skinned—a good conversationalist, intelligent and well read, the perfect dinner guest when a hostess was one man short," why would he have needed intermediaries? Dorothy Dandridge, or anyone else, would surely have welcomed his friendship.

Near the end of Dorothy's life, when her drinking had grown excessive, Joel discussed the problem with Ruby, Dorothy's mother, and urged her to intervene. Typical of alcoholics, Dorothy spewed fury when she found out. She ended her long friendship with Joel, bitterly claiming that he had betrayed her. When I discussed this unhappy rupture with Juanita Moore, she staunchly defended Joel. "He loved Dorothy, he really loved her," Juanita said. "She might be alive today if she had listened to Joel."

In 1984, two decades after Dorothy's death, Joel led the campaign to commemorate her with a star on Hollywood Boulevard's Walk of Fame. Never well-off financially, he contributed his own funds to help defray expenses, even though he was already elderly and in failing health. An example, surely, of what Ivan Dixon had in mind when he said, at Fluellen's memorial service, "Joel was warm, generous, courageous—he was always doing something for someone."

Joel Fluellen would surely have wished to be remembered for two things: his acting and his activism. Long before civil rights became a familiar concept, he worked zealously to pull down barriers in Hollywood.

Just as he himself avoided defamatory portrayals, so he wanted for all black actors the opportunity to play a range of characters—not necessarily positive or politically correct, but true. (Douglas Sirk's use of the handsome black actor James Edwards as an air force fighter pilot in *Battle Hymn* in 1957 is an early, and rare, example of the kind of casting Fluellen, and others, lobbied for.)

In 1947, Fluellen, a member of the Actors Laboratory Theatre in Hollywood, brought in eighteen young black performers, primarily women, one of whom was Juanita Moore. As the red scare spread, those associated with the Lab endured endless harassment because of the supposed left-wing slant of its plays and players. Harassment turned to persecution in the McCarthy era, when some of its members ended up on the blacklist. Among those blacklisted was Betsy Blair, who described the Lab as a place where "we had classes, warm-up exercises, scenes to do, plays to put on. There were excellent teachers. . . . It was a hive of artistic and political activity."

As one of the most liberal organizations in Hollywood, the Actors Lab might be expected to have expunged racism from its precincts. Such, however, was not the case. Shortly after Joel Fluellen managed to enroll his protegés, he accused the Lab of de facto segregation, for these young black actors had been shunted into "special" evening classes. (Dorothy Dandridge was dropped from one of the Lab's important productions because it was thought that white audiences might not accept her in the role.)

As a member of the Screen Actors Guild, Fluellen was a vocal advocate for better treatment of African-American performers in Hollywood. As early as 1938, the SAG had begun collecting articles from black newspapers for a file designated "the Negro Question." These articles included factual accounts of Hollywood discrimination, and editorials deploring it. In 1944, Lena Horne and Rex Ingram were elected to the board. Two years later, Betsy Blair, married at the time to SAG board member Gene Kelly, proposed a resolution that was passed by the membership in the fall of 1946 with 992 in favor and 34 opposed. I reprint that resolution here because it paints a vivid tableau of the Hollywood prejudice that Joel Fluellen and his allies, black and white, battled against.

WHEREAS, Negro actors have a long and honorable history in American theatre and in the motion picture industry and played an important part in the formation of our Guild, and

WHEREAS, unemployment among our Negro Guild members has reached a point more alarming than at any time in Guild history, and

WHEREAS, Negro parts are being omitted from a great many screenplays and are, in many cases, actually being cut out of books and plays when adapted to the screen, and

WHEREAS, in several instances producers have even gone to the length of using white actors in Negro roles,

NOW, THEREFORE, BE IT RESOLVED that the Screen Actors Guild use all of its power to oppose discrimination against Negroes in the motion picture industry, and

BE IT FURTHER RESOLVED that a special committee be set up at once to implement this policy and to meet with representatives of the Screen Writers Guild and the Screen Directors Guild and the Motion Picture Producers Association in order to establish in the industry a policy of presenting Negro characters on the screen in the true relation they bear to American life.

The *Los Angeles Times,* in its obituary of Joel Fluellen, stated that he "introduced resolutions to the Screen Actors Guild asking the group to use all its powers to oppose discrimination against Negroes in the motion picture industry. He also asked SAG to form a committee. His proposals were turned down."

In a letter to the *Times* a few days later, the actress Marsha Hunt corrected one error in the obituary. "That last line," she wrote, "is in error." She explained that she served on the SAG's board of directors in 1946, and "when Mr. Fluellen's resolution came up, it did pass, a committee was formed, and I was on it, along with two others, as I recall. We visited the heads of casting departments at all the major studios, urging them to offer more and better roles, not only to black actors, but to all minority performers. We asked that they help broaden public perceptions, and to show that not all blacks were servants, nor all Filipinos houseboys, not all Chinese ran laundries, not all Japanese were gardeners, not all Indians had been scalpers, not all Italians were gangsters, and so on.

"We were received and heard politely, and told that they would do what they could. But they reminded us that they could only suggest, and that casting decisions remained with producers and directors. They warned us not to expect miracles, and indeed no miracles occurred."

Marsha Hunt concluded her letter, "But now and then, there was a surprise piece of casting, slowly—very slowly—pointing the way to a better and fairer day. So SAG deserves to be credited with a racial conscience as long ago as the mid-40s. And Joel Fluellen deserves to be remembered and honored for his early efforts to 'overcome.'"

Inevitably, Fluellen's civil rights activism, and his politics generally, led to his being blacklisted. For a time he supported himself by working as a waiter. Joel's invisibility, like that of other African-American actors, perhaps saved him from further hounding. The highly visible Paul Robeson, by contrast, endured endless torment.

Not all was acting and activism for Joel Fluellen. Sidney Poitier's remark about carrying two extra inches on his waist because of Joel's cooking might well be literally true. The aromas, and the dishes, that came from his kitchen made him renowned as a host whose invitations were coveted. In 1970, a writer from the *Los Angeles Times* called at Joel's apartment to do a feature on him, titled, "Louisiana-Born Actor's Cuisine International but Still Basically Bayou."

The first line of the article revealed that Joel cooked not only with fresh ingredients and spices, but with wit, as well, for his signature dish bore the name "Poulet Noir Qui Veut Passer Pour Blanc"—Black Chicken Passing for White. Joel told his visitor that he had cooked since childhood, having learned from his grandmother, who came from the French West Indies, and his mother. He recalled standing on a chair to reach the stove when he was seven years old. Even as a child, he pleased family palates with such dishes as baked sea bass; shrimp cooked with diced potatoes, green peppers, and onions; and various preparations of game. Later, during lean times in Hollywood, he used these skills to run a catering business.

Another visitor, Avery Clayton, whose mother was a friend of Joel's, recalled the floor-to-ceiling art in his apartment. "It was a courtyard apartment in the Adams District [southwest of Downtown and north of USC], with a garden in front," he said. "I remember especially the African art on his walls, and the sculpture." When I asked what he remembered about Joel himself, Clayton replied, "His very formal way of speaking. And the proper welcome we received to his home."

Juanita Moore called Joel Fluellen "the love of my life." Describing his final years, as blindness encroached, she recalled his saying obliquely, "Juanita, I can't live like this." She, however, didn't guess what her friend had in mind. She visited him almost every day, and when he committed suicide in February 1990, she was devastated.

Juanita ended that sad remembrance on a lighter note. "When Joel's eyesight started to fail," she said, "he still wanted to drive me places in his Volkswagen, and I'd say, 'Hell no, Joel, I'm not getting in that car with you! You come on with me.'" As this book took shape, I told Juanita that I planned a chapter on Joel, mentioning that it would be the longest piece ever done on him. She said, "Oh, thank you!" And started to cry. Then, as though addressing the spirit world, she added in a small, intimate voice, "Joel, can you hear that?"

26 | THE KIND OF PLAYWRIGHT WHO FLINGS HIS MANUSCRIPT IN THE FIRE

*W*hen Dan O'Herlihy and his wife arrived in Hollywood in 1947, they brought along a lasting touch of Ireland. Almost sixty years later, over midmorning coffee and cake, Mrs. O'Herlihy—"No, no, call me Elsie," she commanded—recalled an afternoon stroll she took when she and her husband were new in town.

Elsie, whose faint brogue, long hair, and feline face make you flash on high-spirited colleens from *The Quiet Man* or *Dancing at Lughnasa,* came upon a tall man in a cap cutting the hedge beside his house. "Hello, Donald," she blurted out, as she might have done over a fence back in Wexford, even though she didn't know him at all. She did recognize him from the screen, however, for the man was Donald Crisp, and no telling how many of his one hundred and fifty movies Elsie had seen. She caught herself: "Oh, excuse my familiarity," she faltered. Crisp brushed off the apology. "Not at all," he replied. "I wish more people would do it."

The O'Herlihys lived, at the time, on Camrose Drive, and from their patio they could hear every concert at the Hollywood Bowl. When Elsie told me this, I pictured their conviviality in the scented night, like countless others before television drove people inside.

By the time I visited, they had long since moved to a steep location in Malibu. There, alighting from my car, I felt oddly displaced, for the physical setting resembled a mountain somewhere west of Dublin. The

O'Herlihy house might have been magically transported from Macgilly-cuddy's Reeks, or grafted from the Hill of Tara. Looking through east windows, I saw wildflowers on the hillside and a far valley gray with mist. In the opposite direction, the sea.

The Sun, The Son

The O'Herlihy house itself is unlike anything you'll find in traditional Ireland. If you subtracted the art and antiques, the family memorabilia, the homey furnishings, those wildflowers on the hill, the coastal fog and salty air, and removed the house from Malibu to, say, Beverly Hills, you would behold the spare, geometrical, Modernist statement it is. Simple as a Robert Ryman white-on-white canvas, with elegant, unadorned, right-angled walls, the house stands perpendicular to the sky, absorbing endless sunlight.

Architecture runs in the family. First Dan, the architect turned actor, then Lorcan, the youngest of the O'Herlihys' five children, whose first house was the one he designed for his parents on these nine dramatic acres in Malibu. Built in 1990, when Lorcan was thirty, the house was a significant debut commission. "I asked him to build a house for the sun," said Lorcan's father, "and that's what he did."

Joseph Giovannini, writing in *Metropolitan Home,* pointed out that Lorcan "wanted to refine the box rather than break it. He designed the house with a simplicity that would let the vegetation, weather, and light register on the outside, the casual lifestyle, within. The living room, with its fourteen-foot ceiling, seems baronial, though its only luxuries are the sheer space and quality of modulated light." Lorcan said of that room, "We use it the way they use roomy kitchens in Ireland. It's an incredible sight at Christmas, when everyone in the family—fourteen of us—shows up."

Lorcan O'Herlihy was born in September 1959, five months after the premiere of *Imitation of Life.* A prodigy who entered college at sixteen, he graduated from Cal Poly San Luis Obispo, then worked

(continued)

with Kevin Roche on the Temple of Dendur at the Metropolitan Museum in New York and with I. M. Pei on the controversial addition to the Louvre. The first of Lorcan's six awards from the American Institute of Architects was for the family home in Malibu. In 1999, he was the subject of a book, *Lorcan O'Herlihy,* compiled by Oscar Riera Ojeda and Anthony Vidler, and in 2004 the Architectural League of New York selected him as one of the eight "Emerging Voices in Architecture" in the United States.

Although Dan O'Herlihy was still alive when I called, he was too ill to see me. Suffering from diabetes and other maladies, he died in February 2005, a few days before Sandra Dee. Thus, my interview with him was by proxy, and I heard about his early years as Elsie remembered them.

After elevenses, she brought out several scrapbooks commemorating her husband's career. The first, a big three-foot-by-two-foot thing, dated from the late thirties, when scrapbooks, in Ireland at least, meant business. It contained letters, clippings from Irish newspapers, and various memorabilia. The second, photos from the filming, in Mexico, of *The Adventures of Robinson Crusoe* (1954), and stills from the picture. (Directed by Buñuel, it earned a Best Actor nomination for O'Herlihy, who lost to Marlon Brando for *On the Waterfront.*)

As an extra feature on the DVD of *Robinson Crusoe,* O'Herlihy, in a 1985 interview, tells how he, as an architecture student at the National University of Ireland, fell unexpectedly into acting: "Some friends of mine went down and applied for crowd work in the Abbey Theatre. And I went down, too, joined them, and we got the work. We got ten shillings a week, which was well worthwhile to us. I started in the theatre that way. And then bigger parts, and smaller parts, and I stayed in the theatre, working at the university at the same time. When I finished the university—by now I was playing young leading roles in the Irish theatre—I was offered a role in *Odd Man Out* by Carol Reed." Reed had spotted O'Herlihy in a small role at the Abbey, Dublin's most famous playhouse.

While still a university student, O'Herlihy took a job as news an-nouncer and disc jockey on Raidió Éireann. Each night, after a stage performance, he would rush to the station on his bicycle to read the midnight news. Elsie told me that her husband ended each broadcast day with the Irish national anthem. Except for the time he didn't. "Being slightly tone deaf," she said, "one night, by mistake, Danny put on in-stead a Bing Crosby recording, which elicited a barrage of phone calls." No doubt the gaffe was forgiven by the time of O'Herlihy's most thrilling moment as an announcer. Late one night, he was handed a commu-niqué to read to the Irish nation. It announced the end of World War Two in Europe.

Soon after the success of *Odd Man Out* in 1947, producer Charles K. Feldman brought O'Herlihy to Hollywood to play Macduff in Orson Welles's *Macbeth* (1948). As a result of that performance, he was offered the role of Charles Dickens in *The Ivy Green* on Broadway in 1949, a part that required him to age from his midtwenties to his midsixties. This feat O'Herlihy accomplished with the help of six separate beards. The play closed quickly, but O'Herlihy repeated the aging process a few years later—helped along this time by eleven beards—in *Robinson Crusoe*. (To play David Edwards in *Imitation of Life,* he grew a trim moustache.)

Beginning in the late forties, O'Herlihy gave dozens of good perfor-mances in films and on television without ever becoming well known to the public. Among his more recognizable titles from the fifties are *The Blue Veil* (1951) with Jane Wyman, *The Virgin Queen* (1955) with Bette Davis, and *Home Before Dark* (1958) with Jean Simmons. After *Imitation of Life*, he made notable appearances in *Fail Safe* (1964), *MacArthur* (1977), in which he played FDR, *RoboCop* (1987), and *RoboCop 2* (1990). (Earlier, O'Herlihy had played another U.S. president. In 1972, he starred as John F. Kennedy at the Abbey Theatre in its production of *The White House*.) He also appeared, unaccountably, in a 1962 stinko "remake," *The Cabinet of Caligari,* which has nothing to do with the original classic.

Versatility was perhaps the strong point of his career: He could play any role well, though his performance is unlikely to be the one that's best remembered. O'Herlihy occupied that unnamed niche between leading man and character actor.

My visit with Elsie O'Herlihy recalled my first trip to Dublin, when the Irish history and literature I had read coalesced, at last, to form a panoramic portrait of a culture I had previously not understood. Here, on the walls, hung portraits and sketches, by Dan O'Herlihy, of James Joyce and other towering figures of the Irish Renaissance whom he had encountered as a young actor. Elsie pointed out other paintings by her husband: several street scenes, including one, with Grecoesque figures, titled *Beggar in Dublin,* and a haunting tableau of Irish fishermen carrying the coffin of one of their number along the beach before making their way to the cemetery. Elsewhere I saw antiques, including an eighteenth-century dining table. And many books, with comfortable, old-fashioned chairs to read them in.

O'Herlihy, born in 1919, came of age just as the legendary Irish writers were growing old. In one of his early appearances at the Abbey, as a super, he got an approving nod from the elderly William Butler Yeats. He played the lead in the original production of Seán O'Casey's *Red Roses for Me* in Dublin in 1943. O'Herlihy once described Yeats's great love, the fiery Irish nationalist Maud Gonne, as the most beautiful woman he had ever seen. "When I met her," he said, "she was ninety-four, dressed in black from head to foot, and with an air of ravaged beauty about her—a great, gaunt woman, six feet two inches tall, with sunken cheeks and burning eyes."

It's fitting that O'Herlihy, with such a background, spoke fluent Gaelic. On a photo for Susan Kohner when *Imitation of Life* wrapped, he wrote a Gaelic inscription, which Elsie translated, when I showed her a copy, as, "May the road rise up before you"—the first line of a traditional Irish blessing that continues, "May the wind be always at your back" and ends, "And may you be half an hour in heaven before the devil knows you're dead!"

One might say that O'Herlihy possessed the gift of language rather than gab. But up against a blarney meister like Orson Welles, he could send back better than he got. A few years after *Macbeth,* when Welles was in New York for a television production of *King Lear*, he wired O'Her-lihy: "Up To My Ears in Method Actors. Come East Do Lear." By then, O'Herlihy was working nonstop for good money. As he said later, "You never got paid if you worked for Orson, so I replied, 'Delighted To Come East Do Lear. You Doing Edgar?'" He received, of course, no reply.

One of O'Herlihy's best roles came late in his career. It was in John Huston's final film, *The Dead*, with O'Herlihy as the increasingly drunk and embarrassing Mr. Browne. As a Protestant—"he's of the other per-suasion," cautions a guest at the Epiphany celebration when the talk turns to religion—Mr. Browne delights in an attack on the pope.

When I asked about *Imitation of Life*, Elsie O'Herlihy assured me that her husband relished the camp side of it. "It's the best soap opera ever made," she exclaimed. He played it deadpan, but if you look closely you might detect a gleam in his eyes. He seems to romp through the part, as though incredulous that they're paying him to have such fun. As play-wright David Edwards, he disses Lana Turner's Lora Meredith because, at the audition, she plays his new comedy not with "delicate reactions" but with "loud, goggle-eyed takes." Just before her lofty departure, how-ever, she informs him that he's "too good a writer to have such a scene in your play." Lora is barely off center stage before he calls her back to con-fer. Humbled, and secretly thrilled at being told off, he seeks the coun-sel of this great actress from the hinterlands: "What would you do with that scene?"

"Drop it entirely," she responds, like Kaufman to Hart.

"That's not a bad idea," he muses. "Let me think. Yes . . . but the scene has a couple of lines that are important."

Lora, like a blonde, smooth-faced Lillian Hellman, knows all about dramaturgy: "Give them to Amy," she says brightly.

"Yes," David Edwards mulls for a split second. "It would work. Huh! Think you could play Amy?"

This audition sequence, a satire on a comedy, provides plenty to laugh at, not least of which is a Douglas Sirk fillip: Lora is right— eliminations from a silly play like this can only better it. Together, she and Edwards turn backstage Broadway into a lark, and then they fall— slightly—in love, though their affair is less about passion than about box office. One could read the playwright as homosexual or bi, especially when Lora confides to Annie that if David Edwards slowed down, "he'd be sure to find out how sad he really is"—"sad" being fifties code for "queer."

When Edwards says, after Lora Meredith's rave reviews on opening night in *Stopover*, "I'm in love with you, Lora"—he qualifies it instantly with: "But I must hasten to add, I always fall in love with my leading ladies." He sounds like a fan swooning over Judy, Barbra, or—well, Lana. And can anyone name a heterosexual playwright who flings his manuscript on the fire when a leading lady turns it down? Would Ibsen? Arthur Miller? Clyde Fitch? (Ibsen did have Hedda Gabler burn the manuscript of her husband's rival.)

Elsie told me that her husband liked Lana Turner because she didn't make star demands. "She was very honest," Elsie said, "and he thought she gave a good performance. Danny liked all the performers and thought they played quite well."

As it turns out, both Elsie and I were wide of the mark: He wasn't fond of Lana or Douglas Sirk, and for him, making the picture was a grind. Thanks to the 1985 interview quoted above from the DVD of *Robinson Crusoe,* I heard O'Herlihy's pointed comments about *Imitation of Life.* Asked what it was like working with Lana Turner, he replied: "She was very much the star. It was difficult to play a love scene with her because it was terribly technical. I didn't realize that, technical as it might be, it worked on screen. I found it difficult to play with her, though. And I found the director extremely difficult. He's a great picture maker, but he didn't know how to handle actors. In a gentle love scene, he would suddenly scream at you—or at somebody else. It was disruptive to a performance, I would say. But a very good picture maker. It's a very good picture. Very slick, yes. But I did not enjoy it. It wasn't my type of picture. It was the only one I was ever in that made a mint of money." (By technical, I take it he means fussbudget camera setups befitting a star, excruciating caution so that Miss Turner's hair isn't mussed or her lipstick smeared, etc.)

By the time he filmed *Imitation of Life,* O'Herlihy was easily the most distinguished actor in the cast, having appeared in "serious" plays and films. One would expect Sirk to respond favorably to O'Herlihy, since the director himself started in theatre, where he seems to have left his professional heart. Sirk, in retirement, always discussed the stage with greater depth of feeling than he mustered for his films, and in greater detail. He remembered incidents and personalities from his German theatre work, while forgetting much of his Hollywood career. By the time of *Imitation of Life,* however, Sirk had been so misused—as he thought—that fatigue obscured whatever rapport he might have found with Dan O'Herlihy.

*I*n 1988, the year after Sirk's death, *American Film* published a "Flashback" feature titled "Magnificent Obsessions: A Remembrance by Ross Hunter." In paying tribute to the man who directed ten Hunter productions, Ross assembled comments that Sirk had made about their films at Universal. In an introductory note, he explained that this commentary was taken "from Sirk's letters, his conversations with me, and his remarks noted in my daily diary."

Here is what Sirk himself said about *Imitation of Life*: "I would have made this picture no matter what, if only for the title. I didn't read the book when you gave it to me, but did read your outline. I didn't see the John Stahl picture either, [the 1934 *Imitation of Life*] because I wanted to avoid any possible influences. [Sirk told Jon Halliday that he saw the Stahl version after he finished his own.] I liked the outline—especially the Negro angle; the Negro girl trying to escape her condition, sacrificing—for the sake of her status in society—her bonds of friendship, family, et cetera, and trying to vanish in an imitation world. The casting of newcomers Susan Kohner and Juanita Moore—who obviously had the best parts—put the leads, Lana Turner and John Gavin, in the background. And although at times it was difficult to work with Lana because of her personal-headlines tragedy, she was always a professional.

"But even though I so much loved and enjoyed working with you, in my mind I was leaving Hollywood even before I made the picture. The studio had forced me to do pictures I didn't want to make, and I was fed up. After the huge success of *Imitation*, I knew I could write my own ticket, but although the Universal people tried to hold me and I hated to leave you and 'my family at the studio,' I knew I had to go. I was ill and the strenuous schedule and the heartache attached to Lana's endless tragedy did me in.

"This became the definitive break with Hollywood and picturemaking. So here I am in Switzerland—wanting to be in Hollywood—like one of those goddamn split characters in my pictures. Know that my heart is often there with you. And perhaps you'll make a picture in Switzerland, and I can see you."

In the following pages, we meet Sirk's studio family, those who never appeared before the camera but whose craft enhanced his artistry. "I liked working with a group of people I knew well," he said. "I am sure this way of working stems from the theatre, where I always had my own troupe."

Sirk's compliments to Ross Hunter sound a bit sugared-up; in interviews, he was less effusive. Sirk's praise of cinematographer Russell Metty, on the other hand, never wavered: "We always agreed about everything. We had just the same way of seeing things, and we had a great time working together."

Metty shot ten of Sirk's films, if not exactly the ten best, then at least five of the most famous: *Magnificent Obsession, All That Heaven Allows, Written on the Wind, A Time to Love and a Time to Die,* and *Imitation of Life.* Their other five collaborations deserve attention, which will come only when the films are more readily available: *Take Me to Town, Sign of the Pagan, Taza, Son of Cochise, Battle Hymn,* and *There's Always Tomorrow.*

Although Metty came to Universal in 1947, and Sirk a bit later, the two worked together for the first time only in 1953. *Take Me to Town* was the visually opulent result of their first collaboration. It's a banquet of color atop the canned-corn story of a backwoods preacher in the Old West (Sterling Hayden) who falls for saloon singer and petty crook Vermilion O'Toole, voluptuously incarnated by Ann Sheridan. Even in this confection, however, Sirk misses no subversive trick. Tweaking fifties notions of good girl/bad girl, he reverses the privileged status of the first to turn Vermilion into a heroine. Wearing a pink corset and pantaloons, she shoots a grizzly that menaces a child, stages a melodrama to raise money for the new church, and ends up marrying the preacher and teaching Sunday school. (If Germans were given to raucous laughter, you might hear a Sirk cackle in the background.)

This is one of Sirk's quasimusicals, like *La Habañera,* made in 1937 for UFA, and two of his early Universal pictures, *Has Anybody Seen My Gal?* and *Meet Me at the Fair,* both from 1952. A tacky ballad that underscores the opening credits tips us off about Vermilion: "At first she stole kisses, then she stole hearts. . . . She started a crime wave when she broke every rule." A bit later there's Sheridan's let-'er-rip signature song: "A flaming redhead, I'm a flaming redhead, If you play with fire, you'll get burned"—and you know she's hot enough to do it.

Sirk wants us to adore Vermilion as much as he does, so he bucks the heart-of-gold cliché by making her a three-dimensional character: She's no assembly-line slut, though she has tried most positions, and her attitude is, so what? ("There's a lot of girl here," she tells the preacher when he lifts her from a swoon after she kills the bear.)

I've never seen Ann Sheridan better used, owing to Sirk's tutelage and to Metty's camera, which frames her large, expressive face like a series of museum portraits—think John Singer Sargent or Elizabeth-Louise Vigée-Le Brun. In a night scene on the porch of a cabin, Metty shadows that face to create the effect of an undulating veil. (Earlier, in 1947, he designed similar shadow patterns for the face of Joan Fontaine in *Ivy.* "He was a genius," Fontaine said sixty years later.)

In *Imitation of Life,* Metty's play of shadow over Lana Turner and John Gavin, in their long sequence on the staircase outside her cold-water flat, enhances the limited emotional range of these two actors. Metty's filigree of shadows—like intermittent clouds and sun over a landscape—moves from light to darker, and without his expert lighting the sequence would grow monotonous. This is a good example of Sirk and Metty operating almost as one: The director avoids stasis by moving the actors constantly in the hallway, then up and down the stairs, while the cinematographer complements the scene's momentum with chiaroscuro lighting. (Metty used similar effects on Lana and Dan O'Herlihy in their love scene after her first opening night smash.)

In other films, Metty used shadows more extensively, along with unconventional, expressionistic camera angles. In *Take Me to Town*, however, his camera is stable, both literally and psychologically, as befits what Sirk considered "a little lyrical poem to the American Western past." Dressed in Bill Thomas's extravagant costumes, Sheridan is photographed like a one-woman Easter parade. Metty shared with Ross Hunter and Sirk the knack for making a Wal-Mart story look moneyed and stylish, as if tailored by Henri Bendel.

When it becomes better known, *Take Me to Town* may attract a following. It has the right ingredients. Though Sirk considered it a poem, it's as demented as a Bollywood spectacle, which it halfway resembles in artificiality, over-the-top music, gaga plot, wildly saturated color, and surreal images (e.g., a piano in front of a waterfall).

Russell Metty (1906–1978) spent his life in Los Angeles, one of the world's sunniest cities, and yet he is celebrated as a sculptor of darkness with his camera. Michael Walker, writing in the British publication *Film Dope*, noted that "as characters [in a Metty film] move around a room they shift in and out of shadowed areas in an unusual way for a Hollywood movie, in which—with certain obvious exceptions such as film noir—a generally 'high key' evenness of illumination prevails." Nowhere is Metty's shadow art more distinctive than in Orson Welles's *The Stranger* (1946), where he uses such melodramatic lighting effects as big shadows and steep high-angle and low-angle shots to create a disturbing small town in Connecticut that might pass for Hades. Metty's cinematography here makes Gregg Toland's in *Citizen Kane* seem almost conservative by comparison.

This was not Metty's first collaboration with Welles. As a "special consultant" on *Citizen Kane,* he shot the trailer. A year later, he did some of the reshoots on *The Magnificent Ambersons*. In 1946, when Welles was forced to turn over to RKO the thirty-seven cans of film he had shot on his ill-fated epic *Pan-American* (later retitled *It's All True*), Metty "offered to arrange the available footage for potential backers, who could then buy it and allow Welles a free hand to cut it. Welles was to explain the film to the audience in an introductory talk, recut it in its entirety, and provide a coherent narrative. The sceening was arranged, the backers were present, but Welles, who had forgotten all about it, did not turn up. It was a grave embarrassment to Metty."

Charles Higham, a Welles biographer who interviewed Metty, described the cinematographer as "powerfully built, brusque, and rude to a degree" with "the appearance and manner of a longshoreman and the soul of a great pictorial artist." Susan Kohner said, "I always thought he must have been a good football player as a young man. He had that kind of physique." Indeed, Metty, in photographs, resembles Vince Lombardi, legendary coach of the Green Bay Packers. Both had thick, full heads of steely gray-and-black hair; large, open faces that nevertheless suggested reserve; and a penetrating gaze with a hint of the brute.

In 1957, when Metty and Welles teamed for the last time on *Touch of Evil,* Charlton Heston wrote in his diary after watching early rushes: "I swear, some of Russ Metty's shots look like Cartier-Bresson stills." Later he called Metty "one of the great cameramen. He is nearly the only one of them who is also fast. Most of the time you hear things like, 'Do you want it fast, or do you want it good?' With Russ, you got both."

Susan Kohner remembers Metty as "pleasant enough, but not very communicative. Sometimes a cameraman will say, for example, 'If you would look to the left a little, otherwise we'll just get the whites of your eyes.' He'll talk to you, or try to give you an indication if there's something wrong with the way you position after a few rehearsals. They'll even say it to the actor instead of telling the director. But not Metty. He didn't speak to the actors at all. He spoke only to Sirk." Metty, like Sirk, Juanita Moore, Lana Turner, and Susan herself, was a client of the Paul Kohner agency. Susan confirmed that her father considered Metty "a fine cameraman," adding, "I don't believe he would have let me make a picture unless he thought I would be in good hands. He knew the work of everyone who made *Imitation.*"

Metty's remoteness on *Imitation of Life* may have reflected the formality of his relationship with Sirk, who rarely socialized with colleagues. On *Touch of Evil,* with the gregarious Welles and a close-knit cast and crew, Metty loosened up. One night, Heston recalled, "Russ cooked up a mess of spaghetti in the trailer, which saved us from that dreary catered stuff."

Metty's triumph, of course, is apparent throughout *Touch of Evil,* although nowhere more so than in the bravura opening shot of the film, a three-and-a-half-minute take that is one long tracking shot. "It was technically an amazing shot," said Heston, "almost impossible, given the precise timing that it required not only from Janet Leigh and me, the couple in the car, and the passing extras, but, most critically of all, the boom grip and the camera operator."

Another feat for Metty, less spectacular although toilsome in its own way, was concealing the cast on Janet Leigh's arm. She broke it a few days before shooting began on *Touch of Evil*, and at first Welles wanted her to wear the cast in plain sight. Soon, however, he changed his mind and instructed Metty to shoot Leigh in such a manner that her arm would always be somewhat concealed.

It's ironic that Metty won his only Oscar for *Spartacus*, in 1961, an ungainly film that seems to lie outside the Kubrick canon. Then, too, Metty and Kubrick clashed because the director tried repeatedly to override Metty's decisions as director of photography. Their turf war explains in part why the film is an artistic patchwork, flawed and unsatisfying.

The Academy had many more auspicious opportunities to honor Metty, from *Bringing Up Baby* in 1938, through the forties and fifties when he worked with Welles and Sirk, up to *The Misfits* in 1961. Like many of Hollywood's great artistic craftsmen, Russell Metty was turned out when the studios collapsed, although he lasted longer than many. At Universal in the sixties, he shot close to a dozen films that Ross Hunter produced, including *Flower Drum Song* (for which he received an Oscar nomination) and *Madame X*. Metty finished his career in the seventies as director of photography on TV shows like *Columbo* and *The Waltons*. A forlorn end, as though a great colorist such as Gauguin or Matisse had been reduced to painting traffic signs on a provincial backroad.

When Alexander Golitzen, art director (with Richard H. Riedel) on *Imitation of Life*, won an Oscar for *Spartacus*, Ross Hunter sent him a telegram: "Congratulations! You won without any white sets." It was their private joke, though Hunter's predilection was well known at Universal. *Imitation of Life* might serve as a textbook case: In Lora Meredith's Connecticut house, we see white walls in her great cathedral of a living room;

a fireplace of white-painted stones; white sofa, creamy beige piano, white armchair. Lora's bedroom is also white, and so is the kitchen. Once she has achieved stardom in the theatre, her dressing room is white.

Barbara Hall, of the Academy of Motion Pictures' Margaret Herrick Library, interviewed Golitzen in 1990, when he was eighty-two years old. Questioning him about Sirk's and Hunter's involvement with art direction and set design on *Imitation of Life* (and other pictures), she reiterated Sirk's penchant "for making films that are almost entirely interiors, and so meticulously designed."

Golitzen responded, "I'd say he was very conscious of the physical domain around himself. But he didn't interfere *at all* in the actual design." Hall followed with, "What kinds of things would he tell you when you would start the film?" Golitzen answered, "First you show him the sketch of what you're preparing to do. And he says, 'Well, that looks pretty good, *but* . . .' And then he would put in two or three little suggestions that you incorporate. And then when you show him the set, he would say, 'Well, we need maybe a lamp on each corner,' and those would be his contributions to it. But he would look around quite a bit before really accepting it."

Ross Hunter, according to Golitzen, exerted more visual control on a Sirk–Hunter film than the director did, which is an unsurprising though controversial claim. It contradicts many Sirk critics who write from opinion untroubled by research, implying, on scant evidence, that Sirk singlehandedly created the mise-en-scène in every frame. Based on Golitzen's testimony, both he and Hunter had greater input than Sirk.

Golitzen continued, "Ross is one of the few producers in this industry, that I've worked with for many years, who really got in on the act, you might say. Because he definitely, especially in wardrobe more than settings, would put his finger in it. [The reason for] white sets was because he *loved* to have a white set in the picture. The pre-production was according to him. And then when the picture started shooting, it was according to Sirk. Period." (Beverly Heisner, in her book *Hollywood Art: Art Direction in the Days of the Great Studios,* notes Ross Hunter's color coding in his productions: "gray means poverty and meanness, white and brighter colors—pink bedrooms—mean affluence and well-being.")

Betty Abbott Griffin, the script supervisor who worked on so many Hunter–Sirk pictures, as well as on Sirk pictures pre-Hunter and Hunter pictures post-Sirk, agrees that the look of the films produced by Ross Hunter and directed by Sirk owe more to Hunter. She sums up the process like this: "Ross told Alex [Golitzen] what he wanted. And Ross was the perfect producer. Once the sets were up, he was attentive without interfering."

One might say, then, that while the surfaces of many Sirk pictures at Universal originated with Ross Hunter, and were executed by Golitzen, the genius came from Sirk. Many sets used in *Imitation of Life,* for instance, have a fraternal twin in later films produced by Ross Hunter. The latter, however, hold scant interest today, as they may resemble a Sirk film in certain particulars but lack the vital elements that Sirk contributed: style, irony, directorial finesse, fluid camera work, and expert editing. Ross Hunter films of the sixties are bland and predictable, each one an example of what happens when the producer is the sole auteur.

Golitzen described Sirk as "always on schedule—I don't recollect a single picture of his that he lost a day." Golitzen would surely know, since he worked on a dozen Sirk films. In the oral history, however, he talks more about Ross Hunter than about Sirk, perhaps because he worked on thirty Hunter productions. Referring to the phrase "a Ross Hunter picture," and what it calls to mind, Golitzen said, "They were very commercial. That's his strong point. Slick is a good word. He was also very visual, and appreciated how things looked. From the smallest prop to the biggest expanse. That's why Ed Muhl [head of Universal] would assign the so-called 'polished' pictures to Ross Hunter. Because Ross had a polished touch."

Alexander Golitzen had a big life and a big career. In a photograph taken for the 1990 oral history, he looks like a native westerner: white hair, receding hairline, a salt-and-pepper moustache, and the kind of large glasses you might see on an older man in a small-town cafe in Wyoming. Who would guess that he was a White Russian aristocrat?

Born in 1908, Golitzen was the grandson of a mayor of Moscow who was also governor of the province. The family lived just outside Moscow on an estate called Petrovskoie. During the Revolution, the family (Golitzen's father was a prominent doctor) fled to China. From there, they emigrated to Seattle in 1923, where Alex grew up. He studied architecture at the University of Washington, graduating in 1931.

Meanwhile, his family had relocated to Los Angeles. After college, Alex found work in the MGM art department as a sketch artist, where he assisted art director Alexander Toluboff on films such as *Grand Hotel* and *Queen Christina*. Laid off at MGM, he went to United Artists, where he worked under renowned art director Richard Day, assisting on such pictures as *Stella Dallas, Dead End,* and *Wuthering Heights.*

For Hitchcock's *Foreign Correspondent* in 1940, Golitzen received his first Academy Award nomination. Subsequently nominated many times, he won Oscars for *Phantom of the Opera* (1943), *Spartacus* (1960), and *To Kill a Mockingbird* (1962). Scattered among his many prestige pictures are a few surprises: *Cobra Woman* in 1944, the Maria Montez concoction that looks like an overdose of Baskin-Robbins, and *Ricochet Romance* (1954), with Marjorie Main as Pansy Jones, a Ma Kettle wannabe. Photographs of Golitzen at his zenith show a resemblence to Claude Rains—similar circumflex eyebrows, a mouth suggesting sardonic amusement.

In 1955, Golitzen became supervising art director of Universal-International. As department head, he hired and supervised the studio's art directors, consulting with them on their projects, and coordinated set construction, location selection, and budgets. By virtue of his position, Golitzen received art direction credit (often with the actual hands-on art director) on many of the films produced by Universal from 1954 to 1973.

Golitzen also worked on the early planning of the Universal Studios Tour, which began in 1964. In those early days, the tour was less megatourist than today and in fact seemed intimate by comparison. Betty Abbott Griffin took the tour when the studio first inaugurated it. She, and other employees, were asked for feedback. "They led us through a dressing room," she recalls, "and the guide said, 'This was Lana Turner's dressing room . . . and oh, my goodness, she left her comb here and there's hair in it!'

"Well, I had to leave the tour," Griffin says, laughing even now at such tomfoolery. "I broke up and couldn't stop. I was hysterical."

Other names often seen in the credits of Universal films, including *Imitation of Life* and other Sirk–Hunter productions:

- Richard H. Riedel, who assisted Golitzen on *Imitation of Life*, spent his entire career at Universal, from 1940 until his death in 1960, aged fifty-six, in a car crash outside Rome, where he was scouting locations for Ross Hunter's remake of *Back Street*. A year earlier, he had been Oscar nominated for his work on *Pillow Talk*, another Hunter production. "He and I got on beautifully together," said Golitzen.

- Russell A. Gausman, set decorator (1892–1963), worked on some seven hundred pictures, beginning with the 1925 silent *Phantom of the Opera*, starring Lon Chaney, and ending with *Spartacus* in 1960, for which he won his second Oscar. He began at Universal as a prop boy in 1915, the year that Carl Laemmle opened Universal City. Later he headed the prop department. Gausman received his first Oscar for the 1943 remake of *Phantom of the Opera*, which tested his resourcefulness at a time of wartime shortages. He was able to build the chandelier that Claude Rains sent crashing down from the theatre ceiling only because he had combed a large swathe of California in search of old chandeliers, which he then tore apart for their crystals. The gas footlights for the theatre scenes were possible because Gausman had bought up the furnishings of a derelict mansion in Menlo Park the year before. He took reflectors that had been used to illuminate oil paintings by gas and converted them into footlights. Every year he spent thousands of studio dollars with impunity, because his purchases paid off in subsequent pictures for years to come.

- Julia Heron was born in Montana in 1897 and began her career around 1918. "The primary objective of any set decorator," she said, "is to get anything required as reasonably as possible." Golitzen considered her "a terrific decorator," and for that reason lured her to Universal from United Artists. "She was very caustic in speech and manner," he said, "often profane, but she knew exactly what was called for, and her crew respected and liked her. Many art directors learned a lot from her." The script of the 1951 comedy *The Groom Wore Spurs,* starring Ginger Rogers and Jack Carson, contained several key scenes set in a Las Vegas gambling casino where the characters were seen playing slot machines. A few days before shooting began, however, California passed an inconvenient law making it illegal to own these one-armed bandits. The prop houses, from which studios usually rented such items, quickly disposed of their machines in compliance. Julia Heron, however, pulled a few strings and no doubt greased some palms so that when filming started, two dozen slot machines were ready to roll. Nominated five times by the Academy, she won an Oscar for *Spartacus.* Heron was one of the founders of the Motion Picture and Television Country House and Hospital, and served on its board of directors. She died there in 1977.

- Milton Carruth, editor, helped make Sirk's films smooth-flowing and seamless, shaping them into a sort of visual chamber music. Sirk himself, an economical director, shot very little excess footage, thus making the editor's job less complex. Carruth (1899–1972) spent his entire career, from 1929 to 1966, at Universal. In the thirties, he directed a handful of minor pictures at the studio and co-directed a couple of others. Carruth was one of three editors who served as the core of Universal's editing department for a span of some forty years. Despite his work on Hitchcock's *Shadow of a Doubt* (1943), Carruth received no nod from the Academy.

*R*oss Hunter should have retired in 1959, after *Imitation of Life*, when Douglas Sirk did. Had he done so, he might now enjoy not only high regard for his financial necromancy, but also a tardy succès d'estime. His productions would perhaps be remembered as bejeweled standouts in the Eisenhower decade, minus that herd of Hunter relics lumbering through the sixties, and beyond.

Hunter's biography, however, would remain unchanged: a meshwork of glossy prevarications, closety denials, and press-release versions of reality. In the words of actor and playwright Terry Kingsley-Smith, who worked with Hunter on several projects, "Ross had a terrible time with the truth." And yet Kingsley-Smith, like other friends and colleagues of Hunter's that I spoke with, didn't really hold that problem against him. "It's hard for me to talk about Ross," he said, "because he was delightful to be around, he had a wonderful sense of humor, and high energy."

Kingsley-Smith explains the mendacity thus: "Ross lived in a fantasy world, and I think he believed all of it." Citing one perplexing experience with Hunter, he recalls writing a story and screenplay called *Jazz Babies* as a proposed sequel to Hunter's *Thoroughly Modern Millie*. When Universal balked, Hunter put other writers on the project. Then, apparently

*A friend of the producer explained, "Ross never said the word 'glamorous.' It was just his little thing; he'd say, 'Very glamoo.'"

owing to frustration with the studio, he told Kingsley-Smith that he, Hunter, had already come up with the same story "before I got yours in the mail." When Kingsley-Smith asked why he hadn't mentioned this before, Hunter claimed to have sent his own story to Isobel Lennart, screenwriter of *Funny Girl*. Kingsley-Smith: "I happened to meet Isobel at a party, and she said she had never seen any such story! So it was some vague idea Ross had, which he mistook for reality."

Ross told Kingsley-Smith, on one of their happier days, that *Jazz Babies* needed a big, show-stopping finish. "Like the one in *Imitation of Life*," Ross added. He expounded on the funeral sequence, admitting the absurdity of such an enormous final turnout for an obscure woman like Annie Johnson. "But the finish!" he exclaimed. "That was our big finish!" And who could gainsay the cinematic rightness of that famous, tear-stained result?

The best assessment of Ross Hunter, in my estimation, is William J. Mann's in his book, *Behind the Screen: How Gays and Lesbians Shaped Hollywood, 1910–1969*. Mann, both an admirer of Hunter's work and an iconoclast, notes that in a Ross Hunter production, "there is no winking at the audience, no self-conscious camp: these were sincere, sumptuous epics of life, loss, and love, all designed according to Hunter's motto, 'Entertainment Through Beauty.'"

Although Hunter's moviemaking credos may seem naively simple— "If you want the girl next door, go next door," and "No woman will leave a sink full of dirty dishes to watch another woman wash a sink full of dirty dishes"—it worked in the dying days of Old Hollywood. If you were a woman (his target audience) in the fifties looking for an enjoyable night at the movies, would you pick the grim, gray violence, and the sermonizing, of *On the Waterfront* . . . or *All I Desire,* starring Barbara Stanwyck as an actress with secrets in her past? *Marty*—about a butcher who meets a wallflower . . . or *Interlude,* with June Allyson, Rossano Brazzi, European locales, a love affair, and "culture"?

Referring to realism in general, and to such unglamorous "T-shirt and psychology" pictures as *The Rose Tattoo* and *The Fugitive Kind,* Ross announced, "I'll leave all that to Tennessee." And he did, once Sirk was no longer there to inject not only psychology but various disturbing isms—pessimism, expressionism, American racism—that Ross Hunter, a Jewish homosexual from Cleveland passing as a fair-haired WASP-about-Hollywood, had no wish to confront. (William Mann, calling *Imitation of Life* Hunter's gayest picture, adds, in an aside, "One cannot help but think of Ross Hunter's own story when viewing this film.")

Ross could have been the youngest Gabor, for all the flurry over his birth year. It was 1924, no—1926, nothing of the kind, it was 1927, or maybe even 1930—unless he was born in 1921, like Lana. In 1984, when Ross did an oral history with Ronald Davis, of Southern Methodist University, he attached this addendum to the legal agreements page, written in his own hand: "I'd like to set the record straight as to birth date—which is all over the place in 20 different versions. Born in Cleveland, Ohio—on May 6, 1926. Real name is Martin Terry Fuss." And yet, on his crypt in Westwood Memorial Park, the dates are 1920–1996.

Beside him rests his partner of some fifty years, Jacque Mapes. Underneath Jacque's name, the inscription "Beloved Friend," and below that "1914–2002." Although Ross and Jacque were one of the most enduring couples in Hollywood, they seem embarrassed about it even post mortem. How coy is "Beloved Friend"? And below Ross's name, "Beloved Producer," as though they were partners in a St. Valentine's Day enterprise. (Their eternal neighbors are Marilyn Monroe, six crypts away, and songwriter Jay Livingston, whose epitaph is his biggest hit: "Que Será, Será.")

"The kind of life I put on the screen," said Hunter, "is the way I want life to be." Martin Terry Fuss made up his mind early on: he wanted more than a semiprosperous home in a Jewish neighborhood in Cleveland. So, at age nine, he went on the stage. Having mastered the banjo, the saxophone, and the harmonica, he toured the RKO–Orpheum circuit in a vaudeville act with six other children.

Papa Fuss, however, disliked his son flitting about like a little bird—in Yiddish, faygelah; translation, "homo." He yanked him out of showbiz and into school, where the youngster did so well that he won a scholarship to Case Western Reserve University. Part of the Hunter mythology has him earning an MA degree before the age of twenty, but the university has no record of such grad school accomplishment. According to their registry, his BA degree was awarded in 1942. (In 1991, the university chose Hunter as recipient of its Creative Achievement Award.)

Hunter's official bio describes a crowded life: army service during World War Two; a discharge owing to injury or unspecified illness; teaching English in a Cleveland high school; newspaper reporter; actor in local theatrical productions. The most questionable segment of this busy backstory is the episode in which several of his female students submit a photograph of their handsome teacher to Paramount Pictures in New York, which summons him for a screen test. It's true that Ross was nice looking—clean-cut, wholesome, safe—but it's likely that he made his beachhead in Hollywood without a boost from swooning bobby-soxers in homeroom. William J. Mann, who checked local newspapers and Cleveland city directories, found Ross listed only as "usher" at a movie theatre, suggesting that the other jobs were part-time or substitute.

A more credible scenario than Ross's own has him noticed on stage at the Cain Park Theatre in Cleveland by Max Arnow, a talent scout for Columbia Pictures. Eventually, that studio signed him to a standard seven-year contract—this part of the story is verifiable from an item that appeared on March 15, 1944, in the Cleveland *Plain Dealer*: "Studio Gives Martin Fuss Film Contract."

In later years, Ross was the first one to laugh when his acting career came up. On that topic, at least, he didn't pretend. Beginning with *Louisiana Hayride* (1944), opposite Judy Canova, he appeared in a score of B pictures. Soon he was noticed by teenagers in such quickies as *Ever Since Venus* (1944), *Hit the Hay* (1945), and *Sweetheart of Sigma Chi* (1946). Ross always claimed that he earned over a thousand dollars a week, and that floods of fan mail, largely from teenage girls, proved his popularity; he said he got more letters than anyone else at Columbia. His celebrity included fan magazine covers and features inside bearing titles like "Get Hep to Hunter"—*Movieland*, June 1946—which described him as "Columbia's latest gift to women." *Modern Screen* named him Most Promising Actor.

Gangsterish Harry Cohn, head of Columbia, didn't agree. He disliked Ross Hunter, describing him as possessing three onscreen expressions: "blank, blanker, blankest." When Hunter badgered the boss for roles in higher-quality pictures, Cohn put him in *The Bandit of Sherwood Forest* (1946) with one line to speak: "Do not worry, Robin, everything will be all right."

Finally, in 1947, Columbia dropped him. A year or so later, according to the Hunter chronology, MGM cast him opposite Esther Williams in *The Duchess of Idaho*. His assignment included a great deal of time in water, and so he was injected with a prophylactic antibiotic. He developed penicillin poisoning and spent close to a year in the hospital. Good-bye, movies.

Once he recovered, his meagre acting career was gone forever. In the Ross Hunter story, it's never easy to tell dream from biography, even for Ross himself. Thus, in later years as he recounted his ups and downs, penicillin was sometimes the villain, and sometimes overlooked. (Penicillin was new in the forties, and it is possible that a doctor unwisely used it as a vaccine.)

A has-been before the age of thirty, Ross again taught high school, this time in Downey. At night, and on weekends, he worked part-time at a small independent studio where he learned editing, budgeting, publicity, and other skills that would serve him well when he became a producer. In 1951 he got a job as assistant to Leonard Goldstein, at Universal, producer of the Ma and Pa Kettle series and many other low-budget pictures.

Soon Ross began coproducing his own cut-rate productions. He quickly got the reputation of a budget slasher whose pictures looked like—well, not a million bucks, but at least several thousand more than they cost. Ross didn't fancy his half-dozen western assignments—*The Battle of Apache Pass, Untamed Frontier*, and the like—so he bootlegged glamour and romance into the mise-en-scène. For *Tumbleweed* (1953), he instructed his set decorators to design "the most ornate tepee ever seen on a screen," and costumed Audie Murphy's leading lady, the ingenue Lori Nelson, as though "she had been dressed by Givenchy."

Ross and Ann Sheridan were close friends, and we've seen already how he, Sirk, and Metty glorified her in *Take Me to Town*, the first Ross Hunter production that Sirk directed (Leonard Goldstein coproduced). The reputations of both Hunter and Sirk depend primarily on their ten pictures produced between 1953 and 1959. Whether you consider Douglas Sirk and Ross Hunter artists, artisans, or washouts, you must argue from the evidence of those ten core films.

After Sirk's departure, Ross produced eighteen more pictures, including *Pillow Talk, Portrait in Black, Midnight Lace,* two additional *Tammy* pictures, *The Chalk Garden, Madame X,* and *Airport* (1970), which topped *Imitation of Life* as Universal's biggest moneymaker up to that time. (It cost ten million to make, and grossed over fifty million.)

But Hollywood had changed, and the new viciousness was more corrosive than studio-era exploitation and paternalism. Lew Wasserman, now the emperor of a vast enterprise that included Universal, had big problems, including shaky job security. Although he and Ross Hunter got along, Wasserman was no Ed Muhl, the old-fashioned Universal production head who green-lighted the Sirk–Hunter pictures.

During Muhl's tenure, if Ross had said around town that Universal was living off the profits from Ross Hunter productions, Muhl might have laughed, knowing it was so. But when Ross made the impolitic boast that he had saved Wasserman's job with those *Airport* millions, and gossip spread the word, Wasserman wasn't amused. He was angry not because Ross fibbed, but because he told the truth. *Airport* "came out three months before MCA's board [the parent company] was due to decide on the renewal of Wasserman's contract." Wasserman stayed on, to the consternation of his enemies on the board, but when Hunter's contract came up for renewal, he was dropped. He made only one other theatrical film, the musical turkey *Lost Horizon* in 1973, followed by four made-for-TV movies and a miniseries. His career as producer ended in 1979.

In private life, Ross Hunter belonged in a Ross Hunter picture. The reality of this assertion became apparent to me during a long conversaton with Robert Osborne, host of Turner Classic Movies and a close friend of Ross and Jacque. Osborne first met the couple in the late sixties, not long after they moved into the seven-thousand-square-foot house built to their design in 1966 on Trousdale Place. This hillside address is located in Trousdale Estates, a northern projection of Beverly Hills above Sunset Boulevard. Earlier, they had lived on Rising Glen Road, in Beverly Hills, in a less opulent house than the one on Trousdale.

I asked Osborne to describe the Trousdale house. "The wonderful thing about it," he began, "is that it looked like a Ross Hunter movie set. Your first thought on entering might be, So that's why he believes his movies are true to life—he lives in a house like Susan Hayward's in *Back Street,* or Lana Turner's in *Imitation of Life.*" Osborne's description conjured a generic Ross Hunter set, high-ceilinged and full of light, with white walls and imported fixtures, elegant with perhaps a soupçon of kitsch.

Osborne mentioned the impressive foyer, the two-tiered living room with adjacent den. "Then," he said, "you go up a short flight of stairs and off to the right are Jacque's quarters, and Ross's off to the left. You go down some stairs, and there is a bar and a screening room." (Ross told another visitor that he had the same projection equipment as Grauman's Chinese.)

In 1966, shortly after moving in, Ross took Bob Thomas, an Associated Press writer who reported on Hollywood, on a tour of the new place. The proud new owner pointed out the "crystal chandelier from Ireland in the dining room, and china from Carol Channing," who had recently appeared in Hunter's *Thoroughly Modern Millie.* The silver closet, Thomas wrote, was "lined entirely in tarnish-proof cloth to eliminate polishing." In the gadget-filled kitchen (think of the modern conveniences in a Hunter film), Ross offered Thomas a cup of coffee: "He pressed a button on the wall and a machine ground the beans, rumbled liquidly, and spouted a hot brown stream into a cup."

Elsewhere in the house was a railing from a Spanish church; a mural, *The Mummers,* by Canadian muralist Douglas Riseborough; and lemons— in ceramics, sculpture, and paintings, including a Matisse still life. ("I have this thing about lemons," said Ross, whose walls in various rooms were painted yellow, white, and beige. Any gift to Ross with a lemon motif was greatly prized. At the close of production on *Madame X,* Lana sent him an arrangement of lemons in an elegant epergne.)

Bob Thomas's outdoor sketch might double as reporter's notes from set construction at Universal: "Although he has lived in the place only a few weeks, the grounds give it an established look. 'That's my instant landscaping,' Hunter explained. 'It was all planted in one day, including the large trees. Even the lawns were rolled out like carpeting.'" Beyond the greenery, on a terrace below, was a marble swimming pool with three massive, bubbling fountains, and a panorama of Los Angeles in the distance.

No mention was made in the article of Jacque Mapes, though Thomas surely knew the score. Four years earlier, Ross had told Hollis Alpert, who profiled him under the knowing title "Diamonds Are a Man's Best Friend," that the earlier house (on Rising Glen) was shared by a stepbrother. Earlier still, when Ross was an actor, he and Jacque passed as "cousins from Ohio." They fooled no one, of course; or only the willfully naive. When they arrived at a party, someone might say, "Oh, the Hunters are here." They were merely following the unwritten code of Hollywood, which, though restrictive, was more liberal than that of the flyover. And when Ross and Jacque went out together in public, they were always accompanied by two female friends, their "dates."

Imitation of Wife

One of Hunter's problems with the truth involved Nancy Sinatra Sr., the ex-wife of Frank Sinatra. In 1967, Ross told a columnist, "It's absolutely true. I asked Nancy to marry me. You know what a wonderful person she is. We're good for each other." That last line sounds borrowed from Lana, in *Imitation of Life*, to John Gavin: "You're so good for what ails me."

The marriage fantasy had a *Waiting for Godot* aroma, and, like the Beckett play, desperation below the surface comedy. Putting the charade in context, however, Ross made that statement two years before Stonewall. He apparently thought he must. Hollywood then, as now, pressured gay men to dabble in heterosexual romance. (One difference today is that the usual suspects not only marry and produce children; they must also join a religious cult.)

Ross was too smart not to know that people were laughing at his tales. One wonders how Jacque Mapes viewed the matter. It's possible

(continued)

that the men, and their very close friend Mrs. Sinatra, had a merry time with their farce.

In 1970, Ross told a reporter from *Newsday* that he had been married briefly in his acting days (not so). About Nancy Sinatra, he said, "a bit shyly": "We're been together three years. It's a lovely relationship." (His bad acting is evident even in interviews.) Then, as disingenuous as Myra Breckinridge, he added this coy bit of tattle: "I never would have taken Nancy to see *Oh! Calcutta!* if I'd had any idea it would be as dirty as it was. Nancy's so sweet and square, that's why I love her so."

When I asked Mrs. Sinatra about Ross, she said: "All I know is we always had a very nice time together, he was good company, he was a very talented man, as his movies have shown, and I still miss him. He was a good friend." She also cautioned me, "as a preface to our little talk," that she does not give interviews because "things that come out in print are never quite what you say. You know what I mean?" Mrs. Sinatra consented to speak to me because of her fondness for Ross, and also because I was recommended by Laura Mako, who was often the fourth member of the party with Ross, Jacque, and Nancy Sinatra.

Laura Mako's happiest memory of Ross: "Fun! Lots of laughs. Always upbeat." I asked her, "When the four of you went out, what was the evening like?" She said, "We always had fourth row center at the theatre. We went to the best restaurants, and Nancy and I went to England with him in 1973 for a command performance of *Lost Horizon*. Which was fitting, because Ross treated people royally." A writer for the *Times* of London reassured the British public: "Going to the pictures can be a bit risky nowadays, but I think the Queen is on safe enough ground with *Lost Horizon*." True enough. Her Majesty, like every lady, was safe with Ross Hunter—even in the dark.

With sympathetic eloquence, Robert Osborne puts their situation in context: "The thing to remember about Ross and Jacque is to place them in their time frame. Living the closeted life they did is not something to be jeered at today just because society is more open. They loved their work, and they wanted to be able to continue it. In the climate where they lived, that required them to behave in accordance with certain expectations. They behaved like Cary Grant, Rock Hudson, and many others, who were acceptable. But you couldn't misbehave if you wanted to stay in Hollywood's good graces. And Ross and Jacque didn't misbehave."

Ross was devastated by the death of Rock Hudson, in 1985. They had been friends for more than three decades. Not long after, he and Jacque became active in STAGE (Southland Theatre Artists Goodwill Event), which was founded in 1984 and is billed today as "the world's longest-running AIDS benefit." (As I write this, in 2008, Ross and Jacque are still listed on the STAGE website as Honorary Chairpersons. Beside their names, in parentheses, are the words "in remembrance.")

By the midnineties, Ross had begun to fail in his long battle against cancer. He was determined, nevertheless, to attend one of the four performances of STAGE's 1996 benefit, "Sondheim III," held at the Doolittle Theatre in Hollywood in March of that year. Robert Osborne, in his column "Rambling Reporter" in *The Hollywood Reporter,* described the event that Ross was so eager not to miss.

"For Saturday's performance," he wrote, "Hunter and Mapes had bought the first four rows of seats and asked forty of their good chums to join them, including Nancy Sinatra [Frank's ex-wife, not their daughter], Betty White, Barbara Rush, Anne Jeffreys, and Stephanie Zimbalist. Ross ultimately couldn't join the party, being too weakened from his long bout with cancer. That made him even more determined to summon the strength to attend Sunday's final performance. But it wasn't to be. The matinee began at three p.m., and Ross had died three hours before, which Carole Cook announced on stage just before the beginning of the show: 'He loved the theatre and was always there for us whenever we needed help. So we dedicate this show to Ross Hunter.'"

He would have loved it. Even Osborne's brief descriptions convey the wit and theatrical pizazz of those on the program. "Using only Sondheim songs that have both lyrics and music by S.S., 'Sondheim III' included Betty Garrett and David MacArthur doing 'Broadway Baby' (from *Follies*) as old-timers traveling on walkers; David, Patrick, and Shaun Cassidy—instead of the usual three frustrated femmes— lamenting 'You Could Drive a Person Crazy' (from *Company*); Michael Jeter, dressed as a French au pair except for the army boots he wore, do- ing 'Everybody Ought to Have a Maid,' (from *A Funny Thing Happened on the Way to the Forum*), then returning throughout the show to tidy up the stage." Other high points, according to Osborne, were Carole Cook's ribald "Can That Boy Fox-Trot," and Glynis Johns singing "Send in the Clowns," which she had introduced in *A Little Night Music*.

"My first love is the theatre"—a showbiz cliché, and yet in Ross Hunter's case, true. His initial acting jobs—whatever the quality—took place on the local stage in Cleveland. What many of his latter-day colleagues did not know was that in the late forties, after he stopped appearing in movies, Ross and Jacque ran two theatres in Los Angeles. At the Parlor Playhouse, Ross recalled, "We created a new kind of theatre at that time. We rented a house in the Valley, and we presented a play in every room. There were only thirty seats, so every scene was a close-up." They also worked at the Tent Theatre, which covered two lots in the Valley. Later, Ross directed a couple of shows at the Las Palmas Theatre in Hollywood, both produced by Jacque.

After his career as producer, Ross took up stage directing once more. In 1981, he directed Vera Miles in Neil Simon's *The Gingerbread Lady* at the Beverly Dinner Theatre in New Orleans, with Jacque as coproducer. In interviews, Ross sounds like a serious director with a distinct vision. He said he went over the play "with a microscope" until he knew every emotion, every laugh, every comma in it. Once his actors were on stage, he sought to avoid what he had seen at other dinner theatres—"the cast standing in a line, like the Ziegfeld Follies." The secret, Ross said, "is to paint a picture on stage. My formula for stage directing is my movie technique. I use close-ups, long shots, background music [as underscore]. I see it all as if I were looking through a camera lens." How do you do a close-up on stage? Hunter said he achieved the effect "by hav-ing all the actors look intently (and very still) at one particular actor. This forces the audience to zero in on him as well."

Betty Garrett, who appeared, along with Jan Sterling and Evelyn Keyes, in *Breaking Up the Act,* Terry Kingsley-Smith's play that Ross di-rected in San Antonio, elaborated on Hunter's stage close-ups. She re-called his telling her, "Now, come on, Betty, get right here for your close-up." Meaning, she added, "that you would be sort of alone on stage, even though other actors were present. Ross would either put a spot on you, or put you in a place where the light fell directly on you. You would almost do the scene out to the audience."

Garrett also recalled his saying, "Cut!" when he wanted a scene to end. If cast members reminded him that the scene still had a little way to go, he would reply, "Yes, but this is where we'd fade in or fade out." She added, "So you see, he still had picture-making on his mind." *Break-ing Up the Act* is about a trio that resembles the Andrews Sisters, except that during the McCarthy era these three break up over the testimony of one of them before a congressional witchhunting committee. Many years later, they reunite for a concert, and, as Garrett explained, "During rehearsal, much of the bitterness comes out, but they settle their differ-ences and fall into each other's arms at the end of the play."

Jacque Mapes designed the set and supervised the costumes, Garrett said, and he, too, seems to have retained a cinematic eye: "Everything was done in shades of beautiful blues and tans and browns. The set had those colors, and my blouse was what I call Williamsburg blue. Jan Ster-ling had a brown dress, and Evelyn's was shades of tan and brown." Jacque had worked for years as a set decorator. Among the famous sets he decorated are those in *The Hunchback of Notre Dame* and *Singin' in the Rain.*

One of Ross's last plays was *The Sound of Murder* in 1982, also in New Orleans. Lee Meriwether was to head the cast, but during re-hearsals she became ill. Although she was hospitalized, and replaced by Dina Merrill, she recalls Hunter's concern when she showed the first signs of illness. "He was a charming gentleman," she said, "old school, always solicitous of your comfort. No unhappiness on the set." Dina Merrill, who had been friends with Ross for years, flew to New Orleans

and learned the role as fast as possible. "A director who has been an actor," she said, "understands the process, and can communicate direc-
tions more easily."

I asked if they worked together again, and she said no. Since she
liked Ross and Jacque a lot, and stayed in touch with them for the rest
of their lives, I asked what Ross did professionally during the last years
of his life. "Not a lot," she answered. "They gave nice dinner parties, and
all their old friends would come. He didn't consider himself retired. He
was waiting for another picture to come along."

A chorus line of friends recalled Ross, and happy times with him and
Jacque. Since they often used the same words—"fun," "terrific," "elegant," "generous"—I call on one, Jan Wahl, for more specific reminiscences. Wahl, the TV and radio host from San Francisco, met Ross and
Jacque on an ocean cruise in the eighties when she was on board to lec-
ture on classic Hollywood pictures. Jan is an exuberant woman, full of
enthusiasm for life and movies, and astute in her evaluations.

"Ross had a huge impact on me," she said. "We talked on the phone
all the time when I couldn't get down to L.A. I'd say, 'Ross, I just sat
through another piece of crap at the movies,' and he would say, 'There
are no producers, so there's no one to tell the directors to cut it shorter,
or take out a character.' He was so right! Today there is no third eye—no
Ross Hunter to shape a movie.

"Yes, of course Ross and Jacque had beards," she said. "Nancy Sinatra Sr.—'Big Nancy,' they called her, to distinguish her from Nancy Jr.—
and others. But they were such sophisticated, elegant gentlemen, both
of them, that any woman would fight for the chance to be in their company.

"Ross told me there was one woman who, when she walked into a
room, made him feel he could have gone after her: Susan Hayward. That's
the only time he ever referred to being gay. He liked women of a certain
age, and he liked them in his pictures. Women who have lived and have
the scars, even though the scars don't show through the glamour. Women
who still carry on. He loved that about Lana Turner. He often said,
'Movies are not life. They should be bigger than life. And if they're not bigger than life, they should at least be more important than life.'"

Their friends agree that Ross and Jacque beautified their own lives, and those of others. One might say, also, that in *Imitation of Life* Ross, more than Douglas Sirk, sought to beautify death. An occurrence at Ross's memorial service, therefore, seems all the more perverse because of its unlovely gaucheness.

Jan Wahl recounted the events of that day. "In the chapel where the service was held, music was playing from *Thoroughly Modern Millie* and *Flower Drum Song*. The printed program had a picture of Ross on the cover, and under the picture, "In Loving Memory of Ross Hunter. Entered this life May 6, 1920. Entered eternal life March 10, 1996. Services Wednesday, March 13, 1996, 1:00 p.m., Peirce Brothers Westwood Village Memorial Park."

Inside the program: "Opening Remarks: Robert Osborne. Remarks by Barbara Rush, Carole Cook, Betty White. Closing Remarks: Robert Osborne." At the bottom of the page: "Good night, sweet prince, and flights of angels sing thee to thy rest."

Elsewhere in the program, a poem:

If I should die and leave you here a while,
Be not like others, sore undone, who keep
Long vigils by the silent dust, and weep.
For my sake—turn again to life, and smile . . .

(The following year, Lady Sarah McCorquodale read the same poem at the funeral of her sister, Princess Diana, in London.)

On the back page of the program, Psalm XXIII, "The Lord is my shepherd."

Jan Wahl added, "After all those people said so many lovely things about Ross, Nancy Sinatra Jr., the daughter of Frank and Nancy Sr., got up there. She said, 'Ross was like a father to me.' Then she seemed to turn bitter. 'In some ways,' she went on, 'more of a father than my own. I would get so fucking mad—' Then she noticed a nun in the back of the room, so she stopped and said, 'Oh, sorry, Sister.' But then she said it again!

"It was so embarrassing, and Ross would have hated it. He was never, ever vulgar. He just didn't like to hear anyone talk about the vulgar parts of life." That faux pas might symbolize the break between Ross Hunter's Hollywood and what followed. He railed against what he considered ugliness, violence, pornography, and though he included many outstanding new films in his denunciations, his point seems increasingly relevant, if misdirected.

As movies become not more sensationalistic, but more incompetent and juvenile, even flaccid Ross Hunter productions such as *Airport* or *Midnight Lace,* even junk like *If a Man Answers,* show the lineaments, the craftsmanship, of a real movie. These pictures are dying echoes of Hollywood, rather than a thud or a splat. Their strength is that, by comparison with later trends, they have well-defined scenes, articulate dialogue (even when it's bad), competent camera work, precise editing, and stars. They also have a point of view, unlike the shapeless muddle that defines so much present-day moviemaking. Why does a mediocre Ross Hunter film look better than what you'll find now at the multiplex? It's a question of craftsmanship. Then, too, those pictures, like all in the studio era, were descended from literature and from other movies, and not, as today, from TV, or video games, with the pointless editing of MTV, and actors who might have been added as CGI (or left behind as pods by invaders from Planet Botox).

I asked Jan Wahl whether Ross was bitter that his career had ended when he was still relatively young. "No," she said. "Ross wasn't bitter about anything. Except, perhaps, what had happened to movies. He said to me, 'We had no idea it would go to the kids. We never imagined that movies would be about what sells to adolescents.'"

Ross knew where magic belonged, even when he didn't get it right. What has happened, in the unmagical meantime, is enough to make anyone, even sweet, gentlemanly Ross Hunter, so fucking mad.

*W*hen I began this book I would have stated unequivocably, "The script was written by two people. Their names are Eleanore Griffin and Allan Scott." That certainty, however, existed prior to my discovery of a set of clues concerning a third writer, well known in Hollywood at the time but whose involvement with *Imitation of Life* was unguessed at then, as now, by all but a few.

The attempt to parse a Hollywood script, to label the parts written by this collaborator or that, is like driving through fog: landmarks remain obscure, or else they loom unforeseen. Biography, though less reliable than radar, can sometimes differentiate strands of literary DNA on the screen—especially, as in the case of *Imitation of Life,* when that's all you have to go on.

For instance, Eleanore Griffin once found herself almost living on the street . . . did she perhaps incorporate her own plight into that of Annie Johnson and Sarah Jane, homeless at Coney Island? Fannie Hurst in the novel made no mention of homelessness. Though it's unprovable, might we construe Griffin as chief architect not only of that early scene but of the second part of *Imitation of Life,* with its emotional blows and enduring regrets?

The life of Eleanore Griffin might have suited a Fannie Hurst novel, had Fannie invented a heroine who wins an Oscar that is later stolen while the lady is potted. The actor Bart Williams, who met Griffin in the seventies when she was brought in to doctor the book of a musical he appeared in, told me her story.

Born in 1904 in St. Paul, Minnesota, Griffin became a newspaper reporter in the twenties. Her arrival in Los Angeles coincided with the advent of talking pictures, and like many journalists of the time she seized her main chance. Unlike novelists and playwrights who considered movie work a sell-out, journalists like Griffin looked on studio employment as a happy advance from ambulance chasing and features on the Boy Scouts.

In 1937, Griffin was hired by Universal as a story writer, meaning that her job was to concoct something resembling a short story—a product later known as a treatment. From this skeletal plot, the screenwriters then fashioned a script with setting, dialogue, and the like. After a couple of years at Universal, Griffin moved to MGM. There success came early, and big: she shared an Oscar with Dore Schary for Best Writing, Original Story, for the 1938 hit, *Boys Town*. (Schary and another writer wrote the actual screenplay.)

It took another ten years, however, for Griffin to receive credit for an actual script, although like many employees of studio writing departments, she may well have contributed to any number for which she received no screen credit. Between 1948 and 1954 she did little work, or none. Certainly her credits played out. Those were the alcoholic years.

Bart Williams stayed in touch with Eleanore Griffin from the time of their association in the seventies until her death in 1995, at age ninety-one. Along the way, he learned that she had won an Academy Award. "I said something about it one day," Williams recalls, "asking where she kept it, since I had never seen it at her house.

"'Oh, I don't have that,' she replied.

"'What do you mean, you don't have it?'

"'Those were my drinking days and I didn't know who was coming in and out of my house. I sure got robbed a lot. They took my jewelry, took just about everything.'"

Williams recalls her adding that when she was on the skids she lost her house in Beverly Hills. Some twenty years later, when Williams knew her, she lived in a small rented house in Sunland, in the San Fernando Valley. Her companions were an old beagle, an old cocker spaniel, and several cats. He recalls her as dressed in timeless tweed and low high heels—"kind of like Miss Marple." Concerned over the missing Oscar, Williams phoned the Academy. "I told them about the theft," he said, "and I asked whether they might be able to replace it." The answer was yes, although replacement costs amounted to several hundred dollars, which Eleanore didn't have. As a compromise, the Academy devised a plaque with pertinent information about her award.

I speculated with Bart Williams as to whether biographical elements might have migrated into Eleanore Griffin's scripts. He said, "I do remember her saying, 'I was forever falling in love with the wrong men.' Actually, I believe she used an old-fashioned term like 'cads' or 'bounders.'" (An instance of screenwriter's bio on the screen: Anita Loos had a weakness for cads and wrote some of them into her screenplays—e.g., the Clark Gable character in *San Francisco*.)

Extant evidence of Griffin's turbulent love life goes back to 1938, the year of her Oscar. In June, an L.A. paper reported that "Mrs. Eleanore Griffin Rankin, scenario writer, went to court to get a divorce and learned, to her surprise, that she had never been legally wed." The snafu occurred when she and William Rankin, also a studio story writer, married in Tijuana in 1937; their marriage, owing to technicalities in Mexican law, was invalid. The judge told the couple, "The first thing you have to prove to get a divorce is that you were married." Failing that, he advised Eleanore's attorney to seek an annulment.

Whether the liaison ended, or resumed, is unclear, although Griffin and Rankin continued working on stories and scripts together, half a dozen in all, including *Only Angels Have Wings* (1939) and *The Harvey Girls* (1946). Nor did Eleanore specialize in pictures about caddish love affairs. Rather, she developed a sideline in sentimental uplift: *Tenth Avenue Angel* (1948), *A Man Called Peter* and *Good Morning, Miss Dove* (both 1955), and her final script, *One Man's Way* (1964), the story of Norman Vincent Peale, as played by Don Murray.

Then there's *Back Street* (1961), Ross Hunter's most masochistic picture, adapted by Griffin and William Ludwig from yet another novel by Fannie Hurst. Throughout the decades that Susan Hayward, as the other woman, worships John Gavin from her high-fashion world, she never loses hope. Thus, it might be read as a left-handed application of the Reverend Peale's famous philosophy—the power of positive thinking. Which works, no thanks to Fannie, but with a big boost from Ross Hunter and his writers: when Gavin dies, Hayward inherits his kids. (In the novel, the other woman dies of starvation! Hurst hated what she considered this rewrite's flabby ending.) The best thing in the picture, however—its one connection with reality—is Vera Miles, in a disturbing performance as Gavin's vicious and pathetic alcoholic wife. Eleanore Griffin surely wrote that one from the gut.

Allan Scott, the other screenwriter of record on *Imitation of Life*, was a gentleman author whose life resembled the debonair, well-to-do characters he wrote for six of the ten Fred Astaire–Ginger Rogers dance musicals. Born in suburban New Jersey, educated at Amherst College, a Rhodes scholar at Oxford, Scott returned home in the early thirties to do what all young men of letters did: write a novel or a play. In Scott's case, *Goodbye Again* (coauthored with George Haight) enjoyed a successful run on Broadway, followed by a film adaptation directed by Michael Curtiz in 1933.

Interspersed with the Astaire–Rogers pictures is lightweight thirties fare, written or cowritten by Scott, that hasn't worn so well: *I Dream Too Much,* starring opera diva Lily Pons and nicknamed "I Scream Too Much"; *Quality Street,* with Katharine Hepburn in box-office-poison mode. Later, Scott wrote three pictures that starred Claudette Colbert, including *So Proudly We Hail* (1943), for which he received an Oscar nomination. (Undeserved. It's a dim script whose trite romance fumbles the main point of the picture—heroic American nurses at Bataan—until well into the second hour.)

Scott's liberal politics led to his involvement with various antifascist and progressive causes, though he escaped the fate of his brother, the screenwriter Adrian Scott, who, as one of the Hollywood Ten, served time in jail for refusing to name names when subpoenaed by a congressional committee.

Asked by an interviewer about his seeming preference for writing women's roles, Allan Scott answered, "I think it was because at RKO in those days the really big stars were women." Scott's daughter, the actress and documentary filmmaker Pippa Scott, said, "My dad became known for writing women's roles particularly well and a number of stars would ask for him. As I recall, that was one of the reasons he was brought into *Imitation of Life*." She recalls "phone calls and visits from Ross Hunter" at the family home.

As an adjunct to my conjecture about Eleanore Griffin as primary source for the darker side of *Imitation of Life*, I nominate Allan Scott as writer-in-chief of the Let-Us-Now-Praise-Lana-Turner first half of the picture. The glide from Fred and Ginger to Lora Meredith surely wouldn't tax a limbered-up screenwriter like Scott: clusters of blond scenes for a blonde star, scenes both light on their feet and lightly satirical. Scott's recipe for his work at RKO might also apply to the Lana Turner apportionment of his late picture for Universal: "The Astaire–Rogers pictures were full of optimism and happy turns of events, slightly tongue-in-cheek and unrelated to the world around us." Sounds like the story of Lora Meredith until Sirk took hold with his brand of Weltschmerz, so alien to the credo of fifties America. Indeed, some of Lana's airiest lines could be outtakes from the suave and swank of *Swing Time* or *Carefree*, e.g., "Walked my feet off, trying to see every agent on Broadway—and some off-Broadway."

Allan Scott never talked about *Imitation of Life* in interviews. When I asked his daughter the reason, she said, "I believe my dad was as willing to talk about that picture as any of the others he worked on. But interviewers always asked about the Astaire and Rogers films. No, he didn't consider it outside his canon. I think he valued it as highly as the others."

Susan Kohner's script, dated July 30, 1958, does not bear the names of Eleanore Griffin and Allan Scott. Instead, the title page of this "Second Revised Final Screenplay" credits Christopher Cooper. The *Imitation of Life* production budget, on the other hand, itemizes "Writers' Salaries" for four persons: Griffin ($22,000) Scott ($20,834) Sy Gomberg ("from 7-15 to 7-21," $2,200), and Inez Cocke ($1,808). What accounts for these contradictions, and why did no one on the picture ever mention the entrances and exits of this quartet of writers?

Inez Cocke was a real person, not a pseudonym. She also worked on Sirk's *Interlude* in 1957. Since her only mention vis-à-vis *Imitation of Life* is in the production budget, and since her small salary suggests minimal involvement, she is hereby excused.

Sy Gomberg, too, was a real person. And so was Christopher Cooper, I learned after much sleuthing, although Mr. Cooper, when the script was written, was six years old. Thus, he might be called an innocent bystander in the case of the missing screenwriter.

After a number of phone calls in Los Angeles, I located Christopher Cooper, or Chris, as he prefers to be called. We arranged to meet for lunch, and he told me how to recognize him in the restaurant: "I look like George Lucas." His description was apt, for Chris, too, has long, salt-and-pepper hair, a gray-white beard, and round glasses. He is, however, some ten years younger than the wizard of *Star Wars* (and not to be confused with another Chris Cooper, the Oscar-winning actor).

Chris's mother is the actress Maxine Cooper, who appeared often on television in the fifties and whom cultists will remember as Velda in *Kiss Me Deadly* (1955) and as the bank teller in *What Ever Happened to Baby Jane?* (1962). Owing to a long and debilitating illness, she was unable to be interviewed. Her son told me that Maxine Cooper and her first husband divorced in the midfifties. She resumed her maiden name, which she also gave to young Chris. In 1957, she married Sy Gomberg, who later became the adoptive father of Chris Cooper. The Gombergs also had two daughters. (Another detail in this complex name game: Chris Cooper, after being adopted by Sy Gomberg, became Chris Gomberg, which is the name he now uses. To avoid further confusion, however, I will call him Chris Cooper here.)

It's relevant to point out that Sy Gomberg was extraordinarily well-liked by his colleagues, and also that he hated shouting, fights, and conflicts—events not unheard of at Universal, where he was under contract in the late fifties. When I contacted James Whitmore, a close friend of Gomberg's, he said, "Sy was a wonderful man, one of my dearest friends and a gentle and a very caring man, with strong impulses to help make things better." Whitmore, however, knew nothing of Gomberg's connection with *Imitation of Life*, since they met only later.

Ray Bradbury said, "We worked together at Universal many years back. It was during that period when Sy was working on *Imitation of*

Life. I'm sure he was going through hell, as most of us went through hell when we were at the studios, but Sy was not one to complain about things when it got rough. But I'm sorry, I can't help further."

James Ragan, a close friend of Gomberg's and a faculty member at USC, where Gomberg taught in the graduate writing program in the nineties, supplied several clues, although speculative ones, to the puzzle of Gomberg's involvement with *Imitation of Life.* Ragan suggested that "Sy might have been brought in to polish the script because he was constantly at work on civil rights, civil liberties, and later, Native American rights. And since he was under contract to Universal at the time, he would have been 'handy' for such a polish. Sirk and Hunter might well have requested someone like Gomberg to make sure the script was not offensive in any way."

Ragan added that it was common practice in those days to bring in a writer like Gomberg for prestige purposes—that is, screenwriters who had won or been nominated for Academy Awards, Writers Guild Awards, and the like. Gomberg was nominated for an Oscar in 1950 for John Ford's *When Willie Comes Marching Home,* and for *Summer Stock* the same year by the Writers Guild. But Gomberg's prestige was no greater than Eleanore Griffin's and Allan Scott's—indeed, Griffin was the only one of the trio who had actually won an Oscar. But she was also a woman.

Gomberg's son, Chris, said, "My father was a big peacemaker who disliked quarrels and fights." The only thing Chris can recall Gomberg saying about *Imitation of Life* is that "there was a lot of conflict with the production." That, in his estimation, is the reason his father removed his own name from the script and added his young stepson's instead. (A year earlier, he had used "Christopher Cooper" for his work on another Universal picture, *Step Down to Terror.*)

Based on scant evidence—that one week in July designated in the production budget, the omission of *Imitation of Life* from Gomberg's credits, the small size of his paycheck—it seems that his involvement went no further than a final polish. According to James Ragan, Gomberg did not claim credit for scripts that he "doctored," neither in conversation nor on his bio sheets.

Speculation on conflicts over the *Imitation of Life* script leads only to further speculation. Since Sirk, Hunter, and studio head Ed Muhl had worked in harmony for years, the fights must have taken place in the writers' building. Did Griffin and Scott dislike working together? Or, did they team up against Gomberg, who was brought in to "improve" their work? Flashback to 1958, when most Americans, including progressives, were capable of language, and opinions, that today would qualify as racist. Might such tiny defamations have crept into the *Imitation of Life* script, only to be removed by Gomberg? It seems unlikely—Allan Scott's liberal credentials were impeccable, and there is no reason to believe that Eleanore Griffin's were any less so.

Perhaps Gomberg's credentials were even more sterling. His sister, Phyllis Spear, told me about a time in the seventies when her brother pulled out of a film because "he could not tolerate the producer's attitude toward blacks, his terrible resentment of the black actors." She added, "They were midway through the shoot when Sy had a falling-out with this big-name producer that I won't name." Indeed, Gomberg's convictions were strong. His son told me that in 1965, both of his parents went to Alabama to march from Selma to Montgomery with Martin Luther King Jr.

On June 2, 1958, William Batliner, casting director at Universal, wrote to Susan Kohner at the Grand Hotel in Rome, where she was traveling with her family. Enclosed with the letter were several pages of script that Susan and Juanita would use as their screen test, viz., the motel room scene. Batliner informed Susan in the letter that "unfortunately, the script is being completely rewritten at the present time and we do not as yet have an appropriate test scene from the new script. I am sending you, however, a scene from the old script which is the type we'll probably use for testing purposes."

Those four script pages provide further clues. Each one has the initials EG in the lower left corner: Eleanore Griffin. This suggests the correctness of my hypothesis: Griffin must have constructed much of the Annie/Sarah Jane part of the screenplay. It's possible that she and Allan Scott even worked separately, perhaps at their respective homes with a treatment as overall blueprint. But, since "the script is being completely rewritten at the present time," as Batliner emphasized, EG may have been odd woman out.

Once that script was indeed rewritten, the initials at the bottom of virtually every page were AS and SG, Scott and Gomberg, suggesting once more that Gomberg did a late polish, although a rather large one. (These initials I verified throughout Susan's script, that "Second Revised Final Screenplay.")

Ironically, that late rewrite changed very little, at least in the motel scene. In Eleanore Griffin's version, which Susan received in Rome, Sarah Jane is working in a gambling casino called the Panhandle rather than the Moulin Rouge. When she leaves work, she returns to the motel, and the dialogue throughout that scene with her mother remains virtually unchanged in the revised script and in the release print of *Imitation of Life*.

Reconstructing the case, it appears that Eleanore Griffin, if put aside in midsummer of 1958, was replaced by script doctor Sy Gomberg, who—owing to conflict and unhappiness of unknown origin—made himself invisible by using his stepson's name rather than his own. (Griffin received screen credit along with Scott; the Writers Guild would have seen to that.) Whatever unhappiness existed, however, the conflict ultimately ended up where it belongs: on the screen, as the great primal clash between Annie Johnson and Sarah Jane. Their scene in the motel, like their other scenes in the film, came from writers at their best. Surely we should honor them all for the dramatic development of *Imitation of Life*, whether their part in writing it was great or small.

Susan Kohner's script, which would have been the version used by other cast members, as well, has a few surprising variations. On page 13 is the early scene where young Susie offers Sarah Jane the black doll, which Sarah Jane refuses. She drops the doll to the floor in disgust, and the camera lingers on it for a long moment. Two pages later, on the morning after Annie and Sarah Jane's arrival, when Lora wakes up and the girls, no longer required to keep quiet, cut loose screaming, the script specifies that Lora and Annie go into the kitchen, where Annie has made Lora's breakfast.

At this point, however, an intriguing vignette is omitted from the final cut. The two girls are left alone. In the script, Sarah Jane says, "I'm afraid we woke up my baby," followed by a deleted shot that Sirk might have kept in for shock value: "She pulls the blanket back. Her doll is Frieda, the white doll."

Besides the scenes written but not used is one absent from the script because it was shot only after the picture wrapped. Susan Kohner explained why: "It was the mother-daughter scene between Lana Turner and Sandra Dee, which wasn't in the script. The scene between Juanita and me was so powerful that it left Lana and Sandra in the dirt without liftup, so that was written and shot afterwards."

Susan isn't certain whether Sirk, or Hunter, or both, decided to add this scene. Although an afterthought, it seems integral to the film because it's the only time Lora and her daughter come into open conflict. Lora, learning from Annie that Susie is in love with Steve, marches from the sickbed to Susie's room. Now it's clear to her why Susie was so upset on hearing of her mother's engagement to Steve. "So Annie told you. Well, that's how you usually find things out about me," Susie responds. For the first time, she is snide.

The scene, well written and well directed, builds as Susie informs her mother that she's going far away to college. Lana makes a high-flown speech about working so hard to provide her daughter a comfortable life, and Susie's response deflates her: "You've given me everything—but yourself!" Followed by a great Lana Turner moment. Chin high, she declaims: "If Steve is going to come between us—I'll give him up. I'll never see him again." And Sandra's exasperated, magnificent retort: "Oh, Mama! Stop acting!"

Then the two women—for Susie is suddenly no longer a girl—play their teary resolution in "white" counterpoint to the heartbreak of Annie and Sarah Jane's melancholy farewell. Susie kneels before her mother and sobs, "Oh, Mama, I'm sorry, I didn't want to hurt you"—a line that echoes Sarah Jane's earlier one to Annie, after the "Fetched-y'all-a-mess-of-crawdads" spectacle: "Oh, Mama, try to understand. I didn't mean to hurt you." These lines resound in Sarah Jane's lamentation on her mother's coffin: "I didn't mean it! Mama! Do you hear me?! I'm sorry!"

Imitation of Life has a Sirkean ending: future happiness vaguely implied, a prospect so false that savvy viewers don't swallow it. The script, however, continued on for a page and a half, thrusting us deep into Ross Hunterland. A wintry, postfuneral scene at Lora's house: she informs Steve that she has decided to adopt Sarah Jane, then take her and Susie—"both my daughters"—far away from New York. He asks, "Where will you go?"

In a mawkish speech—could it be an outtake from a David Edwards play?—she declaims: "I don't know yet. Maybe Iowa. It looks so green from the plane. Or maybe we'll visit the little town where Susie was born—where I was born—and where they still take my talent—such as it is—with a grain of salt. Or perhaps we'll drive up the coast to Maine, rent a house with oil lamps and no plumbing. I'll do the washing—the ironing."

Steve, grinning, has the last word: "You're ham, clean through to the bone, aren't you?" Then, "Lora looks at him, affronted. He leans over and kisses her. Her face becomes soft and happy. As they kiss . . . FADE OUT."

(A couple of still photographs—Lana and Gavin in a snowy landscape, dressed in winter wardrobe not seen in the film—suggest that this scene was actually filmed. If the footage survived, it awaits rediscovery.)

*I*f you're unconvinced that Hollywood glamour is extinct, look at today's gaggle of actresses as they prance interchangeably to the Academy Awards ceremonies. Anorectic, or else too chubby, faces drained of intelligence and pumped with chemicals, nasal-voiced and rather dim overall, they make a spectacle not so different from what you see at the mall. And their dresses, fussed over for days and weeks, are also styleless. That's because the wearer must provide the real style; without it, a dress is just a dress.

And then look at the costumes Jean-Louis designed for any one of some two hundred movies, in a career from 1944 to the early seventies. Or just glance at a still: Rita Hayworth in *Gilda*; Judy Garland in *A Star Is Born*; Kim Novak in *Picnic*; Doris Day in *Pillow Talk*; or get an eyeful of those twenty-nine outfits he designed for Lana in *Imitation of Life*. Even his lesser efforts—outfits for Patricia Knight in the early Sirk film *Shockproof*, for Paulette Goddard in *Anna Lucasta*, for Eva Gabor on several episodes of *Green Acres*—outshine the apparel in that sickly parade of Jennifers, Lisas, and Nicoles.

Ross Hunter, who commissioned Jean-Louis to dress the stars in many of his productions, summed up the designer's genius in a sentence: "Jean is as good at creating an apron as a ball gown."

———

They had figures then . . . and if they didn't, Jean-Louis and those like him molded, revamped, and perfected one for every star. "When I was at Columbia," he said, "some producer wanted flesh [on an actress], and you can't give flesh when you don't have it. The poor girl was skinny, she had a little arm like this, and you give her a big bosom, it doesn't balance. So you give her long sleeves, and try to cover her up, maybe give her a slit and show some leg."

Stars dressed by Jean-Louis and other top designers required personality. If they lacked their own, the studio supplied one. They were taught to walk, speak, smile, and, more important, to shut up. So that a gown, no matter how beautiful, never upstaged the actress. "The best dressed woman," said Jean-Louis, "is the one who's not conspicuous. If a woman is well dressed, you're not aware of what she's wearing." Well, sometimes you are, if it's Marlene Dietrich. For her 1953 nightclub act in Las Vegas, Jean-Louis worked six months on her bugle-beaded, flesh-colored dress made of soufflé, a see-through chiffon.

Jean-Louis (né J. L. Berthault, in Paris, in 1907) spent his early career as a sketch artist with a Parisian couturier. Then a taxicab ran him down. The financial settlement for his broken arm paid for his one-way ticket to New York, where, in 1936, he was hired as a lead designer at Hattie Carnegie's *maison de couture*. "The following year he designed the trim little suit that became a classic, the Carnegie suit, one of the first fashions to become popular as an American name design. The suit, which had a fitted, buttoned top, nipped waist and narrow skirt, was worn by everybody who was anybody in society and fashion at the time."

In 1943, according to Jean-Louis, his contract with Carnegie wasn't renewed. Just then, Columbia Pictures made him an offer, no doubt owing to the good offices of Joan Cohn, wife of the studio head, and a fan of the young designer. Eventually he dressed all the ladies of Hollywood, or close to it, on-screen and off.

Claudette Colbert in *Tomorrow Is Forever* (1946); *The Guilt of Janet Ames* (1947), starring Rosalind Russell—"the way she carries the clothes always made it a pleasure to dress her," he said; Lucille Ball in *Miss Grant Takes Richmond* (1949); Deborah Kerr and Donna Reed in *From Here to Eternity* (1953); Joan Crawford, *Queen Bee* (1955) and *Autumn Leaves* (1956); Vivien Leigh in *Ship of Fools* (1965); and Rita Hayworth and Kim Novak again and again—these are just a few of the stars who looked their best in creations by Jean-Louis.

Nominated by the Academy more than a dozen times, he won but once, for *The Solid Gold Cadillac* in 1956. But Judy Holliday, the star, wasn't a designer favorite, although he dressed her for four other pictures. "When I saw her the first time in the fitting room, I thought, Oh my God, what are we going to do with that? She was standing with a sloping shoulder. But then she came on the screen, a different woman."

Jean-Louis, like other ostensibly heterosexual fashion designers, was gossiped about. It's true he married late: the first time in 1955, when he was forty-eight. The marriage lasted until her death in 1987. In 1993, he married Loretta Young, who had been a close friend of Jean-Louis and his late wife for many years. Loretta told columnist Liz Smith at the time that, hearing Jean-Louis was very depressed after his wife's death, she paid him a visit and persuaded him to come and stay with her in Palm Springs for a while. He stayed for many weeks. Eventually Loretta said, "Let's buy a house here together." And they did. Loretta, righteous as ever, added, "You know me, Liz, I just can't see living with a man I'm not married to." The marriage lasted until his death in 1997.

Their friendship had begun when he costumed Loretta in 1952 for an undistinguished film, *Paula*. The following year he began designing the gowns she wore as hostess of *The Loretta Young Show* on television. Many women viewers reportedly tuned in each week just to watch Loretta sweep through the doorway in yet another stunning creation. (Her grandeur became an object of fun, especially when Carol Burnett made a sweeping entrée—and landed in a crumpled heap with skirt tail over her head.)

Perhaps Jean-Louis's most famous—even notorious—dress was worn by Marilyn Monroe in 1962 when she sang "Happy Birthday, Mr. President" to John F. Kennedy, turning the simple song into extended foreplay. The gown—soufflé again, like Marlene's—was adorned with some six thousand beads. She was sewn into it, as into a winding sheet—a macabre metaphor, though fitting, for the occassion that called for the dress possibly hastened her end. To perform at the birthday bash, she went AWOL from *Something's Got to Give*. Added to her other infractions, that absence proved too much for Fox; the studio fired her. This humiliation destabilized her further. Then, too, her public flirtation alarmed many in Washington, who knew the hidden punch line to Marilyn's naughty joke. Powerful men wanted to stop her dangerous coquetry.

Marilyn had recently bought a white sequined evening gown from Jean-Louis for $1,600. According to several sources, she telephoned his shop on Friday, August 3, 1962, and made plans to meet him on the following Monday—a day that, for Marilyn, didn't come.

Dressing Well Is the Best Revenge

Although an avalanche of press releases claimed that Lana wore thirty-four different outfits in *Imitation of Life,* by my count it's twenty-nine. That's including housecoats; the print dress in the flea powder modeling assignment; that blue tailored suit she wears again and again in the first half of the film, usually with a white blouse; the mink coat she flings at her agent; and her onstage costumes for Lora Meredith's Broadway hits. It's fitting that Lana's wardrobe ascends the ladder of fashion, from off-the-rack summer dress in her opening scene to creations worthy of Marie Antoinette: the dresses keep pace with her character's rise from destitution to superstardom.

Perhaps Lana started with thirty-four outfits; deleted scenes could account for the lower tally in the release print. Certainly Ross Hunter didn't cut corners when it came to his star, for he wanted her to feel beautiful and glamorous. That's why he insisted on real jewels instead of paste. "You couldn't tell the difference in the audience," he said, "but Lana knew they were real. And that's why she radiated on the screen."

The jewelry was said to be worth a million, and it was watched over by armed guards. Even when Lana was filming a scene, they were nearby, strategically positioned behind the camera. Several months before the shoot, Laykin et Cie agreed to lend the jewelry to Universal. By the time filming started, however, a third of the pieces had been sold in Laykin's shop at I. Magnin. All buyers agreed to allow

(continued)

their new jewels to be picked up by armed guards and taken to the studio as needed for use in the picture. And so, from time to time, the production department got calls from wealthy matrons who inquired: "Are my jewels working today?"

Bill Thomas (1921–2000), who dressed everyone but Lana in *Imitation of Life,* concentrated on bringing characters to life on the screen through realistic costumes. His realism complemented Jean-Louis's pyrotechnics with fabric and accessories. Thomas's outfits for Susan Kohner and Sandra Dee are nice looking for every day and properly dressy for the theatre, though in no sense fashion trendsetters. Sarah Jane's skirts and blouses, and Susie's less mature, less form-fitting casuals, are the clothes of well-brought-up teenagers in the late fifties. (According to the production budget, Sandra's wardrobe totaled $6,350, Susan's $945.)

Bill Thomas veered toward conservatism in dress, especially for adolescents. "Today, the American teenage girl's weakness for fads has encouraged fashion designers to promote gimmicks instead of clothes," he said at the time of *Imitation of Life.* "Teenagers, like most women, tend to overdress." He advised all females: "Take an extra two minutes to study yourself in a mirror. If you look overdressed to yourself, remember it will be ten times as obvious to somebody else."

An example of Thomas's realistic approach is the look he gave Juanita Moore. Her costumes—matronly housedresses—intentionally play down her real-life attractiveness, thus reinforcing her character's humility and detachment from worldly things. In her few dressy scenes in *Imitation of Life,* she wears the conventional cuts and dark colors of old age, although Annie Johnson would be about forty. Total cost of her wardrobe: $590. (As for male members of the cast, John Gavin wore $1,650 on his back, while other men either furnished their own suits or wore costumes from the wardrobe department.)

Jean-Louis once said, "I couldn't make a sketch till I know who is the star." Bill Thomas, on the other hand, might well have insisted that for him, it was always the story. If necessary, Thomas could have completed costume designs even before the picture was cast.

Prior to *Imitation of Life,* Bill Thomas dressed the actors in ten other Sirk films of the fifties. Thus, he is a key contributor to the visual integrity of some of Sirk's most important pictures, including *All That Heaven Allows, Magnificent Obsession,* and *The Tarnished Angels.* If he made Jane Wyman appropriately dowdy and repressed, he also pushed *Take Me to Town* over the top by dressing Ann Sheridan in dance-hall haute couture. As the voluptuous redhead Vermilion O'Toole, she wears a parade of high-gloss outfits that verge on vulgarity but never cross the line—because the character doesn't. Lee Patrick, as the cigar-smoking boss lady of the "opera house"—i.e., saloon—wears a shocking green, hoop-skirted gown that alludes to Scarlett O'Hara's improvised dress from recycled draperies. To show Patrick's witty costume to best advantage, Sirk had her play the dance-hall piano while standing up.

A Chicago native, Bill Thomas grew up in Southern California. After army service during World War Two, he took a job at Western Costume, which supplied wardrobe to the studios. In the late forties he became an apprentice to MGM designer Irene, and then to Walter Plunkett, a specialist in historical design who created the costumes for *Gone With the Wind.* Thomas made Judy Garland's clown costume in *The Pirate* in 1948. The following year he left MGM for Universal, where he remained until 1959. Nominated multiple times for an Oscar, he won for *Spartacus* in 1961, an award he shared with Valles. (Thomas designed only the slave garb worn by Jean Simmons in the picture.)

Twice he dressed Lana Turner, the first time in *The Lady Takes a Flyer* (1958), then in *By Love Possessed* (1961). Years later he told an interviewer, "Lana was the most clothes-conscious star I ever worked with. She knew fabric and color, and what worked for her, like nobody I ever met."

Although a member of Sirk's "family at the studio," as well as a friend of Ross Hunter, Bill Thomas was no lackey. Barbara Rush recalls a volcanic quarrel between Hunter and Thomas on one of the Sirk–Hunter pictures she appeared in. "They had a strong disagreement over some outfit I was wearing," she recalled. "Bill threatened to quit. He said to Ross, 'Don't you talk to me like that!' And Ross yelled back, 'I'm the producer and you will do it exactly as I tell you to.' Then Bill said, 'I won't! And I won't be responsible for that disaster.'"

I asked about the outcome of their dispute. Barbara Rush sighed, "Oh, they adored each other. But that doesn't mean you can't get mad."

Only Her Makeup Man Knows for Sure

Reading movie credits—opening or end—was less taxing in the studio era than it is today, when every carpet beater and veggie washer gets a mention. Certain names then were enigmatic: Van Nest Polglaze, Omar Kiam. None, however, was more ubiquitous than Westmore. Indeed, the Westmores pervaded Hollywood beautification like Bonapartes across nineteenth-century Europe. With one exception, they were all men, and all brothers: Mont (1902–1940), Perc (1904–1970), Ern (1904–1968), Wally (1906–1973), Bud (1918–1973), and Frank (1923–1985). Patricia Westmore, Lana Turner's hairdresser on *Imitation of Life*, was their half-sister. All worked as makeup artists, and several became studio department heads, Perc at Warner Bros., Wally at Paramount, Bud at Universal from 1947 until his death in 1973. It was Bud who made up Susan, Juanita, Sandra, and the others for *Imitation of Life*, often assisted by colleagues in his department. (Lana's longtime personal makeup man, Del Armstrong, took care of her.)

Bud and Frank were born in the United States; the others in England, where their father, George H. Westmore, was an expert wig maker. Father and mother moved to Canada in 1909, and from there to various American cities before settling in Los Angeles in 1916, just as the movies needed more and more such artisans. Westmore *père* switched from wigs to makeup, founding the first studio makeup department during the silent era. His older sons served as his apprentices. Following his death in 1931, they in turn taught the family trade to the younger boys. The dynasty still reigns, and if you check the family name on IMDb.com, you'll find a dozen or more of George's descendants at work in movies and TV.

(continued)

If *Imitation of Life* were made today, it's doubtful that Juanita Moore's and Susan Kohner's skin tones would match from shot to shot and scene to scene. But nothing less than perfection would do for Bud Westmore's department. Both women were darkened; Juanita was also made to age dramatically, owing to her character's illness and to grief. Lana, of course, ages not a day from 1947, when the picture opens, to the "present" of 1959. She is kept radiant, and movie-star gorgeous, thanks to a battalion of beautifiers.

Bud Westmore's department comprised some fifty-seven makeup rooms, staffed at peak periods by sixty to seventy experts. "You have to have almost the same professional standards as a doctor or a lawyer," he once told an interviewer, referring not only to professional care but also to confidentiality. "You often hear who's going with whom—and shouldn't be, plus other choice tidbits," he added. "You could fill a column with what you hear." Westmore said the average time needed to make up an actress was around two hours, and about thirty minutes for an actor. That allows ample time for gossip.

He worked on almost five hundred pictures, and along the way he established a prosthesis wing within Universal's makeup department. Among his notable creations were a fishtail for Ann Blyth in *Mr. Peabody and the Mermaid* (she could swim in it); the many faces of Lon Chaney, re-created for James Cagney in *The Man of a Thousand Faces*; and the eponymous *Creature from the Black Lagoon*. (Had Westmore lived to see the schnoz on Nicole Kidman in *The Hours*, he would surely have urged the producers to fire the half-dozen credited prostheticians and bring in one or two young Westmores. Playing Virginia Woolf, an unconventional beauty, Kidman looks more like Golda Meir.)

Westmore understood that makeup, including prosthetics, should not detract from the performer. No matter how spectacular the craftsmanship of his department, it was to remain subsidiary to the actor. "When a performer is properly made up," Westmore said, "he has nothing extraneous to worry about. He can concentrate on the dialogue and thus give the studio the performance they are paying him for."

*G*ary Marmorstein, in his book *Hollywood Rhapsody,* wrote that "If Frank Skinner developed a trademark, it was an overwrought tension that spiced melodramas of the Ross Hunter variety: *Magnificent Obsession, Imitation of Life, Back Street* (the 1941 version as well as the 1961), and *Madame X.*"

"Overwrought" is a loaded word, and I don't entirely agree with Marmorstein's assessment. On the contrary, before the fifties, and the fourteen scores that Skinner composed for Sirk films, plus an additional half-dozen for Ross Hunter productions not directed by Sirk, Skinner's style was noticeably *underwrought.* Although I certainly don't know all of his approximately three hundred scores, I have heard the reputedly better ones, such as *The House of the Seven Gables* (1940), for which Skinner received the second of his five Academy nominations in various musical categories. A puzzling nomination, this one, for the score is interchangeable with any one of a hundred movies from its era. No part of it creates the illusion (as top-notch film scores do) that it's inseparable from the scene it accompanies, except perhaps for the bland ditty "The Color of Your Eyes," which Skinner wrote for Vincent Price to sing at the piano.

Then, *The Naked City* (1948). Skinner and Miklos Rozsa shared credit for this one, owing to an original score by George Bassman that the producer threw out. Rozsa agreed to take on the project, but was given only two weeks to do his work. Finding that time frame untenable, he agreed to score the chase sequence at the end and to leave the first part of the film to Frank Skinner. But that first meagre section, blandly jazz-lite, cannot stand up against Rozsa's forceful and effective finale. At last, you think, a real composer has arrived—as though a great gust of Brahms had swept through a Percy Grainger recital.

Contrast that with Skinner's score for *Imitation of Life*. Although not the extraordinary kind that overflows the screen en route to the concert hall, it does serve the picture, which is the duty of any film score. Using a variety of styles, textures, rhythms, tempi, themes, and variations, Skinner complements and italicizes the onscreen images.

Even before the movie starts up, we're given several big musical cues. As we see the Universal-International logo, that important globe in space, what we hear is a bluesy, gospel-inspired piano accompanied by tense strings. A few bars of this. Then, as jewels start to fall in slow motion for the opening credits, an orchestral allusion to a famous quasi-spiritual. If you were singing along, you'd get as far as "Ol' man river, that ol' man river, he must—" then an abrupt cut-off the very moment Lana Turner's name appears in big white letters on the screen . . . and followed instantly by a sugary segue to Earl Grant singing the lushly orchestrated title song, "Imitation of Life," composed by Sammy Fain, with lyric by Paul Francis Webster.

This musical overture, so redolent of late-fifties moviegoing, was intended to seduce. Most audience members, highly susceptible, found themselves trapped like flies in candy floss. They couldn't have left the theatre if the screen had caught fire.

Immediately after the title and credits music, the jaunty-sad calliope sound of an unseen carousel breaks into the score. It's playing "The Blue Danube," and later, near the end of the Coney Island sequence, a Gay Nineties tune as the little girls balance a beer can on the sleeping fat man's belly. (These carny sounds, apparently loved by Frank Skinner, recur in a number of his scores.) In the rest of the beach sequence, we hear distant late-forties source music, viz., big-band numbers presumably from radios, and barely audible through the beach noise of shrill voices, amusement rides, and PA announcements.

A snatch of jaunty going-home-through-city-streets music, almost a jingle, bridges Coney Island with the next sequence: Lora, Annie, and the girls arrive at Lora's building and make their way upstairs to the cold-water flat. As they enter the dark apartment, several *dark* notes foreshadow the score's later melancholia: minor-key variations that one might call "Sarah Jane's Theme," although on the sound track album it is blended into a cut titled "Home from the Beach."

A bit later, when young Sarah Jane drops the black doll contemptuously on the floor and complains, "Why do we always have to live in the back?" the scene ends with seven piano bass notes played fortissimo—an ominous cue, and certainly not your usual little-girl music in a Hollywood picture, unless she's the Bad Seed.

Frank Skinner (1897–1968) seems to have lived a placid Midwestern life in high-pitched Hollywood. Born in the farming community of Meredosia, Illinois, he was one of five children in a family chronically short of money. But they all loved music; the father was a self-taught keyboardist who played piano for the homespun orchestra that Frank cobbled together at age sixteen. Then Frank quit high school to earn money for the family coffers.

Later, however, the entire Skinner family sacrificed so that he could study at the Chicago Musical College. Frank's youngest brother, Wilbur, for instance, sent Frank half his wages each week. Skinner soon mastered piano, cornet, and trombone. After graduation, he joined a vaudeville orchestra. According to some sources, he played piano on a riverboat. He also played for dance bands and eventually moved to New York, where he got a job as a musical arranger at Robbins Music. In 1924 he married, and in the early thirties he spent six months at MGM as an arranger. Two years later, the studio invited him back to orchestrate its production of *The Great Ziegfeld*. In 1937, Universal offered Skinner a contract, and there he remained for the next thirty years. Among his hundreds of credits, some would have been given for his supervisory role over the work of other composers in the music department. He wrote three books, one on orchestration, another on arranging, and what may have been the first textbook on film composing, *Underscore,* published in 1950.

During his early Hollywood years, Skinner arranged and orchestrated for Deanna Durbin pictures. The first film he scored was *Son of*

Frankenstein in 1939. Hans Salter, another stalwart of Universal's music department, was assigned to orchestrate. Years later, in an oral history, Salter recounted their seat-of-the-pants episode: "If you gave Frank Skinner two months to write a score, he would be behind the eight ball at the end because he didn't start until two weeks before the recording date. On that picture, during the last three or four days, we had to work twenty-four hours a day at the studio. Frank wrote the sequence, I started to orchestrate, he took a nap. When I was through, I told him okay, he got up and wrote another piece, and so on."

Salter wasn't attributing sloth to his colleague and friend; such delays came from overwork. To Salter, Frank Skinner was "an awfully nice fellow. He was extremely helpful to me and you didn't sometimes have to ask him. He offered his help." In 1943, when Salter, an Austrian refugee, became an American citizen, Skinner served as his witness.

Skinner's filmography veers eccentrically, from Hitchcock's *Saboteur* to the Maria Montez opus *Arabian Nights* (both 1942), to the infamous *Bedtime for Bonzo* (1951)—suppressed during the Reagan regime—to the Sirk–Hunter pictures, and *The Ugly American* (1963), into whose score he reportedly incorporated such unusual instruments as the gamelan, marimba, finger cymbals, log drums, tree bells, and harp played with a pick—and produced a lackluster score even so. Skinner retired in 1966, after *Madame X*.

Skinner's most impressive work—opulent scores derived from European romanticism—was done under the aegis of Sirk and Hunter. Perhaps his compositions grew more assertive because Sirk, who knew music, encouraged a distinctive musical idiom. (Sirk liked to point out that "melodrama," a word often used against him, means "drama plus music." A pity Sirk's detractors are less learned than he.) Maybe Hunter, too, encouraged less restraint; certainly the 1961 *Back Street* sounds like a musical Congress of Vienna.

Buttressing this hypothesis is Skinner's score for *Man of a Thousand Faces* (1957), done in the thick of the Sirk and Hunter years, but with no involvement by either. Skinner's score for this lumbering, repetitious movie, badly directed by Joseph Pevney, is amorphous and frustrating. He provided a lovely, melodious musical opening. After that, we hear a surfeit of tiresome vaudeville songs for James Cagney's numbers, and long stretches minus any musical underscore at all. You wait, in vain, for variations on that beautiful intro.

Imitation of Life, on the other hand, abounds in such variations, even though it lacks any single melody to equal the opening of *Man of a Thousand Faces.* In the course of *Imitation,* the title song is worked very hard, but there's a reason: to italicize Lora's imitations—life on stage imitating a lived life; a surrogate mother given to Susie in place of Lora herself; Annie taken for granted and not accorded equal status in the household, despite Lora's genuine love for her. And the imitations of Sarah Jane: her unshakeable belief in the superiority of white blood over black, and the false persona that belief engenders.

Sometimes a variation on this theme song trickles under a scene. Sometimes it's more robust, and occasionally it overjumps the frame in a Wagnerian sweep, as when Lora and Steve quarrel on Christmas Eve, and she storms from the building as he stands, forlorn, on the staircase. Once or twice, this title song is played on a tinkling cocktail piano.

Skinner alternates between blond underscore for Lora, Steve, and Susie, and heavier, ominous motifs for Annie and Sarah Jane, suggestive of jazz and gospel. In the motel scene, musical irony worthy of Sirk himself: a subtle paraphrase of the spiritual, "Sometimes I Feel Like a Motherless Child," which recurs in Annie's deathbed theme.

In spite of Skinner's professionalism with the *Imitation of Life* score, his limitations are not far to seek. As noted, Skinner gives the picture's title song a vigorous workout—but it's someone else's song. Without that Fain–Webster paradigm, and the spirituals sampling, this score might have turned out as paltry as so many others by Skinner, the musical equivalent of vanishing ink.

Title Song

The first line of his obituary in the *Los Angeles Times*, on December 7, 1989, evoked an era: "Sammy Fain, among the last of that select breed

(continued)

of tunesmiths who peddled their songs from the backs of trucks and in the dingy hallways of New York City's legendary Tin Pan Alley, died Wednesday."

Without composers like him, American "standards" might have stopped at "Turkey in the Straw." His unforgettable songs include "I'll Be Seeing You," "Let a Smile Be Your Umbrella," "I Can Dream, Can't I?," "That Old Feeling," and the beautiful ballad, "He's Only Wonderful," from a failed Broadway musical, *Flahooley*. Fain also scored, and wrote for, a number of films, including *Calamity Jane* (winning an Oscar for Best Song, "Secret Love"), *Love Is a Many Splendored Thing* (a second Best Song Oscar, for the title song), and *Tender Is the Night*.

Most of Sirk's films at Universal have an autumnal look, along with the melancholy tone of summer lapsing. Perhaps their most fitting musical accompaniment would have been "The Four Last Songs" of Richard Strauss. Failing that, Sammy Fain and Paul Francis Webster, the lyricist, blended, in the title song "Imitation of Life," wistfulness—"Skies above, in flaming color, without love, they're so much duller"—and an aesthetic dictum to clarify the title: "A false creation, an imitation of life."

Webster found it easier to write lyrics before hearing the music. "I've completed a set of lyrics in an evening," he said, "and I've sweated a month to get a set of lyrics right." He joked that his collaborator had the easier job: "It just drives me wild when I hand a title to Sammy Fain and at about the speed of a fast tennis ball he'll construct music around it."

Webster won Oscars along with Sammy Fain for "Secret Love" and "Love Is a Many Splendored Thing," as well as a third one (with Johnny Mandel) for "The Shadow of Your Smile," from *The Sandpiper*. His legacy, however, is the grace and simplicity of his lyrics, which include "Two Cigarettes in the Dark" (inspired, he said, by seeing Garbo and John Gilbert light each other's cigarettes in a film), "I Got It Bad and That Ain't Good," "Memphis in June," and many more.

(continued)

Less sophisticated, but wildly popular, were "Somewhere My Love" ("Lara's Theme") from *Doctor Zhivago*; "The Loveliest Night of the Year," made famous by Mario Lanza; and "April Love," which Pat Boone at first resisted and which eventually became the biggest single ever released by the Dot record label.

When first offered "Love Is a Many Splendored Thing," Nat "King" Cole turned it down, even though Twentieth Century-Fox, which released the film in 1955, offered him a tax-free Cadillac and a ten-thousand-dollar bonus. (Doris Day, Tony Martin, and Eddie Fisher also nixed the song.) Eventually Cole recorded it—how could he not have known right off how well it suited his voice? It's possible that Fain and Webster, perhaps as a wry joke four years later, intentionally wrote a Nat "King" Cole song for someone else—an imitation called "Imitation of Life."

Earl Grant, who sang the title song with just the right earnest detachment, was one of those creamy-voiced young male vocalists of the late fifties, all of whom learned from Cole the velvety way to caress a ballad. The others were Brook Benton, Sam Cooke, and Otis Redding. They all died tragically, and too soon, and their best recordings have a sad overlay that, in retrospect, sounds like an early good-bye.

Born in Oklahoma, Earl Grant was an accomplished instrumentalist—piano, trumpet, drums, Hammond organ—as well as a singer. In 1958, Grant was preparing a thesis for an MA in music from the University of Southern California, and also teaching school, when he took a job at a club near the USC campus. An impresario heard the act, and soon Grant was performing at the Interlude in Hollywood. A Decca recording contract and TV appearances followed. Among his best recordings are "The End," "If I Only Had Time," and "Imitation of Life." In June 1970, Grant was returning to Los Angeles after a performance in Mexico. He was killed instantly when his Rolls-Royce crashed off the roadway in New Mexico. A young traveling companion, seventeen-year-old Roosevelt Woods, died with him.

*W*hen Ed Muhl died, in 2001, at the age of ninety-four, no obituary appeared. Not in *Variety*, which seldom overlooks a Hollywood death, nor in the *Los Angeles Times*, a paper that would normally publish a career rundown, and a photograph, of a self-made man so central to a major studio. Muhl, who worked at Universal from 1926 until the late sixties, first as a lowly tabulating clerk, and then, from 1953, as head of production, even added his name to the Universal-International logo. In a number of that studio's productions, in the lower left-hand corner not far from the spinning globe, you see the proclamation:

Edward Muhl
In Charge of Production.

When I mentioned this omission to a staff member of the *Los Angeles Times,* she was amazed, and rushed to her computer to search the paper's archives for, as she put it, "at least a paid death notice, wouldn't you think?" But there was none. I almost felt that a great effort had been made to bury the man's name along with the man. Eventually I discovered that in Hollywood, even now, there is one studio official who's eager to hear about Ed Muhl . . . provided you do all the talking. More to come on that. But first, Muhl's backstory.

Ed Muhl is important to our narrative because he fostered the Douglas Sirk–Ross Hunter productions that culminated in *Imitation of Life*. Without Muhl as de facto studio chief, some of those productions might exist, but not in the form we know them today. Muhl, Hunter, and Sirk formed a compatible, and durable, troika. Even more unusual, in Hollywood, was the latitude each man granted the other: Hunter seldom interfered with Sirk, nor did Sirk overstep his director's boundaries; and Muhl left them to their respective tasks, whose results he enjoyed as movies and gloated over as box office earners.

In a sense, Universal was a Midwestern studio. Its founder, Carl Laemmle, though born in Germany, got his start in Chicago, with nickelodeons. Ross Hunter originated in Ohio, Frank Skinner in Illinois, and several stars associated with Universal also came from the heartland: Hoot Gibson from Nebraska, Marjorie Main from Indiana, Rock Hudson from Illinois, Jane Wyman from Missouri. Fannie Hurst, whose novels Universal filmed again and again, was Ohio born and St. Louis bred. And Ed Muhl, in some ways the embodiment of Midwestern values, started out in Indiana.

A certain prairie plainness overspread the vast studio itself during the first half of the twentieth century. Henry Mancini (from Cleveland) described the Universal lot during his early years in the music department as "a very friendly place, homey instead of bustling, and very quiet. We were like a family, and if someone whom none of us knew came into the commissary at lunch, it was an event." Rock Hudson, late in life, recalled knowing "everybody by their first name. You never locked doors, everybody was a friend, everybody knew each other."

According to Muhl's studio biography of 1959, his father was a foundryman in Richmond, Indiana, where Ed was born in 1907. The Muhls, with their several children, moved to Santa Ana, California, in 1922, and two years later Ed graduated from the local high school. After graduation, he held a succession of jobs as foundry worker, used car salesman, clerk in a Long Beach bookstore, and tabulating clerk at a Los Angeles furniture store.

————

At this point, Muhl's eldest son, William, assumes the role of narrator. Born in 1940, William Muhl is the only child of Ed Muhl's first marriage. Later, by his second wife, Muhl fathered six other children.

"I'll tell you how my dad got his first job at Universal, in 1926. Barker Brothers, the furniture store, sold a clock to the studio's accounting department. But it soon broke. So my dad was sent to the studio to fix it. He walked in and someone asked, 'Are you the new clerk?' and my dad said, 'Yes!' The other guy, the actual new clerk, never showed up. And Dad never went back to Barker Brothers.

"From accounting, he moved to the legal department, which he eventually headed. You know how that happened? He became a lawyer through correspondence courses. He passed the bar exam, but he never became a practicing lawyer. He was very smart, and a good organizer.

"Now, Carl Laemmle, who founded the studio in 1915, was still very much in command in the 1920s. But he had an assistant who didn't like my dad. Tried to get him fired, and here's how. Carl Laemmle owned several apartment houses in San Diego, and that assistant persuaded him to send my dad down there. A lot of the apartments stood empty, so it looked like a no-win job. My dad went down, stayed a while, looked the apartments over, and came back to report to the boss. He told Laemmle, 'If you'll cut the rents in half, and work on volume instead of trying to make a million off each apartment, you'll fill 'em up.' That's exactly what Laemmle did, and he was so happy with my dad that he brought him in as his assistant—and fired the other guy!"

I pointed out that Ed Muhl's apartment-renting strategies matched his later philosophy of picture making. "Yes," said his son, "my dad believed in not spending a tremendous amount on a picture. He was content to make back possibly three times what they had put into the movie." Fiscal conservativism led to the topic of Ross Hunter, and his knack for turning the proverbial sow's ear not only into a silk purse, but an entire wardrobe by Jean-Louis, with matching jewels and furs, and glamour queens on minimum wage.

"Ross was one of Dad's favorites," said Ed Muhl's son. "They didn't socialize away from work, but they would have lunch from time to time. My dad liked the producers who didn't want to throw money around."

William Muhl couldn't recall specifics about his dad and Douglas Sirk, although Sirk had this to say: "Muhl was a very nice guy, but he had no showmanship. And in movies you must be a gambler. To produce films is to gamble." Hilde Sirk, friendly with the second Mrs. Muhl, visited her in Beverly Hills, and who knows what ideas they came up with that led to Douglas Sirk pictures.

William Muhl does recall that "*Imitation of Life* was one movie my dad talked about. It was one of his favorites of the big color movies that Universal did. He also liked the old black-and-white movies— *Frankenstein, The Wolf Man,* the Sherlock Holmes pictures—and he'd bring those home on Friday nights and we'd watch them over the weekend."

Muhl, who oversaw production at Universal from 1953 until 1969, was number three in the chain of command. Nate Blumberg ran the studio, while Milton J. Rackmil, in New York, served as president and CEO. (Years later, when asked about Rackmil, Ed Muhl said, "He was smart enough to understand that he didn't know a thing about Hollywood. He once asked me if he should develop personal relationships with stars in order to be a good studio manager." Muhl shot back with a line of Mogulship 101: "No. All you need are two kinds of books: a good screenplay and a fat checkbook.")

Although generally well liked, Ed Muhl could shrink an oversized star ego when necessary. According to his son, when Lana Turner was making *Madame X,* she had a tiff with Ross Hunter and "decided not to report for work one day. So they shut down the stage. The next day, she came in and found the set closed up tight. She went to my dad's office. 'What's going on here?' she asked.

"My dad looked at her and said, 'Who are you?' Because, you see, she had on those huge dark glasses. She said, 'Why, I'm Lana Turner!' and he said, 'Well, I wouldn't have guessed it. Will you take those ridiculous glasses off?' Then Lana said, 'Why aren't the stages open?' and he put it to her straight: 'We're not doing another shot until you decide to work for a living.'"

And what did Lana say after her scolding?

"Well," laughed William Muhl, "I guess she agreed to go back to work. My dad thought it was ridiculous that she went on strike because of some quarrel she had with Ross Hunter." (Between *Imitation of Life* and *Madame X,* filmed in 1965, Lana was big again—but not too big for a comeuppance.) Hitchcock, on the other hand, was too big. Once, following some difference of opinion with the head of production, he sent a memo asking, "Do you believe that audiences say, 'Let's go see the new Ed Muhl movie'?"

It's not an anomaly that Ed Muhl was largely absent from the spotlight during his long career at Universal. That studio didn't have celebrity moguls such as Zanuck and Warner and Mayer. If Fox was Oz, say, and MGM the Emerald City, then Universal was Kansas. And that suited Ed Muhl fine.

"He didn't like the limelight," said his son. "He attended a few premieres, small ones, and a couple of Academy Awards ceremonies, but otherwise he was an executive five days a week, and weekends he spent at the ranch." In 1938, Muhl bought a 120-acre spread near Saugus (a town later absorbed into Santa Clarita), in the northern part of Los Angeles County, for which he paid four dollars an acre, according to his son. William Muhl recalled that "a neighbor up there told him, 'You got taken! I only paid two dollars.'" Actual management of the property, he said, was done by his father's parents.

Whether at home in Beverly Hills, or at the ranch, Ed Muhl read nonstop. "He read countless scripts," said his son. "He had taken that Evelyn Woods speed reading course, so he would go through six or seven a night. They were stacked by his bedside. He also read a lot of books, and at the breakfast table you'd have to set the newspaper on fire in order to talk to him."

When I asked William Muhl to sum up his father's personality and character, he said, "He was a very honest man. He would always tell us, 'Don't lie, don't cheat, don't do this, don't do that.' He was almost like a preacher. And he lived that way. He had a lot of friends in the production end, the lower end of the studio, guys who had worked their way up, like him. He was honest with his bosses and his employees. He never did any throat cutting. Under different circumstances, I think he would have been a farmer. He liked repairing fences and delivering colts up at the ranch."

Muhl's studio biography from 1959 concluded with a line surely applied to no other high muck-a-muck in Hollywood: "He takes almost as much pride in his alfalfa crops, his flock of chickens, and his well-trained horses as he does in turning out a hit movie." (Perhaps he and Sirk, another farmer manqué, spent long hours discussing crops and livestock.)

In photographs from the fifties, Ed Muhl looks a little like Raymond Burr, and also like Burr's *Perry Mason* adversary, William Talman. In those photos, he wears dark suits, with patterned ties, and combs his full head of dark hair back, with a crest to the right. He has narrowed eyes, as if from years of squinting in the sun, and a cautious half-smile while cutting a huge silver anniversary cake in 1952 to celebrate twenty-five years at Universal—his own quarter century, and also that of Mrs. Margaret Teeter, a waitress in the studio commissary, with whom he shares the cake. (That rationed smile has vanished in later photographs taken with Lew Wasserman, who acquired the studio in 1962 and fired many old-timers, although not Muhl.)

Muhl, under Universal's new regime, gradually devolved. By the mid-sixties, he had become a less vital part of studio management. Eventually, he worked as a consultant around Hollywood, and retired in the early seventies. Gradually, Muhl "sold off little bits of the ranch," according to his son. During those long retirement years, added William Muhl, "he liked to get in his car and drive all over California. When he sold the ranch, he got a small condominium up there in the Santa Clarita area. Later, he rented a house. He was interested in a lot of things. For instance, he would go into hardware stores to see what the newest inventions were. He continued reading a lot. He went to Europe a couple of times, and visited the town in Germany where the Muhl family originated. When he visited me, he would complain about how the studios were being run."

Wrapping up his thoughts about his father, William Muhl said: "I was very proud of him. I liked the way he kept a normal family life, as though he were an accountant. Early on, he air-conditioned the writers' building at Universal. That happened after he visited the building one day and found it extemely hot. 'How can anybody be creative in this heat?' he said."

———————

Most voracious readers have a high regard for writers—whether they're stuck in a hot building or in hot water. Perhaps that's why Ed Muhl sided with screenwriter Dalton Trumbo at the time of *Spartacus*. As a blacklisted member of the Hollywood Ten, Trumbo spent almost a year in prison in 1950 for contempt of Congress. After his release, he moved, with his family, to Mexico, where, under various pseudonyms, he wrote a number of scripts during the fifties.

Dalton Trumbo's name, in the Hollywood of 1960, was anathema to such flamboyant McCarthyites as Hedda Hopper. To others—for instance, Kirk Douglas—Trumbo was a friend who had been wronged. Still others respected his writing for the screen, and would welcome his return as a colleague, but considered him too dangerous to touch. Even though Trumbo was the principal screenwriter on *Spartacus,* he had no guarantee that his name would appear in the credits.

Existing evidence suggests that Ed Muhl played a minor role in annulling the blacklist, although Otto Preminger was the first to break it, by putting Trumbo's name on *Exodus,* released in January 1960. I asked Christopher Trumbo, son of the screenwriter, whether Muhl was the one who permitted his father's name to be used on-screen for *Spartacus* when it was released in October of the same year. (Even after Preminger's bold defiance, Trumbo's name on a film still elicited threats of boycott.)

Christopher Trumbo answered, "I would say so. The way I understand it, after Preminger, and *Exodus,* it wasn't until August of 1960 that Kirk Douglas [executive producer, as well as star] announced that Trumbo's name would appear on *Spartacus.* Now, Douglas may well have wanted to make that announcement earlier. But he couldn't. That decision rested with Universal, and it's Ed Muhl who eventually would say yes or no. He said yes."

Trumbo continued, "I think Ed Muhl saw through the hysteria. By 1960, it was possible to do so; the landscape had cleared. Muhl was able to look around and say, 'What's the fuss about? There's nothing wrong with our script, nothing wrong with our movie, and we're willing to stand by our product.' And [Dalton] Trumbo had written it. It was a prestige picture, one of the most expensive up to that time."

Christopher Trumbo recalls his father talking about Ed Muhl at home. What, I inquired, was the tenor of those references? "Reasonable guy," he said. "You have to realize," he added with a laugh, "that for Trumbo, the idea of not having an enemy was good. And Ed Muhl was not the enemy."

Ed Muhl's son William referred me to his half-brother, Phillip Muhl, a lawyer and senior vice president at Disney. I phoned and left a message. A few days later I received a call from the publicity department at Disney. It was soon apparent that the caller was fishing: "We were wondering what you plan to write about the senior Mr. Muhl."

His real concern, although submerged, and the apparent reason for his call, was this: "We were wondering what you plan to write about the senior Mr. Muhl and Rock Hudson." Callers trying to extort information—whether studio executives, or telemarketers—are never as suave as they think they are. Slightly amused at the caller's transparency, I took his inquiry not at face value, but rather at two-face value. With nothing to hide, I told him of my interest in Ed Muhl as an important force in fifties Hollywood, adding that perhaps Phillip Muhl could supply details that his half-brother, William, didn't recall. Neither of us mentioned Rock Hudson; and yet his name hovered like a specter over our conversation.

The caller assured me that he would soon arrange an interview with Phillip Muhl. Meaning, as it turned out, You'll never hear from this studio again. After a couple of weeks, I phoned his office. Then, and on subsequent attempts, I received standard evasions.

At that point, I hadn't planned to write about Muhl and Rock Hudson because I considered the story old news. In *Rock Hudson: His Story,* coauthored by Hudson and Sara Davidson and published in 1986, a year after the actor's death, there was a brief account, with facts jumbled for legal reasons: "[In 1953] Rock had started having an illicit affair with one of the most powerful executives at the Studio, a short, paunchy man who was married and had three children. Rock told his friends stories of how the executive would lock his office door, have his secretary hold the calls, and come after Rock on his knees. Rock did not see the executive frequently, but it was enough to keep the executive hooked and eager to help Rock's cause. . . . Thirty years later, when the executive was retired and had dozens of grandchildren, he saw Rock at a cocktail party. He found a moment to take Rock aside and say, in a lowered voice, 'I still love you.'" Two decades later, another writer quoted Mark Miller, a friend of Rock Hudson's, who recalled the actor saying to him at the time, "Can you believe Ed Muhl? After all these years!"

As I continued my research, it seemed that a series of obscure dots connected those accounts of Hudson and Muhl with the odd fact of no obituary for Muhl. The dots continued right up to the phone call from Disney's publicity department. Was someone still horrified by a reported homosexual liaison from half a century earlier?

Then I came across what seemed another obfuscation. In Edward Muhl's bio page at www.allmovie.com, the writer states that "the following account comes from his son, Phillip Muhl." In that account, which differs in various particulars from the one given me by William Muhl, the early career is set forth in tedious detail. Only the final three sentences, however, are devoted to Muhl's years as a top Universal executive. Not a single film title is given; there is no hint of his importance to the studio. Reading that lopsided biography, I felt as though it were a decoy. But why?

The red scare finally departed, and Ed Muhl helped usher it out, but the great gay scare still haunts Hollywood. If indeed Muhl was bisexual, or gay, and if he loved Rock Hudson, or any other man, an eloquent line from *Imitation of Life* is the best response to anyone who may feel traumatized. It's what Annie Johnson declares outside the school, the first time young Sarah Jane denies her race: "That's what you are, and it's nothing to be ashamed of!"

August, 1958: Lana Turner confers with director Douglas Sirk during first week of filming *Imitation of Life*. *Collection of Lou Valentino*

Ross Hunter,
Mahalia Jackson,
and Juanita
Moore on the set.
*Collection of the
author*

Sammy Davis Jr.
visits Juanita
Moore and Ross
Hunter during
the shoot.
*Collection of the
author*

Lana Turner and Susan Kohner wait for a camera setup. *Collection of Lou Valentino*

Lana in her dressing room on the first day of filming. That dressing room was a forty-two-foot custom-built auto trailer, described as "the most luxurious ever accorded a film star at Universal-International." Even so, it proved too small, and was later expanded.
Collection of Lou Valentino

Everyone was on Lana's side as she began *Imitation of Life*. Flowers, telegrams from well-wishers—but behind the smile she was scared. *Collection of Dwayne Teal*

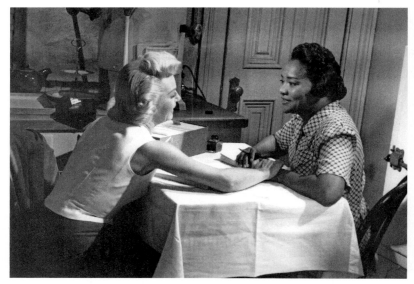

Lana Turner and Juanita Moore in an intimate scene that Sirk composed as carefully as a sonnet. *Collection of Lou Valentino*

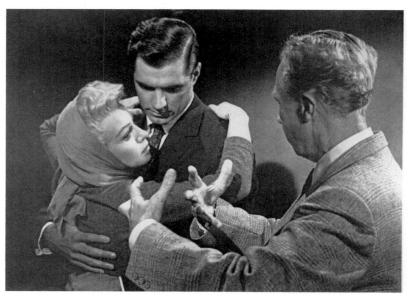

Sirk directs Lana and John Gavin in their big love scene. *Collection of Lou Valentino*

"I'm an actress, and a good one." Sirk made Lana believe that line from the movie, but was he convinced? John Gavin stands behind Lana. *Collection of Lou Valentino*

Sirk directs Dan O'Herlihy and Lana. *Collection of Lou Valentino*

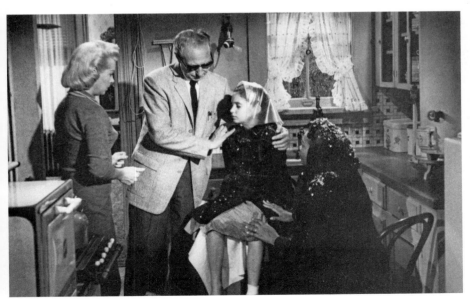

Sirk, a perfectionist, positions Karin Dicker for a shot with Lana and Juanita. *Collection of Lou Valentino*

Lana, as rising Broadway star Lora Meredith, will soon outshine first lady of the stage Geraldine Moore, played by "Queen of the Extras" Bess Flowers. *Collection of Lou Valentino*

Bit player Paul Bradley, John Gavin, Cecily Evans, Robert Alda, and Lana. *Collection of Dwayne Teal*

Three faces of Juanita Moore. Clockwise from left: stylish beauty, as Lena Younger in *A Raisin in the Sun*, as exotic Dominique in *Affair in Trinidad*. *Collection of the author*

Burly cameraman Russell Metty with Zsa Zsa Gabor on the set of *Touch of Evil* the year before he shot *Imitation of Life*. *Photofest*

Art director Alexander Golitzen confers with the producer and director of *Phantom of the Opera*, for which he won an Oscar in 1943. *Photofest*

1297-P.19

At the end of filming,
cast members
exchanged photos.
Juanita inscribed hers:
"To my darling
Susan—All my love,
Juanita Moore."
*Collection of Susan
Kohner*

Dan O'Herlihy's
inscription to Susan is
in Gaelic. It's the first
line of a traditional
Irish blessing that
means "May the road
rise up before you."
*Collection of Susan
Kohner*

As a member of the Sandra Dee Fan Club, the author received an autographed photo from a Hollywood princess. *Collection of the author*

Mahalia equals Hallelujah!
Collection of Dwayne Teal

Sirk in his final years. *Collection of Matthias Brunner and the Douglas Sirk Foundation, Zurich*

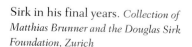

Even in a wardrobe test, Lana is resplendent—and so is the Jean-Louis gown. *Collection of Lou Valentino*

Sarah Jane from sedate . . .

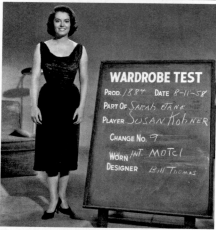

. . . to sophisticated . . .

. . . to bold. (Only the black sheath dress made it to the final cut.) *All photos collection of Susan Kohner*

Lana's personal makeup man, Del Armstrong, and two wardrobe women keep Lana glamorous every moment. *Collection of Lou Valentino*

When Sandra Dee posed for wardrobe shots, her character was still named "Maggie"— later changed to "Susie." *Photofest*

WARDROBE TEST
PROD. *1884* DATE *8-11-5*
PART OF *MAGGIE*
PLAYER *SANDRA DEE*
CHANGE NO. *5*
WORN *GRADUATION*
DESIGNER *Bill Thomas*

The man on the beach, Billy House, surrounded by Karin Dicker, John Gavin, and Terry Burnham. *Collection of Dwayne Teal*

Following *Imitation of Life*, Troy Donahue quickly rose from contract player to superstar. Here on the set of *Palm Springs Weekend* in 1963. *Photofest*

Sandra Gould, Ross Hunter, and Lana. *Collection of the author*

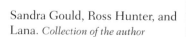

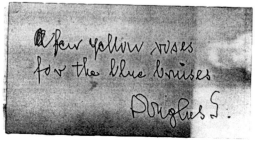

After Troy Donahue hit Susan Kohner so hard that she missed work for a couple of days, Sirk sent flowers, with this card: "A few yellow roses for the blue bruises. Douglas S." *Collection of Susan Kohner*

The world premiere of *Imitation of Life* was held in Chicago. *Collection of the author*

Forty-seven years later, Juanita gets top billing when *Imitation of Life* is the main attraction at the University of Arkansas, Pine Bluff, for its African Film Heritage Festival. Like any great star, she was mobbed by fans. *Photo by Sam Staggs*

Susan and her mother arrive in London for the British premiere of *Imitation of Life*. *Collection of Susan Kohner*

Fannie Hurst shares her Yorkshire terriers with Sandra Dee at press preview of *Imitation of Life* in Hollywood. *Collection of Dwayne Teal*

Fannie Hurst never went out without her trademark calla lily. Her inscription reads: "To Susan, the brightest star on the Horizon—with gratitude for her magnificence in *Imitation of Life*." *Collection of Susan Kohner*

I really don't 'die' in the picture until much later in the filming schedule," Juanita Moore told a visitor to the set in early September of 1958. She was explaining why one brief scene in the funeral sequence had already been completed, even though Annie Johnson's actual funeral—the dramatic showpiece of the film—was yet to come. In that early scene, Juanita filled in for Mahalia Jackson.

It came about like this. In order to complete the roles played by Dan O'Herlihy and Robert Alda, who had commitments elsewhere, Sirk staged their final scene—one shot of them seated among mourners in the church—before he was ready to shoot the full-fledged funeral.

Sirk assembled Alda, O'Herlihy, a dozen extras, and relevant crew members on a sound stage at Universal. They were directed to look appropriately solemn. Since Mahalia Jackson was nowhere near Hollywood, Sirk decided to provide funereal atmosphere of a similar kind. So Juanita, out of camera range, and unrecorded, sang in her place as cinematographer Russell Metty filmed this group of mourners. She had a fine voice, though spirituals were not part of her nightclub repertoire in New York and Europe. Juanita, not superstitious about mourning her character prematurely, said, "It really didn't upset me. After all, that's show busines." (If you look closely at the shot, you'll see that Alda, O'Herlihy, and the extras are seated in front of a backdrop painted to resemble the large, square blocks of stone used in church architecture.

The real giveaway, however, is the lighting, which doesn't match the later scenes filmed in an actual church, a rare gaffe in a Sirk film.)

Filming of the funeral took place at the Hollywood Methodist Church, later renamed the Hollywood United Methodist Church. It stands at 6817 Franklin Avenue, on the northwest corner of Highland. The neo-Gothic structure, built in 1928, has an imposing belltower to which, in 1992, a twenty-foot red AIDS ribbon was added. Although other directors since Sirk have found the church photogenic (part of *Sister Act* was shot there), not one has availed himself so fully of the sanctuary. In fact, Sirk used only that. In *Imitation of Life* we never see the church's exterior; when mourners come through the door, they are not on Franklin Avenue, but on Melrose: a fire on Universal's backlot the previous year having destroyed the New York street, a similar one at Paramount was used as stand-in for Harlem.

Close observers may notice an African-American woman seated on Lana's right in the church, who later, as they exit into the street, grips Lana's arm. This woman would be a "nurse," so called not because of medical training but rather owing to the assistance she stands ready to provide. A tradition in some African-American churches, these women were deaconesses or church mothers dressed in white (sometimes black, as here) who assist the family with tissues and fans. If need be, the "nurse" escorts a keening mourner out of the church during the service or eases the fall of one who faints. These ladies were sometimes present, also, at regular Sunday services, especially in Baptist and Pentecostal churches, to assist the emotionally overwrought.

Annie's death, and Lora's reaction to it, contain in microcosm the major themes of the film. Annie Johnson's last words are, "I'm just tired, Miss Lora. Awfully—tired." But even as her eyes close forever, a quick cut to Lora registers the enormity of Annie's passing. A sharp intake of breath, then she screams, "Annie! Annie!" and sinks into sobbing grief. At that moment, the camera's cruel reminder of Lora's actressy self-absorption: She steals the close-up from her dearest friend.

Then the camera pans slightly left for a weird composition. In the lower left of frame, a mound of Lora's blond hair (her face buried in

Annie's bosom). In lower right, the dead woman's face, turned away, forms a dark dune. Overpowering the center of the frame is a black-and-white photograph of smiling Sarah Jane. Meaning that Annie, in her final moments, gazed on a lifeless image. An imitation of Sarah Jane, whose real presence was Annie's one desire.

On the sound track, a dirge: four descending piano bass notes. The next beat is Mahalia Jackson's, singing "Trouble of the World." We hear her voice for several seconds before we see her. Sirk dissolves from the photograph of Sarah Jane to the great stained-glass window above the choir. At this point, he performs one of the technical tours de force for which he is acclaimed (and which Sirk detractors never seem to notice). A low-angle, canted shot of the predominantly blue stained glass suggests the ascent of Annie's soul to Jesus, who floats, in a red robe, in the center panel. The shot is held for a long moment. Only then does the camera turn back to earth: a slow diagonal descent, panning from upper left to lower right of frame, to pause on Mahalia Jackson in long shot.

"Singing" is hardly an adequate word for Mahalia; in her black robe, she's like a pipe organ with a mouth. The camera moves among the mourners, then returns to her, in the choir. As it cuts to a close-up, we feel ourselves in the presence of a holy woman who prophesies through song. Such was not Sirk's reaction, however, at least not initially. "Before shooting those scenes," he said, "I went to hear Mahalia Jackson at UCLA, where she was giving a recital. I knew nothing about her. But here on the stage was this large, homely, ungainly woman—and all these shining, beautiful young faces turned up to her, and absolutely smitten with her. It was strange and funny, and very impressive. I tried to get some of that experience into the picture. We photographed her with a three-inch lens, so that every unevenness in the face stood out."

Sirk always seemed ambivalent about the funeral, calling it "an irony." And nonplussed by the outpouring of emotion in every theatre that showed *Imitation of Life*. "When I heard how audiences were reacting to that . . . ," he said, leaving his thought unfinished. "But that was the reaction of American audiences. When it was dubbed into German, all they got was the Negro angle." Sirk implied that he considered the funeral sentimental: "I have no talent for sentimentality," he said, "so perhaps I don't recognize it." It's often disappointing to quiz the artist about his art, since the answers cannot possibly match the work itself. Then, too, Europeans, whether behind the camera or in the audience, never see quite the same film that Americans see. Ultimately, Sirk's shortcomings as *Imitation of Life* spectator mean little when measured against his accomplishment as director.

I've observed that people who scoff at the funeral, or seem uncomfortable watching it, are often those who subordinate emotion to intellect, or who hold a strictly pragmatic view of life. Indeed, Sirk himself may have belonged to the former category. James Baldwin touched the real nerve, perhaps, although he wasn't referring to *Imitation of Life*. In *The Fire Next Time,* Baldwin suggested that blacks in America, because of their skin color and their history, remind white Americans of a reality that doesn't fit into the national mythos of progress, materialism, and upward mobility. They "do not believe in death," Baldwin wrote, "and this is why the darkness of my skin so intimidates them . . . the fact that life is tragic."

Sirk, in spite of having "no talent for sentimentality," did possess a talent for dramatic construction. What could have ended *Imitation of Life* except Annie's funeral? "The funeral scene wasn't in the original script," he said. "So of course the front office was very nervous about okaying it. 'Is it against God?' they said. Ross Hunter told them, 'Oh, it's wonderful—it's full of religious touches.' And as usual, he got what he wanted."

Script changes were made right up to September 8, 1958, the day before the funeral. Susan Kohner recalls two days of filming, and the production budget corroborates her memory: one half-day for the church interior, a day and a half outside in the street.

Lana Turner's daughter once said, "For Mother, life was a movie." By this point in the filming of *Imitation of Life,* Lana had become immensely fond of Juanita, almost, it seemed, fusing the real woman with her character, Annie Johnson. That isn't far-fetched when you recall how closely Lana herself resembled Lora Meredith.

Juanita remembers several occasions when Lana, under great career pressure and still distraught from the Stompanato ordeal four months earlier, would whisper, "Juanita, I need to talk," and they would leave the set. No doubt she found Juanita's comforting presence a ballast to steady her against flashbacks to April 4. Whatever Juanita said would have consoled Lana, for one of Juanita's gifts is the power to banish bad emotions. I've discovered that there isn't room enough for Juanita and stress in the same place. (Their talks weren't always solemn. Lana once said, "Juanita, I was on my ass when this picture came along." The rejoinder: "Honey, you can't get any lower than that.")

Lana said, "I most dreaded the part when Annie's repentant daughter would throw herself on the casket," reminding the star of her troubled relationship with her own daughter. Rehearsing the funeral scenes inside the church, Lana recalled later that "I simply broke down. Images of my own life, my own dark fears flooded my mind, and I dissolved in tears. I fled."

When Patti Westmore, Lana's hairdresser on the picture, saw her leave the church pew and rush out through a side door, she followed. Lana's dressing room trailer was parked nearby, and by the time she reached it she was almost hysterical, "running in my high heels and weeping."

Inside the trailer, Lana "slumped onto the chair in front of my little dressing table, burying my face in my arms. By now I was shaking with sobs, unable to control myself. That casket, with its blanket of heavily perfumed gardenias, had wakened unexpectedly all the crushing thoughts of death I had been trying to suppress."

When Patti Westmore arrived, Lana, unable to speak, waved her arms, motioning her away. But Westmore wouldn't leave. Instead, she grasped Lana's shoulders and ordered her to "Stop it! You've got to come back and finish the scene." But Lana couldn't stop.

Then Patti slapped her. Lana said it knocked the breath out of her, but it stopped the hysteria. "Then she put her arms around me and hugged me." Now under control, Lana returned to the church and finished the rehearsal. After a break to repair Lana's hair and makeup, Sirk was ready to shoot. The cameras rolled. "I cried," Lana said, "but I had myself under control now, and the tears rolled silently down my face, as I sat there in the pew with John Gavin and Sandra Dee, and Mahalia singing so beautifully, and that casket, all covered with flowers.

"'Cut and print,' called the director. 'Brilliant!' he said to me. 'You gave it just what it needed.'"

(The deathbed scene, filmed after the funeral, was also emotionally difficult for Lana. Technically, though, her main task was to react: Juanita did the real acting. At first, Juanita played the scene with tears in her own eyes to match Lana's. Sirk corrected her: "You're dying, not crying.")

Sirk had one iron rule: "A camera movement ought to be justified by your actors' movements, and your actors' movements must be justified by the camera." One illustration of this dictum occurs when Susan Kohner bursts through the crowd of mourners, crying out, "Let me through! Please let me through." Pushing aside spectators, she runs into the street, which is kept clear by a mounted policeman.

Some directors might have had her zigzag, or else run straight to the coffin. Not Sirk. Susan, a wild, unravelled look about her, plunges blindly—yet choreographically—in a wide S-curve through ice chunks on the black pavement, barely missing the back end of the horse. Following her movement, the camera mimics her trajectory in a crane shot that also describes an S. The dramatic sweep of this shot matches both her veering physical movement and the desperation of her grief.

As Susan breaks away from a cop telling her to stand back, the camera closes in, as if it, too, were a participant in her frustrated struggle to reach her dead mother. She breaks away from the cop, only to encounter another obstacle: a pallbearer, whom she shoves away, then splays her upper body on the coffin. The camera stops, as though exhausted, like her. For a time it simply stares: at her, and at the white flowers on the white coffin.

Susan calls this scene her most difficult in the film because of the intense emotional preparation that went into it. Increasing her difficulty was the effort of holding the emotion throughout the long run down the street for several additional takes. Owing to crowd control with the large number of extras, her run from offcamera to the hearse was shot four or five times. (Running on wet pavement in high heels couldn't have been an easy feat, either.)

I asked Susan what she felt as she ran down that icy street to the casket. She said, "Once you're on a roll, you start bringing up an emotion— what if this was my mother in there?—and then you start to think of all the times you were perhaps not nice to your mother. You think, Oh my God, what if she were gone . . . and now I'm sorry . . . and I wonder if she ever knew that I really loved her. All of that—it's cumulative. Once you start such an emotion rolling, it's not hard to keep it going. It just pours out." (Susan's mother told me she was in the crowd that day. "She didn't know I was there," said Lupita Tovar Kohner. "I was crying in the back of the crowd. When she ran to the coffin, it got me!")

Susan explained that logistics made it a demanding scene for everyone. "The assistant director is trying to get the extras not to look, telling them, 'Don't notice that she's going to come through but when she does, don't keep her from getting to the street.'"

Even for an economical director like Sirk, wrapping up the entire sequence—funeral, Susan's street scene, procession—in two days was exemplary when you consider the number of people involved and the complexity of the various setups. For example, he used some 350 extras for the church and procession scenes, in addition to actors and a large number of crew members. And all of it "on location"—in Hollywood, to be sure, but on the Paramount lot, away from the familiar surroundings of Universal. (One little oversight: the funeral takes place in winter, but a female mourner in the street wears short sleeves.)

Everywhere irony: for this is Hollywood, and there is Sirk. The funeral, like the rest of the picture, was white-owned, like some latter-day studio plantation. And yet two black women, Juanita Moore and Mahalia Jackson, transcend the petty bounds of business, politics, human injustice, and well-meaning white patronage. In aesthetic terms, this funeral scene marks a second surge of the civil rights movement. One might argue that Juanita Moore, throughout *Imitation of Life,* and Mahalia Jackson singing "Trouble of the World" at the end became touchstones in the struggle. To commemorate them, will there be postage stamps for Black History Month? Juanita Moore High School, and Mahalia Jackson International Airport?

No such thoughts entered Juanita's head when she watched the funeral at the Methodist church, and the procession at Paramount. A day later, the studio issued a press release: "When director Douglas Sirk filmed the funeral, one of the most interested spectators on the sidelines was Juanita Moore." She told the publicist: "I just wanted to see what a lovely funeral I received."

The effects of that funeral were felt more intensely within the African-American community than in any other. At least, that's the assertion of Karla F. C. Holloway, a professor at Duke University and author of *Passed On: African American Mourning Stories*. According to Holloway, "Annie's deathbed moment and her funeral services . . . were to become singularly important in American film history and in African American households as well. The movie was especially poignant to black women."

Holloway points out one of the film's ironic dualities: "It publicly dramatized a private black narrative of passing." Passing for white, and also passing to another world (among African Americans, "to pass" is a widespread euphemism for dying). Holloway, as an observer of African-American attitudes toward death, and of the customs surrounding it, believes that "the dignity and control that Juanita Moore brought to that deathbed scene, and the ornate funeral that [her character] had authorized and directed, provoked the teary-eyed bonding of a generation of mothers and daughters."

The practical results of *Imitation of Life* were also far reaching in the African-American community. Holloway asserts that "many who had not done so before . . . were persuaded to write out their own funeral instructions, just as Annie had done in the film. Countless numbers of envelopes were carefully placed in dresser drawers with these poignant instructions written on the outside: 'To be opened on the occasion of my death.'" Although Annie's famous line—"Our weddin' day—and the day we die—are the great events of life"—was written by a white person, it surely expresses a momentous African-American truth.

*H*allelujah, indeed. I'm listening to Mahalia Jackson sing "Great Gettin' Up Mornin'," and I can't keep still. My feet are tapping, and I'd rather clap than type. Which is the point of her singing: She wants to move you—right into the arms of her Lord. "Move on Up a Little Higher" is the song that catapulted her to stardom; recorded in 1945, it eventually sold over a million copies. Mahalia's autobiography, published in 1966, was titled *Movin' on Up*.

The very name "Mahalia Jackson" preaches a sermon. Like Mother Teresa and the Dalai Lama, she was canonized during her lifetime as both religious icon and secular saint. "The Queen of Gospel Song," as she was often called, started out in New Orleans. The granddaughter of slaves, Mahalia was born in 1911 in a modest, three-room house, the third of six children. Her father held three jobs. Her mother died when Mahalia was four, and the little girl was raised by aunts. As a child, she started singing at the Mt. Moriah Baptist Church. Baptized in the Mississippi River, she later recalled, "Ever since that day, I promised the Lord that I'd dedicate my life to Him in song."

Mahalia left school after eighth grade to earn money for the family as a laundress and maid. At age sixteen, she went to Chicago to live with relatives. There, at the Greater Salem Baptist Church, she joined a gospel quintet, the Johnson Singers. But singing was for Sunday. During the week she worked hard, soon proving herself a shrewd businesswoman, even on limited funds. Eventually, she saved enough to open a beauty parlor and, later, a florist's shop. In 1934, Mahalia recorded "God Gonna Separate the Wheat from the Tares" for Decca Records. Although that first single found an audience in the South, it was not until the midforties that she became well known for her recordings and personal appearances in churches.

Her records brought acclaim at home and in Europe in the late forties, followed by enduring fame. Mahalia's first Carnegie Hall concert took place in 1950, a sold-out event. Throughout her career, Mahalia refused all offers to sing in nightclubs—even from Las Vegas for $25,000 per performance. ("Not a thing wrong with your establishment, honey," she told the owner, "I just don't belong in it.") Nor would she sing anything but sacred songs, although she had learned much, as a girl, from listening to such blues singers as Bessie Smith. Surely the Lord, like her other fans, would have enjoyed Mahalia's version of "Backwater Blues" or "Stormy Weather," but he never got the chance. "Blues are the songs of despair," she said. "Gospel songs are the songs of hope."

According to biographer Hettie Jones, "People were always after Mahalia to sing differently. In 1932, she took a lesson from a certain Professor DuBois, who told her to stop shouting and slow down the tempo, because the way she sang, white people would never understand her and she wouldn't be 'a credit to the Negro race.'"

Mahalia resisted. Many years later, however, she succumbed to similar bad advice. It's not surprising that television diminished her talent. Watching a compendium from her local TV show in Chicago in the fifties, the so-called *Mahalia Jackson Collection* on DVD, I could almost hear a phalanx of producers, sponsors, and directors toning her down. Except for two rousing spirituals on the DVD—"Joshua Fit the Battle of Jericho" and "When the Saints Go Marching In"—the songs lack what Mahalia herself sometimes called "jubilation." They range from the queasy uplift of Rodgers and Hammerstein's "You'll Never Walk Alone" to such insipid hymns as "Sweet Hour of Prayer." Mahalia seems uncomfortable with such glucose; it's as if Aretha Franklin were to take on the John Denver songbook. (Fortunately, another DVD does a better job. *Mahalia Jackson: The Power and the Glory* is an excellent ninety-minute documentary on her life and career.)

In countless appearances, and in three films (*St. Louis Blues* in 1958, *Imitation of Life,* and *The Best Man* in 1964), Mahalia spread her message of divine love. With her great instrument and earthy warmth, she numbered show business colleagues and foreign royalty among her devotees. In 1961, she sang "The Star Spangled Banner" at President Kennedy's inaugural. But life out of church, and away from her public, perhaps disappointed her. Or maybe not. Two marriages ended in divorce—but she had the Lord, whom she loved so passionately that no other man could compete.

At Universal in 1958, for *Imitation of Life,* Mahalia received lavish star treatment, including a dressing room the size of an apartment. She was paid $5,000 for a few hours' work. When it was time to view the rushes of Mahalia's scene, an unprecedented crowd of studio personnel flooded the projection room. To handle the overflow, a second screening was set up. Ross Hunter claimed to have received eleven requests from other studios to view the rushes, though surely such an outpouring of religious fervor would have turned Hollywood into a Jesus camp. If Hunter exaggerated, it was to spread the word: in praise of Mahalia, and to publicize his picture.*

Mahalia once described herself as "just a good, strong Louisiana woman who can cook rice so every grain stands by itself." Duke Ellington recalled that "she always had fine soul food" on the table at her home, and toward the end of her life she brought out a cookbook, titled, naturally, *Mahalia Jackson Cooks Soul.*

She had a mischievous side, also. Once, before a concert in a prosperous church in California, the minister was hesitant to pay her before the service. Mahalia, having been ripped off even by the godly, regarded

---

*On the *Imitation of Life* sound track album, "Trouble of the World" is sung not by Mahalia Jackson but by the actress and singer Lillian Hayman. Mahalia was under contract to Columbia Records at the time, and the company would not allow Decca to record her for its LP. As for Lillian, this would not be her only brush against *Imitation of Life.* In 1968, she began a long career on the daytime soap *One Life to Live.* Her first important story line was as the Annie Johnson–like mother, Sadie Gray, surprised by the reappearance of her daughter (portrayed by the light-skinned African-American actress Ellen Holly), who has spent several years passing as a white woman.

him. Then she touched her throat. In a gravelly voice, she croaked, "Mama hoarse. Don't know if I can sing." Whereupon, the minister anted up. With cash in hand, Mahalia proclaimed: "It's a miracle! Mama's got her voice back, praise the Lord!"

While raw talent accounted for her professional greatness, generosity and a huge heart made her seem good to the core. Her faith was noncatechistical, expressed in private devotion and through charity and activism. One of Mahalia's major concerns was education for poor youngsters, many of whom benefited from the scholarship fund she set up. Early on, she became both a vocal and a financial stalwart of Martin Luther King Jr., singing benefits for his Southern Christian Leadership Conference and also for those arrested during sit-ins and bus boycotts. Moments before Dr. King made his "I Have a Dream" speech at the 1963 March on Washington, Mahalia stood before the multitude and sang, "I been 'buked and I been scorned/I'm gonna tell my Lord/When I get home/Just how long you've been treating me wrong."

Nine years later, Mahalia went home.

Her funeral resembled Annie Johnson's in turnout, although she had made it clear she wanted "no big fanfare when I'm gone." No marching bands, no white horses. There was mourning, of course, but along with it a great celebration of Mahalia's life and art. And it took two funerals to give her a fitting send-off.

The first took place in Chicago, where she had spent most of her life. There, on a frigid January day in 1972, the lines began forming at daybreak outside the Greater Salem Baptist Church. As she lay in state, some fifty thousand persons filed past her mahogany, glass-topped coffin. The following day, as many as six thousand filled the Arie Crown Theatre for a two-hour service "marked not by grief but by joyous song and eulogies which reminded that Mahalia's great talent had been one that evoked happiness, not tears."

Aretha Franklin sang "Precious Lord, Take My Hand," which Mahalia had sung four years earlier at the funeral of Martin Luther King Jr. Ella Fitzgerald was there, and so were Coretta Scott King, Sammy Davis Jr., and Chicago's mayor, Richard J. Daley, who, in 1957, had placed armed guards at Mahalia's new house in a white neighborhood after a shot was fired through a window.

Three days later, in New Orleans, another fifty thousand paid their respects at the visitation in the city's Rivergate Convention Center Auditorium, which remained open all night to accommodate the throngs. On the day of burial, additional eulogies were held in the auditorium, attended by such notables as Dick Gregory, Lou Rawls, the governor of Louisiana, and the mayor of New Orleans. Schoolchildren, whites from the suburbs, and the poor of Rampart and Dryades streets all turned out, united for one day at least. Then a funeral cortege of twenty-four limousines drove slowly past her childhood place of worship, Mt. Moriah Baptist Church, where her recordings played through loudspeakers, and from there to Providence Memorial Park in Metairie, a nearby town, where Mahalia was laid to rest.

36 | NOBODY LIKED IT BUT THE PUBLIC

*B*y 1959, enforcers of Hollywood's self-imposed Production Code—i.e., the censorship arm of the Motion Picture Association of America, or MPAA—wielded less power each year. The moviegoing public wanted more of what these censors had long suppressed: adult subject matter, treatment of controversial topics, and especially sex. Studios—who retained the censors in preference to threatened government censorship of motion pictures—increasingly missed no chance to supply the public's demand.

Race, however, was still a highly sensitive subject, made more visible, and volatile, by the burgeoning civil rights movement. When *Imitation of Life* wrapped in early October 1958, Ross Hunter and his backers at Universal anticipated few obstacles from censors. The filmmakers had tried, at every step of production, to eliminate snags. It helped that the notorious Joseph Breen had retired from the MPAA in 1954 and was succeeded by his longtime deputy, Geoffrey Shurlock, who seemed liberal, even passive, by comparison with his zealously right-wing predecessor.

In 1957, Section II.6 of the Production Code had been deleted, that racist line stating that "Miscegenation (sex relationship between the white and black races) is forbidden." Although *Imitation of Life* does not deal with miscegenation per se, it is likely that Breen, had he still been in command, would have interpreted the Susan Kohner–Troy Donahue romance-gone-sour as such. Fanatical bigot that he was, Breen might conceivably have raised objections even to the close friendship and co-habitation of Lora Meredith and Annie Johnson.

Shurlock, in a letter to Mrs. Kathryn McTaggart of Universal's legal department dated May 13, 1958, made no reference to race. Rather, he was concerned over "Sarah Jane's nightclub number," pointing out that its "acceptability will depend on the discretion with which it is shot in the finished picture. This applies not only to her dance movements, but to her costume as well."

As summer wore on, and revised portions of the script were submitted to Shurlock, he asked for, and received, the removal of the word "damned." Wariness continued over Sarah Jane's club act, and he cautioned that care must also be "exercised with regards to the costumes and routine of the girls in the Tropicana" [i.e., the Moulin Rouge]. He found that "Loomis' following dialogue seems rather offensively pointed: 'If the Dramatists' Club wants to eat and sleep with you, you will eat and sleep with them'"—but did not demand its deletion. The line, risqué for the era, stayed in the script. After mild wrangling over the lyric of Sarah Jane's number at Harry's Club (detailed above), the script was deemed acceptable.

Anticipating resistance to the picture in the South, two versions of the trailer were constructed. The "Southern" trailer showed this exchange between Sarah Jane and her boyfriend:

FRANKIE: "Are you black?"
SARAH JANE: "No! I'm as white as you!"
FRANKIE: "You're lying."
SARAH JANE: "I'm not."

Perhaps the scene was considered acceptable because of its racial antagonism. This trailer included a few seconds of Mahalia Jackson's song, plus a generous amount of Lana, Sandra, and Gavin.

The trailer shown in the North was similar, although in it a voice-over declaimed: "What a daughter says to a mother—" followed by Sarah Jane's "I'm white! White! WHITE!" Sarah Jane's exchange with Frankie was retained, and snippets of the motel scene (absent from the Southern trailer) were put in.

Drafts of the two trailer scripts, labeled "Northern" and "Southern," and preserved at the Academy, suggest a good deal of hesitation and debate over the exact contents of each one. In rough draft form, they contain many typed and handwritten revisions and deletions. Whatever the studio hoped to accomplish—or avoid—was apparently realized when the trailers were screened. No outrage was reported, and the picture found a huge audience on both sides of the Mason-Dixon line.

Controversy, when it came, arose from unexpected quarters. It had nothing to do with sex, one reason being that Ross Hunter and Douglas Sirk did not make "sizzling" films (apart from Sirk's *Written on the Wind,* with a different producer). Sirk's intellectualism excluded Hollywood's garden-variety copulation from his realm of interest, and Ross Hunter found turn-on pictures "dirty." A few years after *Imitation of Life,* Hunter regularly lamented the dearth of G-rated films. "I guess I sound like a real old-fashioned square," he told an interviewer, "but I still think movies should be made for the family. In my pictures, Adam and Eve don't inspire the costumes."

Universal's advertising department surely realized that several of its ads for *Imitation of Life* might stir up a racial hornet's nest. The most daring was a panel showing Susan Kohner and Juanita Moore, along with the ostensible line of dialogue (acutally heard nowhere in the film): "The color line won't stop me, Ma! I look, feel, think white . . . and I'm going to marry white!"

The first paper to reject this ad was the *Pittsburgh Press,* one of the largest papers in Pennsylvania. The assistant editor said, "We are a family newspaper. It is the policy of the paper to refuse advertising considered in bad taste." (The *Press* did accept other ads for *Imitation of Life,* however. Two other Pittsburgh dailies accepted the controversial ad without hesitation.) The studio's reaction was one of puzzlement, since the rejected ad had been accepted by papers much farther south—in Miami and Oklahoma City.

Later, a writer in the *Chicago Defender,* an African-American paper, referring to this same ad, asked the cogent question, "Where do these guys get the stuff that Negroes WANT to be white? In these days when Negroes are achieving success in every field, why would the boys at Universal, who have NO way of knowing how a Negro feels, have the nerve to dramatize and publicize such lines?"

Shortly after the first Hollywood press preview of *Imitation of Life,* on January 27, 1959, the editor of the *Los Angeles Tribune,* an African-American paper, sent a wire to various publications: "*Imitation of Life* is a libel on the Negro race. It libels our children and the Negro mother should be banned in the interest of national unity, harmony, peace, decency, and inter-racial respect. The *Tribune* is refusing all advertising of it and will picket it in the Los Angeles area and call upon the NAACP to condemn, oppose, and picket it, too." (Surely the complaint would be more understandable if made against Sarah Jane than against her mother, unless Annie Johnson struck the editor as an Aunt Jemima offshoot.)

According to *The Hollywood Reporter,* Universal immediately solicited positive comments from other African-American media to counter the *Tribune's* broadside. The *Reporter* printed several of these, including Harry Levette's, of the Associated Negro Press: "*Imitation of Life* is a fine picture, in fact better than the original version. It contains no offense whatever to the Negro race." Hazel Washington, of the *Chicago Defender,* said, "I can't praise it enough and I thought the Negro problem was handled honestly and with excellent taste." From "Doc" Young of the *Los Angeles Continental*: "The studio certainly has made sincere efforts to handle a controversial subject with good taste. Further, it is a fact that passing exists in this country. As to the mother, Juanita Moore handles this role with dignity and I believe turns in one of the outstanding performances of recent times."

Having overcome these hurdles, *Imitation of Life* opened nationwide with few problems. The picture moved audiences of both races, and it's likely that tears were shed for Annie Johnson by many who, had they encountered her in real life, would have required her to enter through the back door.

After that first press preview of *Imitation of Life,* in late January 1959, Harrison Carroll, a columnist for the *Los Angeles Herald and Express,* wrote that "everybody in the U-I commissary was congratulating Susan Kohner, who is just completing another fine role in *The Big Fisherman*." The columnist noted, also, that Dan O'Herlihy and his wife, Elsie, "never got to the theatre. They narrowly escaped death in a four car crash, and were trapped twenty minutes in the wreckage." Lana's escort that evening was Fred May, who, the following year, would become her fifth husband—for two years.

A day later, a second column in the paper was devoted to the preview, this one written by Cobina Wright, who recounted her conversation with Ross Hunter the morning after the press preview. "The producer told me that he had already received two hundred telegrams congratulating him on his success." In the first published reference to the weeping occasioned by *Imitation of Life,* she ended her column with this line: "Tears flowed constantly throughout the picture, but it is so beautifully done that you must go see it."

In lieu of a Hollywood premiere, an "Invitational Press Preview" was held on February 18 at the Screen Directors Guild Theatre. Several persons who worked in the motion picture industry at the time have explained that, while the splashiness of premieres depended on stars and not directors, Lana's notoriety, and her precarious position in 1959, would have militated against a lavish event. Then, too, most Sirk pictures did not open as glamour evenings for "le tout Hollywood." High regard for his work came much later. And since Universal, and Ross Hunter, were not big spenders, the decision to hold a premiere far from Hollywood made sense, especially as there was a chance the picture would bomb. If it did, the fallout would be less damaging the farther it took place from Hollywood's doorstep.

As it turned out, this second press preview accomplished much the same as an actual premiere: It drew a celebrity audience, and it garnered publicity. The *Los Angeles Herald and Express* championed the picture more than any other paper. On the day following the preview, it ran three large photographs: Lana and Cheryl, Ross Hunter escorting Fannie Hurst, and Susan Kohner dancing with her date, the actor John Gabriel. A feature headed "Celebs at Tearful Preview" led with, "Lana Turner, the glamour gal of Hollywood, and her lovely daughter, Cheryl, made a rare public appearance last night . . ." Although the preview was informal, and many came in casual dress, Lana wore a white gown swathed in white ostrich feathers—with matching daughter.

The article quoted Joan Bennett (a friend of Susan's, and costar of Sirk's 1956 picture, *There's Always Tomorrow*) as saying she had cried so copiously that "I can't get my face back on." (Hedda Hopper reported that Lana and her mother, Mildred, did not weep during the funeral scene. They sat in front of her, smoking endless cigarettes.)

George Burns claimed he hadn't wept so since the income tax man came calling. Others who attended the screening, followed by supper at Romanoff's, included the Gavins, the Kohners, the O'Herlihys, and Juanita Moore and her husband. Also, Mr. and Mrs. Edward G. Robinson, Mr. and Mrs. Howard Keel, Mr. and Mrs. Ronald Reagan, Mr. and Mrs. Frank Borzage (he was directing Susan's new picture, *The Big Fisherman*), Mr. and Mrs. Dan Duryea, Dana Wynter and Greg Bautzer, Agnes Moorehead, Red Buttons, and Walter Wanger (Joan Bennett's husband). John Huston sent Susan a telegram from Mexico City: "Everything wonderful for you tonight." The Sirks didn't attend; "I never saw my films after I finished the final cut," he said. "I never went to a preview."

When a columnist asked Fannie Hurst about the new version versus the original 1934 *Imitation of Life*, she said, "I think the casting is better this time and I'm especially glad because the Negro mother is not played as a mammy type but as a dignified woman." Her statement is either disingenuous or dumb, because Hurst, in her novel, made Delilah, the black woman, a more stereotypical mammy than even Margaret Mitchell's.

Years later, Cheryl Crane's snarky description of her evening out with Lana may explain why she declined to be interviewed for this book. In her autobiography, *Detour,* Cheryl wrote that "the film's publicists wanted to show that Mother and I were loving and united, that I liked the film and was happy to join her in exploiting our problem. Dry-eyed afterward, I told reporters that I loved the movie—it was 'so sad' and Mother was 'so wonderful.' Lacking the self-confidence to refuse to help her sell the picture, I denied my feelings instead and went along."

In reality, Cheryl found it grotesque and disturbing that her troubled relationship with Lana was pastiched on billboards with Sandra Dee and the accusatory line: "You've given me everything a mother could but the thing I wanted most . . . your love!" Forever after, apparently, the picture made Cheryl wince: "*Imitation of Life* hardened my feelings of estrangement toward Mother. Its happy ending made me sneer. Mother was back on top again, the great star, but so what? Hers was an empty life."

On the huge marquee of Chicago's Roosevelt Theatre on March 17, 1959: "Fannie Hurst's *Imitation of Life*," followed by the star names, and "World Premiere." A few days earlier, the *Tribune* had headlined, "STARS DE-SCEND ON CHICAGO," naming Lana, Susan, Juanita, Gavin, O'Her-lihy, as well as Fannie Hurst and Ross Hunter. Sirk, Robert Alda, and Sandra Dee did not attend, nor did Mahalia Jackson—the only cast member with a Chicago connection—who was presumably on the road. The *Chicago Defender,* reporting on the opening, noted that "when Sarah Jane returns for the funeral of the mother she rebuked and wished to deny, there is sorrow throughout the theatre."

A day earlier, Lana, Susan, Juanita, Dan O'Herlihy, and Ross Hunter autographed Easter eggs at the corner of State and Madison streets to raise money for the Easter Seal campaign. From Chicago, the terrific word-of-mouth spread east and west as the picture opened nationwide. By April, everyone knew they had a hit. (Had Ross Hunter, and Universal, foreseen such success, they might have booked the premiere for a top-of-the-line Chicago movie house. The Roosevelt was considered second-tier.)

The picture received bad reviews coast to coast. Looking back, it's hard not to regard Bosley Crowther, of *The New York Times,* as the mother hen who hatched generations of junk reviewers for that paper. He was in high dudgeon over *Imitation of Life,* calling it "detergent drama," a "sob story" whose stars give "an imitation of movie acting." So exercised was he that he devoted two columns to the picture, like a double hex. And his spell worked. Decades later, Janet Maslin, the Florence Foster Jenkins of *Times* reviewers, used another dull cliché, calling *Imitation of Life* a "melodramatic chestnut." (The stupidest remark ever published about Sirk also appeared in the *Times.* In 2007, Jeannette Catsoulis, reviewing a Chinese film, opened with, "Like Douglas Sirk without the throw pillows, *Sunflower* is a shamelessly old-fashioned melodrama . . .")

Fact checkers at *The New Yorker* were surely on spring break in April 1959, for the reviewer, John McCarten, carelessly paraphrased dialogue from the picture, which he presented as verbatim. "You are wrong," he has Lana saying to the playwright, "the scene I am reading isn't funny, and doesn't belong in the play." (Her actual line is much sharper: "And if you'll forgive me for saying it, you're too good a playwright to have such a scene in your play.") There are other misquotes in the review, but why linger over the beery writing of one who dismissed the entire cast with: "I can't find much to say in favor of any of them."*

Movie reviews of this ilk soon turn stale, and the only reasons for digging them up are historical and sociological. Why, I wonder, did the reviewer for the Memphis *Commercial Appeal* make no mention of Juanita Moore? Given the time and place, who wouldn't suspect a racist slight? A reviewer for the Dallas *Times Herald* surely set a record for number of errors in a single sentence: "As we recall, in the original *Imitation of Life* Lora and Annie build a little tea-shoppe in a Southern town into a giant Aunt Jemima-type industry." Corrections: In the 1934 film, the white woman is named Bea Pullman and the black woman Delilah; they open their first pancake house on the boardwalk in Atlantic City, as in the novel; Delilah's daughter leaves home and works in a restaurant in Virginia.

In the Dallas *Morning News,* another reviewer, displaying his erudition, suggested that the theatre showing *Imitation of Life* might profitably sell a "new version of the ancient lachrymatories, once used to collect the tears of all who purged themselves with grief." He stated that "both the segregation and the quandry of Miss Kohner seem overdone"—as though Dallas's own segregation in 1959 were other than rigid, and pervasive. (Did that reviewer not know that when Susan and Juanita went on a publicity tour with the picture in the South—including Texas—Juanita appeared at theatres with predominantly black audiences, and Susan where they were mostly white?)

---

*It happened again in 1996, when *New Yorker* panjandrum John Updike wrote a windy memorial tribute to Lana. He mistakenly has "her fictional daughter" in *Peyton Place*, rather than Sandra Dee, tell her to "Stop acting!"

Leonard Mosley in the London *Daily Express* didn't mince words: "I hated this film. And yet I found it fascinating to watch, because Lana Turner and all she stands for in Hollywood hypnotise me." The two most favorable reviews, and the most perceptive, appeared in *Variety* and *The Hollywood Reporter*. (But, said the *Los Angeles Times* critic, "It didn't jerk my tears.")

Even now, reviewers can't leave it alone. Every time the picture is revived, they dust off clichés from a half-century ago: "tearjerker," "weepie," "sudser," and this from *The New Yorker*'s "Goings On About Town" a few years back: "The three-hankie situations . . ." It has also been mocked as a "women's picture," though that dismissal is no longer quite PC. When they can't think of anything else, they call it a "soap opera." (Ross Hunter said: "Critics label any love story soap opera.")

A different cliché comes to mind: Consider the source. Or the sources. The very fact of these wobbly denunciations could be taken as a powerful argument in favor of *Imitation of Life*. Sloppy reviewers, especially the factually challenged, must be viewed as media hacks, or, in the case of more highfalutin papers of record, house lackeys with a pre-set agenda.

A favorite myth of Old Hollywood is the star who saves the studio. Financial matters, of course, are never so simple, but what a seductive piece of lore: Mae West rescuing Paramount, Shirly Temple bailing out Fox in the Depression, even Lucille Ball and Desi Arnaz and the purchase of RKO. The epitome of this fantasy is Norma Desmond, in *Sunset Boulevard,* who declares, "Without me, there wouldn't be any Paramount Studio."

Without Lana Turner, Universal probably would have remained standing, but the millions from *Imitation of Life* pulled the studio out of a hole. All through the summer of 1959, *Variety* and the other trades led the cheers for this surprise blockbuster: "*Imitation of Life,* the picture that revitalized Universal . . ." "This is the *Life* Universal fancies . . ." "How to push critics into the background." The picture eventually brought in a reported six and a half million dollars in North American rentals, and almost as much abroad. (If we estimate, conservatively, that it earned ten million dollars worldwide, and adjust for inflation, the total approaches fifty or sixty million in twenty-first-century dollars.) Even before its release in Western Europe, the picture "clicked," as *Variety* put it, throughout Latin America and in Asia.

Imitation of Life is generally considered the top-grossing picture in the studio's history up to that time. (Every studio dreams of such success: All those millions in box office receipts for a picture that cost $1.5 million to make.) It was the biggest moneymaker of Lana's career, and it made her wealthier than she had ever been. She said, "I had accepted a fairly modest fee because Ross had a limited budget, so he suggested I gamble and work for half the profits. This was a new trend in Hollywood, and I was taking a big chance. But for me the gamble paid off. I don't know exactly how much I made—my managers took care of that— but it was more than the highly publicized million dollars that Elizabeth Taylor got for *Cleopatra* some years later." (Lana's salary, according to the *Imitation of Life* production budget, was $25,000 per week, for a total of $156,000—not so "modest," after all, for a falling star.)

Lana's ultimate take, of course, would have been a percentage of the net profit, not of the grosses quoted above. According to some sources, her total was eventually two million dollars, making her well-off for life. (She struck similar deals with Hunter for *Portrait in Black* and *Madame X*.) Unlike most stars and directors during the studio era, who earned a flat fee for their pictures, Lana also shared residuals every time *Imitation of Life* was shown on television, and, eventually, from VHS sales and the like. She needn't have worked another day. Indeed, her filmography would shine brighter had she retired from the screen while on top, thus avoiding such ratty vehicles as *Who's Got the Action* (1962) with Dean Martin and Walter Matthau, *The Big Cube* (1969) with Lana on LSD, and *Bittersweet Love* (1976) costarring such lesser lights as Celeste Holm, Robert Lansing, and Meredith Baxter Birney.

Following its first-run success, *Imitation of Life* played around the country during most of 1959, first at neighborhood theatres in cities, then at suburban and small-town movie houses and drive-ins. Three years later, it was rereleased on a double bill with Ross Hunter's recent *Flower Drum Song* (1961), with elaborate studio press kits yoking the two pictures like fraternal twins. If you search for similarities, however, you might surmise, vaguely, that Nancy Kwan, as a nightclub entertainer in San Francisco's Chinatown, had watched Susan Kohner's dance routines. True, some of the *Imitation of Life* team was on board: Alexander Golitzen as art director, Russell Metty cinematographer, Milton Carruth edited this minor Rodgers and Hammerstein musical, and everyone involved made it more bearable than a big sticky-cake show like *The Sound of Music*. The point of those press kits, of course, was that both pictures dealt with race, as though *Flower Drum*'s stereotypical chinoiserie had anything to do with life. It was the real imitation on that double bill.

*W*hen black folks get Oscar nominations, you know they *really* deserve it," said Curtis King, founder and director of the Black Academy of the Arts, in Dallas, as he introduced Juanita Moore at a recent event. His epigram drew laughter, for the allusion to fine performances overlooked reverberates among African Americans. In 1959, however, it's likely that Juanita would have won the Academy Award for Best Supporting Actress except for one obstacle: Susan Kohner. And the reason Susan didn't win was Juanita.

Two such performances in the same picture insure that the Oscar goes to a third party, often less deserving, and it did: to Shelley Winters, for *The Diary of Anne Frank*. (The other nominees were Hermione Baddeley for *Room at the Top* and Thelma Ritter for *Pillow Talk*.) The same year, Katharine Hepburn and Elizabeth Taylor, both nominated for best actress in *Suddenly, Last Summer,* lost to dark-horse candidate Simone Signoret. Arthur O'Connell and George C. Scott, both nominated in the Supporting Actor category for *Anatomy of a Murder,* lost to Hugh Griffith in *Ben-Hur*. It's a familiar phenomenon, and unavoidable. Faced with one vote and an impossible choice—Juanita Moore or Susan Kohner—many Academy voters compromised: Shelley Winters, a sentimental favorite, in a film reverenced by all.

———

"I was scared to death at the Oscars," said Juanita, long after the fact.

"I was, too," Susan confessed. "Shelley Winters won that year." Pause. "She remained in my father's black book forever." Surely both she and Juanita, like all nominees who don't win, feel the occasional twinge even now.

Like the other nominees, Juanita and her husband, and Susan and her escort, George Hamilton, were seated down front near an aisle for easy egress. Susan's gown, designed by Bill Thomas, who had costumed her for *Imitation of Life,* was a Grecian draped floor-length creation of imported French oyster white chiffon and was accented with red silk shoes. Juanita recalls wearing a shell pink cocktail dress.

The 32nd Academy Awards Ceremonies took place April 4, 1960, at the Pantages Theatre on Hollywood Boulevard, and was telecast on NBC. The evening, or at least the taped record of it, seems less exciting, less glamorous, than previous ceremonies in the fifties. It lacks the star power and the verve of the 30th (see chapter 8), a diminution perhaps explainable by the waning of traditional studio power; the end of an etiolated decade; and the lame predictability of Bob Hope, who had grown on the event like mistletoe.

The evening opened with a medley of Harold Arlen songs, conducted by André Previn: "Blues in the Night," "That Old Black Magic," "Over the Rainbow." Perky Mitzi Gaynor presented the documentary awards, crisp Ann Blyth accepted for an absent documentary filmmaker, followed by presenters Arlene Dahl and Fernando Lamas, Haya Harareet, Olivia de Havilland, Natalie Wood and Robert Wagner, Hope Lange and Carl Reiner, Edmond O'Brien.

Janet Leigh and Tony Curtis presented the screenwriting awards, John Wayne the award for Best Director—to William Wyler for *Ben-Hur*—followed by winners Charlton Heston as Best Actor (*Ben-Hur*), Simone Signoret for *Room at the Top,* and Sam Zimbalist, producer, for Best Picture, *Ben-Hur.*

Neither Susan nor Juanita was pictured in the telecast, even when their names were read out as nominees.

*I*n 1960, Susan Kohner told a reporter from the *Los Angeles Times,* "If acting was taken away from me right now, I wouldn't be lost at all. I have a lot of interests. I love books, I love music, and eventually I'd like to get married."

To those who knew Susan, and to savvy readers of that interview, her comments must have seemed whimsical. After all, she was a gunpowder talent who had exploded a year earlier in *Imitation of Life*, and even now her name was ubiquitous on marquees, in film and TV credits, in the magazines. No longer an actress on the way up, she was *up*. Oscar nominated; well-liked; a serious professional without personal liabilities. Beautiful, intelligent, cosmopolitan.

In August 1959, *The Big Fisherman* was released, with Susan second-billed after Howard Keel. Directed by Frank Borzage (his last film), and based on a novel by Lloyd C. Douglas, this biblical epic-romance—the story of St. Peter, featuring a Middle Eastern Romeo and Juliet—provided Susan her largest role. She's on screen through most of the film, with a supporting cast of newcomers (John Saxon as her lover, Ray Stricklyn, Martha Hyer) and veterans—Herbert Lom, Beulah Bondi, and Marian Seldes. The film, with its Maxfield Parrish colors and bold N. C. Wyeth shapes, resembles a big book of Bible illustrations for children. Shot and edited like a silent film (not surprising, since roughly half of Borzage's work took place before the advent of sound), it's more subdued and pictorial than many of the era's Judeo-Christian pageants. You could turn off the audio and still follow the plot. (But you'd miss Martha Hyer's camp line. She plays Herodias, and when her husband, Herod Antipas, invites Susan Kohner's Fara, a Judean, to a palace soirée, his petulant wife remonstrates: "We are overwomaned already.")

In December of that year, *The Gene Krupa Story* was released, starring Sal Mineo and Susan; and in 1960, *All the Fine Young Cannibals,* with Robert Wagner, Natalie Wood, Susan, and George Hamilton, who would become Susan's fiancé. In the picture, Susan plays Hamilton's sister. They're Dallas rich kids, and Susan, in a showy role, speaks with a "fetched-y'all-a-mess-of-crawdads" accent. She plays a vixen, and she does it well, recalling Bette Davis in *Cabin in the Cotton*—and also Sarah Jane.

It's intriguing to watch Susan here and think of the feral, sultry roles—and the poignant ones—she might have played. To Robert Wagner, as Chad, her husband (loosely based on Chet Baker), she croons a haunting little speech worthy of a Julie Harris gamine: "You don't have to love me, Chad. Just say that you do. For a little while. And we'll be less lonely." Later he slaps her—hard—for referring to his friend and mentor (Pearl Bailey) with a racial epithet. Susan, in turn, horsewhips the shirtless Wagner with a riding crop.

Natalie Wood and Susan play sisters-in-law, though they could pass for sisters. (Wood had tested for Susan's role in *Imitation of Life,* and around the time of *Cannibals,* Susan tested for Maria in *West Side Story.*) Louise Beavers also has a small part in *Cannibals,* a quarter century after appearing in the original *Imitation of Life.*

Susan appeared once more with Lana Turner, in *By Love Possessed* (1961), which costarred George Hamilton. By then, he and Susan were engaged, and Hollywood seers predicted not only the wedding of the year but an on-screen partnership, as well. This was already their second film together.

Susan and George Hamilton had started dating in 1959, and she chose him as her escort on Oscar night when she was a nominee. The celebrity press doted on the couple, reporting on the engagement ring from "one of the finest jewelers in New York City"; Hamilton's down payment on a twenty-seven-room house for their conjugal life (viz., Grayhall, the hunting lodge at Pickfair); the thrilling mix of young love and young careers. One magazine even published "Scoop Pix! George Hamilton's and Susan Kohner's Honeymoon"—a scoop that didn't happen.

To be sure, the wedding date had been announced: August 19, 1962. In June, they attended the Hollywood premiere of Stanley Kubrick's *Lolita*, and the celebration following, described by *Photoplay* as "a high-class party with low-cut gowns" held in the Trianon Room of the Beverly Wilshire Hotel. Sue Lyon, the sixteen-year-old "nymphet" (as she was called ad nauseam), was guest of honor, and seated prominently at the center of the room. George Hamilton and Susan Kohner sat at a distant table.

According to *Photoplay*, "At about one a.m. those near them say that George turned and said something to Susan. Susan stared at her fiancé and, through what looked like a forced smile, responded with just the slightest shrug of her lovely shoulders. George looked back at Sue Lyon, or what he could see of her through the circle of photographers. In a few moments he spoke to Susan again. This time, allowing for hearsay, she answered, 'If you like, George.'"

A montage of magazine features completes the story: "The Night George Hamilton Danced with Lolita"; "The Doll and the Dance That Broke Susan's Heart"; "The Day Susan Kohner Gave George Hamilton the Gate." Whether Hamilton danced once with Sue Lyon, or once too often, isn't the point. The nymphet was merely the convenient catalyst. Susan's statement, reported in *Photoplay* after she returned the engagement ring, is perhaps the best summation: "George is ready for love, but he is not ready for marriage." (Today, Susan neither denies nor confirms this account, calling it "fan magazinery.")

Susan's last film, *Freud*, directed by John Huston, was released late in 1962. In it, she plays Freud's wife, Martha, and has little to do. Siggy, as she calls her husband (played by Montgomery Clift), is too occupied with complexes and hypnosis to pay her much attention. Susan's most memorable line, spoken wistfully when a colleague of Siggy's tells the Frau Doktor of a romantic Italian vacation: "Venice must be lovely in the spring."

After half-a-dozen TV shows, the last one in 1964, Susan ended her career. On August 30 of that year, she married John Weitz in a ceremony performed in the garden of her parents' home in Bel Air. Susan's wedding gown, made of organdy with hand embroidery, was designed by Bill Blass, who also served as best man. Among the guests were Lana Turner, Agnes Moorehead, Mr. and Mrs. Eddie Albert, Warren Cowan and Barbara Rush, John Gavin, Eva Marie Saint and Jeffrey Hayden, Jerry Lewis, Edward G. Robinson, Otto Preminger, Mr. and Mrs. Billy Wilder, and Jill St. John.

Forty years later, in a rare interview, Susan explained her departure from Hollywood: "I didn't have the passion anymore. The passion went into another direction and I never missed it. The man I married was the most fascinating, erudite, and marvelous individual. I wanted to have children and I didn't think I could handle both—a career and raising a family."

Susan's husband, John Weitz (1923–2002), must have made her Hollywood suitors look pallid and provincial, for he was a man of the world—literally—and an overachiever in several fields. Born Hans Werner Weitz to wealthy parents in Berlin who sent him to school in England in the early thirties, and who themselves emigrated there when Hitler came to power, Weitz first attended St. Paul's School in London, and then Oxford for a year. He apprenticed in Paris with Captain Edward Molyneux, a fashion modernist.

Weitz became an American citizen in 1943. He eagerly served his new country in wartime, eventually joining the Office of Strategic Services (the forerunner of the CIA). After the war, he settled in New York, where he designed women's sportswear collections. In 1964, he launched a menswear line. Weitz pioneered product licensing, and eventually his signature appeared on everything from business suits to housewares and home sewing patterns. In 1974, he won a Coty Award—the Oscar of the fashion world—in recognition of innovative achievements in style.

One of Weitz's interests in the fifties was auto racing, and he drove at Sebring several times. His first book, which combined his interests in fashion and racing, was *Sports Clothes for Your Sports Car,* published in 1958. He eventually extended his hobby into a car-building project: in 1979, Weitz designed the X600, an aluminum-bodied two-seater sports car that was exhibited in the United States, England, and Japan. Later he wrote half-a-dozen other books, including the bestseller *Man in Charge: The Executive's Guide to Grooming, Manners, and Travel; Hitler's Diplomat: The Life and Times of Joachim von Ribbentrop*; and two novels.

Weitz, a tall, handsome man who could probably have become a movie star had he made the attempt, or a designer of men's and women's costumes for films, lived a star's life without benefit of Hollywood. His story reads like a screenplay; indeed, he seems a candidate for a full biography. Today, Susan refers to herself—in correspondence, on the telephone—as "Susan Weitz," or sometimes, if it's a professional connection, as "Susan Kohner Weitz." Indicating, of course, that acts two and three of her life take precedence over that distant first act whose climax was *Imitation of Life*.

39 | A LATE ENCOUNTER WITH L. T.

*W*hen men, especially heterosexuals, write about Lana Turner, they often stop with the sweater. The woman I now introduce is more like an X-ray who sees past that sweater, into Lana's heart.

Until her retirement a few years ago, this woman was well known in the New York publishing world, for she was author, journalist, raconteuse, gadfly, and wit. She also had Hollywood connections, her most important one, for our purposes, being as ghostwriter of Lana's 1982 autobiography, *Lana: The Lady, the Legend, the Truth.* For reasons that I will presently make clear, she agreed to speak only off the record. For convenience, therefore, I assign her the name "Eleanor Fletcher," which is my invention and, I hope, not recognizable to her friends.

I first met "Eleanor" in the eighties, when I interviewed her for a magazine article. During our conversation, she mentioned as one of her projects the Lana Turner book. I asked several questions about Lana, until Eleanor silenced me. "You absolutely must not include that. My name is nowhere on the book, and it's all in the past." Some twenty years later, after Lana's death and Eleanor's increasing debility, I tracked her down and we had the conversation I wanted to have the first day we met. I now turn the chapter over to Eleanor Fletcher, with a minimum of authorial intrusions.

"Lana worked with Hollis Alpert* on her autobiography, and she hated the book. She said to me, 'Eleanor, I don't know how that man could make my fascinating life so dull.' She also had problems with Dutton, and she decided she didn't want them to publish the book. One day, I got a call from an editor there who asked me to go to L.A., spend a weekend working with Lana, buff the book up a little bit, at least make it more to her liking.

"I did that. I came home thinking the job was finished. Apparently, however, even before my plane landed in New York, Lana had phoned Dutton to say, 'You can't publish my book unless Eleanor goes over it with me page by page. I want it entirely rewritten.' Now, Dutton had paid her an enormous advance on the book. So much, in fact, that they couldn't afford to pay me very much.

"Then Lana called me. 'Eleanor, you have to come back. I can't let this book go!' She was right. Hollis Alpert's book was dull, and much longer that what Lana and I did. He crammed every fact into it but had no grasp of how it was to be a beautiful woman in Hollywood during the studio days, when stars were gods and goddesses.

"Lana said, 'Eleanor, you can understand because you're a *wooman*.' She pronounced it like that. So I went back to L.A. and we redid the book from the top. One of the things I'm pleased with is that I got her to tell me about her abortion, about the baby she conceived with Tyrone Power that the studio wouldn't let her keep. She said, 'Oh, I can't tell the world about that,' and I said, 'You can. You can be courageous. It's a changed world.' I said, 'If you want to be a role model, you have to tell how it was in those days.' People who tell the stories of their lives always want to be role models, that's really their agenda.

"She said, 'Do you think?'

"I said, 'Yes, I think.'

"She said, 'And they won't say I'm a whore?'

"'No, Lana.'

"I didn't tell her that when I was going out to L.A. I told my mother

*Born in 1916, Alpert is the author of many books on show business. He was film critic of *Saturday Review* from 1950–1972.

about this assignment, and my mother said, 'That kurveh.' A Yiddish word meaning 'whore.'"

"How do you spell that, Eleanor?" I asked.

"I'm not telling you! Next you'll want to use my real name."

"Well, you're not the only Jew in New York," I said. "Someone will spell it for me."

"Then," Eleanor resumed, "we came to the credits. She wanted to put my name on the book. I said, 'Lana, I think that's a terrible idea. I don't want a fight with Hollis Alpert.' She said, 'I won't have his name on there.' So I said, 'Let's compromise. Let's just put your name on the book. It's yours.'" (The copyright notice reads: "Copyright 1982 by Eltee Productions, Inc., and Hollis Alpert.")

"You don't want to revive the credit story," Eleanor moaned. "I'll give you something good in its place. Here it is: Lana did not remember her husbands as well as she remembered every sitting she ever had for a costume. She loved to talk about her clothes. This is the unvarnished truth! She gave me a cuff-by-collar description of every dress she ever wore on the screen! I didn't put all that in because it would be ridiculous. She also said she was proud to have had the narrowest hips at Metro. The studio had dressmaker's dummies of all their stars so that the wardrobe department could do basic fitting on the dummy while the star was elsewhere. And each star was required to maintain her weight. Anyway, Lana's had the narrowest ass of all the dummies.

"So of course I had to ask, 'And who had the broadest one?' She told me: Greer Garson. But she was a larger woman, taller—Lana Turner was the size of a mouse."

"Did Lana tell you anything about *Imitation of Life* that didn't make it into the book?" I asked.

Eleanor sighed heavily, as though suffering. "I have to tell you," she finally replied. "I never saw *Imitation of Life*. It wasn't my kind of movie. In those days, I went to see Anna Magnani. But whatever Lana told me, I put into the book, I swear to you. I let her furnish all the material. She told me she thought Hollis Alpert was probably in love with her. I don't know him, so I have no idea whether she was his cup of tea. But I do know he was the wrong writer.

"By the way, her lawyer, Melvin Belli, negotiated her contract with

Dutton. One stipulation was that the minute I handed in the manuscript, I had to relinquish the tapes. Belli confiscated them. I don't know whether he kept them or destroyed them. Lana always hired good lawyers.

"I stayed at a hotel in Century City and we worked at Lana's home. She lived in one of the Century City high-rises. It had a minuscule balcony that was covered in plants, and it overlooked the old MGM lot. Everyone warned me she would be late. We were to meet every morning at ten o'clock in her apartment. I always arrived ten or fifteen minutes early. I sat in the lobby chatting with the doorman, and at ten o'clock on the dot he called her to announce me. Lana always answered the door herself, though she had a secretary or a factotum who handled her business. But the secretary was never present at our meetings—only Lana and me. She was always perfectly coiffed, perfectly made up, but not dressed. She wore a fine-looking robe with a zipper up the front. She had a card table, and I would set up my tape recorder on it, and a notebook.

"Lana, who was a neat freak, arranged her cigarettes, the ones that would eventually kill her, and a gold lighter, and she would square the corners with the corners of the table. And we went at it. We didn't stop for lunch, because Lana didn't eat. You don't stay that thin by gorging. I don't know what she ate when I wasn't there, but I can guarantee it wasn't lunch.

"Occasionally she would ask if I wanted a drink of water. I'd say yes, and she would go get it for me. I'd think, I don't believe this—Eleanor Fletcher of Washington Heights is sitting in Lana Turner's apartment and Lana is pouring her water. It was really bizarre.

"I was there on Mother's Day. When I turned up, she said,"—and here Eleanor did a dead-on imitation of Lana's voice and inflections— 'Did you call your mother?' I answered, 'Well, I haven't, Lana, but I'll call her in the evening.'

" 'No, no, no, you'll call her right now,' and she brought the phone and dialed as I told her the number. Lana said to my mother—the one who had said, 'So, you're working with that kurveh'—'I'm here with Eleanor and she wants to wish you Happy Mother's Day.'

" 'Oh, Lana,' gushed my mother, 'Oh, I love you so much! I love all your movies! When are you going to make another one?' "

When I could stop laughing, I asked Eleanor about Lana's apartment.

"She had a long, long wall of paintings. I swear to you, on the life of my cat, she was proudest of the Keanes [big, droopy-eyed portraits by Margaret Keane]. As I stood there looking at those paintings, I said to myself, This woman married into the Topping family, which had a beautiful house where she often stayed. They had gorgeous taste in furnishings and art, and they bought only the finest. But Lana never picked up anything. It's true she was very young when she married Bob Topping, but her taste was incredibly garish.

"At that time I had a lover who lived in Los Angeles. He was one reason I took the assignment. Lana wanted to meet him, so I brought him up. We invited her to join us for dinner at our favorite restaurant, Bangkok One. She demurred. Eventually I realized that she never left home unless it was a definite engagement, such as a film festival. She couldn't bring herself to slip on a pair of jeans, or a skirt, and go out for an informal dinner with a couple of friends. She said, 'I would love for you to bring me one of those fabulous chicken wings you talked about.' So we brought her two. She looked at them and said, 'They're so big! And two of them!' I don't believe she ate those wings, and I wish I had them now.

"She was no old lady at the time. She was only sixtyish. It was that studio discipline, that studio oppression, and many stars never escaped from it. Unless you were an independent spirit like Katharine Hepburn or Bette Davis, the studio was your mother and your father. That's what MGM was to Lana. They held her hand, they dressed her, they coiffed her, and that attention was very important to her. She was picked up at age fifteen and thrown into a sweater and soon she was a star. This was a little girl who knew *nothing*. That's why I think she loved her clothes so much. Because they were the outward proof of how important she was. And so, even when she was retired, and rich, she still couldn't go out unless she met the studio's approval. She always had to be Lana Turner, Movie Star."

"Now, Eleanor," I said, "here's a big question. I know what Lana told you for the book about Stompanato, but what do you think? Do you accept her version of the events of that night, April 4, 1958?"

Eleanor Fletcher: "I accept her story for this reason: I believe that Lana believed it. I also believe that O. J. Simpson actually thought he did not kill his wife. He had talked himself into it so completely that, by the end of the trial, he had convinced himself he was an innocent man. And Lana, too, had told her story one way, and one way only, for a long time. She went for drunks and abusers. I think Stompanato beat her to shit, I'm sure he did. He took everything he could from her. I think the hand on the knife was Lana's.

"Although how that little person could have killed that big guy, I don't know. Maybe she caught him off guard. She might have caught him in bed. I don't believe her daughter killed him. I believe Lana did it. But what difference does it make if the bastard deserved to die? More women should kill abusive men."

Because Eleanor is so shrewd, so intuitive, and because she never misses a subtext, whether written or spoken, I found her assertion unsettling, as though a surprise witness had just stunned the courtroom. That disconcerting paragraph was the climax of our conversation, and I changed the subject.

"How," I wanted to know, "did you capture Lana's voice in the book? Many ghostwritten autobiographies sound processed and generic."

She said, "I led her down paths she didn't want to go down. About the abortion, about Tyrone Power. I believe she really did love him, but not as much as Tyrone Power loved Tyrone Power. The book had to be in Lana's voice. No one will ever take her for a genius, but she lived a very interesting life. I treated her with kid gloves. She said to me many times, 'Oh, we're not going to put that in the book?' Then I would have to go through the litany: 'Lana, you really should include this. If you don't, you're losing sympathy from your readers. These are things that will make women everywhere sympathetic toward you.'"

The book was a success, and Lana made nationwide appearances at book stores, department stores, and the like. At the American Booksellers Convention that year, Eleanor and Lana attended a party together, though as friends and not as coauthors. "She tried to arrive on time," Eleanor said, "but she was in her hotel room, she didn't know what to wear, didn't like the way her makeup looked, wanted her hairdresser, who wasn't even in town.

"So she didn't come down, and didn't come down, and when she finally showed up the man who paid big money for the paperback edition of her book, and who hated her, called her a cunt in front of everyone. He's dead, and he was a bastard, too. He was Ron Busch. Now there's a name, speaking of bastards!"

*P*rior to the present century, one might navigate the vast movie oceans and rarely spot a tributary isle of Sirk. It's true that in the wake of *Imitation of Life,* a measly sixties archipelago popped up, only to sink like the remains of Atlantis. In 1960, a quickie knockoff appeared called *I Passed for White,* starring Sonya Wilde as a young biracial woman who marries a rich white man (James Franciscus) and lives in anguish lest he discover her secret, which those few moviegoers who saw it knew from the pulpy title.

The same year, Dyan Cannon (spelling her name "Diane") played "a Negro girl who tries to pass as white" in *This Rebel Breed,* which also starred aspiring white heartthrob Mark Damon as a half-Latino, half-black police officer. Cannon plays "Wiggles"—who is, according to Leonard Maltin's movie guide, "a gang deb."

Pictures like this, of course, owe nothing to Sirk except for the gimmick of passing, which was looked on at the time as a titillating, and lucrative, subject for exploitation. The first movie to make actual, though indirect, use of *Imitation of Life* was probably *Harlow,* in 1965. (The one starring Carroll Baker, not the other *Harlow* that year with Carol Lynley in the title role.) This awful picture—theme and variations on Harlow rather than a real biopic—has a strange heartbeat that makes you halfway respond to the story. The reason is Carroll Baker. Hers was a Susan Kohner talent that Hollywood seldom used right. Baker's acting style may remind you of Kohner's: both harness their respective New York training so that neither Meisner nor Method runs wild. Indeed, Baker could have played Sarah Jane.

Throughout the picture, the tides of *Imitation of Life* pull certain scenes: scenes in agents' offices, in limousines, cheesy nightclub sequences, family confrontations, even Harlow's deathbed scene. Under Gordon Douglas's direction, however, it's drained of fuel like an exhausted carburetor. The production attempts a Ross Hunter opulence; minus Ross Hunter, however, the decor smacks of Anna Nicole Smith.

Unexpected echoes of *Imitation of Life* reside in the Joan Crawford vehicle *Berserk* (1967), with Joan as a draconian circus owner in England and Judy Geeson as her Sandra Dee-ish daughter. When Joan gives hunk Ty Hardin "twenty-five percent of the circus and one hundred percent of me," blonde daughter turns peevish: "I heard what your plans are with Lover Boy. I was hoping that we could go away together when the season ends—just the two of us." But Mommie Dearest has to work: After all, the big top is so uncertain when there's a murder every week.

The youngster refuses to see Mom's point: "All my memories are of teachers and other people who brought me up."

Joan: "But you certainly never lacked anything."

"No. Except what I needed most—you!"

Mother and daughter have one Ty that binds, but this girl uses wiles—and weapons—beyond the scope of Sandra Dee. Her lessons in man-snatching were surely inspired by the films of Joan Crawford.

The one place where you might expect a whiff of *Imitation of Life* is Sirkless: *Guess Who's Coming to Dinner?* directed by Stanley Kramer in 1967. One reviewer called it "the best picture of 1939." No one, however, would have called *Imitation of Life* the best picture of 1967. Like the entire Sirk oeuvre, it languished in the attic of the sixties like a Victorian antique. Its treatment of race so mismatched the events and the attitudes of the decade that only a prescient midsixties viewer would have seen *Imitation* as racially retro but emotionally timely. (In Europe, on the other hand, Sirk was always taken seriously. A long interview in *Cahiers du cinéma* in 1967 was the real beginning of Sirk awareness.)

Mama, Can You Hear Me?

In 1969, Diana Ross recorded a hit single called "I'm Livin' in Shame," said to be inspired by *Imitation of Life*. Although the lyric doesn't involve passing, it's a teary, masochistic lament for having shunned the old-fashioned, unchic mother, now deceased, who brought the daughter acute embarrassment. "She wore a sloppy dress," with stockings rolled to ankles; tied a ragged scarf around her head; and ate from the pot without using fork or plate.

The speaker has married high, and has a two-year-old that she never brought to see his grandmother. Then came a telegram: "Mama passed away while making homemade jam."

That line is typical of the gauche lyric, which carefully avoids any direct borrowing from the script of *Imitation of Life*. Only the refrain—"Mama, Mama, Mama, can you hear me?"—is lifted from the movie. The song belongs to that genre of Mama songs calculated to jerk a tear from the Sahara: "Mama from the Train," a Patti Page hit; "(Put Them All Together, They Spell) M-O-T-H-E-R," ca. 1915; "My Mother's Eyes," from the 1929 film *Lucky Boy*; and a thousand more. Miss Ross hasn't recorded a Mama album, nor, alas, has Christina Crawford.

Not until the seventies did a coterie of English-language cinephiles begin to examine the films of Douglas Sirk. Even then, however, his work was perplexing and elusive. His biggest pictures—some would say his best—belonged to a decade that no one missed. They also embodied a foreign formalism at odds with current American moviemaking and, unlike the films of such émigré directors as Billy Wilder, William Wyler, and Michael Curtiz, Sirk's never quite lost their continental accent. Although his Universal pictures pleased the public when they came out, they were also hermetic. In that, they resembled the so-called closet dramas of Milton, Goethe, Byron, and Shelley, plays not intended to be performed onstage but rather to be read by initiates as poetry or philosophy. Another factor working against Sirk's recognition: his so-called melodramas displeased American critics (and art-house audiences) because of their operatic story lines and their high quotient of artificiality. The American masses, being literal-minded, went for the cinematic equivalent of Norman Rockwell realism. (It got worse. In the new century, those masses flock to movies as dumb as the forty-third American president.) Then and now, arty films that want decoding don't linger in Pomona and Poughkeepsie.

We encountered the two leading Sirk pioneers back on pages 92–93—Jon Halliday in England, and Michael Stern in the United States. Their books, however, were written far from Hollywood, where few filmmakers paid on-screen homage to Sirk until later. The exception was John Waters, whose raunchy, anarchic pictures seemed to extract the id from Sirk's oeuvre, though never the polish. What's understated in Sirk—repression, dysfunctional families, unrequited love, ambiguous eroticism—in Waters becomes American Dada. (Waters himself has said, "Strive for art in reverse.")

Although *Polyester* (1981) is Waters's flags-flying homage to Sirk—the suburban dream as upside-down comic nightmare—it's in *Female Trouble* (1974) that Waters runs amok in the atelier of the Sirk psyche. That Christmas scene, for instance, where Divine wrecks the tree and beats up her parents because they didn't give her cha cha heels—isn't it the full-blown mental-illness version of many a melancholy Christmas in Sirk?

After Divine runs away (like Sarah Jane), she's at the Red Garter performing a cellulite shimmy in front of a table of lascivious men—a scene as expressionistic, in its demented way, as Sarah Jane at Harry's Club. Like Lora Meredith, Divine as Mother leaves something to be desired. Mink Stole, as her daughter, Taffy, screams: "How could I call you my mother? I wish I'd been an orphan." David Lochary, as Donald Dasher, is a more relentless photographer than John Gavin in *Imitation of Life,* but the way he points his camera at Divine—his "crime model"—sends up Gavin's pictures of Lana as "A Mother in Distress."

At times, all of Sirk seems deconstructed in *Female Trouble.* After Edith Massey throws acid in Divine's face, the victim is mummy-wrapped like Jane Wyman in *Magnificent Obsession.* Then, as the healed

Divine is unveiled, each layer of bandage lifted lovingly, her hairdresser exclaims, "I'm getting a hard-on! Beauty always gives me a hard-on." Bandages off, Divine resembles a Jackson Pollock, which leads her entourage into a deep discussion of makeup for the disfigured face. That bedside confabulation is no more coocoo than its presumptive source in *Magnificent Obsession*: lofty declarations about "the source of infinite power" and a "secret society" of philanthropists whose charity flows like electricity, with "insulation"—i.e., secrecy—insuring that it flows in the right direction. (Sirk called this "trashy stuff" with an "element of craziness"—a description sure to arouse John Waters.)

Every time I watch a Waters film, I feel that the secret, "dirty" history of Hollywood is finally there: everything the studios, directors, and stars wanted to put on-screen in the twentieth century, but weren't allowed to by the censors. On the surface, it's the underside of Baltimore, but beneath that is Hollywood's seething innards.

(In 2007, Waters released a CD compilation, *A Date with John Waters,* which included the theme from *Imitation of Life*. The romantic selections on the CD, described by Waters as "beautiful and touching," were timed for the Valentine's Day market. "It might get you laid," he said.)

When I mentioned above that Jon Halliday's and Michael Stern's books on Sirk were written far from Hollywood, I might have included two filmmakers, equally distant, whose works are often cited as bearing the mark of Sirk. These two, Fassbinder and Almodóvar, started out in the seventies (Fassbinder directed four films in the late sixties), and it's obvious from many of their pictures that they *watched* a lot of Sirk, and copied certain aspects of his films, such as set decoration, use of color, melodramatic scenarios, and troubled female protagonists who are often actresses. Critics trying to nail specific allusions and homages, however, often fall short. Even when these critical fishing expeditions do get a nibble, it's not *Imitation of Life* they've hooked.

Almodóvar, in an interview, summed up his distance from Sirk, whom he called "a marvelous director." Two things, he said, separate his own farcical, amoral work from that of Sirk: "Morality—in all classic melodramas, there are the good guys and the bad guys—and humor. As I said, I admire Sirk's films, but one has to recognize that there is a complete absence of humor. The humor that is there is perhaps in the eye of the one who sees it, but in no way is it the intention of the film."

Fassbinder said that in the early seventies he watched twenty films by Sirk. No doubt that's one reason critics endlessly yoke the names of these two German directors. Fassbinder also befriended Sirk, who claimed to admire the younger man's work. Though I could never gnaw through Fassbinder's three dozen lazy, solipsistic films, I've seen enough to know that whatever he borrowed from Sirk didn't improve his stillborn talent.

Had there been no war to drive Sirk out of Germany, or if he had returned there postwar and made the films he dreamed of making, I'm afraid his own output might have resembled that of Fassbinder. Sirk told Jon Halliday, "One of my dearest projects was to make a picture set in a blind people's home. There would just have been people ceaselessly tapping, trying to grasp things they could not see." Given such uncinematic impulses, Hollywood may be the best thing that ever happened to Sirk. Without studio restraint, he might have attempted the same kinds of indulgent pictures that Fassbinder cranked out between 1965 and his death in 1982.

Now that *Imitation of Life* has become a mainstream classic, its greatest influence perhaps lies ahead. (A survey in the *New York Daily News* in 1995 placed it among the ten most popular movies ever made, though it landed only at number 178 on the AFI's whimsical list of the four hundred pictures nominated for the Top 100 Greatest American Movies.)

On the threshold of Y2K, Quentin Tarantino tossed a bouquet to Sirk in *Pulp Fiction,* thus making him hip and okay to emulate. John Travolta and Uma Thurman go to a supercool fifties retro eatery called Jack Rabbit Slim. From the menu, Travolta orders "the Douglas Sirk steak." It's probably no coincidence that Travolta's Chevy Malibu in the film is as red as Rossano Brazzi's in *Interlude* or Dorothy Malone's in *Written on the Wind*—i.e., Sirk red.

Already, in the twenty-first century, more movies and TV shows have referenced *Imitation of Life* than in the four previous decades since its release. In a 2001 episode of *Will & Grace*, Jack (played by Sean Hayes) receives news that leads him to believe he's biracial. In a parody of Sarah Jane's motel scene, he faces the mirror and declaims: "I'm black! I'm black!"

Much has been written, by reviewers who don't know their Sirk, about Todd Haynes's *Far from Heaven* (2002) as an all-out homage. It's more accurate to call it a loving tribute to *All That Heaven Allows*, since it bears faint resemblance to Sirk's other films. *Imitation of Life*, for instance, intersects *Far from Heaven* only in moments. Raymond, the African-American man played by Dennis Haysbert, has a young daughter named Sarah. When three prepubescent white boys chase her after school, she darts into an alley where they pelt her with stones. Though less violent, the scene is just as horrific as its source, the alley scene where Troy Donahue beats Susan Kohner. In another allusion to that scene, Dennis Quaid, having learned that his wife, played by Julianne Moore, was spotted in a restaurant with a black man, echoes Donahue's Frankie: "Just tell me one goddamn thing. Is it true? What they've been saying?"

François Ozon's *8 Women* (2002) is the comprehensive Sirkorama that American reviewers thought they found in *Far from Heaven*. Behind the opening credits of this Pop-Tart of a movie, vertical strings of rhinestone beads sway like wind chimes. The music, by Krishna Levy, is a honeyed allusion to Frank Skinner's themes for the Sirk–Hunter films. The opening sequence clones *All That Heaven Allows*: a villa surrounded by snowy countryside, and a doe nibbling winter vines, with treacly musical underscore, evokes a vague fifties dream world somewhere on the Universal backlot.

The villa houses a female ménage à huit, most of them *monstres sacrés* of French cinema: Catherine Deneuve, Fanny Ardant, Isabelle Huppert, Danielle Darrieux, et al. Madame Chanel (played by the black actress Firmine Richard) is the cook, a lesbian in love with big-boned glamour puss Ardant. The plot resembles Agatha Christie's *Ten Little Indians* more than any Sirk story. A faux mystery, it's as lame as *Murder by Death*, which it also resembles. There are amusing touches, however. Deneuve's husband is stabbed in bed, a possible nod toward Stompanato. As it turns out, however, he wasn't really stabbed at all. He reappears; it was a put-on.

The glued-on French pop songs that the actresses perform recall Sirk's odd semimusicals made in Germany. A more obvious Sirk touch: Deneuve and her daughter (Virginie Ledoyen) are photographed through a mullioned window in a scene of actressy distress. A good deal of assembly is required, however, in this Douglas Sirk put-it-together-yourself kit. Ozon's attempt to copy Sirk's color fails; his insipid palette looks ready to dribble off the frame like watercolors. As this picture makes clear, only Sirk knew how to make a Sirk film. His imitators, except for Todd Haynes, can't follow instructions. What makes this a charming trifle, however, is the director's unpretentious sense of fun. After a florid speech by Catherine Deneuve, Fanny Ardant applauds, saying, "Fine melodramatic acting!"

It seems 2002 was the year of eights: Curtis Hanson directed *8 Mile*, with Eminem as Rabbit, an aspiring white rapper in a field that's largely black. When Rabbit comes home and finds his mom, Kim Basinger, watching *Imitation of Life* on TV, it's an obvious plot point: to underscore the irony of Rabbit trying to pass as a top-notch white rapper.

The irony is double-edged, however, in a way the filmmakers wouldn't want to acknowledge. This vanity production, showcasing the bantam talent of Eminem, is so heavily weighted in Rabbit's favor that he's bound to win the big freestyle rap contest over his black competitors. *8 Mile* is racially retrograde in a way that *Imitation of Life,* made over four decades earlier, never was. *Imitation* was progressive; *8 Mile* is a Bush-era glorification of Eminem's assault on what he perceives as the glass ceiling of hip-hop. His success—and Rabbit's—might be more applause-worthy if he weren't such a mean little snot.

In earlier times, Eminem's well-documented homophobic lyrics— like the homophobia of the "religious" right—might well have taken the convenient form of racism. But since public racism is now off limits, would-be bigots must look elsewhere. The sick joke of the Eminem story is that this high school dropout would be listened to at all. (Q.E.D.: filmmaking in the rotten age of Bush.)

In *Die Mommie Die!* (2003), Natasha Lyonne, as Edith Sussman, daughter of Angela Arden (Charles Busch), to her grande diva mom: "Oh, Mother, must you always be acting?"

In season four of *Six Feet Under,* which aired in 2004, the following unfocused exchange took place:

KEITH (NOT OUT AT HIS NEW JOB): "It's weird at work. I feel like Sarah Jane from *Imitation of Life.*"

DAVID: "That makes me Troy Donahue."

KEITH: "There's this side of me that feels all puffed up because everybody thinks I'm straight."

In *Hustle and Flow* (2005), Jennifer Bynum Green sings a spiritual in a church in Memphis. The song, and the singer, seem to allude to Mahalia Jackson, though the camera angles are different from Sirk's.

41 | GENTLEMEN PREFER LYPSINKA

*T*he script of *Angels in America*, an HBO miniseries that aired in 2003, is full of allusions: to *The Barefoot Contessa, A Streetcar Named Desire, The Glass Menagerie*, Walt Whitman, etc. Adapted by Tony Kushner, from his play, the film is packed with visual references impossible on the stage. Whether Kushner, and director Mike Nichols, intended to parody the *Imitation of Life* funeral or to pay tribute, the echoes are there. For instance, a funeral at a black church in New York for a man dead of AIDS echoes Annie Johnson's. But this is Kushner, not Sirk, so the funeral is a postmodern celebration that sends the defunct off to a flamboyant gay heaven.

After the service, the coffin is loaded into a horse-drawn carriage while a jazz band plays "Just a Closer Walk with Thee." A drag queen approaches to touch the glass side of the hearse as another one—this one in nun's habit—zips past on roller skates. Lypsinka (aka John Epperson) is among the mourners in *Angels in America,* and fittingly so, since both she and her creator, John, are huge fans of Sirk, and of *Imitation of Life* in particular. At www.lypsinka.com, you'll always find plenty about the picture, from the outré ("I tried to lure Sirk out of retirement to direct my intimate family drama, *Taste the Blood of Lypsinka*") to astute talking points, such as Lypsinka's theory that even Hitchcock borrowed from Sirk: "Look at the last scene of *Imitation of Life* and the last scene of *The Birds*. They're practically the same scene. In Hitchcock's neglected masterpiece, *Marnie,* there is an establishing shot of the facade of a house with a tilted camera so that you can see a person at a downstairs window and another person at an upstairs window on the other side of the house. Sirk had already used this shot in *Written on the Wind.* Also in *Marnie,* in the pretend-psychoanalysis scene with Sean Connery, Tippi Hedren shrieks, 'White! White! WHITE!' Susan Kohner, of course, had delivered the same line reading, in a very different context, five years earlier. Sirk and Hitchcock worked at the same studio."

In a recent conversation, Lypsinka pointed out an *Imitation of Life* detail that no one else seems to have noticed. "In Lana's career montage, twice you see a petite blonde stand up in the audience and clap. I believe it was Lana's stand-in. Maybe Lana said to Sirk, 'Why don't you give her a moment on screen?' That woman looks a lot like Lana, same hair, same shaped face." After taking another look, I think Lypsinka's on the money.

In 2000, Lypsinka starred as Lora Meredith in *Imitation of Imitation of Life,* directed by Kevin Malony in the Tweed Theatre production off-off-Broadway. Another male actress, Flotilla DeBarge, played Annie Johnson. Stephen Pell's adaptation, which retained the framework of the original script, combined parody and heartfelt emotion in the way that such fringe deconstructions often do. (The late Charles Ludlam's Ridiculous Theatrical Company pioneered this aspect of gay theatre.)

Lypsinka recently recalled the play's development. "In rehearsal, we would ad-lib. That's how one scene briefly veered into *Sunset Boulevard*—the scene of Lora and Steve on the staircase. My lines were, 'What's a snapshot of a disgusting old man with a beer can on his belly? Is that your idea of achieving something? Is a beer can real? Going up and down and up and down, like oil wells in Bakersfield pumping, pumping . . .' That's typical of how we transformed the original script. We also added musical numbers. When Lora's star is rising, we put in the song 'Star' from the movie *Star,* only we didn't use Julie Andrews's version but Marilyn Maye's. We also set it up that Flotilla, in the cold-water flat, was providing sexual favors to the milkman so that he wouldn't leave a bill.

"The first act ended with the Troy Donahue scene in the alleyway.

The actor who played Troy wore a full gay leatherman's outfit, with chaps and his butt hanging out. The second act began with Annie massaging Lora's feet. You see, during intermission Flotilla had added gray to her hair, and I piled on more makeup, changed my hairstyle, and put glitter on my lips. By the second act, also, she was no longer Annie, but 'Ahnnie.'

"At the end, Flotilla was confined in a wheelchair—with legs spread apart, so the audience saw right up her dress. She died in that wheelchair, and there was a cardboard mockup of a coffin. Jackie Hoffman, as Sarah Jane, ran in from the audience, pushing people aside as she ad-libbed lines like, 'Get out of my way, faggot.'"

Liza Minnelli, who came backstage after a performance, perhaps spoke for others in the audience when she told Lypsinka, "I found myself caught up in the story, and then you guys would do something so hilarious it would break me out of it."

Though tempted to crown Lypsinka as the world's second-greatest Lora/Lana, I wouldn't dare—fearing revenge from other contenders. There is, for instance, Therese Kotara, as the title character in Blair Fell's *Lana Verner, Lana Verner,* which premiered in 2000 at Theater Lab Houston. A reviewer in the *Houston Chronicle* likened the one-act parody to "a racier version of the old *Carol Burnett Show*'s movie spoofs, extended into a ninety-minute special."

In a nod to *Mildred Pierce,* the playwright named Lana's daughter Vita. Vita falls in love with her mother's beau—played by a mannequin, said to be a mite more convincing than John Gavin. This leading man is rolled around the stage by the other characters. The black girl, named Lima Beena, breaks her mother's heart by passing—as a blonde.

In 2006, Running With Scissors, a theatre group in New Orleans, presented *L'imitation of Life,* with an all-male cast. The plot, as synopsized in a press release, "follows the highs and lows of all-star sweater girl Lana Turner (Ricky Graham) as she seeks to relaunch her sagging career with a really important film about prejudice, parenthood, and prêt-à-porter."

A jump cut from the ridiculous to the academic, viz. Barbara Klinger's *Melodrama and Meaning: History, Culture, and the Films of Douglas Sirk,* a very slow read: "Given its pervasiveness in culture, mass camp acts as a particularly significant manner of appropriating texts from bygone eras. Responding to a difference between past and present conventions, mass camp renegotiates the meaning of films according to modern standards. In so doing, its impact is at the same time profoundly historical and ahistorical. . . . Camp resurrects past artifacts, not to reconstruct their original meaning in some archaeological sense, but to thoroughly reconstitute them through a theatrical sensibility that modifies them by focusing on their artifice."

Frightfully profound, one sighs, digesting such carbohydrate wisdom. The immediate reason for resurrecting "past artifacts" is the poverty of present-day showbiz. If you've ever seen a drag queen taking herself seriously as Céline Dion, Jennifer Lopez, or Whitney Houston, you'll understand the appeal of Lana, Joan, Bette, and Barbra.

Devoted Fans

I heard this story from Brian Kellow, a friend in New York: "When I lived in an apartment on Seventy-second Street at the height of the AIDS crisis, I went into the hall one day and found one of my neighbors weeping inconsolably. Fearing the worst, I said, 'Steve, what's wrong? Can I help?' He wiped his eyes and said, 'Oh, Brian, I've just watched *Imitation of Life!*' "

Manuel Puig, the Argentinian author of *Kiss of the Spider Woman*, was a fervent admirer of Sirk, and his favorite film was *Imitation of Life*. In 1978, his close friend Nestor Almendros, the cinematographer, arrived in New York from Paris. The two had not seen each other for months, and Puig insisted that he come right over and stay at his apartment in the Village rather than in a hotel. According to Puig's biographer, "By around two a.m. their conversation drifted to the subject of Lana Turner. Manuel adored 'the sweater girl' and her campy splendor. Nestor said she was a lousy actress, a whore,

(continued)

and he detested her. Suddenly, Manuel ran to the door, opened it, and ordered his jet-lagged friend, who stared at him speechlessly, to leave. 'A person who hates Lana can't remain under my roof.'" (Eventually the two friends patched up their differences, as Lana surely would have wished.)

The painter David Salle, referring to *Imitation of Life*, once told an interviewer that he "really despaired of ever being able to make...a work of art anywhere near as great as that film."

Genuflection takes many forms. The Mexican director Joselito Rodriguez (1907–1985) is often regarded as having "remade" *Imitation of Life* in his own image, and not once but twice. This is not the case, however, in spite of certain plot resemblances. In 1948, Rodriguez made *Angelitos negros,* meaning, literally, "little black angels." He filmed it in sepia tones. In 1970, Rodriguez made a second version, this time in color, and it is this one that merits inclusion here, for it starred Juanita Moore, dubbed in Spanish.

Fannie Hurst's biographer, Brooke Kroeger, considers *Angelitos negros* a remake derived from Hurst's novel, though further research would have revealed its source as a radio play by the Cuban Félix B. Caignet (1892–1976). Kroeger seems not to have wondered why Hurst didn't prosecute the producers of the original Mexican film, as she surely would have done had it been derived from *Imitation of Life.*

The first *Angelitos negros* has roughly the same status in Mexico as John Stahl's original *Imitation of Life* in this country, i.e., a minor classic. One reason, no doubt, is that the male lead, Pedro Infante, was one of Mexico's greatest stars. Another reason owes to Mexico's diverse racial composition, including a substantial black population estimated at five percent. While Afro Mexicans have not encountered the same institutionalized racism as African Americans, they have nonetheless faced discrimination at all levels. *Angelitos negros,* although conceived as melodrama and acted (in both versions) in the apoplectic style of Mexican soap opera, critiques the privileged status of lighter skin in Mexican society.

Herewith, a brief synopsis of the first version; minor changes were made in the second to bring it up to date. Ana Luisa, a wealthy young woman whose fair skin and blond hair give her a marked resemblance to Eva Perón, works as the director of an exclusive school for daughters of the bourgeoisie. She is cared for by Mercé, the black maid who raised her from infancy after the death of her parents. Ana Luisa, spoiled and blatantly racist, marries a famous singer, José Carlos, played by Pedro Infante. When their daughter is born, the mother is horrified to behold an "angelita negra." Supposing that African blood runs in her husband's veins, she excoriates him and rejects the baby.

Although Ana Luisa, her husband, their daughter, and Mercé live for years under the same roof, they are bitterly divided. In a flamboyant confrontation on the stairs, Ana Luisa slaps Mercé, who tumbles to the bottom, critically injured. On her deathbed, the black woman reveals a secret: seduced by Ana Luisa's father, she is the real mother scorned by the haughty, prejudiced Ana Luisa. At the eleventh hour, Ana Luisa begs Mercé's forgiveness. It is granted, and the older woman dies, surrounded by her weeping family, reconciled at last.

If the 1948 *Angelitos negros* has the visual tone of a minor classic, the 1970 remake could pass for a *fotonovela* at the supermarket checkout. Art direction leans toward the lost and found, and so does the male lead, Manuel Lopez Ochoa, whose oily blandness suggests a Latino Wayne Newton. He is directed to play obtuse when confronted by the racism of his blonde fiancée, Ana Luisa. (She refuses to shake hands with his best friend, who is black.) With one exception, the actors shout, scream, fling themselves about, as if cautioned to avoid subtlety at all costs.

The exception is Juanita Moore, as stately and handsome as a Barbara Stanwyck. Even in a dubbed performance, she shows force, strength, and dignity as Mercé, the secret mother of the racist Ana Luisa. Her characterization is entirely believable, surely a difficult feat when surrounded by such pompous theatricality. Through long scenes of agony, Juanita sustains real emotion. In step with the times, she makes Mercé more assertive than Annie Johnson. Here, as in *Imitation of Life,* Juanita plays an emotionally understated deathbed scene. (It was becoming familiar turf.)

When I asked Juanita about *Angelitos negros,* she said, "The director wanted me really to fall down the stairs. He said, 'We'll have men at the bottom to catch you.' You know what I told him? 'Down the stairs, my ass!'" As it turned out, Juanita didn't take a tumble. Ana Luisa slaps her at the top of the stairs, then a cut to Juanita stretched on the floor. Manuel Lopez Ochoa, the male star, did his own lifting—he picked up Juanita and carried her off the set.

Juanita tried to say as much of the Spanish dialogue as possible, though she knew she would be dubbed. I asked whether her husband accompanied her to Mexico for the film. "He sure did," she answered, "and those Mexican women nearly took him away from me!" Despite her commendable performance, Juanita says she never saw the movie.

42 | THERE ONCE WAS A LADY NAMED FANNIE

*L*ike an improbable cross of Danielle Steele with Eleanor Roosevelt, Fannie Hurst, during her eighty-two years, wrote twenty-nine books and engaged tirelessly in progressive causes. Among her output were eighteen novels, eight short story collections, a volume of autobiography, and two books classifiable as "miscellany." In 1921, when she was thirty-six years old, Fannie became a charter member of the Lucy Stone League, an organization that fought for women's right to retain their maiden names after marriage. Her later activism included membership in feminist and civil rights organizations, including the Urban League. She addressed the twenty-fifth anniversary dinner of the NAACP, and served on the executive committee of the Writers Campaign Against Lynching. Mrs. Roosevelt's husband appointed Fannie to the National Advisory Committee of the Works Progress Administration in 1940. In 1952, she was a delegate to the World Health Organization.

Fannie also had a stupid side. In a preface to Zora Neale Hurston's first novel, *Jonah's Gourd Vine,* published in 1933, Hurst wrote: "Here is negro folk lore interpreted at its authentic best in fiction form of a high order. A brilliantly facile spade has turned over rich new earth. Worms lift up, the hottish smells of soil rise, negro toes dredge into that soil, smells of racial fecundity are about." Fannie's biographer, Brooke Kroeger, adds the dry comment: "Whatever Zora may have had to say to Fannie about the preface is not known."

As though afflicted with a form of literary Tourette's syndrome, Fannie Hurst scribbled down whatever unseemly tic popped into her head, and respectable publishing houses—Harper & Bros., Knopf, Doubleday— peddled her inimitable prose to consumers. It's astounding that in the teens, twenties, and thirties, she was one of the highest-paid writers in the world. Why? In the days before TV, she enthralled a mass audience with her own vast wasteland of sitcorn.

Her widespread acclamation is even more shocking when you pick up *Imitation of Life,* published in 1933 (the year that *Ulysses* was finally allowed into the United States) and read, "There was no suppressing the enormity that was Delilah [the black woman], nor was there the desire to suppress it. Her table might appear frighteningly lavish (how she loved the board that groans), but she had skill immense as it was consistent, in utilizing breakfast's left-over bacon into luncheon's coleslaw served with sizzled bacon cubes, and there was no such thing as too many griddle cakes, because once Delilah herself surrounded them the golden syrup began to pour down their diminishing flanks to form engulfing pools into which she dove with an exaltation not dissimilar to the white-eyed ecstasy with which she soared into her frequent outbursts of Baptist fervor." (In the film, Delilah denies such ecstatic consumption: "I'se very deceiving as to proportions," she says. "I'se very light at the table.")

This descriptive passage is relatively restrained as compared to the Niagara of Negro dialect that Fannie pours into Delilah's mouth throughout the novel. When Bea, Delilah's white patroness, returns home from work: "Gawd bless mah soul if it ain't mah honey-chile! Clean dead-beat to de bone. Off wid dem dar stockin's. Let Delilah rub up dem white little dead-beat feet. Look what Delilah's got heatin' for her dead-beat honey-chile. Hominy what I found in de market and dat you heah don't know nothin' 'bout."

And yet this Margaret Dumont of Publishers Row sometimes wrote with a crude, trashy power. Bea Pullman, who, in *Imitation of Life,* achieves wealth and fame through her nationwide chain of waffle restaurants, falls in love with a man eight years younger than she. But so does Bea's daughter, Jessie. Unaware, Bea rushes ahead in her fantasy that she and Frank will be married. On the last page of the novel, she hands herself over to him at last: "'Don't you see, I'm through now, playing for time. I haven't any pride where you are concerned. Only humility, Frank, and the passionate desire to try to return to you some measure of the incredible happiness you have given me. Age is not necessarily a matter of years, Frank. The eight years between us need not be eight. My capacity for living and loving—'

"'For God's sake,' he almost screamed, his teeth bared beneath the grinding of his palms against his eyes . . . 'For God's sake—don't make me have to be plainer.'

"On his turning, the door swung open to Jessie in her canary-colored frock."

Blind to her mother's love for Frank, Jessie blithely announces, "I love him and he loves me. Relieve his terror, parent; give us the maternal blessing . . . or I may pass out of the pressure of too much happiness."

Fannie, gauche as always, twists her penultimate sentence like—well, as she might put it, like a lock of ear-tumbling hair: "Here was the scene which was to be preserved so perfectly in the retina of her mind's eye, that looking back, looking back at it across the years, the living picture of it, even to the yellow of a frock and the smear of anguish across a face, was never to dim."

For all that, Fannie's final line, uncharacteristically short, resounds with vulgar pathos: "They were so young, standing there . . . so right . . ."

In the novel, although in neither film version, Peola, Delilah's light-skinned daughter, has herself sterilized before marrying a white man. They move to Bolivia, and she is never heard from again. Thus, Delilah's funeral in the novel lacks the harrowing drama of the repentant daughter who returns too late.

Among Fannie's enormous fan mail for *Imitation of Life* was this letter from a woman in Indianapolis: "I know Peola. I am Peola, for I am a Negro. Sometimes, when I feel as though I cannot stand this agony, this torture, this scorn, I'm utterly glad that Peola did what she did. Sometimes when Fannie Hurst is engraved deeply in my mind, I say to myself while I am washing dishes or getting dinner, 'I wonder how Peola and her white husband got along. I wonder if he ever found out.'"

Hollywood made some thirty films from Fannie's novels and short stories, beginning in 1918 and ending in 1961, with the second remake of

Back Street. During those years, Fannie was constantly in the news—the Candace Bushnell of her age. In 1920, for instance, the revelation of her marriage, which had been kept secret for five years, "triggered a publicity firestorm."

Her commentary was solicited on sundry topics: "Juvenile delinquency today cannot be blamed on sexy books, cheap movies, or bang-bang TV programs," she opined in the fifties. In 1967, the year before her death, Fannie penned an upbeat piece for *Family Weekly* called, "How to Grow Old—and Like It." ("Ladies—Keep your chin up, even if it's double.") Said to be the first author ever interviewed over the airwaves—in Newark, in 1922—Fannie was never long absent from the media. In later years, she had her own show on local television in New York.

When she lectured, no topic escaped: the Modern Woman; Marriage; Politics. She served on panels, and judged contests, e.g., to find "The Ideal American College Girl." At these public wisdom-sheddings, Fannie's preferred attire was a black dress with her trademark calla lily, either a brooch or a fresh one, pinned to her bosom, the ensemble topped by a flower-basket hat. When interviewers—e.g., Edward R. Murrow, for *Person to Person*, in 1954—called on her, they found the celebrity authoress ensconced in a fourteen-room triplex at the Hotel des Artistes, on West Sixty-seventh Street, in Manhattan. With Fannie were her lapdogs, Calla Lily and Lily Putian. (Elsewhere in her demesne, there were, at various times during her long tenure, monkeys, cats, and birds.) She spoke in a high-pitched, slightly nasal voice with broad, stagey vowels. Despite her pretentiousness, however, she retained much Midwestern genuineness, and had many friends at all levels of society. (Born in Ohio, Fannie grew up in St. Louis in an assimilated German-Jewish family. Throughout her life, she remained ambivalent about her ethnic background.)

To call *Imitation of Life* Fannie's best-remembered novel is inaccurate, for the title alone is famous. Few people today have read the novel, including Susan Kohner and Juanita Moore. It's also unlikely that others in the cast would have bothered. Nor did Douglas Sirk, who said, "Ross Hunter gave me the book, which I didn't read. After a few pages I had the feeling this kind of American novel would definitely disillusion me.

The style, the words, the narrative attitude would be in the way of my getting enthusiastic." But, Sirk added, "*Imitation of Life* is more than just a good title, it is a wonderful title: I would have made the picture just for the title."

Readers in 1932, however, were famished for another Fannie Hurst story; they had waited a whole year since *Back Street*. When the women's magazine *Pictorial Review* ran the first serial installment of Fannie's new novel in December, the editor used Fannie's alternate title, "Sugar House." The buzz was terrific, and while magazine installments were still appearing, Harper and Bros. brought out *Imitation of Life*— Fannie's better title—in February 1933. "Within three weeks, the book was in its eighth printing and ninth on the bestseller list for the month. Three months later, Fannie sold the movie rights to Universal, which again put her property in the hands of the director John Stahl," who had directed *Back Street* in 1932.

"nstylish," "ordinary," "unnuanced," "orderly"—such words are often used to evoke the films of John M. Stahl, whose work bears an oddly symbiotic relationship to that of Douglas Sirk. In the thirties, Stahl was one of Universal's two top directors (the other was James Whale). Stahl is best remembered for his popular, moneymaking women's pictures—*Back Street* (1932), *Imitation of Life* in 1934, *Magnificent Obsession* (1935), and *When Tomorrow Comes* (1939). Sirk directed remakes of the latter three, keeping the first two titles; under Sirk, *When Tomorrow Comes* became *Interlude*. Both directors are routinely labeled, by unstylish and unnuanced critics, as masters of the "weepie" and the "melodrama."

That word! It's so unspecific that at least half the movies made in Hollywood might so qualify. Sirk stuck with the classic Greek definition of melodrama: drama plus music. A more narrow one, and more useful in criticism, is this, from *A Handbook to Literature,* sixth edition, by C. Hugh Holman and William Harmon: "A work, usually a play, based on a romantic plot and developed sensationally, with little regard for motivation and with an excessive appeal to the emotions of the audience. The object is to keep the audience thrilled by the arousal of strong feelings of pity, horror, or joy. Poetic justic is superficially secured, the characters (either very good or very bad) being rewarded or punished according to their deeds. Though typically a melodrama has a happy ending, tragedies that use much of the same technique are sometimes referred to as melodramatic." Why not call Scorsese's films melodramas? Ron Howard's? P. T. Anderson's? It's a lazy designation, as unhelpful as the word "interesting," and used most often as a patronizing term by monkey-see, monkey-do reviewers.

As Jon Halliday points out, "The power of all Sirk's best films is dramatic, not 'melodramatic.'"

In his youth, John M. Stahl (1886–1950) played minor parts on the New York stage before joining up with itinerant theatrical companies. He later performed in vaudeville. He directed his first picture in 1914 and his last in 1949. Stahl's simultaneous career as film producer ran from 1921 to 1941. Recalling his early days as a Hollywood pioneer, Stahl told an interviewer, "Well do I recall when there was a single narrow road over the Cahuenga Pass and jitney buses rambled over the hill to take people to work at Universal City. Hollywood was a sleepy village and some people weren't sure whether moving pictures were here to stay."

In those early days, Stahl worked with Louis B. Mayer for twelve years, beginning at First National and later at MGM. For a time, he ran his own small company, Tiffany-Stahl Productions, a Poverty Row studio later absorbed by Monogram Pictures. His first directing assignment at Universal was *A Lady Surrenders,* in 1930, and his last, *When Tomorrow Comes,* in 1939. After one picture at Columbia, Stahl moved to Twentieth Century-Fox, where he directed his final ten pictures.

In recent years, Stahl has acquired a dedicated following. In 1999, for instance, his work received a major retrospective in Spain, at San Sebastián, under the auspices of the Filmoteca Española. In the accompanying festival book, Miguel Marias wrote, in an essay titled "The Unknown Mr. Stahl": "He was never very well-known, nor did he enjoy much prestige among 'serious' critics, partly because when he died in 1950 film critics hardly existed, and the few who were writing at that time were scarcely aware of the unassuming figure of John M. Stahl. He was, as far as we can see, appreciated by the film industry. Actors respected him and did not shun working with him. Also, his films were successful enough that they hardly ever lost money. . . . He was what is usually called 'a safe bet,' but was also unquestionably of the 'second rank.' He was never a star director, nor does he seem to have had the pretentions or vanities of an auteur, or even those of an accomplished artist of the visual."

Stahl's belated transfer to Fox in the early forties was his best professional move. Darryl F. Zanuck, head of the studio, seems to have demanded, and received, pictures from Stahl that lacked the sluggishness, the flab, and the visual flatness of his Universal films.

For purposes of comparison, it's worth examining one of Stahl's last efforts at Universal: *Letter of Introduction,* in 1938, with Adolphe Menjou, Andrea Leeds, Eve Arden, and Ann Sheridan. Overall, it lacks rhythm, pacing, and style. This phlegmatic comedy-drama feels ill at ease with itself. Edgar Bergen, that tiresome ventriloquist, and his exhausting alter ego, Charlie McCarthy, get far too much attention as the camera dotes on them for long stretches. Even the great cinematographer Karl Freund couldn't save this unsatisfying little novelty pic.

There is, however, one very good sequence: Adolphe Menjou, as a Barrymoresque alcoholic actor, goes onstage drunk at an important Broadway opening. Here the pacing is impeccable. Stahl extends the agony of the other actors, who are embarrassed and immobilized by the star's unprofessionalism. He also captures the anguish of the ingenue backstage as she realizes that her dreamed-of career is now in ashes, and he transforms the nervous audience, which finally erupts in laughter, into a cruel chorus.

Many directors, believing movie audiences uninterested in stage acting, would truncate a sequence like this one. Stahl, on the other hand, grasps how calamity on a stage, with live actors, can be made cinematic and gripping. Later, however, Menjou's deathbed scene is as stiff and poorly directed as the one in Stahl's *Imitation of Life.*

Stahl's first Fox film, *Immortal Sergeant* (1943), shows improvement, though it's still lopsided. Starring Henry Fonda, Maureen O'Hara, Thomas Mitchell, and Reginald Gardner, it's a standard World War Two drama. Zanuck had not yet broken Stahl's habit of holding shots, scenes, and sequences several beats longer than necessary, which creates drag where momentum is called for. Typically, Stahl's camera seems at odds with the rest of the picture. It's either too close to the subject of a shot, or intrusive in a setting, or else it's off-center and distracted.

Immortal Sergeant moves better than the usual Stahl, however, and it includes a riveting scene where a German plane, shot down by Allied soldiers in the Libyan desert, crashes into an army truck. Here Stahl's timing is impeccable: the plane comes down in a crash landing, careens, lurches forward in what seems an hour-long moment, thus building fright and tension until the final incineration.

One of Stahl's better pictures at Fox was *The Keys of the Kingdom* (1944), starring Gregory Peck, Vincent Price, and Thomas Mitchell, and produced by Joseph L. Mankiewicz, who seems, along with Zanuck, to have ridden herd on Stahl.

Peck, at the start of his career, was already too virtuous. Still, this is the kind of schmaltzy epic that Hollywood did well. You may hate yourself for responding to such Catholic tractarianism, but the moments of screen godliness really are affecting. The picture looks good, too, though you never believe for a moment you're really in Scotland or in China, where Peck spends his adult life as a missionary priest. Stahl, in his late fifties when he made this film, seems at last to have matured as a craftsman.

The following year he made the picture that justifies those who regard him as an artist. *Leave Her to Heaven* is a brooding murder story that insinuates more evil than it states. Its visual realism stops just short of the surreal, and Gene Tierney, playing a warped egomaniac, brings a soupçon of witchery to her performance. The picture epitomizes a certain forties style: disturbingly saturated color; bold acting (at least by Tierney); a story rooted in popular literature; and "natural" locations that waver between dream and tribulation.

Stahl's directorial languor in *Leave Her to Heaven* is not lazy; rather, his rhythm is that of a romantic reverie veering toward nightmare, like Baudelaire crossed with H. P. Lovecraft. After Tierney's character commits suicide, however, the movie turns conventional. Perhaps Stahl isn't to blame: he's left with a cast of predictable actors, viz., Cornel Wilde, Jeanne Crain, and Vincent Price.

In 1946, Zanuck removed Stahl as director of *Forever Amber*. Stahl was behind schedule and over budget; in addition, Zanuck considered both the direction and the female lead, Peggy Cummins, unacceptable. He scrapped every frame of Stahl's footage, instructing the new director, Otto Preminger, to start over, at great cost to the studio.

Some months after Stahl's death in 1950, a daughter from one of his previous marriages (the director was married three times) filed a petition in Santa Monica Superior Court charging that his will, which favored his third wife, was signed under duress. According to the court claim, Mrs. Roxanna Stahl, the director's widow, had threatened to expose her husband's youthful prison record, which included time served in New York and Pennsylvania under the aliases of Jack Stall and John Stoloff. The petition further claimed that he was born Jacob Morris Strelitzsky in Baku, Russia, and not in New York City, as Stahl himself had always claimed.

Whatever his juvenile transgressions, and his later cinematic ones, Stahl did not lack mourners. Close to two hundred persons, including many Hollywood figures, attended funeral services conducted at the Little Church of the Flowers, in Forest Lawn. Jeanette MacDonald sang "Ah, Sweet Mystery of Life." Honorary pallbearers, who surely buried many a hatchet that day as well as an esteemed colleague, included studio executives Darryl F. Zanuck, L. B. Mayer, William Goetz, Joseph M. Schenk, Harry Warner, producer and agent Charles R. Feldman, publicist Harry Brand, costume designer Charles LeMaire, and actors Gene Raymond, George Montgomery, and Jean Hersholt.

*T*o call Universal Pictures in 1934 a racist institution is wide of the mark. To be sure, the studio's portrayal of black characters in its first version of *Imitation of Life* makes us squirm today. Moreover, the studio's treatment of the picture's African-American stars, Louise Beavers and Fredi Washington, seems callous at best, and at worst blatantly discriminatory. For instance, while Claudette Colbert earned $10,833 a week, for a total salary of $90,278, Beavers—who surely worked as hard, and appeared in almost as many scenes—was paid $300 weekly, which amounted to $2,900 for nine weeks.

Fredi Washington's salary of $500 per week, for a total of $3,250, was perhaps justified by her inexperience, for she had appeared briefly in only two previous pictures.* Louise Beavers, by contrast, had been around since the early twenties and had made close to a hundred movies. True, her parts were usually small ones as someone's servant, and often uncredited, but within the Hollywood hierarchy of the time, she deserved higher earnings. (Warren William and Ned Sparks, the

---

*The first, *Black and Tan* (1929), was a nineteen-minute jazz short starring Duke Ellington and his music. Fredi played a dancer. In 2008, the U.S. Postal Service issued a set of five commemorative stamps celebrating vintage black cinema and picturing original posters for the respective films. On the *Black and Tan* poster, Fredi Washington's name is prominently displayed, although she is uncredited in the actual film.

male leads, earned $25,000 and $10,000, respectively—two stiff "talents" who were nevertheless audience favorites. Stahl, as director, collected $60,000.)

Ironically, Universal was probably more enlightened, and less condoning of prejudice, than many places in the United States. One could argue that the studio's Scroogery was color-blind, meaning that, throughout its history, it paid all actors the least amount possible (consider Susan Kohner's $5,750, and Sandra Dee's $6,500, versus Lana's vastly larger paycheck). Universal, unlike many institutions, did not require blacks to come through separate entrances, drink from separate fountains, or eat in a segregated commissary. But whatever fine impulses the studio might have had toward justice and equality, American intolerance began just outside the gates.

That helps to explain why, in the studio's in-house publication, *Universal Weekly,* dated October 13, 1934, Beavers and Washington are virtually invisible. Film scholar Anthony Slide has explained that these studio journals were published "purely to sell an in-house product—motion pictures—and consisted entirely of information on that product and the personalities involved therewith." The target audience of these in-house publications was exhibitors.

On the cover of the lavishly produced issue in question, Claudette Colbert glows in a fetching color illustration whose designer created a come-hither look absent from Colbert's actual face. Inside, on page 1, is a full-page photograph of producer Carl Laemmle Jr., followed by full-page portraits of Fannie Hurst, John M. Stahl, Colbert, Warren William, Rochelle Hudson, Ned Sparks, and Baby Jane Quigley (who plays Colbert's infant daughter). That brings us to page 8, where every *white* supporting player, down to walk-ons, is pictured: Alan Hale, Henry Armetta, Marilyn Knowlden, G. P. Huntley Jr., and Paul Porcasi—the latter three uncredited onscreen. Only on page 9, the first page of text, do we see Louise Beavers pictured with Colbert and the two little girls in a still from the film. The two-by-three-inch photograph is composed so that Beavers might be overlooked.

Spread across pages 22 and 23 is a montage titled "The Most Carefully Selected Cast in Screen History," which includes Beavers twice and Washington once. A few pages on, Beavers makes a final appearance in two small stills, Washington in one—and they are seen no more. Their camouflage was calculated to mislead exhibitors, in the South especially, many of whom would balk at a "Negro story."

Nevertheless, *Imitation of Life* proved a minor watershed in Hollywood's appeal to black moviegoers. For the first time, owing to insistent demand on the part of theatres in African-American neighborhoods for special accessories on the picture, the exploitation department at Universal made up a special trailer, which was to be screened together with the regular production trailer. (This outreach took place some nine months after the picture's initial release.) The special promo consisted of "flashes of newspaper criticisms which highly praise Louise Beavers and Fredi Washington," and was expected to increase the box office of "colored houses" substantially.

At least eight writers worked on the *Imitation of Life* script, including Preston Sturges. In 1934, Sturges had not yet directed a picture; he was known around Hollywood for his screenplays. Sturges got a two-week assignment at Universal, where, according to studio cost sheets, he was paid $4,750—gross overpayment, surely, for his negligible contribution, since only a few lines of his dialogue made it to the screen.

William Hurlbut, the screenwriter of record, who presumably carried out the bulk of adaptation, received $7,675. In simplifying Hurst's plot, he retained none of her dialogue. What he substituted, however, was often as arch and coy as anything you'll hear in that decade when movies were still learning to talk. Hurlbut, possibly aided by his fellow writers, eliminated eleven of Fannie Hurst's characters and replaced them with seven new ones. He streamlined the plot in other ways: in the film, Bea Pullman makes her fortune by boxing the flour for delicious pancakes. In the novel, the flour is not boxed; Bea's fortune results from a chain of restaurants, and her specialty is waffles, not pancakes.

Hurlbut's writing teammates were paid considerably less than he and Sturges, with salaries ranging from $3,400 to $50. (The studio paid Hurst the magnificent fee of $25,000 for rights to the novel, a tidy fortune in the depths of the Depression.)

Filming began June 27, 1934, and finished September 11. At the start of the *Imitation of Life* shoot, however, the script had not been completed.

One reason may have had to do with too many writers creating a muddle. A more immediate cause of disarray was the controversial matter of race, especially passing. In this case, a very light-skinned African American was presumed to be the product of miscegenation, a taboo on American screens.

The Motion Picture Producers and Distributors of America (MPPDA, later the MPAA), Hollywood's self-censorship arm, had been formed in 1922, under the leadership of Will H. Hays, a former postmaster general. This self-policing institution was devised to forestall outside censorship by national and local governments. A regulatory code was drawn up, followed by a stricter one in 1930. Not until 1934, however, with the arrival of Hollywood's Savonarola, Joseph I. Breen, as director of the Production Code Administration, was the Code strictly, and repressively, enforced. *Imitation of Life,* therefore, inadvertently proved something of a racial test case. A few years earlier it might have been more honestly filmed.

The paper trail began March 9, 1934, with a "Memorandum for the Files" of the MPPDA, which summarized a meeting between Breen and two of his subordinates with studio representatives, including Carl Laemmle Jr., executive producer of the picture. The memorandum states that "we emphasized the dangers involved in treating this story as regards the possibilities having to do with negroes [sic]. It was our contention that this part of the plot—the action of the negro girl appearing as white—has a definite connection with the problem of miscegenation. [Until 1957, the Production Code forbade any portrayal or mention of miscegenation.] We pointed out that . . . this was an extremely dangerous subject and surely [sic] to prove troublesome, not only in the south, where it would be universally condemned, but everywhere else. The lynching scene in this story was discussed with the understanding if used at all, it would be considerably modified."

The most surprising phrase in that memorandum is "the lynching scene." Nothing of the sort occurs in the novel, and the subject, although not specifically forbidden by the Code, was rarely portrayed in motion pictures. On March 10, in an interoffice memo from J. B. Lewis to Breen, the matter is addressed once more: "The big dramatic punch of the picture describes the lust of a young negro [sic] buck who believes that a white girl has given him a 'come on' signal and who nearly gets lynched as a result."

On March 22, Breen, in a letter to Will Hays in New York, informed him that "we had a number of conferences with the studio, stating our belief that a story of this type was in violation of the spirit of the Code clause which forbids the treatment of miscegenation on the screen. Hence we stated definitely that it seemed the kind of picture which would be inadmissible under the Code. The studio is giving the matter some further thought."

In a subsequent letter, James Wingate, acting in Breen's absence, informed Maurice McKenzie, of the MPPDA in New York, that "the script has been rewritten several times, and the first half of it was resubmitted yesterday. This script presents indirectly the subject of miscegenation. Although there is none of it in the picture, it portrays a light colored negro girl who desires to go white. This, however, is not the main theme of the story."

In April, attention shifted temporarily to specific language in the script. A number of Delilah's expressions—e.g., "Mah Lo'dy," "Lo'd help," "De Lo'd knows," and the like—were questioned by the MPPDA's McKenzie, in New York: "We are not quite sure whether the numerous references by the colored woman would come under the profanity clause of the Code." This, of course, was patently absurd, since no character could be more reverent than Delilah.

On May 18, Will Hays himself weighed in, stating, "Altogether the picture seems a very unfortunate possibility and Mr. Breen is confronted with a very real worry. . . . In a case like this, it would be hoped that the picture be not made." Not until July 17 did Harry Zehner, assistant general manager of Universal, submit a complete *Imitation of Life* script to Breen. Even then, however, as Zehner hurriedly pointed out in his letter, the script was "not final as to dialogue. Nevertheless, inasmuch as Mr. Stahl has already been shooting over two weeks on the picture, I would like some written reaction from you with regard to this picture so that we may not enounter any unnecessary difficulty. In this connection, may I state that it is very probable that we will shoot the lynching scene which is contained in the blue script but which has not been included in the white script. There are technical reasons in existence here at the studio as to why we do not want this sequence to appear in the final script."

Wrangling continued. On August 3, Breen wrote to Will Hays: "The danger point in this story is the handling of the Negro question. . . . They are going ahead with production and are thoroughly aware of our fears in the matter. We have advised them definitely, however, that the element of lynching would, we believe, be entirely unsuitable for screen presentation, and that we would not pass the picture if it were in."

For a long time, I searched for specifics of that lynching scene, whose inclusion in the script raised such concern among the censors. Finally, I discovered its place in the story, although not the name of the screenwriter who added it. In the *Chicago Defender,* an African-American daily, a short feature appeared on September 12, 1942, under the byline of Harry Levette, a veteran at the paper. Titled "Hollywood Respects Stars' Word on What Is Offensive," the article reported on current protests over "the Negro sequence" in *Tales of Manhattan,* which had just been released. (The stars of that sequence are Paul Robeson, Ethel Waters, and Eddie Anderson.) The writer then cited Hattie McDaniel and Clarence Muse as two actors who had successfully objected to offensive language and derogatory scenes in films they appeared in.

Levette ended his article with Louise Beavers and *Imitation of Life.* "She told the Universal studio officials during a story conference that her people hated the word n____r which ran freely all through the screen story. Out it came, and the word 'black' was substituted by director John Stahl. And then believe it or not, their eyes having been opened, they cut a whole long sequence that depicted a near lynching when Peola, pretending to be white, accused a young colored man of attempting to flirt with her. Just as they have strung him up, she breaks down with remorse and screams, 'Don't, don't do it, I'm a n_____r too.'" Levette made it clear that his assertions were not based on hearsay: "If you doubt my word, I still have the original script and synopsis, and will be glad to let you see it." (Although the word "black" was considered a negative term before the late sixties, it is said nine times in *Imitation of Life*; the word "colored," a polite term in common use before the civil rights era, five times, and "Negro," a somewhat more formal word, and universally acceptable, only once. Fredi

Washington's grandmother used to say, "There's no such thing as a black person. You're colored. The colored race.")

The picture wrapped in early September, and two months later it was screened for Production Code censors. On November 14, Breen wrote officially to Harry Zehner at Universal: "We had the pleasure of viewing a projection room showing of your production, *Imitation of Life*, yesterday, and are glad to inform you that this picture satisfactorily meets the Code requirements, and contains nothing which could be considered censorable."

Nothing censorable—and yet the completed film retains virtually everything, except the lynching, from those original scripts that Breen and Co. considered "extremely dangerous." The "Negro question" is intact. Peola remains a light-skinned African American whose father, Delilah says, "was a very, very light-colored man," pointing, albeit indirectly, toward past miscegenation. Peola is unwavering in her determination to pass. Even one or two of Delilah's expressions like "mah Lo'dy" remain in the picture, and, surprisingly, she sings, "I puts my trust in Jesus" in a scene of comic relief.

It's possible that the studio included the lynching scene solely for trading purposes, as often happened. Scenes, and language, were included that had no chance of passing the censors. When, in such cases, the studio finally dropped the controversial material, its concessionary beau geste would so placate Code administrators that all else in the film might escape tampering. On the other hand, as Harry Levette reported, maybe the studio acted in good faith to avoid both the N-word and its highly disturbing context.

Ironically, the near-lynching might have been the most powerful scene in the film. It would have revealed the unending dangers faced by African Americans, and underscored Peola's desire to escape from constant degradation.

A month into production, no actor had yet been cast as Stephen Archer, Colbert's love interest. Then, in late July, the *Los Angeles Times* announced that Paul Lukas had signed for the part. The paper elaborated that "the particular problem encountered in casting the role was that the portrayer had to appear as if he were a scientist, and also seem highly romantic. It was deemed difficult for anyone to qualify as both."

Two weeks later, the paper reported that Lukas, after filming two scenes of *Imitation of Life*, had been replaced by Warren William. The trade-off was amicable, since Warner Bros., Lukas's home studio, wanted him for a picture and Universal was happy to accept in exchange Warner's reigning matinee idol with the pyramidal proboscis. (Warren William made nine movies that year, seven for Warner Bros., plus *Imitation of Life* on loanout to Universal, and DeMille's *Cleopatra* at Paramount, in which he played Caesar.)

By coincidence, young Rosalind Russell arrived at Universal for a screen test with John M. Stahl during the search for Stephen Archer. The day was going badly for everyone, and she was shunted from makeup to hairdressing only to learn that all hands were occupied with real stars. Finally, she ended up on Stahl's set—"Where's your makeup?" he demanded. "Where's your hairdo? Are you the girl who's supposed to test for me? Don't you know I can't use you like this?"

"Now let me tell you something, Mr. Stahl," she popped off. "Nobody would make me up, and nobody would do my hair, but I know these lines and I'm going to say these lines, because I get a hundred dollars for saying them!"

Stahl growled a bit, then put Russell under the camera. There she sat and fed cues to an actor who was hoping to play opposite Claudette Colbert. Years later, Russell still fumed: "Talk about insults—I wasn't even getting a test of my own, I was doing Claudette's lines because she was already busy shooting the movie and Stahl was desperate to find her a leading man. Over the next several days I did tests for the Colbert picture with nine different men." Russell collected nine hundred dollars, considerably more than many actors in the film.

Finally, with a definitive leading man on board, Stahl was ready to film a big, complex scene. A reporter from *The New York Times* was on the set that day, and since few accounts exist of Stahl at work, it's worth a pause to watch. The reporter pointed out that Stahl "dislikes filming a picture in a series of short scenes. Like many other directors, he believes it breaks the continuity, and he prefers to shoot long scenes in which the camera follows the dialogue from player to player."

The action in G-33 (the number of the scene being filmed) involved a party given in Bea Pullman's New York townhouse. At her first meeting with Stephen Archer (Warren William), he is a guest trying to discover who his hostess is. The party sequence is an old-timey set piece, with a dozen or so couples dancing a smooth fox-trot, wine and cocktails for the thirsty, and in the large room a champagne atmosphere to suggest money, sophistication, and midlist Society.

The *Times* reporter enumerated those just out of camera range: Stahl and his assistant director, two makeup men, three carpenters, and a script girl. "A hundred feet away were the two sound-mixers in their booth, connected with the set by telephones. In the flies above the set were five electricians operating the eighteen overhead lights.

"The warning bell clanged and Mr. Stahl took his usual seat on the dolly—a rubber-tired truck which carries the camera—just beneath the camera lens. At the signal—'Camera!'—the balloon-tired truck moved forward in a perambulator shot as Mr. William stepped onto the set to join Miss Colbert. Two men pushed the dolly while another steered it. Three others tiptoed behind, carrying the electric cables attached to the camera and the lights."

In what sounds like a mechanistic ballet, the cameraman, his assistant, and three sound men stepped in precision, partnering the camera. "The boom-man steered the metal arm from which the microphone was suspended. Another held a small mike at the side of the dolly.

"Five property men joined the procession, their duty being to move the furniture out of the path of the dolly as it advanced and replace it—and remove it again—as the camera retreated." They wore felt-soled shoes because the slightest footfall would spoil the elaborate shot—and call down Stahl's wrath on the perpetrator.

No shoe scuffled, nor did anyone topple a piece of furniture. "The dolly and the camera and the small roving army of experts passed up and down the set, stopping here and there to catch a bit of action or record a few well-chosen words. Mr. William and Miss Colbert chatted and laughed and everyone pretended to ignore the working crew."

In spite of the technical expertise and the precision needed to film the scene, it doesn't stand out as a bravura accomplishment in the completed picture. Stahl apparently strove for perfection; Louise Beavers told an interviewer that some scenes were done twenty times before the director decided they were ready. In the hands of a better director, such as Max Ophüls or Billy Wilder, camera and actors might have joined in a great cinematic dance. But here, as elsewhere, Stahl brought a pedestrian touch. The entire party sequence, of which G-33 is an important part, moves at the same tempo as most other sequences in the film. And the long takes add drag to the picture, rather than liftoff.

he *Imitation of Life* premiere took place on November 27, 1934, at the Pantages Theatre in Hollywood. The day after, a favorable review in the *Los Angeles Times* mentioned a "sufficient testimony of tears" among members of the invited audience, which included many big names in the industry. *Variety's* reviewer called it "a strong picture with an unusual plot." After its Manhattan opening, *The New York Times* labeled it "the most shameless tearjerker of the fall" and noted "the stentorian sobbing of the ladies in the Roxy mezzanine yesterday."

The picture's most enthusiastic reception came in the African-American press, which also carried a measure of rebuke. The *Pittsburgh Courier,* in an editorial, labeled it "a new departure in movies," asking rhetorically, "When before has any screen or stage drama for general attraction pondered the pertinent question of the colored girl who can pass for white? When before have colored people appeared as dignified, intelligent, well-dressed human beings and not as jovial cretins on the silver screen? Here are Negroes who go to college, have beautiful churches and dignified religious services quite contrary to the libelous nonsense of *The Green Pastures,** and who experience all of the finer emotions."

---

*Marc Connelly's Pulitzer Prize–winning play, first performed on Broadway in 1930 and filmed in 1936, is a reenactment of Old Testament stories in which all the characters, including God, speak in black Southern dialect.

The *Chicago Defender* called *Imitation of Life* "a great picture with two Race performers doing more than just a little to make it so." At the end of the year, when the *Defender* picked the "Fifteen Most Important Events in 1935," number one was "Italian army invades Ethiopia" and number fifteen was "Louise Beavers and Fredi Washington selected as stars for *Imitation of Life*."

While many blacks saw only positive aspects of a story that portrayed African Americans as "real" rather than buffoons, others objected that these characters were as insulting as those created by actors like Stepin Fetchit. In the year following the release of the film, *Imitation of Life* provoked nonstop controversy. A typical letter to the *Defender* asked, "What good did it do?" and concluded that the picture's undisturbing, old-school themes accounted for its success "in the minds of movie critics and audiences of the other race."

The most damning condemnation of all came from Sterling A. Brown, a young intellectual writing in *Opportunity* magazine. In his review, published in the March 1935 issue, "he panned both the book and the movie, instigating a volley of letters to the editor in the subsequent issues (all with the exception of one supporting Brown's critical stance). Among Brown's objections to the movie is that, though the film's plot differs from that of the book, no substantive change exists in the characterizations and the social ideas set forth. While singling out the superb acting talent of Louise Beavers and Fredi Washington, Brown insists that his readers reject the characterization and ideas reinforcing images of the stereotyped contented mammy and tragic mulatto. Of particular offense to Brown was 'the inebriation of [Delilah's] language, too designedly picturesque, her unintelligible character, now infantile, now mature, now cataloguing folk beliefs of the Southern Negro, and now cracking contemporary witticisms. Her baby talk to the white child partakes too much of maple sugar; to her own, too much of mustard.'"

An angry Fannie Hurst rebutted Brown's review the following month. But her slipshod prose was no match for Brown's precision. His long reply eviscerated her wordy defense. Hurst accused Brown of "carping, petty angles of criticism," and reprimanded him for being neither grateful for her efforts on behalf of black people nor intelligent in his review.

Brown responded with cool venom: "Far be it from me to dispute such a trivial point [as intelligence] with a lady. . . . Concerning my ungratefulness, let me cheerfully acknowledge this degree of unintelligence: that I cannot imagine what in the world I would have to be grateful for, either to Universal Pictures or to Miss Hurst."

Langston Hughes, a stellar member of the Harlem Renaissance, had his say on the topic in the form of a satirical playlet titled "Limitations of Life," performed in 1938 at the Harlem Suitcase Theatre on a bill with other works by Hughes. In the parody, Mammy Weavers, "a colored lady," enters "in trailing evening gown, with tiara and large Metropolitan Opera program, speaking perfect English with Oxford accent." Her "pretty blonde maid," Audette Aubert, welcomes her: "Mammy Weavers, ah been waitin' up for you-all. Ah thought you might like some nice hot pancakes before you-all went to bed."

Reading the play, I wondered why the Marx Brothers didn't hire Hughes as gagwriter. Mammy Weavers condescends to Audette, telling her she doesn't wish any pancakes because she dined on lobster à la Newburg. Audette, agog, asks, "How did you-all like the opera?"

Mammy Weavers: "Flagstad was divine tonight, but Melchoir was a wee bit hoarse."

Audette: "Oh, ah'ms so sorry, Mammy Weavers! Maybe Melchior ought to use Vicks, like Nelson Eddy."

Later, when Mammy Weavers inquires about Audette's daughter, Riola, she is told that the girl "just loves Harlem. She's lyin' out in the backyard in de sun all day long tannin' herself, ever' day, tryin' so hard to be colored."

Fannie Hurst, a fawning admirer of Hughes, didn't take umbrage. But then, neither did Margaret Dumont.

Further afield, Will Rogers acknowledged that "this picture shows that Hollywood has at last realized there is a color problem." He criticized, however, its business-as-usual portrayal of blacks. At Tuskegee Institute, a black college in Alabama, *Imitation of Life* was screened, to great acclaim, as a Christmas treat for students and faculty in December 1935, a year after its release.

Indeed, most black moviegoers seem to have found more to praise than to dislike in the picture. They, like whites, thronged theatres for months after its opening. Numerous press accounts mention a lack even of standing room in large theatres in Chicago, New York, and elsewhere, necessitating added matinees and held-over runs. Many in those audiences were so thrilled to see black people on screen at all, and in substantial parts, that gratitude, not affront, was their primary emotion.

Imitation of Life made so much money in its first six months that Universal announced, in June 1935, several forthcoming pictures to include black players, among them James Whale's *Show Boat*. Studio head Carl Laemmle vowed, "We are out to cast the foremost stars in our new films and to give opportunity to deserving new screen personalities regardless of color." But the studio soon lost its courage. The white Helen Morgan played Julie, the mulatto, in *Show Boat*.

When Oscars were awarded for 1934, Claudette Colbert won— although not for *Imitation of Life*. Rather, she was voted Best Actress for *It Happened One Night*. *Imitation of Life* was nominated as Best Picture, but lost to *It Happened One Night*. Stahl's film won two nonacting awards.

Although I am no partisan of the 1934 version, many are. For seventy-five years it has drawn an audience, in revivals, on television, and on DVD. Once, in the late sixties, Jane Withers got a call around one o'clock in the morning. When she answered, Rock Hudson said, "Were you in *Imitation of Life*? I've got a thousand-dollar bet here that it's you."

Withers laughed as she told me the story: " 'Good gravy,' I said, 'that's a lot of money just to find out whether that was me or not.' But Rock won his bet. Yes, I was in that schoolroom scene where Louise Beavers brings a raincoat and galoshes to her little daughter. I was on the set for one day, as an extra, and I got paid five dollars."

While researching this book I encountered, if not an army, at least a battalion of foot soldiers, ready to defend their choice of Stahl's film as the better *Imitation*. From the ranks, I call upon four whose viewpoints are particularly provocative.

————

Robert Osborne, host of Turner Classic Movies: "I look at the 1959 *Imitation of Life,* and it's so pretty and so glamorous—but I don't think it holds a candle to the Claudette Colbert version. Why? Because those Aunt Delilah pancakes worked as legitimate story points. That's why the two women are together: One makes those great pancakes and the other turns them into an industry. That's the bond. In the later version, it doesn't seem as logical for an actress to have a servant with whom she has the same kind of bond. We were all thrilled, of course, that Lana had a hit movie after what she had been through, but I think her version is kitschy. The Colbert version, however, is a great film."

Vivian Hewitt, a Harlem businesswoman and art collector who was personally and professionally acquainted with various members of the Harlem Renaissance, including Fredi Washington: "I prefer the original version because Fredi was a genuine African American who looked like she was white and could pass. That was authentic. And Louise Beavers, a fine actress, added to the authenticity. That's what the second version lacked."

James Sheldon, a television director and a friend of Susan Kohner (whom he directed in the late fifties in a couple of TV shows): "I saw the first *Imitation of Life* in 1934, when I was thirteen years old. I like that version better. Fredi Washington was so real. And yes, it did make me cry. Maybe because it's the first one I saw, but to me it was terribly moving because the racial issue was so much more pronounced in 1934. Then, segregation and racism were fixed conditions, like the Depression. Civil rights, as a movement, was far in the future. So that, sociologically, one had a different reaction in 1934. The picture wasn't yet fighting for a cause, because the cause hadn't started up. Whereas in 1959, with the civil rights movement underway, it was easier to take sides."

A few years ago, when the 1934 *Imitation of Life* was to be shown on TCM, Michael Henry Adams, a Harlem activist, author, and architectural historian, gave a dinner party. Among his guests was Isabel Powell, sister of the late Fredi Washington. "She said she hadn't seen the picture in many years," Adams told me. "She was happy to watch it again, and we all agreed that it was very poignant. But one problem we all had with the picture was Delilah's refusal to accept a twenty per-cent share of the pancake business. I remember Isabel saying how idi-otic that was."

Of the dinner guests, Adams said, about half were black and the other half white. In the discussion following the movie, the whites were the first ones to bring up the various injustices portrayed in the film. "The blacks were more philosophical," Adams averred. "Our attitude was, What else would you expect in this country in the thirties?"

I asked whether anyone at the party felt as uncomfortable as I do while watching the scene where Claudette Colbert's character conde-scends so cruelly to Louise Beavers's. (Colbert, as Bea Pullman, tells Delilah that the new man in her life is an ichthyologist. As Delilah fum-bles with the meaning of the word, Colbert eggs her on, barely control-ling her mirth.)

"We have a suspicion," Adams replied, "that the black girl would know the meaning of the word 'ichthyologist' better that Colbert's char-acter. And Colbert's daughter, Jessie, doesn't know what it means until she hurriedly looks it up. The white girl has no ambition. She's ready to drop out of school and marry. Whereas the black girl's great desire is a better life, without the shackles of discrimination."

Although the 1934 version seems generally well-intentioned, it does little to challenge the deplorable racial injustices of the day. One im-plied denunciation by those who made the picture, however, is the living arrangements in Bea Pullman's house on Sutton Place: she and her daughter live upstairs, while Delilah and Peola are relegated to the bot-tom floor. The two black women are not even invited to the lavish party taking place on the main floor of the townhouse. Michael Henry Adams said that his dinner guests commented on the irony of that situation: Those who made the party possible are not invited to attend. (In the 1959 version, all the bedrooms in the Connecticut house are upstairs. Thus, on one level at least, all four women are equal.)

Adams added that he sees the picture as "trying to suggest, in the bizarre, conflicted reality of that era, some great injustice in the U.S." He, and those at his dinner party, agreed that "the one indisputably courageous thing in 1934 was casting Fredi Washington, a black ac-tress, as the black girl trying to pass, rather than hiring a white actress, as they did for years afterward. And they didn't try to burden her with the same Negro dialect as her mother. Thus, the filmmakers pointed out the contrast between generations, implying that with education and opportunity, African Americans could achieve the same dignity as anyone else."

*U*niversal's shortage of big-name stars forced it to borrow Claudette Colbert from Paramount, where she was becoming a box-office queen. In 1934, the year of *Imitation of Life,* Colbert had also appeared in *Cleopatra* at Paramount, and in Frank Capra's *It Happened One Night* at Columbia, for which she won her Oscar.

Many years later, Colbert told her biographer, Lawrence J. Quirk, that the reason *Imitation of Life* appealed to her was because "it was a drama with a difference, and so refreshing in its theme, especially for that period." The blandness of that statement matches her performance in the film. And yet she no doubt meant well. Louise Beavers praised her, calling Colbert "one of the finest, sweetest, unaffected" costars.

Among critics and commentators, it's de rigueur to dislike Lana Turner's work and to crow over Colbert's. She has thus been overpraised for her one-note performance in *Imitation of Life,* where she wears fashionable outfits better than she wears the role of Bea Pullman. (Not all the blame rests on Colbert. The script and the direction enable her vapid impersonation.)

When the picture opens, the widow Pullman peddles large cans of maple syrup on the boardwalk, and elsewhere, in Atlantic City. Poverty and overwork rest lightly on Colbert's shoulders, however; her face, hair, silvery laugh, and emotional reactions are the same here as at the end of the picture, when she's as famously successful as—well, Fannie Hurst.

Colbert glides through the role like Gertrude Lawrence in a Noël Coward drawing room. But this is the wrong picture for Colbert's champagne tricks: the plummy voice and sweeping gestures, the contrived theatrical accent, that tic of biting her lower lip to express pleasure, amusement, flirtation—these techniques soon begin to grate. Colbert is miscast; what's needed is an earthy Barbara Stanwyck. That's who could play this Cinderella of the pancakes, from bowls of batter to Sutton Place.

Those who pardon Colbert's offenses will howl in protest, but to me the sincerity of her Bea Pullman is inferior to Lana Turner's Lora Meredith. Lana acts—too hard—but she does inhabit the role. The result isn't meant as realism; true to the title, it's imitating life, not duplicating it for the screen. (Lana also imitates acting, which is the point of her character.) Through the imitation, however, Lora's real heart pumps for those she loves: Susie and Annie Johnson foremost, but also Sarah Jane, Steve Archer. And for herself, Lora the star. Lora knows passion; she just isn't clear about the real and the mock.

Whereas the heart of Colbert's Bea Pullman is well regulated, like a metronome. Everyone in the picture—her daughter, her lover, the manager of Bea Pullman's pancake empire, and Delilah, so doggedly devoted to her white mistress—gets a mild *thump-thump* from that moderate heart. (Bea's blood pressure surely doesn't rise above 110/65.) She passes around emotion like after-dinner mints. If you've seen ten minutes of Colbert here, you've seen it all. Even her glycerine tears at Delilah's deathbed, and later at the funeral, deliquesce like fluid glitter.

Although in my opinion Colbert seldom gave first-rate performances, two pictures prove she was capable of doing so: Mitchell Leisen's 1939 comedy, *Midnight,* and the World War Two drama *Three Came Home* (1950), directed by Jean Negulesco. In both pictures, she had good scripts and skilled directors. As an airy vixen in *Midnight,* she eludes that tiresome Hollywood dichotomy of good girl/bad girl. She's both. A penniless American in Paris, Colbert's Eve Peabody wears her virtue not on her sleeve but on her garter belt. The foolproof script, by Charles Brackett and Billy Wilder, predestined Colbert to give the best comic performance of her career.

Nunally Johnson wrote *Three Came Home*, in which Colbert plays an American woman imprisoned on Borneo by invading Japanese. Separated from her British husband and their small son, she is literally trapped, and also psychologically. Sans makeup, Colbert downgrades her facial expression from worry to despair as the bleak story unfolds. Here, helpless and distraught, she sheds "Claudette Colbert," a feat she apparently deemed unnecessary through most of her career.

The obsequious Aunt Delilah of *Imitation of Life* wouldn't recognize feisty Louise Beavers, the woman behind the role. To encounter a likeness of the real Beavers, take a look at *Bullets or Ballots,* a minor gangster movie from 1936 starring Edward G. Robinson and Humphrey Bogart. Beavers, dolled up in furs and fancy duds, and full of sass, plays Nellie LaFleur, who runs a Harlem numbers racket in cahoots with downtown operative Joan Blondell. Beavers must have rejoiced at this rare chance to lose her maid's uniform and show her stuff.

Offscreen, Beavers "liked baseball, prizefights, and a good game of poker." At her home on Hobart Boulevard in Hollywood, lively card parties took place, with viands spread out for her guests and laughter growing louder as more bottles were opened through the night. "Beavers did not spend time in the kitchen, however. She had a husband who could do that—Leroy Moore, an interior decorator who had come to Los Angeles from Gainesville, Texas, in 1942. Seven years younger than Beavers, Moore prepared and helped serve the food and drinks."

"I am the worst cook in the world," Beavers announced to an interviewer around the time of *Imitation of Life,* explaining that her mother ran the kitchen. (This was before the arrival of Leroy Moore.) Despite her lack of culinary talent, however, Beavers worked for several years as maid to silent star Leatrice Joy. It was not uncommon for African Americans to seek domestic work while trying to break into movies; sometimes their employers helped them make contacts. Years after Beavers had left domestic service offscreen to take it up in pictures, Leatrice Joy sent her a huge box of congratulatory roses upon completion of *Reap the Wild Wind* in 1942. And yes, in that DeMille picture, Beavers played a maid.

Like Juanita Moore, Louise Beavers had to acquire a Southern dialect. Born in Cincinnati in 1902, and raised in Los Angeles, she had never been in the South when she began playing Southern roles. Beavers learned the dialect from books—novels and poems, which she studied assiduously as though it were a foreign language. Her efforts paid off, since, as she said, "Every part calls for me to talk like that."

For *Imitation of Life,* she also studied the art of pancake making. She and Claudette Colbert practiced for hours at a time, using batter prepared by professional cooks. Both actresses learned how to do it, but the experience put Beavers off pancakes forever. On the train to New York to publicize *Imitation of Life,* the steward was crestfallen when she refused to touch the stack of breakfast pancakes he presented so proudly. The kitchen crew had made them in her honor.

In 1937, when David O. Selznick was casting *Gone With the Wind,* Beavers was a top contender for the role of Mammy. She reportedly lost the part because, at her first interview with Selznick, she came dressed as a bejeweled glamour queen swathed in furs—an image that Selznick's eye couldn't transpose to Mammy's homespun garb. (Earlier, Hattie McDaniel, who played Mammy, had coveted Beavers's role in *Imitation.*)

Owing in part to the success of *Imitation of Life,* Louise Beavers was, for a time, the best-known African-American actress in Hollywood. A few years later, however, her career began a long decline that was reversed in 1952, when Beavers replaced the ailing Hattie McDaniel on the popular TV sitcom *Beulah.* (Earlier, McDaniel had replaced Ethel Waters.) After the series ended, in 1953, Mae West hired Beavers for her campy nightclub act, a vehicle that showcased the eternal youth of Mae (on the shady side of sixty). Onstage, six bulging musclemen paraded around the cooing Mae, who leered and rolled her eyes while Beavers, dressed in a maid's uniform, served tea to her corseted mistress.

When Beavers died, in 1962, some four hundred people of all races attended her funeral, while hundreds more visited the church throughout the day to view the body. Her favorite hymn, "City Called Heaven," was sung during the service, and her pastor at the People's Independent Church of Christ read Psalm XCI. The *Los Angeles Herald-Examiner* reported that "the beloved actress was best known as *Beulah* for the TV show she made famous. Many of the floral wreaths surrounding her bier bore only that name in simple tribute."

———

Fredi Washington (1903–1994), who played Louise Beavers's daughter, Peola, was one year younger than her on-screen mother. A startling fact, highlighted by the women's total dissimilarity. Beavers, born matronly, was passive on-screen. In real life, she seemed resigned to the status quo. Devout, with middle-class values and a determination to do well in show business, Louise Beavers fulfilled the expectations of white America. Although she did protest against derogatory language in the original *Imitation of Life* script, and in others, she also did not disturb the peace.

If the cards hadn't been stacked against Fredricka Washington, of Savannah, Georgia, she might have been labeled the black Bette Davis. She possessed the same brand of quicksilver intelligence, nervous drive, and tightly coiled energy with a dash of bitters. Whether her acting talent matched Davis's is difficult to ascertain, for Washington appeared in only half-a-dozen pictures, two of them musical shorts that ran no more than twenty minutes.

Her stiff performance in *Imitation of Life* suggests inexperience rather than lack of talent. In a picture with few cinematic high points, she conveys a stony disdain for the environment of the story and for her place in it—a disdain that possibly includes director, studio, script, and the crooked world at large. Whatever the level of Peola's—and Washington's—vulnerability, she's determined not to show it. Fredi Washington, in the role, is as adamant as a Lauren Bacall.

Cheryl Black, a professor of theatre at the University of Missouri, wrote in the journal *Theatre Survey* that Washington's "light complexion, blue-gray eyes, and unaccented speech did not signify 'Negro.' In a white-supremacist culture that depended on fixed racial identities . . . to maintain hierarchy, Fredi Washington was an unintelligible sign."

Meaning that Hollywood had no idea what to do with her. Washington herself, fiercely independent, had little use for studio dreams. Her passion was justice for her people. Had she come along a couple of generations later, she might have raised her fist in a Black Power salute beside Kathleen Cleaver or Angela Davis.

Fredi Washington had nine siblings. When she was eleven, her mother died and her father sent her from Savannah to a convent in Pennsylvania. Postconvent, Fredi moved to Harlem to be with her grandmother and an aunt. "My first job," she recalled, "was in the stock room of a dress house for $17 a week. Then I got hired as a bookkeeper at W.C. Handy's Black Swan Record Company. That's where I heard about a dance audition for *Shuffle Along,* an all-black Broadway musical that ran between 1922 and 1924. The pay was $35 a week, so I went down and applied." Composed by Eubie Blake and Noble Sissle, *Shuffle Along* is said to be the first Broadway musical entirely created, produced, and performed by African Americans.

Fredi said, "I had never seen a play or a show until I went into *Shuffle Along.* I had never had lipstick on until that day. I knew nothing about makeup and I bought everything they told me I needed and I proceeded to put it on. I looked like a clown." An older, more experienced chorus girl took one look at the novice and ordered her back to the mirror, declaring, "I got to get this off and make you look human." The two women remained friends for the rest of their lives; the more seasoned one was Maude Russell (1897–2001), who claimed to have introduced the Charleston on Broadway. Another of Fredi's lifelong friends from the same chorus line was Josephine Baker.

Washington, who lacked both a singing voice and a knack for comedy, sharpened her dancing skills during the two years she spent in the chorus of *Shuffle Along.* Later she danced in a nightclub act in this country and in Europe. Her second Broadway musical, *Singin' the Blues,* ran for five weeks in 1931. Before that, however, Fredi appeared with Paul Robeson in *Black Boy,* a drama that closed after thirty-seven performances in 1926. In it, she played a young African-American woman passing for white. During the run, Robeson and Washington reportedly began a love affair that went on for two decades.

In 1933, Washington was back on Broadway, in *Run Little Chillun!* The same year, she appeared with Paul Robeson in her first feature film, *The Emperor Jones.* In a small role as Undine, she's a tigress ready to shred any other female who approaches her man.

Those who celebrate Fredi Washington—a passionate coterie—base their passions on her performance in *Imitation of Life.* Fredi herself didn't dwell on the picture. When she talked about it, she seemed proud of the fact that she had "received the privilege of making suggestions for changes, and as a result, dialogue and situations were altered and the entire ending of the picture changed." That statement, made in 1943, perhaps refers to the deleted lynching scene. In 1978, she told an interviewer, "I had to fight the writers on lines like, 'If only I had been born white.' They didn't seem to realize that a decent life, not white skin, was the issue."

John Stahl reportedly interviewed several hundred young women for the role of Peola. As he searched for the perfect "white Negro," as one newspaper headline described the part, Stahl said, "This girl is the daughter of a colored mammy and this point obviously makes it impossible to use an established screen player or, in fact, any girl of Caucasian birth."

On a trip to New York, Stahl spotted Fredi Washington. Soon after, she received a telegram from Universal informing her they would like her to test for *Imitation of Life,* which she did. Not until several months later, however, did she learn the results. The studio, having learned that Fredi was due to arrive in Los Angeles with her husband, Lawrence Brown, a member of Duke Ellington's orchestra, sent a representative to Union Station to meet her. After a great deal of haggling—Universal wanted her to sign a long-term contract, but Fredi refused—all parties agreed to a one-picture deal for this aloof, independent woman from the East. (Although married to Brown for over fifteen years, the great love of Fredi's life was Duke Ellington. She was rumored to have married Brown as a compromise when Ellington took another lover. It was also said that she never got over Duke.)

While filming *Imitation of Life,* Fredi Washington lived at Louise Beavers's home, one reason being that Fredi's husband was on the road with Ellington and she was alone in an unfamiliar city. Fredi soon became her costar's protégée. Beavers, offscreen, functioned as a combined social arbiter and den mother for black Hollywood. As such, she tutored Fredi in which contacts, personal and professional, to cultivate, as well as those to shun.

Fredi made her last screen appearance in 1937, in *One Mile from Heaven.* In it, she played a nurse who adopts an abandoned white child. Her greatest Broadway success came in 1939, when she appeared, with Ethel Waters, as one of *Mamba's Daughters.* During the forties, Fredi appeared in other plays on and off Broadway, and gave her final stage performance in *How Long Till Summer,* which closed after seven performances in 1949.

Fredi Washington's total acting career amounts to roughly five years of her long lifetime. No doubt frustrated by the dearth of suitable parts, she found her calling elsewhere. Her most fulfilling job seems to have been as a journalist on *The People's Voice,* a weekly Harlem newspaper founded by Fredi's brother-in-law, Adam Clayton Powell Jr., the future congressman from New York's twenty-second district. In 1942, Fredi took a full-time job at the paper. "Hired to do public relations, she soon became theatrical editor, and for the next five years waged a crusade in print against racist representations in theatrical media and the correlative lack of opportunity for African American artists."

Fredi's younger sister, Isabel Powell, was married to Adam Clayton Powell Jr. from 1933 to 1945. Prior to her marriage, Isabel had a brief career in nightclubs and on Broadway, including one show, *Singin' the Blues,* with Fredi. When I visited Mrs. Powell in 2006, a few months before her death at the age of ninety-eight, I asked, "What is your favorite memory of your sister?" She said, "Wonderful, gracious, precious. Just beyond anything I can think of that's wonderful, my sister." The sitting room was full of family photographs, and Mrs. Powell pointed out several of her and Fredi in their youth. They looked like twins, each one a knockout.

After her divorce, Isabel Powell never remarried. "Those twelve years were the best anyone could have," she said. Fredi Washington apparently took a different view of the man who devastated her sister when he left her to marry the singer Hazel Scott. I was told by the widow of a man who worked with Fredi at *The People's Voice* in the forties: "She *despised* Adam. She hated his guts because of the way he treated her sister."

A Complex and Painful Phenomenon

"Early in my career," said Fredi Washington, "it was suggested that I might get further by passing as French or something exotic. But to pass, for economic or other advantages, would have meant

(continued)

that I swallowed the idea of black inferiority. I'm a black woman, and proud of it." In several interviews at the time of *Imitation of Life*, Fredi expressed regret for her light skin, insisting that she wished for a darker complexion.

Nevertheless, Fredi sometimes took a "racial furlough"—meaning that, because of her light skin, she could enter a segregated restaurant, hotel, or other establishment unchallenged. Often, when on tour or traveling with other African Americans, she was the designated one to purchase ice cream or other items for the group—since she didn't "look black," she was the only one who would be served.

Both the 1934 and the 1959 versions of *Imitation of Life* acquainted white audiences with the complex and painful phenomenon of passing. For the majority of African Americans, then and now, it was not news. They either knew, or knew of, people who passed. In many instances, the light-skinned person was a family member.

Such was the case in Fredi Washington's own family. Details are sketchy, but I learned that one sister spent much of her life in the guise of a white woman. Although estranged from the family, she attended the funeral of Isabel Powell in 2007. A family friend told me she looked "very old, almost as old as Isabel." Several members of the Powell family spoke on condition of anonymity, and then reluctantly. One suggested that I might try to locate the woman's daughter—"the daughter who found us." Another said: "No one had heard from that sister in a long time." Still another stated, "That's something I wouldn't even want to get into. It's been so long that this particular aunt of mine has been passing for white, that it has nothing to do with us, and I have nothing to do with her."

Beyond her career in journalism, Fredi's activism included working with the NAACP; lobbying Congress for an antilynching bill; seeking clemency for two African-American soldiers accused of rape; and striving to secure hotel accommodations for black performers on tour. She was a founder of the Negro Actors Guild, and she also campaigned for the reelection of President Roosevelt. Curiously, Fredi seems to have been overlooked by compilers of the blacklist, though she made no effort to hide her association with members of the political left. Her final column in *The People's Voice,* in 1947, was a denunciation of red-baiting.

Fredi Washington's second marriage, in 1952, was to a Connecticut dentist, Dr. Anthony H. Bell, who died in the early eighties. Fredi died in June 1994, and on October 21 of that year a memorial service was held at St. Peter's Church in New York. Participants included Jean-Claude Baker, a member of Josephine Baker's "Rainbow Tribe" of adopted children; David Dinkins, former mayor of New York City; Bobby Short; Isabel Powell; and Donald Bogle, an author who had interviewed Fredi and subsequently chronicled her life and career in several books on African Americans in show business.

By coincidence, Susan Kohner was walking down Lexington Avenue that day. Glancing at the church, she saw a poster announcing the memorial service, which was to begin presently. "I walked in and sat at the back," Susan said. "Quite a few people spoke. I wrote a note afterwards to her family and said I really felt like paying my respects because she did such a lovely job in that first *Imitation of Life.*"

If you're fond of movie-based trivia games, try this one: How many young actresses can you name whose careers petered out after playing daughter to a big-name female movie star? Think of Diana Scarwid/Faye Dunaway in *Mommie Dearest*; Joey Heatherton/Susan Hayward in *Where Love Has Gone*; Anne Shirley/Barbara Stanwyck in *Stella Dallas*; and Rochelle Hudson/Claudette Colbert in *Imitation of Life.*

As Colbert's daughter, Jessie, young Rochelle Hudson—eighteen at the time—could have phoned in sick every day and we'd have hardly noticed. Her part is built on teen chatter, and at the end, when her mother postpones her marriage because of this girl's puppy crush on Mom's fiancé, you wonder why someone at Universal didn't dock the screenwriters' pay.

More exciting than any of her screen roles was Hudson's World War Two adventures as a spy. In 1939, she married a Hollywood story editor who was also a member of the naval reserve and, as such, was called to active duty after Pearl Harbor. By the early forties, Hudson's small movie career was receding, so she joined her husband as a government employee. As part of their work, the couple made a number of fishing trips to Baja California and elsewhere in the waters of Mexico and Central America. But they were angling for intrigue. Their assignment: to spot secret enemy activity. On one mission, they discovered an airstrip in a remote part of Baja and, hidden nearby, a cache of aviation gas supplied by German operatives as part of a planned Japanese invasion of the West Coast of the United States.

"Want My Quack Quack"

That's the opening line of the 1934 *Imitation of Life,* spoken by Colbert's three-year-old splashing in her bath with a rubber duck. Every studio was looking for a Shirley Temple, and when Universal found this child—Baby Jane, as she was credited—they kept her busy until MGM snatched her a few years later. Eventually she worked all over town, resuming her real name, Juanita Quigley, by age five. After playing Elizabeth Taylor's sister in *National Velvet* (1944), her career was over. In 1951, Quigley entered the novitiate of the Daughters of Mary and Joseph. Taking her first vows to become a nun, she assumed the name Sister Quentin Rita (the given names of her brother and sister). A few years later, realizing she had made a mistake, she left the convent and married. Juanita Quigley died in 1989.

Born in Oklahoma, Rochelle Hudson was pushed into movies by an ambitious mother. After a string of bit parts and walk-ons, she moved up to larger roles in such pictures as *She Done Him Wrong* (1933), with Mae West. Will Rogers, a fellow Oklahoman, cast her in four of his own pictures.

In *Les Misérables* (1935), she's better directed (by Richard Boleslawski) than in *Imitation of Life.* As Cosette, Hudson looks like an early model of Charlotte Rampling: those wide-set eyes that seem to view the world in long shot; the lengthy, well-shaped nose in a full oval face; an early look of disdain. Hudson is doll-like, but she's a doll who's been handled. She has the kind of screen face that conceals more the longer you gaze at it. And she's always too pert; you wish she'd reduce the caffeine.

Hudson never quite left pictures, though her role as Natalie Wood's mother in *Rebel Without a Cause* in 1955 was hailed as a comeback. Her next movie role was in *Strait-Jacket*, nine years later, as sister-in-law to Joan Crawford's madwoman ax-murderess. The first day on the set, Crawford looked her up and down, then said, "You still have the prettiest legs in Hollywood." At age forty-eight, Rochelle's face bore an unfortunate resemblance to Lady Bird Johnson's, the First Lady who had recently replaced Jacqueline Kennedy.

Her next-to-last film was *The Night Walker* (1964), which was Barbara Stanwyck's final appearance on the big screen. In 1967, Hudson appeared in *Dr. Terror's Gallery of Horrors,* and that was the end. She died of pneumonia five years later.

*I*n a recent conversation with Susan Kohner's older son, Paul Weitz, I asked, "What do you, as a filmmaker, consider the flaws, and the greatness, of *Imitation of Life*?"

He said, "I think you can't separate the flaws from what makes the film great. The primary greatness, and the primary flaw, are its artificiality. But the true strangeness of it is, that the artificiality is coupled with such emotion."

Encountering *Imitation of Life* for the first time, some respond to its flaws, which congregate in what I've earlier dubbed "the blond side" of the movie. Those viewers are the ones who laugh, though what's emitted is hollow laughter. Others, responding only to the emotional, dark side, can't stanch the tears.

That first long, juvenile afternoon when I watched it three times, I took it literally. Like Cheryl Crane back on page 297, who found the picture "so sad," and Lana "so wonderful"—even as it fed on their own troubled lives—I, too, found it "sad" and the actors, the story, "wonderful." Perhaps the movie fed on my life, as well; or vice versa. I didn't have the same mother problems as Cheryl Crane in real life or Sarah Jane and Susie in the film, but I did come home that afternoon a brand-new mutineer. I had no label for the picture's jarring communiqué, but it must have been an encouragement. . . . Be who you are. Or, more eloquently,

To thine own self be true. (Most Hollywood pictures of the period said, Be who you aren't, and to yourself be false.)

Later, having grown up, I sometimes made sport of the more flamboyant parts of *Imitation of Life*. Its flaws seemed delicious, like naughty words encountered for the first time. And yet, contrary to the airy title of Lora Meredith's Broadway hit, I was not "Born to Laugh."

Meanwhile, Sirk was rediscovered, and in New York, where I lived at the time, we began discussing *Imitation of Life* as a unique film in its piercing insight into how children wrong their mothers—or was it the other way around? Both, said someone, but the implied rage and guilt of that subject silenced us. The talk veered instead to the technical expertise of Sirk's direction, his cameraman, his editor; to the famous irony and its myriad manifestations; and, of course, to camp.

Why did we change the subject? Because Sirk's counternarrative, unlike the film itself, felt dangerous. It had no aesthetic resolution. The secret, locked part of *Imitation of Life* is its grip on the unconscious. Susan Kohner knew this intuitively when, throwing herself on the coffin, she imagined it was her own mother lying dead inside. The picture's transmigration through the viewer's emotional corridors rouses a nightmare: the struggle of a mother to possess, and the child's counterstruggle for autonomy. That primal battle invokes the will to pass, in the eyes of the world, for who one wants to be, which contradicts what the mother says one is. As in a dream play, there is no awakening until the foe has been fought, perhaps subdued. Sometimes both contenders fall.

Imitation of Life maps the journey away from one's mother—or one's parents—as a circular road that leads always back to the starting place. Only death puts paid to that circumference. No, not even death. We, like Sarah Jane, may have escaped. But what we have escaped *from* is so much ourselves, that it becomes our tragedy. The real ending of *Imitation of Life*, after the funeral, should have been Sarah Jane, to Lora: "You and my mother ruined the first years of my life. Now she—she will torment me forever."

More than an imitation, Sirk's picture, when we take it personally, turns into a reflection of life—in Sirk's devastating mirror. At the juncture of Sarah Jane's hungry need for her mother, and chaotic rejection of her—we enter the picture. Suddenly, as in a slow zoom, we catch sight of ourselves in that strange waltz of anger and guilt that bedevils Sarah Jane even more than her race. It's enough to make you cry.

That's why, when you've talked and talked about Sirk's subtext, his palette, his painterly compositions, his cinematic brilliance, and his theatricalized discussion of American society—that's why we then change the subject. Because watching *Imitation of Life* is like reading your mother's diary—and finding yourself on every page.

At the
Hollywood
preview, Lana
wore a white
gown swathed
in white ostrich
feathers—with
matching
daughter.
*Collection of Lou
Valentino*

In Cleveland for
the opening of
Imitation of Life,
Ross Hunter,
Juanita Moore,
Susan Kohner,
and Lana
Turner attend a
fund-raiser for
Easter Seals.
Photofest

Juanita Moore and her husband, Charles Burris, at a party following the 32nd Academy Awards ceremonies. Though she and Susan Kohner were both nominated as Best Supporting Actress for *Imitation of Life*, they lost to Shelley Winters for *The Diary of Anne Frank. Photofest*

Hayley Mills, Ross
Hunter, Sandra Dee,
and Universal's
"unknown mogul," Ed
Muhl, in the early
sixties. *Photofest*

Jacque Mapes, Rosalind
Russell, and Ross Hunter
in the mid-sixties. Ross
and Jacque were devoted
partners for half a century.
In death, they are together
at the Westwood Village
Memorial Park in Los
Angeles. *Photofest*

Susan Kohner and Sal Mineo in *Dino*
(1957). *Collection of Dwayne Teal*

Susan Kohner in a glamour photo at the time of *Imitation of Life*. Susan sent it to the author following their first interview, with the inscription: "For Sam Staggs, from his fan Susan Kohner." *Collection of the author*

Susan Kohner with her parents at the time of *Imitation of Life*. *Collection of Susan Kohner*

Carlos Villarías and Lupita Tovar in the 1931 Spanish-language *Dracula*. *Collection of the author*

Lupita Tovar on 1981 stamp commemorating fifty years of sound films in Mexico. *Collection of Lupita Tovar Kohner*

Joel Fluellen (seated, far right) with fellow members of the Screen Actors Guild, including Wendell Corey, Leon Ames, Ronald Reagan, Hilary Brooke, and Rosemary DeCamp. *Photofest*

Sarah Jane's dream come true: passing for white as a showgirl at the Moulin Rouge in Hollywood. *Collection of Susan Kohner*

Ageless Juanita Moore celebrates a birthday in New York, October 19, 2005.
Photo by Jim Willis

Juanita Moore and her godson, the actor and writer Ken Sagoes (right), with some of her fans after a screening of *Imitation of Life* at the University of Arkansas, Pine Bluff, in 2006. *Photo by Sam Staggs*

Even in long shot, a star is a star. Lana on tour in Cleveland for *Imitation of Life*. *Collection of Lou Valentino*

Susan Kohner, accompanied by her mother, publicizes the picture in Miami. *Collection of Susan Kohner*

Part of the lyric in Susan's "Empty Arms" number at Harry's Club was too much for the censors, who refused to let her sing about her "equipment." *Photofest*

Susan rehearsing Sarah Jane's humiliating departure from Harry's Club. The coat in this photograph was discarded in favor of a skirt and blouse. *Collection of Susan Kohner*

The kind of playwright who flings his manuscript in the fire? Lora Meredith has just rejected David Edwards's latest comedy for a drama with "no clothes, no sex"—she'll play "a dull social worker with high dreams and low heels." *Collection of the author*

In a scene deleted from the film, Lora Meredith and Annie Johnson examine a hat. Annie explains that it was given to her "by the lady I worked for a while back," who loaned it to Annie "to wear to a funeral. Then she didn't want it back. I don't know whether she didn't like wearin' it after a colored woman, or because she didn't want anythin' connected with funerals." *Collection of Dwayne Teal*

Rehearsing the funeral sequence, Lana holds a cigarette. She needed it to steady her nerves after a hysterical flood of tears that sent her running from the church. *Collection of Lou Valentino*

Susan Kohner and John Gavin rehearse the funeral sequence. *Collection of Dwayne Teal*

The greatest funeral Hollywood ever filmed was not in the original script of *Imitation of Life*. *Collection of Dwayne Teal*

The original ending of *Imitation of Life*, wisely deleted by Sirk, had Lora Meredith and Steve Archer in a snowy anticlimax, with Lora planning to retire from the stage. *Collection of Lou Valentino*

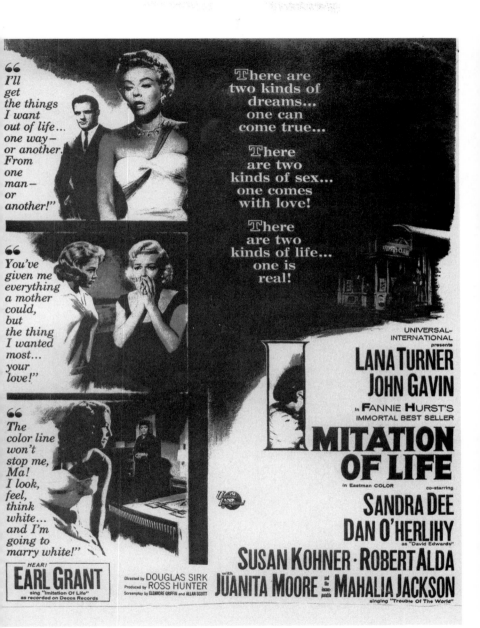

A controversial ad that several newspapers refused to run, owing to the line "I'm going to marry white."

Louise Beavers and Claudette Colbert in the 1934 *Imitation of Life*. *Collection of the author*

In 1934, Rochelle Hudson and Warren William played the roles that Douglas Sirk gave to Sandra Dee and John Gavin. *Collection of the author*

Fredi Washington. *Photofest*

Director John M. Stahl on the set of the 1934 *Imitation of Life*. *Photofest*

Baby Jane, aka Juanita Quigley, spoke the first line in the 1934 version: "Want my quack quack." After several years as a child star, she became a nun. *Collection of Bob Grimes*

Susan Kohner, Ann Robinson, and Juanita Moore backstage at the Egyptian Theater, Hollywood, for the 45th anniversary screening of *Imitation of Life*, April 2004. *Photo by Joseph Valdez*

Juanita Moore and Susan Kohner in New York, October 2005. *Collection of Susan Kohner*

ACKNOWLEDGMENTS

That first day, as a kid at a sad movie, I didn't imagine the long journey I had set out upon. Certainly it never occurred to me that I'd tell Susan Kohner, while going through scrapbooks in her New York apartment, "You know, this is the first time I've written about a movie whose star is in the same room!" Nor laughing so hard with Juanita Moore that my jaw ached. It's literally true that without their friendship and enduring help, there would be no *Born to Be Hurt*. It is an honor to dedicate the book to them.

Others who were there, in 1958, when *Imitation of Life* was filmed, have been equally cordial. They are Ann Robinson, Lupita Tovar Kohner, and Elsie O'Herlihy.

Betty Abbott Griffin, although not on the set, worked as script supervisor on thirteen other Douglas Sirk pictures, and she provided insights available nowhere else. She also drove me to Van Nuys one afternoon to look at the Sirks' house, now much changed. Pippa Scott answered questions about her father, Allan Scott, one of the credited screenwriters, and Bart Williams told me more about his friend, Eleanore Griffin, the other credited writer, than I would have heard from anyone else. Chris Gomberg, Kathy Gomberg, and Phyllis Spear provided clues to Sy Gomberg's uncredited contribution to the script. William Muhl unveiled the backstory of his father's career at Universal. Effie Grubb entertained me with stories about her brother, Lee Goodman.

It was my good fortune to locate several persons with direct or indirect connections to the 1934 *Imitation of Life*. They are Jane Withers; the late Isabel Powell, sister of Fredi Washington; and Jean-Claude Baker, a friend to Fredi Washington in her later years.

Anyone who writes about Douglas Sirk must start with Jon Halliday's invaluable books, and other writings, on the director. Those documents are so complete that I had few remaining questions, but the ones I did have Jon deftly answered. In addition, he introduced me to Matthias Brunner, in Zürich, who heads the Douglas Sirk Foundation. This new acquaintance became a virtual friend via e-mail, and an actual one when we met. Matthias opened his archive to me, spent hours recalling Douglas and Hilde Sirk, his close friends during their final years, and took me to dinner at the Sirks' favorite restaurant in Zürich, all of which added texture, and a new dimension, to my work.

To name every person who contributed to my vast project would equal the end credits for a blockbuster. And since I'm one to stick around for credits, I include here everyone who made my job easier and more fun. First, I must spotlight those who joined me at various stages and stayed on—available 24/7, or so it seemed—until the last page. They read various sections and offered pungent suggestions; provided documents, photographs, and leads; spoke to me in person, by phone, and in e-mails. Indeed, they supplied many of the materials, and the psychological support, needed for a monumental, and complex, history. They are: Michael Henry Adams, Ron Bowers, Warren Butler, Donald D'Aris, John Epperson (aka Lypsinka), Tucker Fleming, Gary Gabriel, Max Gordon, Harry Haun, John Hewitt, Vivian Hewitt, Charles Higham, Foster Hirsch, Vernon Jordan, Brian Kellow, Terry Kingsley-Smith, Berri McBride, William J. Mann, Howard Marren, Joseph Masteroff, Phil Poulos, Curtis Roberts, Glenn Russell, Leigh W. Rutledge, Ken Sagoes, Robert Sanchez, Tom Stempel, Dwayne Teal, Christopher Trumbo, Lou Valentino, and Jan Wahl.

I am equally grateful to those in Hollywood who were friends and colleagues of Douglas Sirk, Ross Hunter, or others who made *Imitation of Life* a picture worth writing about: Valerie Allen, Christiana Benson, Ray Bradbury, Carole Cook, Joan Fontaine, Rita Gam, Betty Garrett, Earl Holliman, Robert Hooks, Linda Hopkins, A. C. Lyles, Carol Lynley, Laura Mako, Lee Meriwether, Dina Merrill, Bob Osborne, Barbara

Rush, Lizabeth Scott, the late Mel Shavelson, James Sheldon, Steffi Sidney, Nancy Sinatra Sr., Paul Weitz, Marvin Westmore, James Whitmore, and Bob Willoughby.

Also, for miscellaneous assistance, Robert Aiken (aka Ford Dunhill), Wavey Austin, Nicholas Bascuez, Wanda Bateman, John Blankenchip, William Bonner Owen, Jerry Boscia, Tim Boss, William Branch, Dorith Bustan, Marc Cave, Avery Clayton, Eric Coleman, Norma Darden, Andrew Davis, Joann Duff, David Durston, Roger Farabee, Robert Fischer, Daniel Frank, Ken Freehill, J. R. Giesen, Alex Gildzen, Grace Godin, Bob Grimes, Ayana Haaruun, Gwen Hargrove, Avanelle Harris, Patrick Harrison, Sharyl Holtzman, Julia Hotton, Guy Hubbard, Marc Huestis, Steven Hughes, Jen Huszcza, Gertrude Jeannette, Sirlouis Jones, Louis Kimble, Curtis King, Laird Koenig, Daniel Kusner, Steve Lambert, Victoria Larimore, Rhea Lewis-Woodson, Kathy Majewska, Kevin Malony, Howard Mandelbaum, Ron Mandelbaum, Joe Martinez, Rose Masterantonio, Evan Matthews, Enid Metz, Joe Milicia, Lawrence Nash, Charles Nelson, Ward Nixon, Karola Noetel, Gabi Norman, Joel Norman, Fifi Oscard, James Robert Parish, Chris Pawlicki, Karen Pedersen, Jeff Pirtle, James Ragan, Carl A. Redus Jr., Frances Ricca, Benjamin Salisbury, Delia Salvi, Stephen Shearer, Preston J. Shumaker, Robert Smith, Drew Talley, Sherry Tanksley, Fredrick Tucker, Joseph Valdez, Steve Vaught, Heather von Rohr, Kelly Wallace, Marc Wanamaker, Bill Warlow, John Waxman, the Reverend Dr. Hank Wilkins IV, Jim Willis, and Valerie Yaros. I am grateful, also, to those who wished to remain anonymous.

Writers, according to legend, aren't given due respect by Hollywood studios. Such is emphatically *not* the case at the famous research institutions in Los Angeles. For instance, Ned Comstock at USC gives me movie star treatemnt each time I use the Cinema-Television Library there. The same goes for Barbara Hall, Special Collections, at the Margaret Herrick Library of the Academy of Motion Picture Arts and Sciences, and for Sandra Archer, Stacy Behlmer, Jenny Romero, Warren Sherk, and many others at the same institution. Thanks, also, to Snowden Becker, who screened for me the thirtieth Academy Awards ceremonies (1958) and the thirty-second (1960). Christopher Frith, at the Billy Rose Theatre Collection of the New York Public Library for the Performing Arts, is always the first one I look for.

My agent, Jim Donovan, and my editor, Elizabeth Beier, are such pillars that I can't imagine writing without their support. A bow to Elizabeth's editorial assistant, Michelle Richter, who made the right phone calls to locate Jon Halliday, the foremost Sirk authority. Kevin Sweeney, production editor at St. Martin's Press, allays much prepublication anxiety by doing all the right things. Carly Sommerstein is such an astute copy editor that I booked her services a year in advance, and Michael Cantwell made the legal vetting a painless experience.

To all of these, tremendous gratitude. Whatever strengths this book may have, they would be fewer without those named here. The flaws, however, are mine alone.

SELECTED BIBLIOGRAPHY

Several minor sources not listed here—books, magazine and newspaper articles, archival materials—are cited in the notes section.

Alpert, Hollis. *The Dreams and the Dreamers*. New York: Macmillan, 1962.

Bacon, James. *Hollywood Is a Four Letter Town*. Chicago: Henry Regnery, 1976.

Baker, Jean-Claude, and Chris Chase. *Josephine: The Hungry Heart*. New York: Cooper Square Press, 2001 (original 1993).

Baldwin, James. *Collected Essays*. New York: Library of America, 1998.

Basinger, Jeanine. *Lana Turner*. New York: Pyramid, 1976.

Berry, Sarah. *Screen Style: Fashion and Femininity in 1930s Hollywood*. Minneapolis: University of Minnesota Press, 2000.

Blair, Betsy. *The Memory of All That*. New York: Knopf, 2003.

Bogle, Donald. *Blacks in American Films and Television: An Encyclopedia*. New York: Garland, 1988.

———. *Bright Boulevards, Bold Dreams: The Story of Black Hollywood*. New York: One World/Random House, 2005.

———. *Dorothy Dandridge: A Biography*. New York: Armistad, 1997.

———. *Toms, Coons, Mulattoes, Mammies, and Bucks: An Interpretive History of Blacks in American Films*. New York: Viking, 1973.

Bronfen, Elisabeth. *Home in Hollywood: The Imaginary Geography of Cinema*. New York: Columbia University Press, 2004.

Bruck, Connie. *When Hollywood Had a King: The Reign of Lew Wasserman, Who Leveraged Talent into Power and Influence*. New York: Random House, 2003.

Cook, Pam, ed. *The Cinema Book*. New York: Pantheon, 1985.

Crane, Cheryl. *Detour: A Hollywood Story*. New York: Arbor House, 1988.

Cripps, Thomas. *Making Movies Black: The Hollywood Message Movie from World War II to the Civil Rights Era*. New York: Oxford University Press, 1993.

————. *Slow Fade to Black: The Negro in American Film, 1900–1942*. New York: Oxford University Press, 1977.

Darin, Dodd, and Maxine Paetro. *Dream Lovers: The Magnificent Shattered Lives of Bobby Darin and Sandra Dee by Their Son*. New York: Warner Books, 1994.

Davis, Ronald L. *Hollywood Beauty: Linda Darnell and the American Dream*. Norman, OK: University of Oklahoma Press, 1991.

Dick, Bernard F. *City of Dreams: The Making and Remaking of Universal Pictures*. Lexington: University of Kentucky Press, 1997.

Duberman, Martin Bauml. *Paul Robeson*. New York: Knopf, 1988.

Dunaway, Faye, with Betsy Sharkey. *Looking for Gatsby: My Life*. New York: Simon & Schuster, 1995.

Editors of Time-Life Books. *True Crime: Death and Celebrity*. Alexandria, VA: Time-Life Books, 1993.

Ehrenstein, David. *Open Secret: Gay Hollywood 1928–2000*. New York: HarperCollins, 2000.

Ellington, Edward Kennedy [Duke]. *Music Is My Mistress*. New York: Doubleday, 1973.

Everson, William K. *Claudette Colbert*. New York: Pyramid, 1976.

Filmoteca Española. *John M. Stahl: Edición bilingüe español/inglés*. San Sebastián/Madrid: Festival internacional de cine de San Sebastián, 1999.

Finler, Joel. *The Hollywood Story*. New York: Crown, 1988.

Finstad, Suzanne. *Natasha: The Biography of Natalie Wood*. New York: Three Rivers Press, 2001.

Fischer, Lucy, ed. *Imitation of Life*. New Brunswick, NJ: Rutgers University Press, 1991.

Fleming, E. J. *Carole Landis: A Tragic Life in Hollywood*. Jefferson, NC: McFarland, 2005.

Goreau, Laurraine. *Just Mahalia, Baby*. Waco, TX: Word Books, 1975.

Graham, Allison. *Framing the South: Hollywood, Television, and Race During the Civil Rights Struggle*. Baltimore: The Johns Hopkins University Press, 2001.

Guilaroff, Sidney. *Crowning Glory: Reflections of Hollywood's Favorite Confidant*. Santa Monica: General Publishing Group, 1996.

Hall, Barbara. *An Oral History With Alexander Golitzen* (unpublished). Beverly Hills: Oral History Program, Margaret Herrick Library, Academy of Motion Picture Arts and Sciences, 1992.

Halliday, Jon. *Sirk on Sirk: Conversations with Jon Halliday*. New and revised ed. London: Faber and Faber, 1997.

————. *Sirk on Sirk: Interviews with Jon Halliday*. New York: Viking, 1972.

Harbin, Billy J., Kim Marra, and Robert A. Schanke, eds. *The Gay and Lesbian Legacy: A Biographical Dictionary of Major Figures in American Stage History in the Pre-Stonewall Era*. Ann Arbor: University of Michigan Press, 2005.

Harvey, James. *Movie Love in the Fifties*. New York: Knopf, 2001.

Heisner, Beverly. *Hollywood Art: Art Direction in the Days of the Great Studios*. Jefferson, NC: McFarland, 1990.

Hershfield, Joanne, and David R. Maciel, eds. *Mexico's Cinema: A Century of Film and Filmmakers*. Wilmington, DE: Scholarly Resources, 1999.

Heston, Charlton. *The Actor's Life: Journals 1956–1976*. New York: Dutton, 1978.

Heston, Charlton, and Jean-Pierre Isbouts. *Charlton Heston's Hollywood: 50 Years in American Film*. New York: GT Publishing, 1998.

Higham, Charles. *Orson Welles: The Rise and Fall of an American Genius*. New York: St. Martin's Press, 1985.

Hill, Errol G., and James V. Hatch. *A History of African American Theatre*. Cambridge, UK: Cambridge University Press, 2003.

Hofler, Robert. *The Man Who Invented Rock Hudson: The Pretty Boys and Dirty Deals of Henry Willson*. New York: Carroll and Graf, 2005.

Holloway, Karla F. C. *Passed On: African American Mourning Stories*. Durham, NC: Duke University Press, 2002.

Hudson, Rock, and Sara Davidson. *Rock Hudson: His Story*. New York: William Morrow, 1986.

Hurst, Fannie. *Imitation of Life*. New York: Permabooks, 1959 (original 1933).

Jackson, Carlton. *Hattie: The Life of Hattie McDaniel*. Lanham, MD: Madison Books, 1990.

Jackson, Mahalia, with Evan McLeod Wylie. *Movin' on Up*. New York: Hawthorn, 1966.

Jackson, Ronald L., II, and Elaine B. Richardson. *Understanding African American Rhetoric*. New York: Routledge, 2003.

Jacobs, Diane. *Christmas in July: The Life and Art of Preston Sturges*. Berkeley: University of California Press, 1992.

Jeffers, H. Paul. *Sal Mineo: His Life, Murder, and Mystery*. New York: Carroll and Graf, 2000.

Jones, Hettie. *Big Star, Fallin' Mama: Five Women in Black Music*. New York: Viking, 1974.

Kashner, Sam, and Jennifer MacNair. *The Bad and the Beautiful: Hollywood in the Fifties*. New York: Norton, 2002.

Kawin, Bruce F. *How Movies Work*. Berkeley: University of California Press, 1992.

Kisch, John, and Edward Mapp. *A Separate Cinema: Fifty Years of Black Cast Posters*. New York: The Noonday Press, 1992.

Klinger, Barbara. *Melodrama and Meaning: History, Culture, and the Films of Douglas Sirk*. Bloomington: Indiana University Press, 1994.

Kobal, John. *Gods and Goddesses of the Movies*. London: Roxby Press Productions, 1973.

————. *People Will Talk*. New York: Knopf, 1985.

Kohner, Frederick. *The Magician of Sunset Boulevard: The Improbable Life of Paul Kohner, Hollywood Agent*. Palos Verdes, CA: Morgan Press, 1977.

Kroeger, Brooke. *Fannie: The Talent for Success of Writer Fannie Hurst*. New York: Times Books, 1999.

Lamparski, Richard. *2nd Annual Lamparski's Whatever Became Of . . . ?* New York: Bantam, 1977.

Landy, Marcia, ed. *Imitations of Life: A Reader on Film and Television Melodrama*. Detroit: Wayne State University Press, 1991.

Lant, Antonia, and Ingrid Periz, eds. *Red Velvet Seat: Women's Writings on the First Fifty Years of Cinema*. London: Verso, 2006.

Läufer, Elisabeth. *Skeptiker des Lichts: Douglas Sirk und seine Filme*. Frankfurt am Main: Fischer Taschenbuch Verlag, 1987.

Leab, Daniel J. *From Sambo to Superspade: The Black Experience in Motion Pictures*. Boston: Houghton Mifflin, 1975.

Leigh, Janet, with Christopher Nickens. *Psycho: Behind the Scenes of the Classic Thriller*. New York: Harmony Books, 1995.

Levine, Suzanne Jill. *Manuel Puig and the Spider Woman*. New York: Farrar, Straus and Giroux, 2000.

McDougal, Dennis. *The Last Mogul: Lew Wasserman, MCA, and the Hidden History of Hollywood*. New York: Da Capo, 2001.

McGilligan, Pat, ed. *Backstory: Interviews with Screenwriters of Hollywood's Golden Age*. Berkeley: University of California Press, 1986.

Maltby, Richard. *Hollywood Cinema*. Second ed. Malden, MA: Blackwell, 2003.

Maltin, Leonard. *The Art of the Cinematographer: A Survey and Interviews with Five Masters*. New York: Dover, 1978.

Mancini, Henry, and Gene Lees. *Did They Mention the Music?* Chicago: Contemporary Books, 1989.

Mann, William J. *Behind the Screen: How Gays and Lesbians Shaped Hollywood, 1910–1969*. New York: Viking, 2001.

Marks, Carole, and Diana Edkins. *The Power of Pride: Stylemakers and Rulebreakers of the Harlem Renaissance*. New York: Crown, 1999.

Marmorstein, Gary. *Hollywood Rhapsody: Movie Music and Its Makers, 1900 to 1975*. New York: Schirmer Books, 1997.

Matthews, Charles. *Oscar A to Z*. New York: Doubleday, 1995.

Meisner, Sanford, and Dennis Longwell. *Sanford Meisner on Acting*. New York: Vintage, 1987.

Mordden, Ethan. *The Hollywood Studios*. New York: Knopf, 1988.

Morella, Joe, and Edward Z. Epstein. *Lana: The Public and Private Lives of Miss Turner*. New York: Citadel, 1971.

Mulvey, Laura. *Death 24 x a Second: Stillness and the Moving Image*. London: Reaktion Books Ltd., 2006.

Mulvey, Laura, and Jon Halliday, eds. *Douglas Sirk*. Edinburgh: Edinburgh Film Festival, 1972.

Murray, James P. *To Find an Image: Black Films from Uncle Tom to Superfly*. Indianapolis: Bobbs-Merrill, 1973.

Oppenheimer, Jerry, and Jack Vitek. *Idol: Rock Hudson, the True Story of an American Film Hero*. New York: Villard Books, 1986.

Peary, Danny, ed. *Close-ups: Intimate Profiles of Movie Stars by Their Co-Stars, Directors, Screenwriters, and Friends*. New York: Workman, 1978.

———. *Cult Movies 3*. New York: Fireside, 1988.

Pero, Taylor, and Jeff Rovin. *Always, Lana*. New York: Bantam, 1982.

Poulson-Bryant, Scott. *Hung: A Meditation on the Measure of Black Men in America*. New York: Doubleday, 2005.

Quirk, Lawrence J. *Claudette Colbert: An Illustrated Biography*. New York: Crown, 1985.

Rains, Bob. *Beneath the Tinsel: The Human Side of Hollywood Stars*. Danville, IL: Three Lions Publications, 1999.

Rampersad, Arnold. *The Life of Langston Hughes. Vol. I, 1902–1941*. New York: Oxford University Press, 1986.

Rebello, Stephen. *Alfred Hitchcock and the Making of* Psycho. New York: Dembner Books, 1990.

Root, Eric. *The Private Diary of My Life with Lana*. Beverly Hills: Dove Books, 1996.

Roud, Richard. *Cinema: A Critical Dictionary*. Vol. 2. New York: Viking, 1980.

Russell, Rosalind, and Chris Chase. *Life Is a Banquet*. New York: Random House, 1977.

Sennett, Robert S. *Setting the Scene: The Great Hollywood Art Directors*. New York: Harry N. Abrams, 1994.

Sharp, Kathleen. *Mr. & Mrs. Hollywood: Edie and Lew Wasserman and Their Entertainment Empire*. New York: Carroll and Graf, 2003.

Sherk, Warren M. *An Oral History with Hans J. Salter* (unpublished). Beverly Hills: Oral History Program, Margaret Herrick Library, Academy of Motion Picture Arts and Sciences, 1994.

Skal, David J. *Hollywood Gothic: The Tangled Web of Dracula from Novel to Stage to Screen*. Rev. ed. New York: Faber and Faber, 2004.

Skinner, Frank. *Underscore*. Los Angeles: Skinner Music Co., 1950.

Spoto, Donald. *Madcap: The Life of Preston Sturges*. Boston: Little, Brown, 1990.

Stern, Michael. *Douglas Sirk*. Boston: Twayne, 1979.

Thomson, David. *America in the Dark: The Impact of Hollywood Films on American Culture*. New York: William Morrow, 1977.

———. *The New Biographical Dictionary of Film*. New York: Knopf, 2002.

Turner, Lana. *Lana: The Lady, the Legend, the Truth*. New York: Dutton, 1982.

Valentino, Lou. *The Films of Lana Turner*. Secaucus, NJ: Citadel Press, 1976.

Wakeman, John, ed. *World Film Directors, Vol. I (1890–1945)*. New York: H. W. Wilson, 1987.

Watts, Jill. *Hattie McDaniel: Black Ambition, White Hollywood*. New York: HarperCollins, 2005.

Westmore, Frank, and Muriel Davidson. *The Westmores of Hollywood*. Philadelphia: J. B. Lippincott Co., 1976.

Willoquet-Maricondi, Paula. *Pedro Almodóvar: Interviews*. Jackson, MS: University Press of Mississippi, 2004.

Zicree, Marc Scott. *The Twilight Zone Companion*. New York: Bantam, 1982.

NOTES

A few sources not included in the bibliography are given here. Unless otherwise indicated, statements from Juanita Moore and Susan Kohner are to the author. Such designations as "LTK to SS" mean, of course, Lupita Tovar Kohner to the author. I have, however, omitted endnotes when it is obvious in the text that an interview subject is speaking with the author, e.g., "Lupita Tovar Kohner told me; Ann Robinson explained to me." I have followed this practice, also, with published sources.

Initials of those interviewed are listed below under "Persons." Abbreviations of institutions, also listed, are similarly sourced.

Quotations from both versions of *Imitation of Life* (and from other films) are from the release dialogue, i.e., what you hear spoken by the actors on-screen. Exceptions are designated as "script" or "shooting script."

PERSONS

RB—Ray Bradbury
AC—Avery Clayton
TF—Tucker Fleming
JF—Joan Fontaine
GG—Gary Gabriel
RG—Rita Gam
BG—Betty Garrett
BAG—Betty Abbott Griffin
RH—Robert Hooks
TKS—Terry Kingsley-Smith
LTK—Lupita Tovar Kohner
SK—Susan Kohner

CL—Carol Lynley
LM—Laura Mako
JMa—Joseph Masteroff
LMe—Lee Meriwether
DM—Dina Merrill
JM—Juanita Moore
BO—Bob Osborne
IP—Isabel Powell
JR—James Ragan
BR—Barbara Rush
PS—Pippa Scott

INSTITUTIONS

AMPAS—Academy of Motion Picture Arts and Sciences, Margaret Herrick Library, Beverly Hills

NYPL—Billy Rose Theatre Collections at the New York Public Library

SMU—DeGolyer Library, Southern Methodist University, Dallas

USC—University of Southern California, Cinema-Television Library, Los Angeles

UT—University of Texas, Austin

INTRODUCTION: RECAPTURING THE PAST

10 "The Ross Hunter touch"—Alpert, p. 80.

1: A SMALL GIANT

16 Oddly, in a letter to Hurst (and subsequent Hunter-Hurst correspondence)—Harry Ransom Center, UT, Austin.

17 "I thought it was a beautiful name"—JMa to SS.

19 "We wanted Pearl Bailey for the role"—Ross Hunter oral history, SMU.

20 "I found Juanita sitting"—Ross Hunter oral history, SMU.

2: THE GOOD AND FAITHFUL SERVANT

26 "Los Angeles itself seemed to be"—Bogle, *Bright Boulevards*, pp. 16–17.

26 "home to the black elite"—Bogle, *Bright Boulevards*, p. xii.

26 "a gallery of famous entertainers"—Bogle, *Bright Boulevards*, p. 79.

27 "Juanita, you can become"—*Los Angeles Times*, July 9, 2000.

27 "the finest and most beautiful theatre"—Bogle, *Bright Boulevards*, p. 67.

27 "I scrambled up enough money"—*Los Angeles Times*, July 9, 2000.

28 "was one of my inspirations"—ibid.

3: A FEW THINGS IN MOVIES

35 "I didn't know how to make a film"—Elia Kazan, *A Life*, p. 374.

38 "I remember so well"—JM, interviewed in documentary *Playboy Presents Rita*, 2004.

4: SUSAN SIGHTINGS

42 "We worked all night"—LTK to SS.

43 "scrubbed, primped, and so antiseptic"—*Motion Picture*, Sept. 1959.

43 "an idyllic childhood"—ibid.

44 "Susan Kohner leaned back"—*Modern Screen*, Aug. 1959.

44 "I'll come to the theatre with her"—LTK to SS.

44 "You know that education"—LTK to SS.

47 like his contemporaries at the Group Theatre—Sidney Pollack, in Meisner and Longwell, p. xiv.

48 "living truthfully . . . you ain't got it"—Meisner and Longwell, pp. 15 and 87.

48 "My approach is a hell of a lot"—Harbin et al., p. 279.

5: AN INTIMATE CONFESSION FROM SUSAN KOHNER

49 "An Intimate Confession from Susan Kohner"—*Modern Screen*, Aug. 1959.

7: IF LOVE COULD KILL

62 "All he wants is to send"—editors of Time-Life Books, p. 77.

63 "Lana was funny"—BO to SS.

63 "was always popular with film crews"—Basinger, p. 42.

63 "I came on the set"—BAG to SS.

64 "For all its other problems"—Crane, p. 322.

64 "You'll never get away from me"—editors of Time-Life Books, p. 98.

65 "What are you doing at Pioneer Hardware?"—Guilaroff, pp. 194–95.

65 drove around town that Friday—Crane, p. 22.

65 Stompanato himself bought the knife—Turner, p. 235.

66 "a hush fell over the crowd"—editors of Time-Life Books, p. 102.

66 "I saw him once do"—Ehrenstein, p. 73.

67 "We were sitting in our suite"—Root, pp. 184–86.

67 "There was, I decided"—Crane, pp. 320–21.

68 "gleaming butcher knife"—Crane, p. 29.

68 "I took a step forward"—ibid.

68 "Out of the corner of my eye"—Turner, p. 240.

8: WILL LANA WIN THE OSCAR?

70 "I had never seen Mother"—Crane, p. 3.

71 "The ballroom sparkled with color"—Turner, p. 225.

72 "You no-good bitch!"—Crane, pp. 13–14.

9: "TAKE AWAY THE SWEATER AND WHAT HAVE YOU GOT?"

74 "Lana Turner can act"—Kobal, *People Will Talk,* p. 458.

74 "When sound came to the movies"—Pero and Rovin, p. 189.

75 "I think Lana learned"—Kobal, *People Will Talk,* p. 389.

77 "I was determined to read"—Turner, p. 254.

77 "When they asked who"—*The Hollywood Reporter*, June 5, 1990.

77 "Katharine Hepburn wanted it"—ibid.

78 "See him, Lana"—Turner, p. 255.

78 "Ross has a great track record"—ibid.

78 "his rosy-cheeked face"—Turner, p. 256.

79 Lana had never reached—ibid.

79 "No, I can't do it"—ibid.

79 "Then he and Paul"—ibid.

10: A PORTRAIT OF THE ARTIST AS HERO AND BULLY

84 Sandra Dee recalled—Castro Theatre, San Francisco, July 1998.

84 Sandra Dee will serve as technical advisor—U-I press release, June 16, 1958.

84 statement from a family friend—*Los Angeles Times*, Feb. 21, 2005.

84–85 "the loneliest classroom"—U-I press release, n.d.

85 "There she sat in class"—Darin and Paetro, p. 85.

87–88 "a Viking, very tall"—BR to SS.

88 "just plain delicious!"—Rock Hudson oral history, SMU.

88 an "actor's director"—Halliday, 2nd ed., p. 38.

88 "Not a lot of rehearsing"—RG to SS.

89–90 "I adopted a position"—Halliday, 2nd ed., p. 80.

90 "tired, embarrassed, and was almost"—Davis, pp. 82–83.

90 Jimmy Hunt opinions—to Stephen Shearer, author of *Patricia Neal: An Unquiet Life*; Shearer to SS.

91 Sirk lost his temper—Oppenheimer and Vitek, pp. 43–44.

11: SIRK DU SOLEIL

93–94 "Sirk was never able to meet"—Halliday, 2nd ed., p. 3.

94–95 "With my last one thousand dollars"—Halliday, 2nd ed., p. 64.

95 "I couldn't hire"—Halliday, 2nd ed., p. 67.

95 "not even a B-feature"—Halliday, 2nd ed., p. 71.

95 shot in one week—Halliday, 2nd ed., p. 181.

95 "naked women frolicking"—Tom Ryan, www.senseofcinema.com.

96 "I went to Berlin"—Halliday, 2nd ed., p. 89.

96–97 "a smaller plane crashed"—Halliday, 2nd ed., p. 92.

12: *HITLER'S MADMAN*

101 "I brought him in"—Halliday, 2nd ed., p. 73.

102 "John Carradine . . . *was* Heydrich"—Halliday, 2nd ed., pp. 71–72.

13: THE SHAKY MEGASTAR AND THE SEPIA HOLLYWOOD HOPE

104 "When Lana Turner walked on"—Ross Hunter oral history, SMU.
104 In fact, she was terrified—Morella and Epstein, p. 217.
104 "Lana needed all the friends"—Morella and Epstein, p. 216.
105 Most of the reporters—Morella and Epstein, p. 217.
106 "was famous for the way"—Crane, pp. 260–61.
106 "Suddenly, Mother would metamorphose"—Crane, p. 260.
107 "as a defense mechanism"—Crane, p. 261.
107 Accessible to the press—Morella and Epstein, pp. 216–17.
107 "Such a gentle man"—*Bright Lights*, Winter 1977–78.
107 "she was very compliant"—*Film Comment*, July/Aug. 1978.

14: LOCATIONS, LOCATIONS

113 "begin with similar shots"—Stern, p. 42.
114 "sweaty passions"—Pauline Kael, *5001 Nights at the Movies*, p. 592.
115 "a spangle-clad bevy"—unsourced clipping, AMPAS.
117 "when they were shooting on location"—Crane, p. 261.
117 The *Ziegfeld* Mothers Club story, TF to SS.

18: THE ROCKING CHAIR BLUES

131 "dubbing was done in films"—GG to SS.
135 "the suspension of narrative"—Maltby, p. 449.

19: THE LADY AND THE BULLFIGHTER

141 "Sirk's films are filled"—Mulvey and Halliday, p. 38.
142 "Everything, even life"—Halliday, 2nd ed., p. 51.
142 One of her first jobs—*Los Angeles Times*, Sept. 7, 1977.
143 "My life is pretty much"—*Los Angeles Examiner*, Sept. 21, 1952.
147 "Working in films"—*Los Angeles Times*, Sept. 7, 1977.

20: NO BEEFCAKE, PLEASE, WE'RE REPUBLICAN

148 "The only time my shirt"—U-I press release, n.d.
148 "a business opportunity"—*Look*, July 22, 1958.
148 His other business ventures—*Current Biography*, 1962, p. 149.
149 "I was thinking about"—*Look*, July 22, 1958.
149 "Why should I hire"—ibid.
150 "There's no Gavin here"—*New York Post Magazine*, Oct. 29, 1961.

150 "Quite frankly, this may sound"—Hofler, p. 332.

150 "Gavin, naturally, was not"—Halliday, 2nd ed., p. 146.

153 "Don't get the idea"—U-I press release, Aug. 12, 1958.

153 "budget constraints forced Hitchcock"—Rebello, p. 65.

153 "grew visibly more riled"—Rebello, pp. 86–87.

153 "I think you and John could be"—Leigh and Nickens, p. 55.

153 "In discreet but descriptive terms"—Rebello, p. 87.

153 nicknamed him "the Stiff"—ibid.

155 "Diplomatic sadism"—New York Times, Mar. 14, 1981.

155 "If they're going to send"—Dallas Times Herald, Feb. 27, 1981.

155 "Perhaps we should name Cantinflas"—New York Times, Mar. 14, 1981.

155–56 "a two-sided role in Mexico"—Dallas Morning News, May 2, 1982.

156 claimed he was feeling ill—ibid.

156 "a controversial ambassador"—Los Angeles Times, Apr. 8, 1986.

156 "socially correct at all times"—New York Post Magazine, Oct. 29, 1961.

156 "He does not want to be reminded"—LTK to SS.

157 To practice for his scenes—U-I press release, Sept. 17, 1958.

21: PRETTY BABY

161 "I'm looking at this article"—Darin and Paetro, p. 80.

162 "I didn't understand"—Darin and Paetro, p. 36.

162 "From that day on"—People, Mar. 18, 1991.

162 "I'll give you this special"—Modern Screen, Aug. 1959.

162 "We were really good buddies"—CL to SS.

162–63 "My mother wanted a cripple"—Darin and Paetro, p. 91.

163 "the best girlfriend"—Darin and Paetro, p. 25.

163 "so white it looked like"—Darin and Paetro, p. 46.

163 "She would say something"—John Saxon, on Larry King Live, Feb. 23, 2005.

164 "My first year and a half"—People, Mar. 18, 1991.

165 "She had a great knack"—Darin and Paetro, p. 84.

165 "By the end of the first week"—Darin and Paetro, p. 86.

165 Discussing the scene years later—Castro Theatre, San Francisco, July 1998.

167 "Will you marry me?"—Darin and Paetro, p. 135.

168 "Why don't we go for"—Darin and Paetro, p. 137.

168 "He told Mary"—Darin and Paetro, p. 138.

168 "But, honey, you can't"—Darin and Paetro, p. 141.

169 "Something of a milestone"—New York Post, Dec. 21, 1965.

169 "She shot her career"—Darin and Paetro, p. 224.

169 "Look at her"—New York Times Magazine, Dec. 25, 2005.

22: "IF TROY DONAHUE CAN BE A MOVIE STAR, THEN I CAN BE A MOVIE STAR"

172 "began waiting tables"—*TV Guide*, Aug. 9, 1961.
172 "This is the story of"—*McCall's*, Sept. 1962.
174 "a terrible temper"—*Hollywood Citizen-News*, July 20, 1961.
174 Her lawsuit for assault and battery—*TV Guide*, Feb. 22, 1962.
174 "The violence I have been associated with"—ibid.
174 During the confrontation—Peter Manso, *Brando: The Biography*, pp. 778–79.
175 "He looks like Young America wants to look"—*TV Guide*, Feb. 22, 1962.
177 "After that film came out"—Hofler, p. 305.
178 "He was stationed in Germany"—*The New Yorker*, Sept. 13, 1999.
178 "What was fascinating to me"—Karl Malden, *When Do I Start?*, p. 284.
179 "Finally," said Faye, "one of them"—Dunaway and Sharkey, p. 109.
180 "The character who moved me so"—Dunaway and Sharkey, pp. 52–53.

23: FURTHER DOWN THE CREDITS

188 "Geeze, kid, I didn't know"—*TV Guide*, July 11, 1970.
188 His initial preparation—U-I press release, n.d.
191 "I was paid $24.50 a week"—*Los Angeles Times*, May 5, 1986.
191 "when Perc Westmore, the makeup man"—*Cleveland Plain Dealer Pictorial Magazine*, Dec. 16, 1945.

24: JACK WESTON AND THE CITIZEN'S ARREST IN BEVERLY HILLS

195 "Bess Flowers was noted"—*Films in Review*, June/July 1984.
196 "I got a job the first day"—ibid.
196 "who is naked except for a band of cloth"—ibid.
196 "I made a good living"—ibid.
197 "Every afternoon at three"—*New York Times*, May 5, 1996.
197 "faces are vaguely recognizable"—*New York Times*, Mar. 14, 1965.
199 "the ladies presented their case"—ibid.

25: JOEL FLUELLEN

200 "I have this theory"—*The New Yorker*, Oct. 30, 2006.
200–01 "I carry two extra inches"—*Variety*, Feb. 12, 1990.
203 "Joel knew his craft"—RH to SS.
203 Fluellen as a "social climber"—Bogle, *Bright Boulevards*, p. 207.
203 "ruthless snob"—Bogle, *Bright Boulevards*, p. 210.

203 and a "gossip"—Bogle, *Dorothy Dandridge*, p. 161.

203 "When *The Green Pastures*"—Bogle, *Bright Boulevards*, p. 208.

204 "also designed hats"—ibid.

204 "At one time he had"—Bogle, *Bright Boulevards*, p. 209.

204 "We knew he was gay"—RH to SS.

204 "an attractive man"—Bogle, *Bright Boulevards*, p. 207.

205 "we had classes, warm-up exercises"—Blair, p. 201.

205 Dorothy Dandridge was dropped—Bogle, *Bright Boulevards*, p. 285.

205 better treatment for African-American performers—Bogle, *Dorothy Dandridge*, pp. 157–58.

205 In 1944, Lena Horne—Blair, pp. 149–50.

206 "introduced resolutions to the Screen Actors Guild"—*Los Angeles Times*, Feb. 7, 1990.

206 "That last line," she wrote—*Los Angeles Times*, Feb. 18, 1990.

207 "Louisiana-Born Actor's Cuisine"—*Los Angeles Times*, Sept. 3, 1970.

207–08 "It was a courtyard apartment"—AC to SS.

26: THE KIND OF PLAYWRIGHT WHO FLINGS HIS MANUSCRIPT IN THE FIRE

210 "I asked him to build"—*Metropolitan Home*, Nov. 1991.

210 "wanted to refine the box"—ibid.

213 "When I met her"—to Arlene Dahl, for her column "Let's Be Beautiful," *Chicago Tribune*, Apr. 25, 1955.

27: "MY FAMILY AT THE STUDIO"

217 "Magnificent Obsessions: A Remembrance by Ross Hunter"—*American Film*, Apr. 1988.

218 "I liked working with a group"—Halliday, 2nd ed., p. 100.

218 "We always agreed"—ibid.

219 "He was a genius"—JF to SS.

220 "a little lyrical poem"—Halliday, 2nd ed., p. 100.

220 "as characters . . . move around a room"—*Film Dope*, no. 42, Oct. 1984.

220 "offered to arrange the available footage"—Higham, pp. 219–20.

221 "powerfully built, brusque, and rude"—Higham, p. 225.

221 "I swear, some of Russ Metty's shots"—Heston, pp. 21–22.

221 "Russ cooked up a mess"—Heston, p. 23.

222 "It was technically an amazing shot"—Heston and Isbouts, p. 80.

222 concealing the cast on Janet Leigh's arm—ibid.

222 "Congratulations! You won without"—Alex Golitzen oral history, AMPAS.

223 "gray means poverty and meanness"—Heisner, p. 299.
224 "Ross told Alex [Golitzen] what he wanted"—BAG to SS.
225 "They led us through a dressing room"—BAG to SS.
226 "The primary objective of any set decorator"—*The Hollywood Reporter*, Nov. 13, 1950.

28: THE BUSINESS OF GLAMOO

228 "Ross had a terrible time"—TKS to SS.
229 "there is no winking at the audience"—Mann, p. 349.
230 "One cannot help but think"—Mann, p. 355.
230 "The kind of life I put"—Mann, p. 351.
230 he toured the RKO–Orpheum circuit—Mann, p. 352.
231 "usher" at a movie theatre—ibid.
232 "the most ornate tepee ever seen"—Mann, p. 354.
233 *Airport* "came out three months before"—Sharp, p. 255.
234 Lana sent him an arrangement of lemons—Turner, p. 279.
234–35 "Although he has lived"—*New York Post*, Sept. 24, 1966.
235 shared by a stepbrother—Alpert, p. 95.
235 "It's absolutely true"—Mann, p. 358.
236 "We've been together three years"—*Newsday*, Mar. 17, 1970.
236 "Fun! Lots of laughs"—LM to SS.
236–37 "The thing to remember about Ross"—BO to SS.
237 "For Saturday's performance"—*The Hollywood Reporter*, Mar. 12, 1996.

29: "TURN AGAIN TO LIFE, AND SMILE"

239 "My first love is the theatre"—*The Hollywood Reporter*, Feb. 12, 1981.
239 went over the play "with a microscope"—unsourced clipping, AMPAS.
240 "Now, come on, Betty"—BG to SS.
240 "He was a charming gentleman"—LMe to SS.
241 "A director who has been an actor"—DM to SS.

30: THE CASE OF THE MISSING SCREENWRITER

247 "I think it was because at RKO"—McGilligan, p. 324.
247–48 "My dad became known"—PS to SS.
248 The Astaire–Rogers pictures were full of optimism"—McGilligan, p. 331.
249–50 "We worked together at Universal"—RB to SS.
250 "Sy might have been brought in"—JR to SS.

31: GOWNS BY JEAN-LOUIS

256 "When I was at Columbia"—Kobal, *People Will Talk,* p. 447.

256 "The best dressed woman"—unsourced clipping, AMPAS.

256 "The following year he designed"—*New York Times,* Apr. 24, 1997.

256 "the way she carries the clothes"—Kobal, *People Will Talk,* p. 446.

257 "When I saw her the first time"—ibid.

257 "Let's buy a house here"—*Los Angeles Times,* Sept. 17, 1993.

259 "Today, the American teenage girl's"—U-I press release, n.d.

260 "Lana was the most clothes-conscious"—*Los Angeles Times,* Jan. 2, 2000.

260 "They had a strong disagreement"—BR to SS.

262 "You could fill a column"—*Hollywood Citizen-News,* Mar. 14, 1970.

32: UNDERSCORE

263 "If Frank Skinner developed a trademark"—Marmorstein, p. 326.

266 "If you gave Frank Skinner two months"—Hans Salter oral history, AMPAS.

266 Sirk liked to point out—Halliday, 2nd ed., p. 49.

268 "I've completed a set of lyrics"—*Films in Review,* Aug./Sept. 1971.

268 "It just drives me wild"—*Los Angeles Times,* Mar. 24, 1984.

33: THE UNKNOWN MOGUL

271 "a very friendly place"—Mancini and Lees, p. 62.

271 knowing "everybody by their first name"—Rock Hudson oral history, SMU.

273 "Muhl was a very nice guy"—*Bright Lights,* Winter 1977/78.

273 "He was smart enough to understand"—Sharp, p. 147.

277 "Rock had started having an illicit affair"—Hudson and Davidson, p. 71.

278 "Can you believe Ed Muhl?"—Hofler, p. 237.

34: "GOIN' TO GLORY"

279 "I really don't die in the picture until"—U-I press release, Sept. 2, 1958.

281 "Before shooting those scenes"—*Film Comment,* July/Aug. 1978.

281 "When I heard how audiences were reacting"—ibid.

282 They "do not believe in death"—Baldwin, p. 339.

282 "The funeral scene wasn't in the original"—*Film Comment,* July/Aug. 1978.

282 "For Mother, life was a movie"—Crane, p. 60.

283 "I most dreaded the part"—Turner, p. 257.

283 "I simply broke down"—ibid.

283 "running in my high heels"—ibid.

283 "slumped onto the chair"—Turner, p. 258.

283 "'Cut and print,'"—ibid.
284 Sirk corrected her—Harvey, p. 419.
284 "A camera movement ought to be"—*Bright Lights*, Winter 1977/78.
285–86 "When director Douglas Sirk filmed"—U-I press release, Sept. 11, 1958.
286 "Annie's deathbed moment"—Holloway, pp. 104–06.
286 "many who had not done so before"—Holloway, pp. 106–07.

35: HALLELUJAH!

287 "Ever since that day"—*Ebony*, Apr. 1972.
288 "Blues are the songs of despair"—*New York Times*, Jan. 28, 1972.
288 "People were always after Mahalia"—Jones, p. 80.
289 When it was time to view the rushes—U-I press release, Sept. 11, 1958.
289 "just a good, strong Louisiana woman"—*Ebony*, Apr. 1972.
289 "she always had fine soul food"—Ellington, p. 256.
289 Once before a concert in a prosperous church—anonymous source to SS.
290 "no big fanfare when I'm gone"—*Ebony*, Apr. 1972.
290 "marked not by grief"—ibid.
291 Three days later, in New Orleans—ibid.

36: NOBODY LIKED IT BUT THE PUBLIC

293 Shurlock, in a letter (and subsequent Production Code correspondence)—Production Code files, AMPAS.
293 two versions of the trailer—AMPAS and Universal Collection, USC.
294 "I guess I sound like"—*Los Angeles Times*, Jan. 20, 1972.
294–95 "Where do these guys get the stuff"—*Chicago Defender*, Apr. 27, 1959.
295 "*Imitation of Life* is a fine picture"—*The Hollywood Reporter*, Feb. 2, 1959.
296 "everybody in the U-I commissary"—*Los Angeles Herald and Express*, Jan. 29, 1959.
296 "Tears flowed constantly throughout"—*Los Angeles Herald and Express*, Jan. 30, 1959.
297 "I never saw my films after I finished"—*Film Comment*, July/Aug. 1978.
297 "I think the casting is better this time"—unsourced clipping, AMPAS.
297 "the film's publicists wanted to show"—Crane, p. 274.
298 "*Imitation of Life* hardened my feelings"—ibid.
298 Bosley Crowther reviews, *New York Times*, Apr. 18 and 19, 1959.
298 "melodramatic chestnut"—*New York Times*, Oct. 29, 2001.
299 John McCarten review—*The New Yorker*, Apr. 25, 1959.
299n John Updike tribute to Lana Turner—*The New Yorker*, Feb. 12, 1996.
300 "Critics label any love story"—*New York Herald Tribune*, May 10, 1959.
301 "I had accepted a fairly modest fee"—Turner, pp. 258–59.

38: MR. AND MRS. WEITZ

305 "If acting was taken away from me"—*Los Angeles Times*, May 15, 1960.

308 "I didn't have the passion anymore"—*Los Angeles Times*, Apr. 4, 2004.

40: IMITATION OF HALF-LIFE

317 "a Negro girl who tries to pass"—*Chicago Defender*, May 10, 1960.

321 Almodóvar, in an interview—Willoquet-Maricondi, p. 28.

322 "One of my dearest projects"—Halliday, 2nd ed., p. 111.

322 A survey in the *New York Daily News*—Kroeger, *Fannie*, p. xvi.

41: GENTLEMEN PREFER LYPSINKA

329 "Given its pervasiveness in culture"—Klinger, p. 141.

329 "By around two a.m. their conversation"—Levine, p. 293.

330 The painter David Salle—*Village Voice*, July 11, 1989.

42: THERE ONCE WAS A LADY NAMED FANNIE

333 preface to Zora Neale Hurston's first novel—Kroeger, *Fannie*, p. 190.

334 "There was no suppressing the enormity that was Delilah"—*Imitation of Life*, ch. 16.

335 "They were so young, standing there"—*Imitation of Life*, ch. 47.

335 "I know Peola"—Kroeger, *Fannie*, p. 204.

336 "triggered a publicity firestorm"—Kroeger, *Fannie*, p. 65.

336 "Ross Hunter gave me the book"—Halliday, 2nd ed., p. 148.

337 "*Imitation of Life* is more than just a good title"—Halliday, 2nd ed., p. 140.

337 "Fannie sold the movie rights to Universal"—Kroeger, *Fannie*, p. 197.

43: JOHN M. STAHL

339 "The power of all Sirk's best films"—Halliday, 2nd ed., p. 2.

339 "Well do I recall"—*Hollywood Citizen-News*, Sept. 1, 1944.

339 "He was never very well-known"—Filmoteca Española, p. 22.

44: NO FALLING DIAMONDS

343 salaries of those in 1934 version—Cinema-TV Library, USC.

344 Slide, *International Film, Radio, and Television Journals*.

345 "flashes of newspaper criticisms"—*Chicago Defender*, Sept. 7, 1935.

345 eliminated eleven of Fannie Hurst's characters—*New York Herald Tribune*, Dec. 2, 1934.

345 Hurlbut's writing teammates—cost sheets at Universal Collection, Cinema-TV Lib., USC.

346 correspondence and memoranda of MPPDA—AMPAS.

349 Fredi Washington's grandmother—IP to SS.

349–50 "the particular problem encountered"—*Los Angeles Times*, July 17, 1934.

350 Lukas, after filming two scenes—*Los Angeles Times*, Aug. 8, 1934.

350 "Where's your makeup?" he demanded—Russell and Chase, p. 54.

350 "dislikes filming a picture"—*New York Times*, Nov. 18, 1934.

351–52 Louise Beavers told an interviewer—*Chicago Defender*, Feb. 16, 1935.

45: THE BIZARRE, CONFLICTED REALITY OF THE ERA

353 "a new departure in movies"—*Pittsburgh Courier*, Dec. 22, 1934.

354 "a great picture with two Race performers"—*Chicago Defender*, Jan. 12, 1935.

354 "Fifteen Most Important Events of 1935"—*Chicago Defender*, Jan. 4, 1936.

354 "he panned both the book and the movie"—*African American Review*, Fall 1997.

355 "Far be it from me"—ibid.

355 Will Rogers acknowledged—*Chicago Defender*, Jan. 26, 1935.

356 "We are out to cast the foremost stars"—*Chicago Defender*, June 19, 1935.

46: MISS BEA, AUNT DELILAH, THE TRAGIC MULATTO, AND THE MOVIE STAR SPY

360 "it was a drama with a difference"—Quirk, p. 3.

360 "one of the finest, sweetest"—*Chicago Defender*, Feb. 16, 1935.

362 Beavers "liked baseball, prizefights"—Bogle, *Bright Boulevards*, p. 262.

362 "Beavers did not spend time in the kitchen"—ibid.

363 the steward was crestfallen—unsourced clipping, AMPAS.

363 "the beloved actress was best known"—*Los Angeles Herald-Examiner*, Nov. 2, 1962.

364 "light complexion, blue-gray eyes"—*Theatre Survey*, vol. 45 (May 2004).

364–65 "My first job," she recalled—*Essence*, Sept. 1978.

365 *Shuffle Along* is said to be—*Theatre Survey*, vol. 45 (May 2004).

365 "I had never seen a play"—Fredi Washington, in unpublished interview with Jean-Claude Baker.

365 "I got to get this off"—ibid.

365 During the run, Robeson and Washington—*Theatre Survey*, vol. 45 (May 2004).

365 "received the privilege of making suggestions"—ibid.

366 "I had to fight the writers"—*Essence*, Sept. 1978.

366 "This girl is the daughter of a colored mammy"—Bogle, *Bright Boulevards*, p. 129.

367 "Hired to do public relations"—*Theatre Survey*, vol. 45 (May 2004).

367 "Early in my career"—*Essence*, Sept. 1978.

368 Fredi expressed regret for her light skin—*Theatre Survey*, vol. 45 (May 2004).

368 Fredi's activism included—*Theatre Survey*, vol. 45 (May 2004).

INDEX

Young, Loretta, 43, 75
  Jean-Louis' relationship with, 257
Yurka, Blanche, 98

Zanuck, Darryl, 35, 340–41
Zehner, Harry, 347–48
Ziegfeld Girl, 76, 117

Zuck, Mary
  Darin, Bobby, courting Dee and, 167–68
  Dee on mothering of, 162–63
  Dee's diary writing of, 165
  Douvan marrying, 161–62
  parenting of, 161
Zugsmith, Al, 18, 95